287. **GYPSIES.** The Land Beyond the Forest. Facts, Figures, and Fancies from Transylvania. By E. Gerard. ILLUSTRATED. N. Y., 1888. *8vo, cloth*..............$1.75
Gypsy, Saxon, and Roumanian Superstitions, Manners and Customs.

OLD TOWN GATE AT HERMANSTADT (ELIZABETH THOR).

THE

LAND BEYOND THE FOREST

FACTS, FIGURES, AND FANCIES

FROM

TRANSYLVANIA

By E. GERARD

AUTHOR OF
"REATA" "THE WATERS OF HERCULES" "BEGGAR MY NEIGHBOR" ETC.

WITH MAP AND ILLUSTRATIONS

NEW YORK

HARPER & BROTHERS, FRANKLIN SQUARE

1888

PREFACE.

In the spring of 1883 my husband was appointed to the command of the cavalry brigade in Transylvania, composed of two hussar regiments, stationed respectively at Hermanstadt and Kronstadt—a very welcome nomination, as gratifying a long-cherished wish of mine to visit that part of the Austrian empire known as the Land beyond the Forest.

The two years spent in Transylvania were among the most agreeable of sixteen years' acquaintance with Austrian military life; and I shall always look back to this time as to something quaint and exceptional, totally different from all previous and subsequent experiences.

Much interested in the wild beauty of the country, the strange admixture of races by which it is peopled, and their curious and varied folk-lore, I recorded some of my impressions in short, independent papers, of which three were published in *Blackwood's Magazine*, one in the *Nineteenth Century*, and one in the *Contemporary Review*. It was only after I had left the country that, being desirous of preserving these sketches in more convenient form, I began rearranging the matter for publication; but the task of retracing my Transylvanian experiences was so pleasant that it led me on far beyond my original intention. One reminiscence awoke another, one chapter gave rise to a second; and so, instead of a small volume, as had been at first contemplated, my manuscript almost unconsciously developed to its present dimensions.

When the work was completed, the idea of illustrating it occurred to me: but this was a far more difficult matter; for, though offering a perfect treasure-mine to artists, Transylvania has not as yet received from them the attention it deserves; and had it not been for obliging assistance from several quarters, I should have been debarred the satisfaction of elucidating some of my descriptions by appropriate sketches.

In this matter my thanks are greatly due to Herr Emil Sigerus, who was good enough to place at my disposal the blocks of engravings designed by himself, and belonging to the Transylvania Carpathian Society, of which he is the secretary. Likewise to Madame Kamilla Asboth, for permission to copy her life-like and characteristic photographs of Saxons, Roumanians, and gypsies.

I would also at this place acknowledge the extreme courtesy with which every question of mine regarding Transylvania people and customs has been responded to by various kind acquaintances, and if some parts of my work do not meet with their entire approval, let them here take the assurance that my remarks were prompted by no unfriendly spirit, and that in each and every case I have endeavored to judge impartially according to my lights.

Emily de Laszowska-Gerard.

CONTENTS.

Contents.

ILLUSTRATIONS.

THE LAND BEYOND THE FOREST.

CHAPTER I.

INTRODUCTORY.

LEAVING Transylvania after a two years' residence, I felt somewhat like Robinson Crusoe unexpectedly restored to the world from his desert island. Despite the evidence of my own senses, and in flat contradiction to the atlas, I cannot wholly divest myself of the idea that it is in truth an island I have left behind me—an island peopled with strange and incongruous companions, from whom I part with a mixture of regret and relief difficult to explain even to myself.

Just as Robinson Crusoe, getting attached to his parrots and his palm-trees, his gourds and his goats, continued to yearn for them after his return to Europe, so I found myself gradually succumbing to the indolent charm and the drowsy poetry of this secluded land. A very few years more of unbroken residence here would no doubt suffice to efface all memory of the world we had left behind and the century in which we live.

I remember reading in some fairy tale, long ago, of a youthful princess who, stolen by the gnomes and carried off into gnomeland, was restored to her parents after a lapse of years. Their joy was great at recovering their child, but it turned to grief when they discovered that she had grown estranged from them, and had lost all interest in the actual world. The sun was too bright, she said, it hurt her eyes, and the voices of men were too loud, they scorched her ears; and she could never feel at home again amid the restless glitter of her surroundings.

I do not recollect how the story concludes—whether the young lady became in time reconciled to her father's brilliant court, or

1

whether she ran away and married a gnome; but this tale somehow reminded me of my own experiences, and I caught myself wondering whether a few years hence, perhaps, the summons to return to the world might not have come too late.

Parrots and palm-trees are all very well, no doubt, to fill up the life of a stranded mariner, but it is questionable whether it be wise to let such things absorb the mind to the extent of destroying all taste for wider interests. Life in an island is apt to consist too entirely of foreground—the breadth of a panorama and the comprehensiveness of a bird's-eye view, only gained by constant friction with the bustling, pushing outer world, being mostly here wanting.

Luckily, or unluckily, as one may choose to view it, the spirit of the nineteenth century is a ghost very difficult to be laid. A steady course of narcotics may lull it to rest for a time; but the spirit is but stupefied, not dead; its vitality is great, and it will start up again to life at the first trumpet-blast which reaches from without, eager to exchange a peaceful dream for the movement of the arena and the renewed clank of arms.

Some such feelings were mine as I beheld the signal waving from the ship which was to carry me back to a world I had almost forgotten; and though I heaved a sigh of regret, and possibly may have dropped a tear or two in secret for the peaceful and familiar scenes I was leaving, yet I would not have steered round the vessel to return to my island.

Not the mere distance which separates Transylvania from Western Europe gives to it this feeling of strange isolation. Other countries as far or farther off are infinitely more familiar even to those who have never visited them. We know all about Turkey, and Greece is no more strange to us than Italy or Switzerland. But no one ever comes to Transylvania in cold blood, unless it be some very rabid sportsman eager for the embrace of a shaggy bear; and as for those rushing travellers, bound for the Black Sea, who sometimes traverse the country in hot-headed haste, they mostly resemble the superficial swallow which skims the surface of a placid lake, without guessing the secrets of the blue depths below.

Situated by nature within a formidable rampart of snow-tipped mountains, and shielded by heavy curtains of shrouding forests against the noise and turmoil of the outer world, the very name of Transylvania tells us that it was formerly regarded as something apart, something out of reach, whose existence even for a time was enveloped in mystery. In olden times these gloomy forest gorges were tenanted only by the solitary bear or packs of famished wolves, while the mistrustful lynx looked down from the giddy heights, and the chamois leaped unchecked from rock to rock. The people who lived westward of this mountain rampart, knowing but little or nothing of the country on the other side, designated it as Transylvania, or the land beyond the forest, just as we sometimes talk of the "land beyond the clouds."

Nothing, however, can remain undiscovered on the face of our globe. That enterprising creature man, who is even now attempting, with some show of success, to probe the country beyond the clouds, has likewise discovered the way to this secluded nook. The dense forests, once forming such impenetrable barriers against the outer world, have in great part disappeared; another voice is heard besides that of the wild beasts of the wood; another breath comes mingled along with the mountain vapors—it is the breath of that nineteenth-century monster, the steam-engine.

This benefactor of the age, this harbinger of civilization, which is as truly the destroyer of romance, and poetry's deadly foe, will undoubtedly succeed in robbing this country of the old-world charm which yet lingers about it. Transylvania will in time become as civilized and cultivated, and likewise as stereotyped and conventional, as the best known parts of our first European States—it will even one day cease to be an island; but as yet the advent of the nineteenth-century monster is of too recent a date to have tainted the atmosphere by its breath, and the old-world charm still lingers around and about many things. It is floating everywhere and anywhere—in the forests and on the mountains, in mediæval churches and ruined watch-towers, in mysterious caverns and in ancient gold-mines, in the songs of the people and the legends they tell. Like a subtle perfume evaporating under the rays of a burning sun, it is growing daily fainter and fainter, and all lovers of the past should hasten to collect this fleeting fragrance ere it be gone forever. This is what I have endeavored to do, to some small extent, since fate for a time cast my lines in those parts.

And first and foremost let me here explain that my intentions in compiling this work are nowise of an ambitious or lofty nature.

I desire to instruct no one, to influence no one, to enlist no one's sympathies in favor of any particular social question or political doctrine. Even had such been my intention, I have been therein amply forestalled by others; nor do I delude myself into the belief that it is my proud vocation to correct the errors of all former writers by giving to the world the only correct and trustworthy description of Transylvania which has yet appeared. I have not lived long enough in the country to feel myself justified in taking up the gauntlet against the assertions of older inhabitants of the soil, but have lived there too long to rival that admirable self-possession which induces the average tourist to classify, condemn, ticket, and tie up every fact which comes within his notice, never demeaning himself to grovel or analyze, nor being disturbed by any doubts of the reliability of his own unerring judgment.

Whoever wishes to study the history of Transylvania in its past, present, and future aspects, who wants to understand its geological formation or system of agriculture, who would thoroughly penetrate into the inextricable net-work of conflicting political interests which divide its interior, must seek his information elsewhere.

Do you wish, for instance, to see Transylvania as it was some forty years ago? If so, I can confidently advise you to read the valuable work of Mr. Paget and the spirited descriptions of Monsieur de Gérando.

Do you want to gain insight into the geological resources of the country, or the farming system of the Saxon peasant? Then take up Charles Boner's comprehensive work on Transylvania. And would you see these Saxons as they love to behold themselves, then turn to Dr. Teutsch's learned work on "Die Siebenbürger Sachsen;" while if politics be your special hobby, you cannot better indulge it than by selecting Mr. Patterson's most interesting work on Hungary and Transylvania.

If, moreover, you care to study the country "contrariwise," and would know what the Roumanians are utterly unlike, read the description of them in the aforementioned book of Mr. Boner; while for generally incorrect information on almost every available subject connected with the country, I am told that the German work of Rudolf Bergner cannot be too highly recommended.

Recognizing, therefore, the superiority of the many learned predecessors who each in their respective lines have so thoroughly worked out the subject in hand, I would merely forewarn the reader that no such completeness of outline can be looked for here. Neither is my book intended to be of the guide-book species—no sort of ornamental Bradshaw or idealized Murray. I fail to see the use of minutely describing several scores of towns and villages which the English reader is never likely to set eyes upon. If you think of travelling this way, good and well, then buy the genuine article for yourself—Murray or Bradshaw—unadulterated by me; or, better still, the excellent German hand-book of Professor Bielz; while if you stay at home, can you really care to know if such and such a town have five churches or fifty? or whether the proportion of carbonate of magnesia exceed that of chloride of potassium in some particular spring of whose waters you will never taste?

All that I have attempted here to do is to seize the general color and atmosphere of the land, and to fix—as much for my own private satisfaction as for any other reason—certain impressions of people and places I should be loath to forget. I have written only of those things which happened to excite my interest, and have described figures and scenery such as they appeared to me. For some of the details contained in these pages I am indebted to the following writers: Liszt, Slavici, Fronius, Müller, and Schwicker—all competent authorities well acquainted with their subject. Some things have found no place here because I did not consider myself competent to speak of them, others because they did not chance to be congenial; and although not absolutely scorning serious information whenever it has come in my way, I have taken more pleasure in chronicling fancies than facts, and superstitions rather than statistics.

More than one error has doubtless crept unawares into this work; so in order to place myself quite on the safe side with regard to stern critics, I had better hasten to say that I decline to pledge my word for the veracity of anything contained in these pages. I only lay claim to having used my eyes and ears to the best of my ability; and where I have failed to see or hear aright, the fault must be set down to some inherent color-blindness, or radical defect in my tympanum. Nor do I pretend to have seen everything, even in a small country like Transylvania, and every spot I have failed to visit, from lack of time or opportunity, is not only to me a source of poignant regret, but likewise a chapter missing from this book.

CHAPTER II.

HISTORICAL.

TRANSYLVANIA is interesting not only on account of its geographical position, but likewise with regard to the several races which inhabit it, and the peculiar conditions under which part of these have obtained possession of the soil.

Situated between 45° 16′ and 48° 42′ latitude, and 40° to 44° of longitude (Ferro), the land covers a space of 54,000 square kilometres, which are inhabited by a population of some 2,170,000 heads.

Of these the proportion of different races may be assumed to be pretty nearly as follows :

Roumanians	1,200,400	Gypsies	79,000
Hungarians	652,221	Jews	24,848
Saxons	211,490	Armenians	8,430

Some one has rather aptly defined Transylvania as a vast store-house of different nationalities; and in order to account for the *raison d'être* of so many different races living side by side in one small country, a few words of explanation are absolutely necessary to render intelligible the circumstances of daily life in Transylvania, since it is to be presumed that to many English readers the country is still virtually a "land beyond the forest."

Not being, however, of that ferocious disposition which loves to inflict needless information upon an unoffending public, I pass over in considerate silence such very superfluous races as the Agathyrsi, the Gepidæ, the Getæ, and yet others who successively inhabited these regions. Let it suffice to say that in the centuries immediately preceding the Christian era the land belonged to the Dacians, who were in course of time subjugated by Trajan, Transylvania becoming a Roman province in the year 105 A.D. It remained under the Roman eagle for something over a century and a half; but about the year 274 the Emperor Aurelian was compelled to remove his legions from the countries over the Danube and abandon the land to the all-ravaging Goths.

I have only here insisted on the Dacian and Roman occupation of Transylvania, because one or other or both of these peoples are supposed to be the ancestors of the present Roumanian race. The Roumanians themselves like to think they are descended directly from the Romans; while Germans are fond of denying this origin, and maintain this people to have appeared in these regions at a much later period. According to the most reliable authorities, however, the truth would seem to lie between these two opposite statements, and the Roumanians to be the offspring of a cross-breed between the conqueror and the conquered—between Romans and Dacians.

After the Roman evacuation the country changed hands oftener than can be recorded, and the rolling waves of the *Völkerwanderung* passed over the land, each nation leaving its impress more or less upon the surface, till finally the Magyars began to gain something of a permanent hold, towards the eleventh century. This hold, however, was anything but a firm one, for the Hungarian king had alike outward enemies and inward traitors to guard against, and was in continual fear lest some affectionate relation should rob him of one of his crown-jewels.

To add to this, the province of Transylvania was but thinly peopled, and ill qualified to resist attacks from without. In view, therefore, of all these circumstances, King Geisa II. bethought himself of inviting Germans to come and establish colonies in this scantily peopled land, promising them certain privileges in return for the services he expected. Hungarian heralds began, consequently, to appear in German towns, proclaiming aloud in street and on market-place the words of their royal master. Their voices found a ready echo among the people, for this promised land was not absolutely unknown to the German yeomen, who many of them had passed through it on their way to and from the Crusades; besides, this was the time when feudal rights weighed most oppressively on unfortunate vassals, and no doubt many were glad to purchase freedom even at the price of expatriation.

As a German poet sings:

"When castles crowned each craggy height
 Along the banks of Rhine,
And 'neath the mailèd warriors' might
 Did simple burghers pine;

"When bowed the common herd of men,
 Serfs to a lord's commanding,

8   *The Land Beyond the Forest.*

The holy Roman Empire then
For free men had no standing.

"Then off broke many and away,
Another country questing;
'We'll found another home,' said they—
'A house on freedom resting.

"'Hungarian forests, wild and free,
Are refuge for us keeping;
From home and home's dear ties will we
Emancipate us, weeping.'"

Or in the words of another:

"We'll ride away to the east,
Away to the east we go—
O'er meadows away,
O'er meadows so gay;
It will be better so.

"And when we came to the east,
'Neath the lofty house came we,
They called us in,
O'er meadows so gay,
And bade us welcome be."

In thus summoning German colonists to the country, the Hungarian monarch showed wisdom and policy far in advance of his century, as the result has proved. It was a bargain by which both parties were equally benefited, and thereby induced to keep the mutual compact. The Germans obtained freedom, which they could not have had in their own country, while their presence was a guarantee to the monarch that this province would not be torn from his crown.

In the midst of a population of serfs, and side by side with proud and overbearing nobles, these German immigrants occupied a totally different and neutral position. Without being noble, they were free men every one of them, enjoying rights and privileges hitherto unknown in the country. Depending directly from the King, they had no other master, and were only obliged to go to war when the monarch in person commanded the expedition. For this reason the country inhabited by the Germans was often termed the Königsboden, or Kingsland, and on their official seal were engraved the words, "Ad retinendam coronam."

The exact date of the arrival of these German colonists in Transylvania is unknown, but appears to have been between **1141** and

1161. That they did not all come at the same time is almost certain. Probably they arrived in successive batches at different periods; for, as we see by history, all did not enjoy exactly the same privileges and rights, but different colonies had been formed under different conditions.

Also the question of what precise part of the German father-land was the home of these out-wanderers is enveloped in some obscurity. They have retained no certain traditions to guide us to a conclusion, and German chronicles of that time make no mention of their departure. The Crusades, which at that epoch engrossed every mind, must have caused these emigrations to pass comparatively unnoticed. Only a sort of vague floating tradition is preserved to this day in some of the Transylvania villages, where on winter evenings some

SAXON BURGHER IN OLDEN TIMES.

old grandam, shrivelled and bent, ensconced behind the blue-tiled stove, will relate to the listening bairns crowding around her knees how, many, many hundred years ago, their ancestors once dwelt on the sea-shore, near to the mouth of four rivers, which all flowed out of a yet larger and mightier river. In this shadowy description probably the river Rhine may be recognized, the more so that in the year 1195 these German colonists are, in a yet existing document, alluded to as *Flanderers.* The name of *Sachsen* (Saxons), as they now call themselves, was, much later, used only as their general designation;

and it is more than probable, from certain differences in language, customs, and features, that different colonies proceeded from widely different parts of the original mother-country.

Although the Hungarian kings generally kept their given word right nobly to the immigrants, yet these had much to suffer, both from Hungarian nobles jealous of the privileges they enjoyed, and from the older inhabitants of the soil, the Wallachians, who, living in a thoroughly barbaric state up in the mountains, used to make frequent raids down into the valleys and plains, there to pillage, burn, and murder whatever came into their hands. If we add to this the frequent invasions of Turks and Tartars, it seems a marvel how this little handful of Germans, brought into a strange country and surrounded by enemies on all sides, should have maintained their independence and preserved their identity under such combination of adverse circumstances. They built churches and fortresses, they formed schools and guilds, they made their own laws and elected their own judges; and in an age when Hungarian nobles could scarcely read or write, these little German colonies were so many havens of civilization in the midst of a howling wilderness of ignorance and barbarism.

The German name of Transylvania—Siebenbürgen, or Seven Forts —was long supposed to have been derived from the seven principal fortresses erected at that time. Some recent historians are, however, of opinion that this name may be traced to *Cibinburg*, a fortress built near the river Cibin, from which the surrounding province, and finally the whole country, was called the land of the Cibinburg—of which, therefore, Siebenbürgen is merely a corruption.

Transylvania remained under the dependence of the Magyars till the year 1526, when, after the battle of Mohacs, which ended so disastrously for the Hungarians, Hungary was annexed to Austria, and Transylvania became an independent duchy, choosing its own regents, but paying, for the most part, a yearly tribute to Turkey.*

---

* The Turkish sway does not seem to have been a very oppressive one, if we are to believe this account of how the Turkish tax-collector used to gather his tithes:

"In a cart harnessed with four horses, the Turkish tax-collector used to drive round the villages in Transylvania; and when he cracked his whip the people came running out and threw, each according to his means, a piece of money into the vat. Sometimes it was but a groat, sometimes even less, for there was but little money in the land at that time; but the Turk was satisfied with what he got, and drove on without further ado."

After something more than a century and a half of independence, Transylvania began to feel its position as an independent State to be an untenable one, and that its ultimate choice lay between complete subjection to either Turkey or Austria. Making, therefore, a virtue of necessity, and hoping thereby to escape the degradation of a conquered province, Transylvania offered itself to Austria, and was by special treaty enrolled in the Crown lands of that empire in 1691.

Finally, in 1867, when the present emperor, Francis Joseph, was crowned at Pesth, Transylvania was once more formally united to Hungary, and, like the rest of the kingdom, divided into *komitats*, or counties.

CHAPTER III.

POLITICAL.

IT is not possible, even in the most cursory account of life and manners in Hungary, to escape all mention of the conflicting political interests which are making of Austro-Hungary one of the most curious ethnographical problems ever presented by history. Taking even Transylvania alone, we should find quite enough to fill a whole volume merely by describing the respective relations of the different races peopling the country. In addition to various minor nationalities, we find here no less than three principal races diametrically opposed to each other in origin, language, habits, and religion—to wit, the Magyars, the Saxons, and the Roumanians, whose exact numbers I have given on a preceding page. The gypsies, whose numbers figure next in the list after the Saxons, need not here be taken into consideration, being absolutely devoid of all political character; but of the other three races, each has its individual aspirations and interests, and each a political object in view which it pursues with dogged persistency.

The Hungarians are at present the masters of the position, having wealth and nobility on their side, besides the reins of government. Since the year 1867, when Hungary, having regained her former independence with extended rights and privileges, re-established a purely Hungarian ministry and an independent Hungarian militia, the progress achieved in the country, both intellectually and commercially, has been remarkable, affording brilliant proof of what can be done by a handful of energetic and intelligent men against a vast majority of other races.

The total population of Hungary, rated at fifteen millions, counts four millions only of purely Hungarian individuals; the rest of the population is made up of Serbs, Croatians, Roumanians, Slovacks, and Germans, all of which (if we except the Germans, whose numbers are insignificant) are far inferior to the Magyars in point of civilization; and here, as elsewhere, when intelligence and wealth are supported by energy, the right of might belonged to the Hungarians, who have always been able to produce skilful and efficient statesmen, knowing their own minds, and clear-sighted as to the country's requirements.

Those now at the helm have had the discernment from the very outset to foresee the danger likely to arise from the ever-increasing spirit of nationality gaining ground among the non-Hungarian inhabitants of the soil. Two courses were here open to them: either seeking to conciliate the various nationalities by concessions to their pretensions; or else, by pursuance of an inflexible policy, to sacrifice all alien considerations to purely Hungarian interests, and impose their own nationality on all without exception.

This latter course was the one adopted by Hungary, who for the last ten years, introducing measures as practical as they are far-sighted, has pursued this object with undeviating consistency.

First of all, the Hungarian tongue was everywhere established as the official language. In all schools, whether of Serbs, Roumanians, or Germans, it became compulsory to teach Hungarian; without a thorough knowledge of the language no one was competent to aspire to any official position; the courts of justice, even in completely non-Hungarian districts, are held in Hungarian, and Hungarian likewise is the word of command throughout the Honved army. Such are the means by which the Government hopes to effect the Magyarization of all its subjects.

But within the last few years we have beheld two new kingdoms spring up at Hungary's very door, Roumania and Serbia—incentive enough to induce all Roumanians and Serbs living in Hungary strenuously to resist this Magyarizing influence, and inspire them with the hope of being one day amalgamated with their more independent countrymen. In Croatia the case is more or less the same, for, being united by similarities of language, custom, and religion to their Serbian neighbors, the Croats far rather incline to assimilate with these than with the tyrannical Magyars; while the Slovacks, continually stirred up by Russian, Ruthenian, and Bohemian agitators, have likewise their reasons for resistance. Add to this that the German colonies, which, far more isolated than the races aforenamed, can never have a serious chance of independent existence, are yet infatuated enough to harbor impossible visions of a union with their father-land, and have consequently ranged themselves among the most vehement opposers of Hungarian rule, and it will be seen that the task which the Magyars have set themselves, of bending all these conflicting interests to their own ends, is indeed a stupendous one. But Hungary, in self-preservation, could not have acted otherwise: it was for her a question of life or death; and having the choice of becoming the hammer or the anvil, who can blame her for choosing the former?

Whether this portentous struggle will outlast our generation, or find its issue within the next few years, will depend upon outward political constellations. So much, however, is certain, that should the Magyars be able to carry through their system during a sufficient space of time, they will have created a State which, by virtue of the richness of its soil, the extent of its domains, and the vigor of its race, will have acquired incontestable right to independent existence.

Should, however, the Oriental question, and with it the Panslavonian one, bring about the inevitable collision of nationalities so long foreseen; should the Balkan races begin to agitate ere Hungary have accomplished her herculean task—then her downfall is certain. The Magyars may, indeed, continue to exist as a nation, but not as a State, and their fate will be that of Poland.

While in the one half of the Austro-Hungarian empire this system of centralizing the power and assimilating all minor interests to the Hungarian idea is being pursued with inflexible ardor, the Cis-Latin provinces — that is to say, Austria proper — are being governed in diametrically opposed fashion.

Till within a few years ago, the German language was the official one in all Cis-Latin provinces, and Germans had there everywhere the upperhand, as to-day the Magyars in the Trans-Latin countries; but since the advent of Count Taafe's Ministry, now seven years ago, the situation has completely changed. The present government, wishing to conciliate the different nationalities, such as Bohemians, Poles, Ruthenians, etc., granted to each of these the free use of its own tongue in school and office—a concession which may be said to mark the beginning of Austria's decomposition. The results of this deplorable system as yet have been that the Germans, who in Austria form the wealthiest and most intelligent part of the population, imbittered at finding themselves degraded from their former position of leaders of the State, have become the most formidable opponents of the Government; while the minor races, only stimulated by the concessions received, are ever clamoring for more. The Taafe Ministry has marvellously succeeded, during the incredibly short space of seven years, in establishing chaos in the administration of the Cis-Latin provinces, contenting no one, and fostering racial contentions which can have but the most melancholy results for the stability of the empire.

Whether a State, not only composed of such heterogeneous racial elements, but, moreover, governed by two such diametrically opposed systems, will have strength to resist attacks from without, who can say? —for it still remains to be practically proved which of the two governments has chosen the right road to success. So much, however, is certain—the Hungarians know what they want, and pursue their preconceived line of political action with consistent energy; while the Austrian Government, never knowing its own mind, is swayed at hazard by whichever of the minor nationalities happens to have the momentary ascendancy, and behindhand, as ever, of "an idea and of an army," may almost be said to deserve the definition of one of its own statesmen,* of being the "land of improbabilities."

CHAPTER IV.

ARRIVAL IN TRANSYLVANIA—FIRST IMPRESSIONS.

THE War Office, whose ways are dark and whose mysteries are inscrutable, had unexpectedly decreed that we were to exchange Galicia for Transylvania.

The unaccountable decisions of a short-sighted Ministry, which, without ostensible reason, send unfortunate military families rolling

---

* The late Count Beust.

about the empire like gigantic foot-balls—from Hungary to Poland, down to Croatia, and up again to Bohemia, all in one breath—too often burst on hapless German *ménages* like a devastating bomb, bringing moans and curses, tears and hysterics, in their train, according as the sufferer happens to be of choleric or lachrymose temperament. Only those who have lived in this country, and tasted of the bitter-sweets of Austrian military life, can tell how formidable it is to be forced to pack up everything—literally everything, from your stoutest kitchen-chairs to your daintiest egg-shell china—half a dozen times during an equal number of years.

For my own part, however—and I am aware that I am considered singular in my views—I had little objection to being treated in this sportive fashion, as long as it gave me the opportunity of seeing fresh scenes and different types of people. There are two sides to every question, a silver—or at least a tin-foil—lining to every leaden cloud, and it is surely wiser to regard one's self as a tourist than as an exile?

What if crockery perish and mirrors be shivered in the portentous flitting? Dry your eyes, and console yourself by gazing at mountains new and lakes unknown. And if furniture be annihilated, and your grand piano-forte reduced to a wailing discord, what of that? Such loss is only gain, for in return you will hear the music of unknown tongues and the murmur of strange waters. If the proceeding be often illogical, the change is always welcome; and on this particular occasion I secretly blessed the playful impetus which had sent our ball of fate thus high up in the air, to alight again in the land beyond the forest.

It was in the beginning of April that we started on our journey, and in Galicia we left everything still deep in ice and snow; but scarce had we passed the Hungarian frontier, and got down on to the broad plains, when a warm, genial breeze came to meet us and tell us that winter was gone. The snow left us by degrees, and with it the poverty-stricken, careworn expression peculiar to Poland; spring flowers ventured out of their hiding-places, singly at first, then in groups of twos and threes, till they grew to extensive patches of gold or sapphire blue, pressing up to the rails on either side of our way. Greasy *kaftans* began to give place to sheepskin *bundas*, and pointed mustaches became more numerous than corkscrew ringlets. The air seemed full of joyous music—the voice of the lark and the strains of

a gypsy fiddler alternately taking up the song of triumph over the
return of spring.

The railway communications are very badly managed, so that it was
only on the evening of the second day (fully forty-eight hours) that
we arrived at Klausenburg, where we were to stop for a night's rest.
It would hardly have taken longer to go from Lemberg to London.

Coming from the Hungarian plains, the entrance into Transylvania is very striking, as the train dashes along narrow winding valleys,
where, below, a green mountain torrent is breaking over gray bowlders;
and above, the cliffs are piled up so high and so near that only by
craning our necks out of the carriage-window can we catch a glimpse
of the sky above. Unfortunately, the early darkness had set in long
before we reached Klausenburg, so that I had no opportunity of observing the country immediately round the town.

Fresh from Polish hotels as we were, the inn where rooms had
been secured struck us as well kept and appointed, though I dare say
that had we come from Vienna or Paris it would have appeared just
fairly second-rate. The beds were excellent, the rooms clean; the
doors could actually be locked or bolted without superhuman effort;
the bells could really ring, and what was stranger yet, their summons
was occasionally attended to.

I was somewhat disappointed next morning when daylight came
round again and showed me the environs of the town. Pretty
enough, but tame and insignificant, with nothing of the sublime grandeur which the entrance into the land had led me to expect. The
town itself differed but little from many other Hungarian towns I
had seen before, and had indeed an exclusively Hungarian character,
being the winter resort of the Magyar aristocracy of Transylvania.

The present town of Klausenburg, or, in Hungarian, Kolosvar,
lying three hundred and thirty-five metres above the sea-level, and
built on the site of Napoca, a Roman city, was founded by German
colonists about the year 1270–1272, and was for many years exclusively a German town, where Hungarians were only tolerated on
sufferance and in one restricted quarter. By degrees, however, these
latter obtained a preponderance; and finally, when the Unitarian sect
made of Klausenburg its principal seat, the Saxons withdrew in dis-
gust from the place altogether.

In the year 1658, Klausenburg was besieged by the Tartars
The Turkish Sultan having deposed George Rakoczy II. for acting

against his will, sent hither the barbarians to devastate the land. Burning and pillaging, the wild hordes reached Klausenburg (then a Saxon city), and standing before its closed gates, they demanded a ransom of thirty thousand thalers for sparing the town.

Martin Auer, the Klausenburg judge and a brave Saxon man, went out to meet the enemy with a portion of the required money. The Tartars threatened to murder him for not bringing the whole of what they asked, but Auer divined that not even the payment of the entire thirty thousand thalers would save the town from pillage. The Tartars intended to take the sum, and then to sack the city. So he begged to be suffered to go as far as the town gates in order to persuade his fellow-citizens to deposit the rest of the money; but when he had reached within speaking distance, he cried out to his countrymen,

"Friends and citizens! I have come hither under the feint of persuading you to pay the rest of the fine demanded by the Tartars; but what I really advise is for you to keep your money and resist the enemy to the last; trust them not, for however much you pay, they will not spare you. For my part, I gladly lay down my life for the good of my people." But hardly had he finished speaking when the Tartars, guessing at the purport of his words, laid hold of the brave Saxon and dragged him off to a cruel death.

A peculiar characteristic of Klausenburg are the Unitarian divorces, which bring many strangers on a flying visit to this town, where the conjugal knot is untied with such pleasing alacrity, and replaced at will by more congenial bonds.

To attain this end the divorcing party must be a citizen of Klausenburg, and prove his possession to house or land in the place. This, however, is by no means so complicated as it sounds, the difficulty being provided for by a row of miserable hovels chronically advertised for sale, and which for a nominal price are continually passing from hand to hand.

House-buying, divorce, and remarriage can therefore be easily accomplished within a space of three or four days—a very valuable arrangement for those to whom time is money. By this convenient system, therefore, if you happen to have quarrelled with your first wife on a Sunday, you have only to take the train to Klausenburg on Monday, become Unitarian on Tuesday, buy a house on Wednesday, be divorced on Thursday, remarried on Friday, and on Saturday sell

2

your house and turn your back on the place with the new-chosen partner of your life, and likewise the pleasant *arrière-pensée* that you can begin again *da capo* next week if so pleases you.

I went to visit this street for sale, which presents a most doleful aspect. As the houses are continually changing hands, none of the transitory owners care to be at the expense of repairs or keeping in order; therefore rotten planking, hingeless gates, broken windows, and caved-in roofs are the general order of the day. A row of card-houses merely to mark this imaginary sort of proprietorship would equally fulfil the purpose.

The town is said to be unhealthy, and the mortality among children very great. This is attributed to the impurity of the drinking-water, several of the springs which feed the town wells running through the church-yard, which lies on a hill.

To our left, about an hour after leaving Klausenburg, we catch sight of the Thorda Cleft, or *Spalt*—one of the most remarkable natural phenomena which the country presents. It is nothing else but a gaping, unexpected rift, of three or four English miles in length, right through the limestone rocks, which rise about twelve hundred feet at the highest point. Deep and gloomy caverns, formerly the abode of robbers, honey-comb these rocky walls, and a wild mountain torrent fills up the space between them, completing a weirdly beautiful scene; but on our first view of it from the railway-carriage it resembled nothing so much as a magnified loaf of bread severed in two by the cut of a gigantic knife.

I do not know how geologists account for the formation of the Thorda Cleft, but the people explain it in their own fashion by a legend:

The Hungarian King Ladislaus, surnamed the Saint, defeated and pursued by his bitterest enemies the Kumanes, sought refuge in the mountains. He was already hard pressed for his life, and close on his heels followed the pagans. Then, in the greatest strait of need, with death staring him in the face, the Christian monarch threw himself on his knees, praying to Heaven for assistance. And see! He forsaketh not those that trust in Him! Suddenly the mountain is rent in twain, and a deep, yawning abyss divides the King from his pursuers.

The rest of the country between Klausenburg and Hermanstadt is bleak and uninteresting—it is, in fact, as I afterwards learned, one of the few ugly stretches to be found in this land, of which it has so

THE THORDA SPALT.

often been said that it is all beauty. A six hours' journey brought us
to our destination, Hermanstadt, lying at the terminus of a small and
sleepy branch railway. Unfortunately, with us also arrived the rain,
streaming down in torrents, and blotting out all view of the landscape
in a persistent and merciless manner; and for full eight days this dis-
mal downpour kept steadily on, trying our patience and souring our
tempers. What more exasperating situation can there be? To have
come to a new place and yet be unable to see it; as soon be sent into
an unknown picture-gallery with a bandage over the eyes.

There was, however, nothing to be done meanwhile but to dodge
about the town under a dripping umbrella and try to gain a general
idea of its principal characteristics.

A little old-fashioned German town, spirited over here by supernatural agency; a town that has been sleeping for a hundred years,
and is only now slowly and reluctantly waking up to life, yawning
and stretching itself, and listening with incredulous wonder to the account of all that has happened in the outside world during its slumber
—such was the first impression I received of Hermanstadt. The top-
heavy, overhanging gables, the deserted watch-towers, the ancient ramparts, the crooked streets, in whose midst the broad currents of a
peaceful stream partly fulfil the office of our newer-fashioned drains,
and where frequently the sprouting grass between the irregular stone
pavement would afford very fair sustenance for a moderate flock of
sheep, all combine to give the impression of a past which has scarcely
gone and of a present which has not yet penetrated.

There are curious old houses, with closely grated windows whose
iron bars are fancifully wrought and twisted, sometimes in the shape
of flowers and branches, roses and briers interlaced, which seem to
have sprung up here to defend the chamber of some beautiful princess
lying spellbound in her sleep of a hundred years. There are quaint
little gardens which one never succeeds in reaching, and which in
some inexplicable manner seem to be built up in a third or fourth
story; sometimes in spring we catch a glimpse of a burst of blossom
far overhead, or a wind-tossed rose will shower its petals upon us, yet
we cannot approach to gather them. There is silence everywhere,
save for occasional vague snatches of melody issuing from a half-open
window—old forgotten German tunes, such as the "Mailüfterl" or
"Anchen von Tharau," played on feeble, toneless spinnets. There
are nooks and corners and unexpected flights of steps leading from the

upper to the lower town, narrow passages and tunnels which connect opposite streets.

"These are to enable the inhabitants to scuttle away from the Turks," I was told, my informant lowering his voice, as if we might expect a row of turbans to appear at the other side of the passage we were traversing. "There is our theatre," he continued, pointing to a dumpy tower bulging out of the rampart-wall. One of the principal strongholds this used to be, but its shape now suited conveniently for the erection of a stage, and the narrow arrow-slits came in handy for the fixing-up of side-scenes.

Many more such old fortress-towers are to be found all over the town, some of which are now used as military stores, while others have been converted into peaceable summer-houses. At the time when Hermanstadt was still a Saxon stronghold each tower had its own name, as the Goldsmiths' Tower, the Tanners', the Locksmiths', etc., according to the particular guild which manned it in time of siege.

From one of these towers it was that the Sultan Amurad was killed by an arrow when besieging the town in 1438 with an army of seventy thousand men.

The whole character of Hermanstadt is thoroughly old German, reminding me rather of some of the Nuremberg streets or portions of Bregenz than of anything to be seen in Hungary.

The streams which run down the centre of each street are no doubt as enjoyable for the ducks who swim in them, as for young ladies desirous of displaying a neat pair of ankles; but for more humdrum mortals they are somewhat of a nuisance. They can, it is true, be jumped in dry weather without particular danger to life or limb; but there are many prejudiced persons who do not care to transform a sober round of shopping into a species of steeple-chase, and who will persist in finding it hard to be unable to purchase a yard of ribbon or a packet of pins without taking several flying leaps over swift watercourses.

Much of the life and occupations of our excellent Saxon neighbors is betrayed by these telltale streamlets, which, chameleon-like, alter their color according to what is going on around them. Thus on washing-days the rivulet in our street used to be of a bright celestial blue, rivalling the laughing Mediterranean in color, unless indeed the family in question were possessed of much scarlet hosiery of inferior quality, in which case it would assume a gory hue suggestive of secret murders. When the chimney-sweep had been paying his rounds in the neighborhood, the current would be dark and gloomy as the turbid waters of the Styx; and when a pig was killed a few doors off— But no; the subject threatens to grow too painful, and I feel that a line must be drawn at the pig.

Such is the every-day aspect of affairs; but in rainy weather these little brooklets, becoming obstreperous, swell out of all proportions, and for this frequent contingency small transportable bridges are kept in readiness to be placed across the principal thoroughfares of the town. After a very heavy thunder-plump in summer, even these bridges do not suffice, as then the whole street is flooded from side to side, and for an hour or so Hermanstadt becomes Venice — minus the gondolas.

These occasional floodings give rise to many amusing incidents, as that of an officer who, invited

OLD FORTRESS-TOWER ON THE RAMPARTS AT HERMANSTADT.*

to dinner by the commanding general, beheld with dismay the dinner-hour approach. He had only to cross the street, or rather the canal, for at that moment it presented the appearance of a navigable river. Would the waves subside in time? was his anxious question as he gazed at the clock in growing suspense, and dismally surveyed his beautifully fitting patent-leather boots. No, the waves did not sub-

* Reprinted from a publication of the Transylvanian Carpathian Society.

side, and no carriage was to be procured, the half-dozen *fiacres* of which Hermanstadt alone could boast being already engaged. The clock struck the quarter. "What is to be done?" moaned the unhappy man in agony of spirit, while the desperate alternatives of swimming or of suicide began to dance before his fevered brain. "A boat, a boat, a kingdom for a boat!" he repeated, mechanically, when it struck him that the quotation might as well be taken literally in this case, and that in default of a boat, he had three good steeds in his stables. "Saddle my horse—my tallest one!" he cried, excitedly; "I am saved!" —and so he was. The gallant steed bore him through the roaring flood, bringing him high and dry to the door of his host, with patent boots intact.

Meanwhile—to return to the subject of my first days at Hermanstadt—the rain had continued to fall for a whole week, and I was beginning to lose all patience. "I don't believe in the mountains you all tell me about!" I felt inclined to say, when my first eight days had shown me nothing but leaden clouds and dull gray mists; but even while I thought it, the clouds were rolling away, and bit by bit a splendid panorama was unfolding before my eyes.

Sure enough, they were there, the mountains I had just been insulting by my disbelief, a long glittering row of snowy peaks shining in the outbursting sunshine, so delicately transparent in their loveliness, so harmonious in their blended coloring, so sublimely grand in their sweeping lines, that I could have begged their pardon for having doubted their existence!

As one beautiful picture often suffices to light up a dingy apartment, so one lovely view gives life and interest to a monotonous county town. It takes the place of theatres, art galleries, and glittering shop-windows; it acts at times as a refreshing medicine or a stimulating tonic; and though I saw it daily, it used to strike me afresh with a sense of delightful surprise whenever I stepped round the corner of my street, and stood in face of this glorious tableau.

The town of Hermanstadt lies in the centre of a large and fertile plain, intersected by the serpentine curves of the river Cibin, and dotted over by well-built Saxon villages. To the north and west the land is but gently undulating, while to the east and south the horizon is bounded by this imposing chain of the Fogarascher Hochgebirg, their highest peaks but seldom free from snow, their base streaked by alternate stretches of oak, beech, and pine forests.

At one point this forest, which must formerly have covered the entire plain, reaches still to the farther end of the town, melting into the promenade, so that you can walk in the shade of time-honored oak-trees right to the foot of the mountains—a distance of some eight English miles.

To complete my general sketch of the town of Hermanstadt, I shall merely mention that although our house was situated in one of the liveliest streets, yet the passing through of a cart or carriage was a rare event, which, in its unwonted excitement, instinctively caused every one to rush to their windows; that the pointed irregular pavement, equally productive of corns and destructive to *chaussure*, seems to be the remnant of some mediæval species of torture; that gas is unknown, and the town but insufficiently lighted by dingy petroleum lamps.

Probably by the time that Hermanstadt fully wakens up to life again, it will discover to its astonishment that it has slept through a whole era, and skipped the gas stage of existence altogether, for it will then be time to replace the antediluvian petroleum lamps, not by the already old-fashioned gas ones, but by the newer and more brilliant rays of electric light.

CHAPTER V.

SAXON HISTORICAL FEAST—LEGEND.

As I happened to arrive at Hermanstadt* precisely seven hundred years later than the German colonists who had founded that city, I had the good-luck to assist at a national festival of peculiarly interesting character.

Of the town's foundation, old chronicles tell us how the outwanderers, on reaching the large and fertile plain where it now stands, drove two swords crosswise into the ground, and thereon took their oath to be true and faithful subjects of the monarch who had called

---

* The Hungarian name of Hermanstadt is Nagy-Szeben, and its Roumanian appellation Sibiin.

them hither, and with their best heart's-blood to defend the land which had given them shelter. The two swords on which this oath was registered were carefully preserved, and sent, one to Broos and the other to Draas—two towns marking the extremities of the Saxonland—there to be treasured up forever. But in consequence of evil . times which came over the land, and of the war and bloodshed which devastated it, one of these swords—that of Broos—got lost. But we are told that the other is still to be seen in the church of Draas. It is of man's length, from which it is argued that these Saxon immigrants were well-grown and vigorous men.

Who this Herman was who gave his name to the city can only be conjectured—probably one of the leaders of the little band, for, as we see by the names of some of the surrounding villages, each has been called after some old German, whose identity has not transpired, as Neppendorf from Eppo, Hammersdorf from Humbert, etc.

Some old chronicles, indeed, tell us that when the Hungarian King Stephen I. was married to Gisela, sister of the German King Henry II., there came in her suite a poor Baron Herman, along with his family, from Nuremberg to Transylvania, and he it was who founded the settlement which later developed into the present town of Hermanstadt. It is said that the first settlement was formed in 1202; likewise that the said Herman lived to the age of a hundred and twenty-five, and was the progenitor of a renowned and powerful race.

Another legend accounts for the foundation of Hermanstadt with the old well-worn tale which has done duty for so many other cities, of a shepherd who, when allowed to take as much land as he could compass with a buffalo's hide, cut up the skin into narrow strips, and so contrived to secure a handsome property. This particular sharp-witted peasant was, by profession, a keeper of swine; and there is a fountain in the lower town which still goes by the name of the *funtine porcolor,* or swineherd's well.

With all these conflicting statements staring one in the face, there did not seem to be (so far as I could learn) any very authentic reason for supposing Hermanstadt to have been founded precisely in 1184; but everybody had apparently made up their minds that such was the case, so the date was to be commemorated by a costumed procession, extensive preparations for which kept the quiet little town in a state of fermentation for many weeks beforehand.

All the tradesmen of the place seemed to have suddenly gone mad, and could hardly be induced to attend to the every-day wants of commonplace mortals whose ancestors had not the *prestige* of a seven-centuried expatriation. If I went to order a pair of walking-boots, I was disdainfully informed that I could not hope for them that week, as all hands were employed in fashioning high-peaked leather boots of yellow pig-skin for Herman and his retainers. If I looked in at the glove-maker's I fared no better, for he had lost all interest in pale kids or *gants de suède;* and the solitary pair of Sarah Bernhardt gloves, hitherto the pride of his show-window, had been ruthlessly cast aside to make way for ponderous gauntlets of heroic dimensions. The tailors would have nothing to do with vulgar coat or trousers, but had soared unanimously to the loftier regions of jerkins and galligaskins; even the tinsmith had lost his mental equilibrium, apparently laboring under the delusion that he was an ancient armorer who could not possibly demean himself by mending a simple modern pudding-mould.

We unfortunate strangers, bootless, gloveless, coatless, and puddingless as we were in those days, had a very hard time of it indeed while this national fever was at its height, and keenly felt the terrible disadvantage of not having been born as ancient Saxons. At last, however, the preparations were complete, and forgetting our privations, we were fain to acknowledge the sight to be one of the most curious and exceptional we had ever witnessed. The old-fashioned streets made a fitting background for this mediæval pageant, in which peasants and burghers, on foot and on horseback; groups of maidens, quaintly attired, plying the distaff as they went along; German matrons, with jewelled head-dresses and cunningly wrought golden girdles; gayly ornamented chariots, bearing the fruits of the field or the trophies of the chase, passed us in solemn procession; while on a sylvan stage erected in the depths of the old oak forest a simple but moving drama set forth the words and actions of the forefathers of those very actors—the German colonists who, seven hundred years previously, had come hither to seek a home in the wild Hungarian forests.

The costumes and procession had been arranged by native artists, and, as a work of art, no doubt many parts of the performance were open to criticism. Some of our fashionable painters would assuredly have turned sick and faint at sight of the unfortunate combinations

of coloring which frequently marred the effect of otherwise correctly
arranged costumes.   Whoever has lived in large towns must have
seen such things better done, over and over again; but what gave
this festival a unique stamp of originality, not to be attained by any
amount of mere artistic arrangement, was the feeling which penetrated the whole scene and animated each single actor.

MOUNTED PEASANTS, FROM THE HISTORICAL PROCESSION.

It is difficult to conceive, as it is impossible to describe, the deep
and peculiar impression caused by this display of patriotism on the
part of Germans who have never seen their father-land—Rhinelanders
who are not likely ever to behold the blue rushing waters of the
Rhine.   Until now we had always been taught that Germany was inhabited by Germans, France by Frenchmen, and England by Englishmen; but here we have such a complex medley of nationalities as
wellnigh to upset all our school-room teaching.   Listening to the
words of the German drama, we can easily fancy ourselves at Cologne

or Nuremberg, were it not for the dark faces of Roumanian peasants pushing forward to look at the unwonted scene, and for the Hungarian uniforms of the gendarmes who are pushing them back.

More primitive but not less interesting than the historical procession just described is the way in which the arrival of these German immigrants is still yearly commemorated in the village of Nadesch. There, on a particular day of the year, all the lads dress up as pilgrims, in long woollen garments, rope girdles, and with massive staves in their hands. Thus attired, they assemble round the flag; a venerable old man takes the lead, beating the drum; and, singing psalms, they go in procession down the street, now and then entering some particularly spacious court-yard, where a dance is executed and refreshments partaken of. A visit to the pastor is also *de rigueur*, and the procession only breaks up at evenfall, after having traversed the whole village from end to end. When questioned as to the signification of this custom, the people answer, " Thus came our fathers, free people like ourselves, from Saxonia into this land, behind the flag and drum, and with staves in their hands. And because we have not ourselves invented this custom, neither did our ancestors invent it, but have transmitted it to us from generation to generation, so do we, too, desire to hand it down to our children and grandchildren."

How these Germans came to settle so many hundred miles away from their own country has also formed the subject of numerous tales, none prettier nor more suggestive than their identification with the lost children of Hameln—a well-known German legend, rendered familiar to English readers through Browning's poem.

"It was in the year 1284" (so runs the tale) "that, in the little town of Hameln, in Westphalia, a strange individual made his appearance. He wore a coat of cloth of many colors, and announced himself as a rat-catcher, engaging to rid the town of all rats and mice for a certain sum of money. The bargain being struck, the rat-catcher drew out of his pocket a small pipe, and began whistling; whereupon from every barn, stable, cellar, and garret there issued forth a prodigious number of rats and mice, collecting in swarms round the stranger, all intent upon his music.

" All the vermin of the place being thus assembled, the piper, still playing, proceeded to the banks of the river Weser, and rolling up his breeches above the knee, he waded into the water, blindly followed by rats and mice, which were speedily drowned in the rushing current.

"But the burghers of Hameln, seeing themselves thus easily delivered from their plague, repented the heavy sum of money they had promised, putting off the payment, under various excuses, whenever the stranger claimed the reward of his labors.

"At last the piper grew angry and went away, cursing the town which had behaved so dishonorably; but he was seen to haunt the neighborhood, dressed as a huntsman, with high-peaked scarlet cap; and at daybreak on the 26th of June, feast of St. John, the shrill note of his pipe was again heard in the streets of Hameln.

"This time neither rats nor mice responded to the summons, for all vermin had perished in the waters of the Weser; but the little children came running out of the houses, struggling out of their parents' arms, and could not be withheld from following the sinister piper. In this way he led the infantine procession to the foot of a neighboring hill, into which he disappeared along with the children he had beguiled. Among these was the half-grown-up daughter of the burgomaster of Hameln, a maiden of wondrous grace and beauty.

"A nurse-maid who, with a little one in her arms, had been irresistibly compelled to join the procession, found strength enough at the last moment to tear herself away, and, reaching the town in breathless haste, brought the sad news to the bereaved parents. Also one little boy, who had run out in his shirt, feeling cold, went back to fetch his jacket, and was likewise saved from his comrades' fate; for by the time he regained the hill-side the opening had closed up, leaving no trace of the mysterious piper nor of the hundred and thirty children who had followed him."

Nor were they ever found again by the heart-broken parents; but popular tradition has averred the Germans who about that time made their appearance in Transylvania to be no other than the lost children of Hameln, who, having performed their long journey by subterranean passages, reissued to the light of day through the opening of a cavern known as the Almescher Höhle, in the north-east of Transylvania.

CHAPTER VI.

THE SAXONS: CHARACTER—EDUCATION—RELIGION.

W HOEVER has lived among these Transylvanian Saxons, and has taken the trouble to study them, must have remarked that not only seven centuries' residence in a strange land and in the midst of antagonistic races has made them lose none of their identity, but that they are, so to say, *plus catholiques que le pape*—that is, more thoroughly Teutonic than the Germans living to-day in the original father-land. And it is just because of the adverse circumstances in which they were placed, and of the opposition and attacks which met them on all sides, that they have kept themselves so conservatively unchanged. Feeling that every step in another direction was a step towards the enemy, finding that every concession they made threatened to become the link of a captive's chain, no wonder they clung stubbornly, tenaciously, blindly to each peculiarity of language, dress, and custom, in a manner which has probably not got its parallel in history. Left on their native soil, and surrounded by friends and countrymen, they would undoubtedly have changed as other nations have changed. Their isolated position and the peculiar circumstances of their surroundings have kept them what they were. Like a faithful portrait taken in the prime of life, the picture still goes on showing the bloom of the cheek and the light of the eye, long after Time's destroying hand, withering the original, has caused it to lose all resemblance to its former self; and it is with something of the feeling of gazing at such an old portrait that we contemplate these German people who dress like old bass-reliefs of the thirteenth and fourteenth centuries, and continue to hoard up provisions within the church walls, as in the days when besieged by Turk or Tartar. Such as these Saxons wandered forth from the far west to seek a home in a strange land, such we find them again to-day, seven centuries later, like a corpse frozen in a glacier which comes to light unchanged after a long lapse of years.

From an artistic point of view these Saxons are decidedly an unlovely race. There is a want of flowing lines and curves and a superfluity of angles about them, most distressing to a sensitive eye. The women may usually be described as having rather good hair, indifferent complexions, narrow shoulders, flat busts, and gigantic feet. Their features, of a sadly unfinished wooden appearance, irresistibly reminded me of the figures of Noah and his family out of a sixpenny Noah's ark. There is something Noah's-ark-like, too, about their attire, which, running entirely in hard straight lines, with nothing graceful or flowing about them, no doubt helped to produce this Scriptural impression. The Saxon peasant is stiff without dignity, just as he is honest without being frank. Were the whole world peopled by this race alone, our dictionaries might have been lightened of a good many unnecessary words, such as elegance, grace, fascination, etc.

Of course, now and then one comes across an exception to this general rule and finds a pretty girl, like a white poppy in a field of red ones; but such exceptions are few and far between, and I have remarked that on an average it takes three well-populated villages to produce two bonnie lassies.

The men are on the whole pleasanter to look at than the fair sex, having often a certain ungainly picturesqueness of their own, reminding one of old Flemish paintings.

Something hard and grasping, avaricious and mistrustful, characterizes the expression of most Saxon peasants. For this, however, they are scarcely to blame, any more than for their flat busts and large feet —their character, and consequently their expression, being but the natural result of circumstances, the upshot of seven centuries of stubborn resistance and warfare with those around them. "We Saxons have always been cheated or betrayed whenever we have had to do with strangers," they say; and no doubt they are right. The habit of mistrust developed almost to an instinct cannot easily be got rid of, even if there be no longer cause to justify it.

This defensive attitude towards strangers which pervades the Saxons' every word and action makes it, however, difficult to feel prepossessed in their favor. Taken in the sense of antiquities, they are no doubt an extremely interesting people, but viewed as living men and women, not at first sight attractive to a stranger; and while compelling our admiration by the solid virtues and independent spirit which have kept him what he is, the Saxon peasant often shows to disadvantage beside his less civilized, less educated, and also less honest neighbor the Roumanian.

As a natural consequence of this mistrust, the spirit of speculation is here but little developed—for speculation cannot exist without some degree of confidence in one's neighbor. They do not care to risk one florin in order to gain ten, but are content to keep a firm grasp on what they have got. There are no beggars at all to be seen in Saxon towns, and one never hears of large fortunes gained or lost. Those who happen to be wealthy have only become so by the simple but somewhat tedious process of spending half their income only, during a period of half a century; and after they have in this manner achieved wealth, it does not seem to profit them much, for they go on living as they did before, nourishing themselves on scanty fare, and going to bed early in order to save the expense of lights.

The townsfolk are weaker and punier editions of the villagers, frequently showing marks of a race degenerated from constant inter-marriage; and, stripped of their ancient Noah's-ark costume, lose much of their attraction.

They are essentially a *bourgeois* nation, possessing neither titles nor nobility of their own, although many can boast of lengthy pedigrees. Those who happen to be *adel* (noble) have only obtained their *von* in some exceptional manner in later times, and the five-pointed crown seems somewhat of an anomaly.

Although the Saxons talk of Germany as their father-land, yet their patriotic feeling is by no means what we are accustomed to understand by that word. Their attachment to the old country would seem rather to be of prosaic than romantic sort. "We attach ourselves to the German nation and language," they say, endeavoring to explain the complicated nature of their patriotism, "because it offers us the greatest advantages of civilization and culture; we should equally have attached ourselves to any other nation which offered us equal advantages, whether that nation had happened to be Hungarian, French, or Chinese. If the Hungarians had happened to be more civilized than ourselves, we should have been amalgamated with them long ago." *

Such an incomprehensible sort of patriot would probably have been condemned by Scott to go down to his grave "unwept, unhonored, and unsung." But I suppose that allowances must be made for

---

* This, however, may be doubted, as I do not believe that, under any circumstances, a natural amalgamation between Germans and Magyars could ever have come about. There is a too deeply inrooted dislike between the two races.

3

their peculiar position, and that it is difficult to realize what it feels
like to be a grafted plant.

There is one village in Transylvania which, isolated in the midst
of a Hungarian population, offers an instance of a more complex species of nationality than any I have yet heard of. This is the village
of Szass Lona, near Klausenburg, which used to be Saxon, but where
the people have gradually forgotten their own mother-tongue and
can only speak Hungarian. There is, however, no drop of Hungarian blood in their veins, as they marry exclusively among themselves; and they have retained alike the German type of feature and
the national Saxon dress intact in all its characteristics. Also the
family names throughout the village are German ones—as Hindrik,
Tod, Jäger, Hubert, etc.

Though none of these people can speak a word of German, and
no one can remember the time when German was spoken in the village, yet during the revolution of 1848 these Hungarian-speaking
Germans rose to a man to fight against the Magyars.

The Saxon dialect—totally distinct from modern German—has, I
am told, most resemblance to the patois spoken by the peasants near
Luxemburg. It is harsh and unpleasant to the ear, but has in some
far-off and indefinable way a certain caricatured likeness to English.
Often have I been surprised into turning round sharply in the street
to see who could be speaking English behind me, only to discover two
Saxon peasants comparing notes as to the result of their marketing.

The language, however, differs considerably in different neighborhoods; and a story is told of natives of two different Saxon villages,
who, being unable to understand one another, were reduced to con-
versing in Roumanian.

The *Sachsengraf* (Count), or Comes, was formerly the head of the
nation, chosen by the people, and acknowledging no other authority
but that of the King. He was at once the judge and the leader of
his people, and had alone the power of pronouncing sentence of death,
in token of which four fir-trees were planted in front of his house.
The original meaning of this I take to be, that in olden times the
malefactors were executed on the spot, and suspended on these very
trees, in full sight of the windows — a pleasant sight, truly, for the
ladies of the family.

Nowadays the Saxon Comes has shrunk to a mere shadow of his
former self; for though there is still nominally a Comes who resides

at Hermanstadt, his position is as unlike what it used to be as those four trumpery-looking little Christmas-trees stuck before his door resemble the portentous gallows of which they are the emblem. It is, in fact, merely as a harmless concession to Saxon national feeling that the title has been preserved at all—a mere meaningless appendage tacked on to the person of the Hungarian *obergespan,* or sheriff.

The principal strength of these Saxon colonists has always lain in their schools, whose conservation they jealously guard, supporting them entirely from their own resources, and stubbornly refusing all help from the Government. They do not wish to accept favors, they say, and thereby incur obligations. These schools had formerly the name of being among the very best in Austria; and I have heard of many people who from a distance used to send their children to study there, some twenty to thirty years ago. That this reputation is, however, highly overrated is an undoubted fact, as I know from sad experience with my own children, though it is not easy to determine where the fault exactly lies. The Saxons declare their schools to have suffered from Hungarian interference, which limits their programme in some respects, while insisting on the Hungarian language being taught in every class; but many people consider the Saxons themselves quite as much to blame for the bad results of their teaching. Doubtless, in this as in other respects, it is their exaggerated conservatism which is at fault; and, keeping no account of the age we live in, what was reckoned good some thirty years ago may be called bad to-day.

Anyhow, between the reforming Hungarians and the conservative Saxons, unfortunate stranger boys have a very hard time of it indeed at the Hermanstadt Gymnasium, and it is a fact beginning to be generally acknowledged that children coming to Austria from Transylvanian schools are thrown two classes back.

But the whole question of education in Austria is such a provoking and unsatisfactory one that it is hardly possible to speak of it with either patience or politeness; and by none are its evil effects more disastrously felt than by hapless military families, who, compelled to shift about in restless fashion from land to land, are alternately obliged to conform their children to the most opposite requirements of utterly different systems.

Thus the son of an officer serving in the Austrian army may be obliged to study half a dozen different languages (in addition to Latin,

Greek, German, and French) during a hardly greater number of years. He must learn Italian because his father is serving at Trieste, and may be getting on fairly well with that language when he is abruptly called upon to change it for Polish, since Cracow is henceforth the town where he is to pursue his studies. But hardly has he got familiar with the soft Slave tongue when, ten to one, his accent will be ruined for life by an untimely transition to Bohemia, where the hideous Czech language has become *de rigueur*. Slavonian and Ruthenian may very likely have their turn at the unfortunate infant before he has attained the age of twelve, unless the distracted father be reduced to sacrifice his military career to the education of his son.

It is not of our own individual case that I would speak thus strongly, for our boys, being burdened with only seven languages (to wit, Polish, English, German, French, Greek, Latin, and Hungarian), would scarcely be counted ill-used, as Austrian boys go, having escaped Bohemian, Slavonian, Ruthenian, and Italian ; yet assuredly to us it was a very happy day indeed when we made a bonfire of the Magyar school-books, and ceased quaking at sight of the formidable individual who taught Hungarian at the Hermanstadt Gymnasium..

O happy English school-boys, you know not how much you have to be thankful for !—your own noble language, adorned with a superficial layer of Greek and Latin, and at most supplemented by a little atrocious French, being sufficient to set you up for life. Think of those others who are pining in a complicated net-work of Bohemian, Polish, Hungarian, Slavonian, Italian, Croatian, and Ruthenian fetters; think of them, and drop a sympathizing tear over their mournful lot !

That the Saxon school-professors are well-educated, intelligent men is no proof in favor of the schools themselves, for here another motive is at work, namely, no man can aspire to be pastor without passing through the university, and then practising for several years at a public gymnasium ; and as these places are very lucrative, there is a great run upon them. Now, as formerly, most young men are sent to complete their studies at some German university town—Heidelberg, Göttingen, or Jena—an undertaking which, before the days of railroads, must have required considerable resolution to enable those concerned to encounter the hardships of a journey which took from ten to twelve weeks to perform. It was usually conducted in the following manner: Some enterprising Roumanian peasant har-

nessed twelve to fourteen horses to some lumbering vehicle, and, laden
with a dozen or more students thirsting for knowledge, pilgered thus
to the German university town some eight or nine hundred miles off.
Returning to Transylvania some six months later, he brought back
another batch of young men who had completed their studies.

The weight which these Saxons have always attached to education
may be gathered from the fact that in almost each of their fortified
churches, or burgs, there was a tower set apart for the inculcation of
knowledge, and to this day many such are still in existence, and known
as the *schul thurm* (school-tower). Even when the enemy was standing outside the walls, the course of learning was not allowed to be in-
terrupted. It must have been a strange sight and a worthy subject
for some historical painter to see this crowd of old-fashioned fair-
haired children, all huddled together within the dingy turret; some
of the bolder or more inquisitive flaxen heads peering out of the narrow gullet-windows at the turbans and crescents below, while the grim-
faced mentor, stick in hand, recalls them to order, vainly endeavoring
to fix their wandering attention each time a painim arrow whizzed
past the opening.

Why these Saxons, who have shown themselves so rigidly conservative on all other points, should nevertheless have changed their
religion, might puzzle a stranger at first sight. The mere spirit of
imitation would not seem sufficient to account for it, and Luther's
voice could hardly have penetrated to this out-of-the-way corner of
Europe at a time when telegraphs and telephones were yet unknown.
The solution of this riddle is, however, quite simple, and lies close at
hand, when we remember that even before the Reformation all those
preparing for the Sacerdoce went to Germany to complete their studies. These, consequently, caught the reforming infection, and brought
it back fresh from headquarters, acting, in fact, as so many living telephones, who, conveying the great reformer's voice from one end of
Europe to the other, promulgated his doctrines with all the enthusiasm and fire of youth.

Every year thus brought fresh recruits from the scene of action;
no wonder, then, that the original Catholic clerical party grew daily
smaller and weaker, and proved unable to stem this powerful new
current. The contest was necessarily an unequal one: on one side,
impassioned rhetoric and the fire of youth; on the other, the drowsy

resistance of a handful of superannuated men, grown rusty in their theology and lax in the exercise of their duties.

In the year 1523 Luther's teaching had already struck such firm roots at Hermanstadt that the Archbishop of Gran, to whose diocese Hermanstadt then belonged, obtained a royal decree authorizing the destruction of all Lutheran books and documents as pernicious and heretical. Accordingly an archiepiscopal commissary was despatched to Hermanstadt, and all burghers were compelled to deliver up their Protestant books and writings to be burned in the public market-place. It is related that on this occasion, when the bonfire was at its highest, the wind, seizing hold of a semi-consumed Psalter, carried it with such force against the head of the bishop's emissary that, severely burned, he fainted away on the spot. The book was thrown back into the fire, where it soon burned to ashes; but on the third day after the accident the commissary died of the wounds received.

Another anecdote relating to the Reformation is told of the village of Schass, which, while Luther's doctrine was being spread in Transylvania, despatched one of its parishioners, named Strell, to Rome in quest of a Papal indulgence for the community. More than once already had Strell been sent to Rome on a like errand, and each time, on returning home with the granted indulgence for his people, he was received by a solemn procession of all the villagers, bearing flying banners and singing sacred hymns. He was, therefore, not a little surprised this time, on approaching the village, to see the road deserted before him, though he had given warning of his intended arrival. The bells were dumb, and not a soul came out to meet him; but his astonishment reached its climax when, on nearing the church, he perceived the images of the saints he had been wont to revere lying in the mire outside the church walls. To his wondering question he received the reply that in his absence the villagers had changed their faith. Strell, however, did not imitate their example, but raising up the holy images from their inglorious position, he gave them an honorable place in his house, remaining Catholic to the end of his days.

Nevertheless, in spite of many such incidents, the change of religion in Transylvania brought about fewer disturbances than in most other places. There was little strife or bloodshed, and none of that fierce fanaticism which has so often injured and weakened both causes The Saxon peasantry did this as they do everything else, calmly and practically; and the Government permitting each party to follow its own religion unmolested, in a comparatively short time peace and order were re-established in the interior of the country.

Without wishing to touch on such a very serious subject as the respective merits of the two religions, or attempting to obtrude personal convictions, it seems to me, from a purely artistic point of view, that the sterner and simpler Protestant religion fits these independent and puritanical-looking Saxon folk far better than the ancient faith can have done; while the more graceful forms of the Oriental Church, its mystic ceremonies and arbitrary doctrines, are unquestionably better adapted to an ardent, ignorant, and superstitious race like the Roumanian one.

CHAPTER VII.

SAXON VILLAGES.

SAXON villages are as easily distinguished from Roumanian ones, composed of wretched earthen hovels, as from Hungarian hamlets, which are marked by a sort of formal simplicity. The Saxon houses are larger and more massive; each one, solidly built of stone, stands within a roomy court-yard surrounded by a formidable stone wall. Building and repairing is the Saxon peasant's favorite employment, and the Hungarian says of him ironically that when the German has nothing better to do he pulls down his house and builds it up again by way of amusement.

Each village is usually formed of one long principal street, extending sometimes fully an English mile along the high-road; only when the village happens to be built at a junction of several roads, the streets form a cross or triangle, in the centre of which mostly stands the church. From this principal street or streets there sometimes branch off smaller by-streets on either side; but these are seldom more than five or six houses deep, for the Saxon lays great stress on the point of locality, and the question of high-street or by-street is to him every whit as important as the alternative of Grosvenor Square or City would be to a Londoner.

Formerly no Roumanians or gypsies were tolerated within Saxon villages, but of late these people have been gradually creeping nearer, and now most German villages have at one end a shabby sort of *faubourg*, or suburb, composed of Roumanian and gypsy hovels.

The principal street, often broad enough to admit of eight carts driving abreast, presents but little life at first sight. The windows of the broad gable-end next the street have often got their shutters closed, for this is the best room, reserved for state occasions. Only when we open the gate and step into the large court-yard can we gain some insight into the life and occupations of the inhabitants.

Near to the entrance stands the deep draw-well, and all round are built the sheds and stables for sheep, horses, cows, and buffaloes, while behind these buildings another gate generally opens into a spacious

.SAXON PEASANT HOUSE.

kitchen-garden. From the court five or six steps lead up to a sort of open veranda, where the peasant can sit in summer and overlook his farm laborers. From this passage the kitchen is entered, to the right and left of which are respectively the common and the best room, both good-sized apartments, with two windows each. In addition to these there is often a smaller one-windowed room, in which reside a young married couple, son or daughter of the house, who have not yet had time to found their own hearth-stone; or else there lives here the old widowed father or mother, who has abdicated in favor of the young people. A ladder or rough flight of steps leads to the loft; and below the veranda is the entrance to the cellar, where stores of pickled sauerkraut, the dearly beloved national dish of the Saxons, and casks of their pearly amber-colored wine, are among the principal features of the provisions.

In the village street, in front of each peasant house, there used formerly to stand a large fruit-tree—pear, apple, or sometimes mulberry—whose spreading branches cast a pleasant shade over the stone bench placed there for the convenience of those who like to enjoy a "crack" with the neighbors on fine evenings after the work is done. Many of these trees have now been cut down, for it was found that the godless gypsies used to make their harvest there while the pious Saxons were at church; or else unmannerly school-urchins in pelting down the fruit with stones would sometimes hit the window-panes instead, and thus cause still greater damage. The result is, therefore, that most Saxon villages now present a somewhat bleak and staring appearance, and that on a burning summer day it is not easy to find a shady bench on which to rest a while.

It may be of interest here to quote the statistical figures relating to a large and flourishing village in the north-east of Transylvania:

Houses, 326 (of these 32 are earth hovels).

Heads of population, 1416—of these the proportion of different nationalities as follows:

Saxons—481 male, 499 female.
Hungarians—2.
Roumanians — 118 male, 83 female (mostly farm-servants).
Tziganes—104 men, 106 women.
Jews—14 male, 9 female.

In this village, which is exceptionally rich in cattle, the different animals number:

Bulls	3	Horses	475
Cows	357	Goats	182
Young cattle	575	Pigs	734
Oxen	1200	Sheep	1000–1500
Buffaloes	120		

Most of the sheep in Transylvania are in the hands of the Roumanians, while the pigs invariably belong to the Saxons. Among these latter, 1000 men possess on an average 215 horses, while among the Szekels only 51 will be found to the same number of heads.

The Saxon peasant, being an enemy to all modern improvements, goes on cultivating his fields much as did his forefathers six hundred years ago. Clinging to the antiquated superstition that a field is the more productive the longer it lies fallow, each piece of ground is ploughed and sowed once only in three years; and having, owing to the insufficient population, rarely enough hands to till his land himself, he is obliged to call in the assistance of Roumanian farm-servants.

Other people, too, have taken advantage of this agricultural somnolency of the Saxons; so the Bulgarians, who pilger hither in troops every spring-time to rent the Saxons' superfluous fields, bringing with them their own tools and seed, and in autumn, having realized the profit of their labor, wend their way back to their homes and families. The great specialty of these Bulgarian farmers is onions, of which they contrive to rear vast crops, far superior in size and quality to those grown by the natives. A Bulgarian onion field is easily distinguished from a Saxon one by its trim, orderly appearance, the perfect regularity with which the rows are planted, and the ingenious arrangements for providing water in time of drought.

Of the numerous Saxon villages which dot the plain around Hermanstadt, I shall here only attempt to mention two or three of those with which I have the most intimate acquaintance, as having formed the object of many a walk and ride. First, there is Heltau—which, however, has rather the character of a market-town than a village—lying in a deep hollow at the foot of the hills south of Hermanstadt, and with nothing either rural or picturesque about it. Yet whoever chances first to behold Heltau, as I did, on a fine evening in May, when the fruit-trees are in full blossom, will carry away an impression not easily forgotten. From the road, which leads down in serpentine curves, the village bursts on our eyes literally framed in a thick garland of blossom, snowy white and delicate peach color combining to cast a fictitious glamour over what is in reality a very unattractive place.

The inhabitants of Heltau, nearly all cloth-makers by trade, fabricate that rough white cloth, somewhat akin to flannel, of which the Roumanians' hose is made. It is also largely exported to different parts of the empire, and Polish Jews are often seen to hover about the place. Such, in fact, is the attraction exercised by this white woollen tissue that a colony of the children of Israel would have been

OLD TOWN GATE AT HERMANSTADT (ON THE HELTAU SIDE).

formed here long ago had not the wary Saxons strenuously opposed such encroachment.

Once riding past here in autumn, I was puzzled to remark several fields near Heltau bearing a white appearance almost like that of snow, yet scarcely white enough for that; on coming nearer, this whiteness resolved itself into wool, vast quantities of which, covering several acres of ground, had been put out there to dry after the triple washing necessary to render it fit for weaving purposes.

The church at Heltau rejoices in the distinction of four turrets affixed to the belfry-tower, which turrets were at one time the cause of much dissension between Heltau and Hermanstadt. It was not allowed for any village church to indulge in such luxuries—four turrets being a mark of civic authority only accorded to towns; but in 1590, when the church at Heltau was burned down, the villagers built it up again as it now stands—a piece of presumption which Hermanstadt at first refused to sanction. The matter was finally compromised by the Heltauers consenting to sign a document, wherein they declared the four turrets to have been put there merely in guise of ornamentation, giving them no additional privileges whatsoever, and that they pledged themselves to remain as before submissive to the authority of Hermanstadt.

Some people, however, allege Heltau, or, as it used to be called, "The Helt," to be of more ancient origin than Hermanstadt—concluding from the fact that formerly the shoemakers, hatters, and other tradesmen here resided, but that during the pest all the inhabitants dying out to the number of seven, the land around was suffered to fall into neglect. Then the Emperor sent other Germans to repeople the town, and the burghers of Hermanstadt came and bought up the privileges of the Heltauers.

The excellence of the Heltau pickled sauerkraut is celebrated in a Saxon rhyme, which runs somewhat as follows:

> "Draaser wheaten bread,
> Heltau's cabbage red,
> Streitford's bacon fine,
> Bolkatsch pearly wine,
> Schässburg's maidens fair,
> Goodly things and rare."

But more celebrated still is Heltau because of the unusually high stature of its natives, which an ill-natured story has tried to account for by the fact of a detachment of grenadiers having been quartered here for several years towards the end of last century.

To the west of Heltau, nestling up close to the hills, lies the smaller but far more picturesque village of Michelsberg, one of the few Saxon villages which have as yet resisted all attempts from Roumanians or gypsies to graft themselves on to their community. Michelsberg is specially remarkable because of the ruined church which, surrounded by fortified walls, is situated on a steep conical mound rising some two hundred feet above the village. The church itself, though not much to look at, boasts of a Romanesque portal of singular beauty, which many people come hither to see. The original fortress which stood on this spot is said to have been built by a noble knight, Michel of Nuremberg, who came into the country at the same time that came Herman, who founded Hermanstadt. Michel brought with him twenty-six squires, and with them raised the fortress; but soon after its completion he and his followers got dispersed over the land, and were heard of no more. The fortress then became the property of the villagers, who later erected a church on its site.

The Michelsbergers make baskets and straw hats, and lately wood-carving has begun to be developed as a native industry. They have also the reputation — I know not with what foundation — of being bird-stealers; and I believe nothing will put a Michelsberger into such a rage as to imitate the bird-call used to decoy blackbirds and nightingales to their ruin. This he takes to be an insulting allusion to his supposed profession.

In the hot summer months many of the Hermanstadt burghers come out to Michelsberg for change of air and coolness, and we ourselves spent some weeks right pleasantly in one of the peasant houses which, consisting of two rooms and a kitchen, are let to visitors for the season. But it was strange to learn that this remote mountain village is the self-chosen exile of a modern recluse—a well-born Hanoverian gentleman, Baron K——, who for the last half-dozen years has lived here summer and winter. Neither very old nor yet very young, he lives a solitary life, avoiding acquaintances; and though I lived here fully a month, I only succeeded in catching a distant glimpse of him.

Midsummer idleness being usually productive of all sorts of idle thoughts and fancies, we could not refrain from speculating on the reasons which were powerful enough thus to cause an educated man to bury himself alive so many hundred miles away from his own country in an obscure mountain village; and unknown to himself, the mysterious baron became the hero of a whole series of fantastic air-castles, in which he alternately figured as a species of Napoleon, Diogenes, Eugene Aram, or Abelard. Whichever he was, however—and it certainly is no business of mine—I can well imagine the idyllic surroundings of Michelsberg to be peculiarly fit to soothe a ruffled or

MICHELSBERG.

wounded spirit. Wrecked ambition or disappointed love must lose much of its bitterness in this secluded nook, so far removed from the echoes of a turbulent world.

Another village deserving a word of notice is Hammersdorf, lying north of Hermanstadt—a pleasant walk through the fields of little more than half an hour. The village, built up against gently undulating hills covered with vineyards, is mentioned in the year 1309 as Villa Humperti, and is believed to stand on the site of an old Roman settlement. Scarcely a year passes without Roman coins or other antiquities being found in the soil.

From the top of the Grigori-Berg, which rises some one thousand eight hundred feet directly behind the village, a very extensive view may be enjoyed of the plains about Hermanstadt, and the imposing chain of the Forgarascher mountains straight opposite.

Hammersdorf is considered to be a peculiarly aristocratic village, and its inhabitants, who pride themselves on being the richest peasants in those parts, and on their womankind possessing the finest clothes and the most valuable ornaments, are called arrogant and stuck-up by other communities.

It is usual for the name of the house-owner and the date of building to be painted outside each house; but there are differences to be remarked in each place — slight variations in building and decoration, as well as in manner, dress, and speech of the natives, despite the general resemblance all bear to each other.

Some houses have got pretty designs of conventional flowers painted in black or in contrasting color on their gable-ends, and in many villages it is usual to have some motto or sentence inscribed on each house. These are frequently of a religious character, often a text from the Bible or some stereotyped moral sentiment. Occasionally, however, we come across inscriptions of greater originality, which seem to be a reflection of the particular individual whose house they adorn, as, for instance, the following:

> "I do not care to brag or boast,
> I speak the truth to all,
> And whosoever does not wish
> Myself his friend to call,
> Why, then, he's free to paint himself
> A better on the wall."

Or else this sentence, inscribed on a straw-thatched cottage:

> "Till money I get from my father-in-law,
> My roof it, alas! must be covered with straw."

While the following one instantaneously suggests the portrait of some stolid-faced, sleepy individual whose ambition has never soared beyond the confines of his turnip-field, or the roof of his pigsty:

> "Too much thinking weakens ever—
> Think not, then, in verse nor prose,
> For return the past will never,
> And the future no man knows."

Many of the favorite maxims refer to the end of man, and give a somewhat gloomy coloring to a street when several of this sort are found in succession:

> "Man is like a fragile flower,
> Only blooming for an hour;
> Fresh to-day and rosy-red,
> But to-morrow cold and dead."

Or else—

> "Within this house a guest to-day,
> So long the Lord doth let me live;
> But when He bids, I must away—
> Against His will I cannot strive."

Here another—

> "If I from my door go out,
> Death for me doth wait without;
> And if in my house I stay,
> He will come for me some day."

The mistrustful character of the Saxon finds vent in many inscriptions, of which I give a few specimens:

> "Trust yourself to only one—
> 'Tis not wise to trust to none;
> Better, though, to have no friend
> Than on many to depend."

> "If you have a secret got,
> To a woman tell it not;
> For my part, I would as lieve
> Keep the water in a sieve."

> "When I have both gold and wine,
> Many men are brothers mine;
> When the money it is done,
> And the wine has ceased to run,
> Then the brothers, too, are gone."

> "Hardly do a man I see
> But who hates and envies me;
> Inside them their heart doth burn
> For to do an evil turn,
> Grudge me sore my daily bread;
> More than one doth wish me dead."

> "Those who build on the highway,
> Must not heed what gossips say."

The four last I here give are among the best I have come across, the first of these having a slightly Shakespearean flavor about it:

> "Tell me for what gold is fit?
> Who has got none, longs for it;
> Who has got it, fears for thieves;
> Who has lost it, ever grieves."

4

"We cannot always dance and sing,
Nor can each day be fair,
Nor could we live if every day
Were dark with grief and care;
But fair and dark days, turn about,
This we right well can bear."

"Say, who is to pay now the tax to the King?
For priests and officials will do no such thing;
The nobleman haughty will pay naught, I vouch,
And poor is the beggar, and empty his pouch;
The peasant alone he toileth to give
The means to enable those others to live."

"How to content every man,
Is a trick which no one can;
If to do so you can claim,
Rub this out and write your name."

Among the many house inscriptions I have seen in Transylvania, I have never come across any referring to love or conjugal happiness. The well-known lines of Schiller—

"Raum ist in der kleinsten Hütte
Für ein glücklich liebend Paar,"*

of which one gets such a surfeit in Germany, are here conspicuous by their absence. This will not surprise any one acquainted with the domestic life of these people. Any such sentiment would most likely have lost its signification long before the wind and the rain had effaced it, for it would not at all suit the Saxon peasant to change his house motto as often as he does his wife.

CHAPTER VIII.

SAXON INTERIORS—CHARACTER.

THE old-china mania, which I hear is beginning to die out in England, has only lately become epidemic in Austria; and as I, like many others, have been slightly touched by this malady, the quaintly decorated pottery wine-jugs still to be found in many Saxon peasant houses offered a new and interesting field of research.

---

* "There is space in the smallest hut
To contain a happy, loving couple."

These jugs are by no means so plentiful nor so cheap as they were a few years ago, for cunning *bric-à-brac* Jews have found out this hitherto unknown store of antiquities, and pilger hither from the capital to buy up wholesale whatever they find. Yet by a little patience and perseverance any one living in the country may yet find enough old curiosities to satisfy a reasonable mania; and while seeking for these relics I have come across many another remnant of antiquity quite as interesting but of less tangible nature.

SAXON PEASANT AT HOME.

Inside a Saxon peasant's house everything is of exemplary neatness and speaks of welfare. The boards are clean scoured, the window-panes shine like crystal. There is no point on which a Saxon *hausfrau* (housewife) is so sensitive as that of order and neatness, and she is visibly put out if surprised by a visit on washing or baking day, when things are not looking quite so trim as usual.

If we happen to come on a week-day we generally find the best room, or *prunkzimmer*, locked up, with darkened shutters; and only on our request to be shown the embroidered pillow-covers and the best jugs reserved for grand occasions will the hostess half ungraciously proceed to unlock the door and throw open the shutter.

This prunkzimmer takes the place of the state parlor in our Scotch farm-houses; but those latter, with their funereal horse-hair furniture and cheerless polished table, would contrast unfavorably beside these quaint, old-fashioned German apartments. Here the furniture, consisting of benches, bunkers, bedsteads, chest of drawers, and chairs, are painted in lively colors, often festoons of roses and tulips on a ground of dark blue or green; the patterns, frequently bold and striking, if of a somewhat barbaric style of art, betray the Oriental influence of Roumanian country artists, of whom they are doubtless borrowed. A similarly painted wooden framework runs round the top of the room, above the doors and windows, with pegs, from which are suspended the jugs I am in search of, and a bar, behind which rows of plates are secured.

On the large unoccupied bedsteads are piled up, sometimes as high as the ceiling, stores of huge, downy pillows, their covers richly embroidered in quaint patterns executed in black, scarlet, or blue and yellow worsted. They are mostly worked in the usual tapestry cross-stitch, and often represent flowers, birds, or animals in the old German style—the name of the embroideress and the date of the work being usually introduced. Many of the pieces I saw were very old, and dates of the seventeenth and eighteenth centuries are constantly turning up; but alongside are others of recent date, for the custom of thus employing the long winter evenings is still kept up among the village girls.

I asked some of them whence they took their patterns, whether they had any sampler books or printed designs to copy from. Nothing of the sort, I was told; they just copy from one another and from old pieces of work. Thus it comes about that many of them to-day go on reproducing some old bird or flower, first introduced by an ancestress of the worker many hundred years ago.

This system of copying is clearly to be traced in the different villages. As each village forms a separate body or community, and

SAXON EMBROIDERY.

intercourse and intermarriage hardly ever take place, these patterns become localized, and one design is apt to run in one particular place to the exclusion of others. Thus I remarked one village where flourishes a peculiar breed of square-built peacocks, alternated with preposterous stags in red and blue worsted, but these fabulous animals are rarely wont to stray beyond the confines of their own parish; while in another community there is a strongly marked epidemic of embroidered double-eagles, perhaps explainable by the fact that part of the population is of Austrian extraction.

The Saxon hausfrau will generally receive us in a surly, mistrustful manner, and the Saxon peasant will not dream of rising from his seat when he sees a lady enter the room. If we happen to be tired we had better sit down unbidden, for neither he nor she is likely to offer us a chair.

Our question as to whether they have any jugs or plates is usually met with a sort of ungracious affirmative. "Will they sell them?" "Not on any account whatsoever! these jugs belonged to some dearly beloved great-grandfather or grandmother, and must be preserved in their memory. Not for unheard-of sums of gold could they bear to separate themselves from such a relic," etc.

These assertions must, however, be taken for what they are worth, and whoever has tried the experiment will have found by experience that it is merely a question of money, and that sometimes an extra bid of ten or twenty kreuzers (twopence or fourpence) will turn the scale, and induce these pious grandchildren to consign to oblivion the memory of the beloved ancestor.

These jugs, which are destined to hold wine (one for each guest) on the occasion of their baptismal, wedding, or funeral banquets, are from nine to eleven inches high, and have a metal lid attached to the handle. Every variety of coloring and pattern is to be found among them; sometimes it is an uncouth design of dancing or drunken peasants, sometimes a pair of stags, or a dog in pursuit of a hare, or else a basket filled with fruit, or raised medallions with sprigs of flowers in the centre.

My inquiries were usually met by the suspicious counter-questions, "Why do you want to buy our jugs? What are you going to do with them?" and the answer I gave, that I was fond of such old things, and that they would be hung up in my dining-room, was often received with evident disbelief.

These people are not easily induced to talk about themselves, and have little sense of humor or power of repartee. They have an instinctive distrust of whoever tries to draw them out, scenting in each superfluous question a member of a species they abhor—namely, " a chiel among them taking notes;" or, as the Saxon puts it, " one of those incomprehensible towns-folk, ever fretting and ferreting after our ways and customs, and who have no sensible reason for doing so either."

Two analogous incidents which I met with, soon after my arrival in Transylvania, seemed to give me the respective clews to Saxon and Roumanian character. The first was in a Saxon peasant's house, where I had just purchased two jugs and a plate, for which, being still a stranger in those parts, I had paid considerably more than they were worth, when on leaving the house the hostess put a small bunch

SAXON EMBROIDERY AND POTTERY.

(This and the illustration on p. 53 are from the collection of Saxon Antiquities in possession of Herr Emil
Sigerus at Hermanstadt.)

of flowers into my hand. The nosegay was somewhat tumbled and faded, for this was Sunday afternoon, and probably the woman or her daughter had worn these flowers at church earlier in the day. In my ignorance of Saxon character I took this offering in the light of a courteous attention, and accepted the bouquet with a word of thanks.

My error did not last long, for as I stepped into the court-yard the wooden, Noah's-ark faced woman hurried after me, and roughly snatching the nosegay out of my hand, she harshly exclaimed,

"I do not give my flowers for nothing! unless you pay me two kreuzers (a halfpenny), I shall keep them for myself!"

Very much amused, I paid the required sum, feeling that, in spite of the crushed condition of the flowers, I had got more than a half-penny's worth out of my hostess after all.

Two or three days later, when out riding, we lost our way in the mazes of the Yungwald, the large oak-forest which stretches for miles over the country to the south of Hermanstadt. It was near sunset when we found ourselves in a totally strange neighborhood, not know-ing which turn to take in order to regain the road back to the town. Just then a Roumanian peasant woman came in sight. She had on her back a bundle of firewood, which she had probably stolen in the forest, and in her hand she carried a large bunch of purple iris flow-ers, fresh and dripping from some neighboring marsh.

I suppose that I must have looked longingly at the beautiful purple bunch, for while my husband was asking the way as well as he could by means of a little broken Italian, she came round to the side of my horse, and with a pretty gesture held up the flowers for my acceptance. With the Saxon lesson fresh in my mind I hesitated to take them, for I had left my purse at home; so I explained to her by pantomime that I had no money about me. She had not been think-ing of money, it seems, and energetically disclaimed the offer of payment, continuing her way after a courteous *buna sara* (good-evening).

Since then, in my walks and rides about Hermanstadt, I have often been presented with similar offerings from perfectly unknown Rou-manian peasants, who would sometimes stop their galloping horses and get out of the cart merely for the purpose of giving me a few flowers; but never, never has it been my good-luck to receive the smallest sign of spontaneous courtesy from any Saxon, and I grieve to say that frequently my experience has been all the other way.

One day, for instance, when walking in a hay-field through which ran a rapid mill-stream, I suddenly missed my dog, a lively rat-terrier, which had been running backward and forward in search of field-mice. " Brick, Brick, Brick !" I called in vain over and over again, but Brick was nowhere to be seen. Only a stifled squealing, apparently proceeding from the mill-stream some way off, met my ear; but I did not immediately think of connecting this sound with my truant terrier. Some Saxon peasants were at work near the water stowing up hay on to a cart. " Have you not seen my dog ?" I called out to them.

One of the men now slowly removed his pipe from his mouth. "Your dog?" he asked, stolidly. " Oh yes; he's just drowning yonder in the stream." And he lazily pointed over his shoulder with a pitchfork.

I rushed to the bank, and there sure enough was my poor half-drowned Brick struggling to keep himself above water, but almost exhausted already. He had fallen in over the treacherous edge, which was masked by overhanging bushes; and the banks being too steep to effect a landing, he must inevitably have perished had I not come up in time. With considerable difficulty, and at the risk of falling in myself, I managed to drag him out, the worthy Saxons meanwhile looking on with indolent enjoyment, never dreaming of offering assistance.

The hard and grasping characters of the Saxons appear in every detail of their daily life; they taint their family relations, and would almost seem to put a marketable price on the most sacred affections. Thus a Saxon mother in her cradle-song informs the sleeping infant that she values it as high as a hundred florins; while the grief over a beloved corpse often takes the form of counting up the exact pecuniary loss to the family sustained from the decease.

Their family life does not appear to be happy, and divorces are lamentably numerous. It seems, in fact, as if divorce had grown to be an established habit among these people; and despite all efforts of the clergy to discourage this abuse, and the difficulties purposely put in the way of divorcing parties, there is little prospect of improvement as yet. No improvement can possibly take place till Saxon parents give up forcing their children to wed against their will, merely for mercenary reasons, and till girls are allowed to attain a reasonable age before binding themselves down to a contract of such importance. When want of sympathy towards the proposed husband is urged on the part of the girl, such objections are usually settled by the practical advice of the long-sighted parents. "Try him for a time, and maybe you will get to like him ; and if not—well, the misfortune is none so great, and you can always seek for a divorce." Brides of fifteen are quite the order of the day, and few are suffered to reach so mature an age as seventeen or eighteen; the consequence of these arrangements being that fully a third of the couples go asunder, each choosing another mate, with whom they usually fare better than with their first venture.

Often in the course of my visits to Saxon peasant houses have I come across one of these unfortunate young females returned to her parents' house, sometimes after a few weeks only of matrimony, there to await the divorce which is to set her free to choose again.

The reasons which induce these people to sue for a separation are frequently so exceedingly futile and ridiculous as hardly to deserve that name. Often it is the food which is made a cause of complaint —either the husband declaring that his wife will take no trouble to please him with her cookery, or else the wife complaining of his being capricious and hard to please. An underdone potato may prove so very indigestible as to sever the conjugal bond, or an ill-baked loaf of bread assume such dimensions as to constitute a barrier for life.

Village pastors whose parishes lie in the wine-bearing districts affirm that the season immediately following upon the vintage, when the cellars are full of new wine, is the most quarrelsome time in the year, and the one which engenders most separations. But even without the aid of stimulants, and when no thought of divorce is in their minds, quarrelsome *ménages* are numerous; and the old story of the Tartar carrying off the shrewish wife of a thoroughly resigned husband may well have had its origin here. This legend, told all over Hungary, relates how a peasant, as he calmly watched the retreating figure of the Tartar bearing off the wife of his bosom, was heard to murmur, "Poor Tartar! thou hast made a bad bargain."

In Transylvania this same story is told of a Saxon peasant, but with a sequel; for this version relates how the bereaved widower settled himself down to a hearty supper that same evening, ever and anon murmuring, as his eye rested on the empty chair opposite his own, the words, "Poor Tartar!" for he was a kind-hearted man, and felt compassion even for the sufferings of a barbarian. But of a sudden the door flies open, and the wretched man once more beholds his lost wife standing before him. Her temper had proved too much even for a Tartar, who had wisely flown, leaving his captive behind.

The words "Poor Tartar!" now gave place to another form of ejaculation; and whenever he deemed himself out of ear-shot, the Saxon muttered bitterly between his teeth "Rascally Tartar! Rascally Tartar!"

But for this unfortunate *dénouement,* who knows whether Saxon husbands of to-day might not frequently be moved to regret the good old times when an obliging Tartar might be expected thus to relieve them of such superfluous blessings?

The bond between parent and child seems to be hardly more commendable. Perhaps my experience has been exceptionally infelicitous, but certainly never in any country has it been my ill-fortune to listen to such shocking and disrespectful language from children to their parents as what I have occasionally overheard in Saxon cottages.

The Saxon peasant being a declared enemy of large families presents a striking contrast to his Roumanian neighbor, with whom six or eight bairns are a very common allowance, and who regards each new addition to the family as another gift of God. The oft-repeated insinuation that the Transylvanian Saxons seek to limit their progeny by unnatural means does not seem to be entirely without foundation. It is said that to have two children only is considered the correct thing in a Saxon household, and that the Saxon mother who, when cross-questioned as to her offspring, has to acknowledge three bairns, turns away her head shamefacedly, as though she were confessing a crime.

It is because the Saxon does not care to see his fields cut up into small sections that he desires his family to be small; and the consequence of this short-sighted egotism is, that the population of many villages shows a yearly decrease, and that houses often stand empty because there is no one to live there.* Thus one village near Hermanstadt can show twenty-seven, another twelve such deserted dwellings. A man whose whole family consisted of two daughters, both married to peasants with houses of their own, was asked what would

* This abuse, however, is entirely confined to the villages, the towns showing a far more favorable rate of increase among the Saxon population.

become of his fine well-built home after his decease. "It will just stand empty," was the stolid reply. In some villages these empty Saxon houses have been taken possession of by Roumanians, who look strangely incongruous within these massive stone walls, reminding one somehow of sparrows which have taken up their residence in a deserted rookery.

Saxon political economists, alive to the danger of their race becoming extinct, think of trying to get new batches of German colonists to settle here, in order to freshen up and increase the number of the race; but there is little chance of such projects being successful. The inducements which formerly tempted strangers no longer exist; and there are probably few Germans who would think it worth their while to settle in a country where every inch of land has already been appropriated, and where the Government seeks to rob each one of his nationality.

The besetting fault of this whole Saxon nation seems to be an immoderate spirit of egotism, so short-sighted as frequently to defeat its own end, leading each man to consider only his individual welfare, to the exclusion of every other feeling. It is strange and paradoxical that these honest, moral, thrifty, industrious, and educated Saxons should live thus in their well-built, roomy houses in a constant state of inward dissension and strife; while their neighbors, the poor, ignorant, thieving Roumanians, crowded together in their wretched hovels, are united by the bonds of a most touching family affection.*

---

* The assertion that the Transylvanian Saxons—taken as a body—show a yearly decrease is, however, incorrect, as has been conclusively proved by Dr. Oskar von Meltzl, in his recent interesting work, "Statistik der Sächsischen Landbevölkerung in Siebenbürgen." By the author's own acknowledgment, however, the increase within the last thirty-two years has been but insignificant; while of 227 Saxon communities established in the country 92 have diminished in number between the years 1851–1883 to the extent of nearly 11 per cent.

CHAPTER IX.

SAXON CHURCHES AND SIEGES.

THE words "church" and "fortress" used to be synonymous in Transylvania, so the places of worship might accurately have been described as churches militant. Each Saxon village church was surrounded by a row, sometimes even a double or triple row, of fortified walls, which are mostly still extant. The remains of moat and drawbridge are also yet frequently to be seen. When threatened by an enemy the people used to retire into these fortresses, often built on some rising piece of ground, taking with them their valuables as well as provisions for the contingency of a lengthy siege. From these heights the Saxons used to roll down heavy stones on to their assailants, sometimes with terrible effect; but when they had in this way exhausted their missiles, the predicament was often a very precarious one. Some of these stones still survive, and may occasionally be seen—as within the fortress walls of the old ruined church which I have already mentioned as standing on a steep incline above the picturesque village of Michelsberg.

The church itself, having been replaced by a more conveniently situated one down in the village, is now deserted, and is used only as a storehouse by the villagers. The fortified walls are crumbling away, and the passage round the church is choked up by weeds and briers, among which lie strewn about many old moss-grown stones, circular in shape and resembling giant cannon-balls. These were the missiles which lay there in readiness to be rolled down on to an approaching enemy; and there was a law compelling each bridegroom, before leading his bride to the altar, to roll uphill to the church-door one of these formidable globes. This was so ordained in order to exclude from matrimony all sick or weakly subjects; and as the incline was a steep one, and each stone weighed about two hundred-weight, it was a considerable test of strength.

Would that these old stones, lying here neglected among the nettles, had the gift of speech! What traits of love and of bloodshed might we not learn from them! Only to look at them there strewn

FORTIFIED SAXON CHURCH.

around, it is not difficult to guess at the outlines of some of the stories they are dumbly telling us. Many are chipped and worn away, and have evidently been used more than once in their double capacity, alternately rolled up the hill by smiling Cupid, to be hurled down again by furious Nemesis.

Here near a clump of burdock-leaves is a shabby-looking globe of yellow sandstone, whose puny size plainly speaks of a *mariage de convenance*—a mere union of hands without hearts; perhaps some old widower, with trembling hands and shaky knees, in quest of a wife to look after his house, and to whom the whole matter was very uphill work indeed!

Close alongside, half hidden beneath the graceful tangles of a wild-rose bush, is a formidable bowlder of gigantic, nay, heroic size, which forcibly suggests that it must have been a mighty love indeed which brought it up here—so mighty, no doubt, that to the two strong young arms which rolled it up the hill it must have seemed light as a feather's weight.

And how many of these, might one ask, have been rolled up here in vain, in so far as the love was concerned? When the fire of love had grown cold and its sweetness all turned to vinegar, how many, many a former lover must heartily have wished that he had never moved his stone from the bottom of the hill!

Such thoughts involuntarily crowd on the mind when sitting, as I have done many a time, within this lonely ruin on fine summer evenings, the idyllic peacefulness of the scene the more strongly felt by contrast with the bloody memories linked around it. It is so strange to realize how completely everything has passed away that once used to be: that the hands which pushed these heavy globes, as well as the Moslem crania for which they were intended, have turned alike to dust; that hushed forever are the voices once awaking fierce echoes within these very walls; and that of all those contrasting passions, of all that tender love and that burning hatred, nothing has survived but a few old stones lying forgotten near a deserted church!

The history of the sieges endured in Transylvania on the part of Turk or Tartar would in itself furnish matter for many volumes. Numberless anecdotes are yet current characterizing the endurance and courage of the besieged, and the original means often resorted to in order to baffle or mislead the enemy.

Once it was the ready wit of a Szekel woman which saved her people besieged by the Tartars within the Almescher cavern. As the whole land had been devastated from end to end, a severe famine was the consequence, and both besiegers and besieged were sorely in want of victuals. The Szekels had taken some provisions with them into the cave, but these were soon exhausted; and the Tartars, though starving themselves, were consoled by thinking that hunger would soon compel their enemy to give in. One day, when, as usual, the barbarians had assembled shouting and howling in front of the cavern, whose entrance was defended by a high wall, a Hungarian woman held up before their eyes a large cake at the end of a long pole, and cried out, tauntingly, "See here, ye dogs of Tartars! Thus are we feasting in plenty and comfort, while you are reduced to eat grass and roots of trees." This much-vaunted cake was but kneaded together of water and ashes, with a few last remaining spoonfuls of flour; but the Tartars, taken in by the feint, abandoned the field.

Another time it was nothing more than a swarm of bees which turned the scale in favor of the Saxons, hard pressed by the enemy outside. Already they had begun to scale the walls of the fortified church, and death and destruction seemed imminent, when the youthful daughter of the church-warden was struck by a bright idea. Behind the church was a little garden full of sweet-scented flowers, and containing a dozen beehives, which it was Lieschen's (such was her name) pride to watch over. Seizing a hive in each hand, she sprang up on the fortress wall, and with all her strength hurled them down among the approaching besiegers. Again and again she repeated this manœuvre till the hives were exhausted, and the bewildered enemies, blinded by the dense swarm of infuriated bees, deafened by the angry buzzing in their ears, and maddened by hundredfold stings, beat an ignominious and hasty retreat.

This occurred in the village of Holzmengen towards the end of the seventeenth century, and of this same village it is related that, when peace was finally restored to the land, the population was so reduced that most houses stood empty. Of four hundred landholders there used to be, but fifteen now remained; and many years passed by without any wedding being celebrated in the place. When, however, at last this rare event came to pass, the bridegroom received the name of the "young man," which stuck to him until his end. The bride was no other than Lieschen, the bee-maiden, and Thomas was the name of her husband; and to this day whoever is in possession of that particular house goes by the name of "*den jung mon Thomas*," even though he happen to have been christened Hans or Peter, and be, moreover, as old as Methuselah. If you ask the name of such another house in the same village, you are told that it belongs to *Michel am Eck* (Michael at the corner). It is not a corner house, neither does its proprietor answer to the name of Michel; but where it stands was once the corner of a street, and Michel the name of one of the fifteen landholders who divided the property after the war; hence the appellation.

There is a story told of an active Saxon housewife who, after she had been shut up for three days within the fortress awaiting the Tartars reported to be near, began to weary of her enforced idleness, and throwing open the gate of the citadel, impatiently called out, "Now, then, you dogs of Tartars, are you never coming?"

When the Tartars had succeeded in capturing prisoners they used to fatten them up for eating. A woman from the village of Almesch, being sickly, refused to fatten, and, set at liberty, came home to relate the doleful tale. The little Hungarians and Saxons were regarded as toys for the young Tartars, who, setting them up in rows, used to practise upon them the merry pastime of cutting off heads.

Living in Transylvania, we are sometimes inclined to wonder whether to be besieged by Turks and Tartars be really a thing of the past, and not rather an actual danger for which we must be prepared any day, so strangely are many little observances relating to those times still kept up. Thus in the belfry tower at Kaisd there hangs a little bell bearing a Gothic inscription and the date 1506. It is rung every evening at the usual curfew-hour, and until within a very few years ago the watchman was under the obligation of calling forth into the night with stentorian voice, "Not this way, you villains! not this way! I see you well!"

Also the habit of keeping provisions stored up within the fortified church-walls, to this day extant in most Saxon villages, is clearly a remnant of the time when sieges had to be looked for. Even now the people seem to consider their goods to be in greater security here than in their own barns and lofts. The outer fortified wall round the church is often divided off into deep recesses or alcoves, in each of which stands a large wooden chest securely locked, and filled with grain or flour, while the little surrounding turrets or chapels are used as storehouses for home-cured bacon. "We have seven chapels all full of bacon," I was once proudly informed by a village church-warden; but, with the innate mistrust of his race, he would not indulge my further curiosity on the subject by suffering me to inspect the interior of these greasy sanctuaries, evidently suspecting me of sinister intentions on his bacon stores.

This storing up of provisions is a perfect mania among the Saxons, and each village has its own special hobby or favorite article, vast quantities of which it hoards up in a preposterous, senseless fashion, reminding one of a dog who buries more bones than he can ever hope to eat in the course of his life. Thus, one village prides itself on having the greatest quantity of bacon, much of which is already thirty or forty years old, and consequently totally unfit for use; while in another community the oldest grain is the great *specialité*. Each article, case, or barrel is marked with the brand of the owner, and the whole placed under the charge of the church-warden.

Some parishes can still boast of many curiously wrought pieces of church plate remaining over from Catholic days—enamelled chalices, bejewelled crucifixes, remonstrances, and ciboriums, richly inlaid and embossed. The village of Heltau is in possession of many such valuable ornaments which, during the Turkish wars, used to be buried in the earth, sometimes for a period of many years, the exact spot where the treasure was hidden being known only to the oldest church-warden, who was careful to pass on the secret to the next in rank when he felt himself to be drawing near the end of his life. Thus, in the year 1794, the church at Heltau, struck by lightning, was seriously damaged, and urgently demanded extensive repairs. How to defray these expenses was the question which sorely perplexed the village pastor and the church elders, when the old warden came forward and offered to reveal to the pastor and the second warden the secret of a hidden treasure of whose existence none but he was aware. The man himself had never set eyes on the treasure, but had received from his predecessor precise directions how to find it in case of necessity. Accordingly, under his guidance the pastor, accompanied by the younger warden, repaired to the church, where, entering the right-hand aisle, the old man pointed to three high-backed wooden seats fixed against the wall, saying, "The centre one of these chairs has a movable panel, behind which a door is said to be concealed. After some effort—for the panel was jammed from long disuse—it yielded, moving upward, and disclosing a small iron door with a keyhole, into which fitted an old-fashioned rusty key produced by the warden. When this door was at last got open, the three men stepped into a small vault paved with bricks. "One of these bricks is marked by a cross, and under it we have to dig for the treasure," were the further instructions given by the old man. A very few minutes proved the truth of his words, bringing to light a small wooden chest containing a chalice, a silver remonstrance, and various other valuables, which may still be seen at the Heltau parsonage; likewise a bag of gold and silver coins, dating from the time of the Batorys, which leads to the supposition that the treasure had been lying here concealed ever since the beginning of the seventeenth century.

Great was the pastor's surprise and delight at this unexpected windfall; but he only took from the bag sufficient money for the necessary repairs, replacing the rest of the treasure where it had been found. None of the other parishioners were informed whence had come the money, so the secret remained a secret.

Only many years later, in the present century, when the son-in-law of the former clergyman had become pastor in his turn, the story of the treasure was imparted to him by the successor of former wardens. The necessity for concealment had now gone by, and peace and prosperity reigned in the country; so the church ornaments were once more disinterred, and finally restored to the light of day, while the antiquated gold and silver pieces, exchanged into current coinage, were applied to useful purposes. Thus it was that the secret oozed out, and came to be generally known.

Saxon village churches of the present day are generally bare and unornamented inside, for all decorations had been dismantled at the time of the Reformation; stone niches have been emptied of the statues they contained, and rich pieces of carving stowed away in lumber-rooms. Only the old Oriental carpets, brought hither from Turkish campaigns, which frequently adorn the front of the pews or the organ-gallery, have been suffered to remain, and hang there still, delicately harmonious in coloring, but riddled through with holes like a sieve, and fed upon by the descendants of a hundred generations of moths, which flutter in a dense cloud round the visitor who inadvertently raises a corner of the drapery to investigate its fleecy quality.

Curious old tombstones and bass-reliefs may often be seen carelessly huddled together in the church entrance or outside the walls, treated with no sort of appreciation of their historical value or care for their ultimate preservation. Also the numerous frescos which used to cover many church walls have been obliterated by the barbarous touch of a whitewashing hand. It would almost seem as if this Saxon people had originally possessed some degree of artistic feeling, which has been, however, effectually extinguished by the Reformation; for it is difficult otherwise to explain how a nation capable of raising monuments of real artistic value in the troubled times of the barbarous Middle Ages should be thus heedless of their conservation in the present enlightened and peaceful century.

RUINED ABBEY OF KERZ.

Of this lamentable indifference to the conservation of their historical and artistic treasures, the ruined Abbey of Kerz, situated in the valley of the Aluta, offers a melancholy instance. This wealthy Cistercian monastery was founded by King Bela III. towards the end of the twelfth century; but being abolished by King Mathias three centuries later, on account of irregularities into which the monks had fallen, it passed, with its lands, into possession of the Hermanstadt church.

The choir of the ancient abbey church, built in the time of Louis the Great in the transition style, is still used as a place of worship by the small Lutheran congregation of Kerz, but the nave has been suffered to fall into decay; many of the richly carved stones of which it was formed have been carried off by the villagers, who have utilized them for building their houses, or degraded them to yet baser purposes. We ourselves crossed the little stream, which runs close by the parson's house, on stepping-stones evidently taken from the ancient building. Likewise a lime-tree of gigantic dimensions in front of the western portal, and supposed to have been planted when the foundation-stone of the church was laid, is now in imminent danger of splitting in twain for want of the trifling attention of an iron waistband to keep its poor old body together. Such the present lamentable condition of one of the most interesting relics in the country which has been named the Melrose of Transylvania.

CHAPTER X.

THE SAXON VILLAGE PASTOR.

The contrast between the domestic lives of Roumanian and Saxon peasants is all the more surprising as their respective clergies set totally different examples; for while many Roumanian priests are drunken, dissolute men, open to every sort of bribery, the Saxon pastor is almost invariably a model of steadiness and morality, and leads a quiet, industrious, and contented life.

On the other hand, however, it may be remarked that if the Saxon pastor be steady and well-behaved, he has very good and solid reasons for so being. Certainly he is most comfortably indemnified for the virtues he is expected to practise.

When a pastor dies the villagers themselves elect his successor by votes. Usually it is a man whom they know already by sight or reputation, or from having heard him preach on stray occasions in their church. Every Saxon pastor, in order to be qualified for the position, must have practised for several years as professor at a public gymnasium—a very wise regulation, as it insures the places being filled by men of education.

The part which a village pastor is called upon to play requires both head and heart, for the relation between shepherd and flock is here very different from the conventional footing on which clergy and laity stand with regard to each other in town life. Whereas in the city no congregation cares to see its spiritual head outside the church walls, and would resent as unpardonable intrusion any attempt of his to penetrate the privacy of the domestic circle, the villager not only expects but insists on his pastor taking intimate part in his family life, and being ready to assist him with advice and admonition in every possible contingency.

The peasants are therefore very circumspect about the choice of a pastor, well aware that the weal or woe of a community may depend upon the selection. They have often seen how some neighboring village has awakened to new life and prosperity since the advent of a worthy clergyman; while such another parish, from a rash selection, has saddled itself with a man it would fain cart away as so much useless straw, were it only possible to get rid of him. For although the power of choice lies entirely with the peasants, they cannot likewise undo their work at will, and only the bishop has power to depose a pastor when he has investigated the complaints brought against him and found them to be justified.

Not only the pastor *in spe*, but also his wife, is carefully scrutinized, and her qualifications for the patriarchal position she has to occupy critically examined into; for if the clergyman is termed by his flock the "honorable father," so is she designated as the "virtuous mother." The candidate who happens to have a thrifty and benevolent consort finds his chances of election considerably enhanced; while such another, married to a vain and frivolous woman, will most likely be found awanting when weighed in the balance.

The funeral of a village pastor has been touchingly described by a native author,* whose words I take the liberty of quoting:

"The old father had gone to his long rest: more than once during the last few years he had felt that the time had come for him to lay down the shepherd's crook; for the world had become too stirring, and he no longer had the strength and activity of spirit to do all that was expected of him. There were serious repairs to be undertaken about the church, and the question of building a new school-house

---

* Dr. Fronius.

was becoming urgent. Likewise many of the new church regulations were harassing and distasteful exceedingly; most especially was he troubled by inward quakings at the idea that at the bishop's next official visit he would be expected to submit to him the manuscripts of all the sermons he had preached within the year, and which, neatly tied up together with black worsted, were lying on the lowest shelf of the bookcase.

"All these thoughts had reconciled him to the prospect of death; and when sitting before his door on fine summer evenings he would sometimes remark to the neighbors who had lingered near for a passing chat, 'It cannot last over-long with me now: one or two pair of soles at most I shall wear out, and I should be glad to remain in the village, and to sleep there under the big lime-tree, in the midst of those with whom my life has been spent. Therefore kindly bear with me a little longer, good people, for the few remaining days the Lord is pleased to spare me.' And these words never failed to conciliate even the more turbulent spirits, who were apt

SAXON PASTOR IN FULL DRESS.

to think that the Herr Vater was over-long in going, and that the parish stood in need of a younger head.

"Now at last the coffin has been lowered into the earth, and the fresh mound covered with dewy garlands of flowers. All the villagers have turned out to render the last honors to the father they have lost. The eldest son of the defunct, standing near the grave, addresses the congregation. In a few simple words he thanks them for the good they have done to his father and to his whole family, and, in name of the dead man, he begs their forgiveness for whatever wrongs the pastor may unwittingly have done; and when he then lays down the keys of both church and parsonage into the hand of the church-warden, scarcely an eye will remain dry among the spectators. For forty years is a long time in which a good man, even though he often errs and be at fault, can yet have done much, very much, good indeed, and resentment is a plant which strikes no root in the upturned clods of a new-made grave."

But the orphaned congregation must have a new pastor; the flock cannot be suffered to remain long without a shepherd; and this is the topic which is being discussed with much warmth at an assemblage of village elders. On the white-decked table are standing dishes of bread-and-cheese, flanked by large tankards of wine. The first glass has just been emptied to the memory of the dead pastor, and now the second glass will be drunk to the health of his yet unknown successor.

These meetings preceding the election of a new shepherd are often long and stormy; for when the wine has taken effect and loos-ened the tongues, the different candidates who might be taken into consideration are passed in review, and extolled with much heat, or abused with broad sarcasm. One man is rejected on account of an impediment in his speech, and another because he is known to be unmarried; a third one, who might do well enough for any other parish, cannot be chosen here because his old parents are natives of the village; for it is a true though a hard word which says that no one can be a prophet in his own country. One man who ventures to suggest the vicar of a neighboring village is informed that no blacker traitor exists on the face of the earth; and another, who describes his pet candidate as an ideal clergyman, with the figure of a Hercules and the voice of a Stentor, is ironically asked whether he wishes to choose a pastor by weight and measure. If only his head and heart be in the right place the clergyman's legs are welcome to be an inch or two shorter.

After a longer or shorter interval a decision is finally arrived at. From a list of six candidates one has been elected by the secret votes of the community, each married land-owner having a voice in the mat-ter, and the name of the successful aspirant is publicly made known in church. Meanwhile a group of young men on horseback are wait-ing at the church door, and hardly has the all-important name been pronounced when they set spurs to their steeds and gallop to bear the news to the successful candidate. A hot race ensues, for the foremost one can hope to get a shining piece of silver—perhaps even gold—in exchange for the good tidings he brings. In a carriage, at a more leisurely pace, follow the elders who have been deputed to hand over the official document containing the nomination.

An early day is fixed for the presentation of the new shepherd to his flock, and at a still earlier date the new Frau Pastorin precedes him thither, where she is soon deep in the mysteries of cake-baking, fowl-killing, etc., in view of the many official banquets which are to accompany the presentation. In this employment she has ample assistance from the village matrons, as well as contributions of eggs, cream, butter, and bacon. The day before the presentation the pastor has been fetched in a carriage drawn by six white horses. The first step to his installation is the making out and signing of the agreement or treaty between pastor and people—all the said pastor's duties, obligations, and privileges being therein distinctly specified and enumerated, from the exact quantity and quality of Holy Gospel he is bound to administer yearly to the congregation down to his share of wild crab-apples for brewing the household vinegar, and the precise amount of acorns his pigs are at liberty to consume.

After this treaty has been duly signed and read aloud, the keys of the church are solemnly given over and accepted with appropriate speeches. The banquet which succeeds this ceremony is called the "key-drinking." Then follows the solemn installation in the church, where the new pastor, for the first time, pronounces aloud the blessing over his congregation, who strain their ears with critical attention to catch the sound and pass sentence thereon. The Saxon peasant thinks much of a full sonorous voice; therefore woe to the man who is cursed with a thin squeaky organ, for he will assuredly fall at least fifty per cent. in the estimation of his audience.

Then follows another banquet, at which each of the church officials has his place at table marked by a silver thaler piece (about 3s.) lying at the bottom of his large tankard, and visible through the clear golden wine with which the bumper is filled. Etiquette demands that the drinker should taste of the wine but sparingly at first, merely wetting the lips and affecting not to perceive the silver coin; but when the health of the new pastor is drunk, each man must empty his tankard at one draught, skilfully catching the thaler between the teeth as he drains it dry. This coin is then supposed to be treasured up in memory of the event.

This has been but a flying visit to his new parish, and only some weeks later does the new pastor hold his solemn entry into the parish, the preparations for the flitting naturally occupying some few weeks. The village is bound to convey the new pastor, his family, as well as all their goods and chattels, to the new home, and it is considered a distinction when many carts are required for the purpose, even though the distance be great and the roads bad, for the people would have no opinion at all of a pastor who arrived in light marching order, but seem rather to value him in proportion to the trouble he gives them. As many as eighteen to twenty carts are sometimes pressed into service for this patriarchal procession.

The six white horses which are to be harnessed to the carriage for the clergyman and his wife have been carefully fattened up during the last few weeks, their manes plaited with bright ribbons, and the carriage itself decorated with flower garlands. At the parish boundary all the young men of the village have come out on horseback to meet them, and with flying banners they ride alongside of the carriage. In this way the village is reached, where sometimes a straw rope is stretched across the road to bar his entrance. This is removed on the pastor paying a ransom, and, entering the village, the driver is expected to conduct his horses at full gallop thrice round the fortified walls of the church before entering the parsonage court-yard.

The village pastor, who lives among his people, must adopt their habits and their hours. It would not do for him to lie abed till seven or eight o'clock, like a town gentleman: five o'clock, and even sooner, must find him dressed and ready to attend to the hundred and one requirements of his parishioners, who, even at that early hour, come pouring in upon him from all sides.

Perhaps it is a petition for some particularly fine sort of turnip-seed which only the Herr Vater has got; or else he is requested to look into his wise book to see if he can find a remedy for the stubborn cough of a favorite horse, or the distressing state of the calf's digestion. Another will bring him a dish of golden honey-comb, with some question regarding the smoking of the hives; while a fourth has come to request the pastor to transform his new-born son from a pagan into a Christian infant.

Various deputations of villagers, inviting the pastor to two different funerals and to six weddings, have successively been disposed of: then will come a peasant with some Hungarian legal document which he would like to have deciphered. Has he won the lawsuit which has been pending these two years and more? or has he lost it, and will he be obliged to pay the damages as well? This is a riddle which only the Herr Vater can read him aright by consulting the big Hungarian dictionary on the shelf.

The next visitor is perchance an old white-bearded man, bent double with the weight of years, and carrying a well-worn Bible under his arm. He wants to know his age, which used to be entered somewhere here in the book; but he cannot find the place, or else the bookbinder, in mending the volume last year, has pasted paper over it. Perhaps the Herr Vater can make it out for him; and further to facilitate the search, he mentions that there was corn in the upper fields, and maize in the low meadows, the year he was born, and that since then the corn has been sown twenty-four times on the same spot, and will be sown there again next year if God pleases to spare him. The pastor, who must of course be well versed in this sort of rural arithmetic, has no difficulty in pronouncing the man to be exactly seventy-three years and three months old, and sends him away well pleased to discover that he is a whole year younger than he had believed himself to be.

Often, too, a couple appear on the scene for the purpose of being reconciled. The man has beaten his wife, and she has come to complain—not of the beating in the abstract, but of the manner in which this particular castigation has been administered. It was really too bad this time, as, sobbing, she explains to the Herr Vater that he has belabored her with a thick leather thong in a truly heathenish fashion, instead of taking the broomstick, as does every respectable man, to beat his wife.

The virtuous Frau Mutter has likewise her full share of the day's work. An old hen to be made into broth for a sick grandchild, a piece of cloth to be cut out in the shape of a jacket, or a handkerchief to be hemmed on the big sewing-machine, all pass successively into her busy hands; and if she goes for a day's shopping to the nearest market-town she is positively besieged by commissions of all sorts. Six china plates of some particular pattern, a coffee-cup to replace the one thrown down by the cat last week, a pound of loaf-sugar, the whitest, finest, sweetest, and cheapest that can be got, or a packet of composition candles. Even weightier matters are sometimes intrusted to her judgment, and she may have to accept the awful responsibility of selecting a new mirror or a petroleum lamp.

Letter-writing is also another important branch of the duties of both pastor and wife. It may be an epistle to some daughter who is in service, or to a soldier son away with his regiment, a threatening letter to an unconscientious debtor, or a business transaction with the farmer of another village. In fact, all the raw material of epistolary affection, remonstrance, counsel, or threat is brought wholesale to the parsonage, there to be fashioned into shape, and set forth clearly in black upon white.

Altogether the day of a Saxon pastor is a busy and well-filled one, for his doors, from sunrise to sunset, must be open to his parishioners, so that after having " risen with the lark " he is well content further to carry out the proverb by " going to bed with the lamb."

A great deal of patience and natural tact is requisite to enable a clergyman to deal intelligently with his folk. His time must always be at their disposal, and he must never appear to be hurried or busy when expected to listen to some long-winded story or complaint. Nothing must be too trifling to arouse his interest, and no hour of the day too unreasonable to receive a visit; yet, on the whole, the lot of such a village pastor who rightly understands his duties seems to me a very peaceful and enviable one. He is most comfortably situated as regards material welfare, and stands sufficiently aside from the bustling outer world to be spared the annoyances and irritations of more ambitious careers. The fates of his parishioners, so closely interwoven with his own, are a constant source of interest, and the almost unlimited power he enjoys within the confines of his parish makes him feel himself to be indeed the monarch of this little kingdom.

One parsonage in particular is engraved on my mind as a perfect frame for such Arcadian happiness. An old-fashioned roomy house, with high-pitched roof, it stands within the ring of fortified walls which encircle the church as well. A few wide-spreading lime-trees are picturesquely dotted about the turf between the two buildings; and some old moss-grown stones, half sunk in the velvet grass where the violets cluster so thick in spring, betray this to be the site of a long-disused burying-place. Up a few steps there is a raised platform with seats arranged against the wall, from which, as from an opera-box, one may overlook the village street and mark the comings and goings of the inhabitants; and a large kitchen-garden, opening through the wall in another direction, contains every fruit and vegetable which a country heart can desire. But the greatest attraction, to my thinking, was a long arcade of lilac - bushes, so thickly grown that the branches closed together overhead, only admitting a soft, tremulous, green half-light, and scented with every variety of the dear old-fashioned shrub, from the exquisite dwarf Persian and snowy white to each possible gradation of lilac pink and pinky lilac. Along this fragrant gallery old carved stone benches are placed at intervals; and hither, as the venerable pastor informed me, he always comes on Saturday evenings in summer to compose his sermon for the morrow. "It is so much easier to think out here," he said, "among the birds and flowers and the old graves all around. When the air is scented with the breath of violets, and from the open church window comes the sound of the organ, ah, then I feel myself another man, and God teaches me quite other words to say to my people than those I find for myself inside the house!"

CHAPTER XI.

THE SAXON BROTHERHOODS—NEIGHBORHOODS AND VILLAGE HANN.

AMONG the curiosities I picked up in the course of my wanderings about Saxon villages is a large zinc dish sixteen inches in diameter, curiously engraved and inscribed. On the outside rim there is a running pattern of hares and stags; on the inside a coat-of-arms, and this inscription:

"NEU JAHRS GESCHENK VON DER
EHRLICHEN BRUDERSCHAFT.*
ALT GESEL GEORG BAYR,
JUNGER TOMAS FRAYTAG
1791."

The dish makes a convenient tray for holding calling-cards, and its origin is an interesting addition to the history of these Saxon people, as it comprises two noteworthy features of their organization— namely, the Bruderschaften (brotherhoods) and the Nachbarschaften (neighborhoods).

The Bruderschaft is an association to which belong all young men of the parish, from the date of their confirmation up to that of their marriage. This community is governed by strict laws, in which the

---

* New-year's gift from the honorable brotherhood.

duties of its members respectively, as citizens, sons, brothers, suitors, and even dancers, are distinctly traced out. In their outward form these brotherhoods have some sort of resemblance to the religious confraternities still existing in many Catholic countries, and most probably they originated in the same manner; but while these latter have now degenerated into mere outward forms, the Saxon brotherhoods have retained the original spirit of such institutions, principally consisting in the reciprocal watch its members kept over one another's morality. Mr. Boner, in his book, very aptly compares the Saxon Bruderschaften to the Heidelberg Burschenschafts; and spite of the great difference which may at first sight appear, these institutions are the only ones to which the Saxon brotherhoods may at all be likened. In the towns these confraternities have now completely disappeared; but in villages they are still in full force, and have but little or nothing of their original character.*

The head of the Brotherhood is called the Alt-knecht. He is chosen every year, but can be deposed at any time if he prove unworthy of his post. It is his mission to watch over the other members, keep order, and dictate punishments; but when he is caught erring himself he incurs a double forfeit. When a new Alt-knecht is about to be chosen, the seven oldest brothers are proposed as candidates. With money received from the treasurer these repair to the public-house, there to await the decision of the confraternity. The other members meanwhile proceed to vote, and when they have made a decision, send a deputation of two brothers to invite the candidates to come and learn the result.

Twice the deputation is carelessly dismissed, the candidates affecting to feel no interest in the matter; only when the ambassadors appear for the third time two glasses of wine are filled for them, and they are desired to salute the new Alt-knecht.

The two emissaries then take place on either side of the newly chosen leader and drink his health, with the words, "Helf Gott, Alt-knecht." They then all proceed back to the assembly-room, where the senior candidate says,

---

* The late King of Bavaria, Ludwig II., made an attempt at reviving these brotherhoods, such as they existed in Germany in the Middle Ages. He himself was the head of the confraternity, and designed the costumes to be worn by its members, who, with their long pilgrim robes, cockle-shells, and wide flapping hats, were among the most conspicuous figures at the royal funeral last summer.

"God be with you, brother: you have sent for us; what do you want?"

The eldest among the voters answers for the others,

"We have chosen N. N. for our Alt-knecht; the other six can sit down."

The lucky candidate is now expected to play the shamefaced, modest *rôle*, and say,

"Look farther, brother; seek for a better one."

"We have already looked," is the answer.

"And is it in truth your will that I and no other should be your head?"

"It is our will."

"And shall it then be so?"

"It shall be so."

"And may it be so?"

"It may be so."

"Then God help me to act righteously towards myself and you."

"God help you, Alt-knecht."

The senior brother then solemnly presents him to the assembly, saying,

"See, brothers, this is the Alt-knecht you have chosen for the coming year. He is bound to undertake all journeys on behalf of the affairs of the confraternity, he will preside at our meetings, superintend the maids at their spinning evenings, and will punish each one according to his deserts; but when he is himself at fault, he shall be doubly visited (punished) by us."

Six other brothers occupy different posts of authority under the Alt-knecht. The first in rank of these is the Gelassen Alt-knecht, who takes the place of the Alt-knecht when absent; he is likewise treasurer, and has the office of presenting newly chosen members to the pastor. Once or twice a month there is a meeting of the Brotherhood at which the affairs of the confraternity are discussed and misdemeanors judged. In presiding at these meetings the Alt-knecht has in his hand, as insignia of his office, a wooden platter, with which he strikes on the table whenever he wishes to call the brothers to order.

Whoever, on these occasions, freely accuses himself of his faults incurs only half the penalty; but I am told that this contingency rarely occurs. The finable offences are numerous, and are taxed at six, ten, twenty kreuzers and upwards, according to the heinousness of the offence. Here are some of the principal delinquencies subject to penalties:

1. Carelessness or slovenliness of attire — every missing button having a fine attached to it.

2. Bad manners at table, putting the elbows on the board, or striking it with the fist when excited.

3. Irregularity in church attendance, falling asleep during the sermon, yawning, stretching, etc., a particularly heavy fine being put upon snoring.

4. Having, on fast-days, whistled loudly in the street, or worn colored ribbons in the hat.

Whoever be discontented with the punishment assigned to him, and forgets himself so far as to grumble audibly, incurs a double fine.

Four times yearly, before the Sacrament is administered in church, the Brotherhood hold what they call their Versöhnungs-Abend (reconciliation evening), at which they mutually ask pardon for the injuries done.

Eight days after Quasimodo Sunday the Alt-knecht sends round an invitation to all newly confirmed youths to enter the confraternity. Their incorporation is accompanied by various ceremonies, one of which is that each newly chosen member is laden with a burden of heavy stones, old rusty pots and pans, broomsticks, and such-like rubbish, secured round his neck by means of ropes, this somewhat obscure ceremony being supposed to signify the subjection of the new member to the rules of the Brotherhood.

On his marriage a man ceases to be a member of the Brotherhood, on leaving which both he and his bride must pay certain taxes in meat, bread, and wine. Henceforth he belongs to the *Nachbarschaft*, or neighborhood. Every village is divided into four neighborhoods, each governed by a head, called the Nachbarvater. This second confraternity is conducted in much the same manner as the Brotherhood, with the difference that its regulations apply to the reciprocal assistance which neighbors are bound to render each other in various household and domestic contingencies. Thus a man is only obliged to assist those who belong to his own quarter in building a house, cleaning out wells, extinguishing fires, and such-like. He must also contribute provisions on christening, marriage, and funeral occasions occurring within his neighborhood, and lend plates and jugs for the same.

The Nachbarvater has the responsibility of watching over the order and discipline in his quarter, enforcing the regulations issued by the pastor or the village *maire*, or *Hann*, and assuring himself of the cleanliness of those streets which lie under his jurisdiction. When an ox or calf has perished through any accident, it is his duty to have the fact proclaimed in the neighborhood, each family in which is then obliged to purchase a certain portion of the meat at the price fixed by the Nachbarvater, in order to lighten the loss to the afflicted family. His authority extends even to the interior of each household, and he is bound to report to the pastor the names of those who absent themselves from church. He must fine the men who have neglected to approach the Sacrament, as well as the women who have lingered outside the church wasting their time in senseless gossip. Children who have been overheard speaking disrespectfully of their parents, couples whose connubial quarrels are audible in the street, dogs wantonly beaten by their masters, vain young matrons who have exceeded the prescribed number of glittering pins in their head-dress, or girls surpassing their proper allowance of ribbons—all come under his jurisdiction ; and the Nachbarvater is himself subject to punishment if he neglect to report a culprit, or show himself too lenient in the dictation of punishment.

Of the third confraternity, to which belong the girls—viz., the *Schwesterschaft*, or Sisterhood—there is comparatively little to say ; but the description of one of these Saxon village communities would not be complete without mention of the *Hann*, who, after the parson, is the most important man in the village.

The designation *Hann* has been derived by etymologists from the Saxon word *chunna* (hundred), out of which successively Hunna, Hund, Hunne, Honne, and Hann have been made. A Hundding or Huntari was a district comprising a hundred divisions (but whether heads of families or villages is impossible now to ascertain), and the Hund, Honne, or Hann was the title given to the man who governed this district. The appellation Hann is to be found in documents of the fifteenth century in the Rhine provinces, but seems to have disappeared there from use since that time.

The Saxon village Hann is chosen every three years ; and though but a peasant himself like the neighbors around, he becomes, from the moment when he is invested in "a little brief authority," an influential personage, whose word none dare to question. He is forthwith

spoken of as the " Herr Hann," his wife becomes the " Frau Hanin,"
and *euer Weisheit* (your wisdom) is henceforth the correct formula of
address.

In one village it is customary for the newly elected Hann to be
placed on a harrow (the points turned upward), and thus drawn in
triumph round the village. The election takes place by votes, much

SAXON PEASANT GOING TO WORK.

in the same way as the nomination of a pastor, and with like circum-
spection. It is by no means easy to find a man well qualified for the
office, for the Hann requires to have a very remarkable assortment
of the choicest virtues in order to fit him for the place. He must be
upright, honest, energetic, and practical, impervious to bribery, and
absolutely impartial; moreover, he must not be poor, for *noblesse*

oblige, and his new dignity brings many outlays in its train. The modest supply of crockery which has hitherto been ample for the requirements of his family no longer suffices, for a Hann must be prepared to receive guests; such luxuries as coffee, loaf-sugar, and an occasional packet of cigars, must now find their way into his house, to say nothing of paper, pens, and ink: who knows whether even a new table or an additional couple of chairs may not become necessary?

Of course the Hann can only be chosen from among those residing in the principal street, and it is considered to be rather an indignity if he has taken his wife from some side-street family—a disadvantage only to be condoned for by very exceptional merit on his own part.

It would be endless were I to attempt enumerating all the duties of a village Hann; so let it suffice to say that the whole responsibility of the arrangements for the health, security, cleanliness, and general welfare of the village rests upon his shoulders. School attendance, military conscription, and tax-collecting are but a few of the many duties which devolve on him. His it is to decide on what day the corn is to be cut or the hay brought home; through which street the buffaloes are to be driven to pasture, and at which fountain it is permitted for the women to wash their linen. He must assure himself that no cart return to the village after the curfew-bell has sounded; that the night-watchmen—one in each neighborhood—are punctual in going their rounds; and that the Nachbarväter make discreet and worthy use of their authority.

CHAPTER XII.

THE SAXONS: DRESS—SPINNING AND DANCING.

Not without difficulty have these Saxons succeeded in keeping their national costume so rigidly intact that the figures we meet to-day in every Saxon village differ but little from old bass-reliefs of the thirteenth and fourteenth centuries. Here, as elsewhere, even among these quiet, practical, prosaic, and unlovely people, the demon of vanity has been at work. Many severe punishments had to be prescribed, and much eloquence expended from the pulpit, in order to subdue the evil spirit of fashion which at various times threatened to spread over the land like a contagious illness. So in 1651 we find a whole set of dress regulations issued by the bishop for the diocese of Mediasch.

"1. The men shall wear neither red, blue, nor yellow boots, nor shall the women venture to approach the Holy Sacrament or baptismal font in red shoes; and whoever conforms not to this regulation is to be refused admittance to church.

"2. All imitation of the Hungarians' dress, such as their waistcoats, braids, galloons, etc., are prohibited to the men.

"3. Be it likewise forbidden for men and for serving-men to wear their hair in a long, foreign fashion hanging down behind, for that is a dishonor; for 'if a man have long hair, it is a shame unto him' (1 Cor. xi. 14).

"4. The peasant-folk shall wear no high boots and no large hats of wool, nor yet trimmed with marten fur, nor an embroidered belt, for he is a peasant. Who is seen wearing such will thereby expose himself to ridicule, and the boots shall be drawn off his legs, that he shall go barefoot.

"5. The women shall avoid all that is superfluous in dress, nor shall they make horns upon their heads.* Rich veils shall only be worn by such as are entitled to them, neither shall any woman wear gold cords beneath her veil, not even if she be the wife of a gentleman.

"6. Silk caps with golden stars are not suitable for every woman. More than two handsome jewelled pins shall no woman wear, and should a woman require more than two for fastening her veil, let her take small pins. Not every one's child is entitled to wear corals round its neck. Let no woman copy the dress of noble dames, for it is not suitable for us Saxons.

"7. Peasant-maids shall wear no crooked (probably puffed) sleeves sewed with braids, for they have no right to them. They may wear no red shoes, and also on their best aprons may they have two braids only; one of these may be straight and the other nicked out, but neither over-broad. Let none presume to wear high-heeled shoes, but let them conform to the prescribed measure under heavy penalty.

---

* This would seem to be an allusion to the Roumanian fashion in some districts of twisting up the veil into a horn-like shape on the head.

" 8. Let the womenkind remember that such things as are forbidden become them but badly. Let them wear the *borten**** according to the prescribed measurements. Let the *herren töchter* (gentlemen's daughters, meaning probably burghers) not make the use of gold braids over-common, but content themselves with honorable fringes. The serving-girls shall go *absolutely* without fringes, nor may they buy silk cords of three yards' length, else these will be taken from their head and nailed against the church wall.

" 9. Among the women are beginning to creep in gold rings which cover the half-finger *ad formam et normam nobilium*—after the fashion of nobles; let these be *completely* forbidden."

The worthy prelate who issued all these stern injunctions appears to have been so uncommonly well versed in all the intricacies of female costume as to make us wonder whether he had not missed his vocation as a man-milliner. It must have been a decidedly nervous matter for the women to attend service at his cathedral, with the consciousness that this terrible eagle-glance was taking stock of their clothes all the time, mentally appraising the value of each headpin, and gauging the breadth of every ribbon. Most likely he succeeded in his object of keeping poor human vanity in check for a time, though not in rooting it out, for scarcely a hundred years later we find a new set of dress rules delivered from another pulpit:

" First of all, it is herewith forbidden to both sexes to wear anything whatsoever which has not been manufactured in Transylvania. Furthermore, it is prohibited to the men—

" 1. To wear the so-called broad summer foreign hats.

" 2. The double-trimmed hats, with head of outlandish cloth; only the jurymen and officials are allowed to wear them.

" 3. Trousers of outlandish cloth, or trimmed with braids.

" To the womenkind let it be *completely* forbidden to wear—

" 1. Fine blue-dyed head-cloths.

" 2. White-starred caps. Only the wives of officials and jurymen in the market-towns may wear yellow-starred caps.

" 3. Silver head-pins costing more than two, or at the outside three, Hungarian florins.

" 4. Outlandish ribbons and fringes.

---

* The *borten* is the high, stiff head-dress worn by all Saxon girls, and which they only lay aside with their marriage.

"5. Borten (cap) 1 foot 8½ inches high, or lined inside with any material better than bombazine or glazed calico.

"6. Neck-handkerchiefs.

"7. All outlandish stuffs, linen, etc."

Here follow several more regulations, concluding with the warning that whosoever dares to disregard them will be punished by having the said articles confiscated, besides paying a fine of from six to twelve florins Hungarian money, the offender being in some cases even liable to corporal punishment.

How strangely these old regulations now read in an age when lady's-maids are so often better dressed than their mistresses, and every scullion girl thinks herself ill-used if she may not deck herself out with ostrich-feathers of a Sunday!

A story which bears on this subject is told of Andrew Helling, a well-known and much-respected burgher of the town of Reps, about the beginning of last century. He was repeatedly chosen as judge and burgomaster in his native place, and had a daughter celebrated for her beauty who was engaged to be married. On the wedding morning the girl had been decked out by her friends in her best, with many glittering ornaments and long hanging ribbons in her head-gear. But what pleased the young bride most was the bright silken apron, a present from her bridegroom received that same morning. Thus attired, before proceeding to church, she repaired to her father to ask his blessing, and thank him for all the care bestowed on her; and he, well pleased with and proud of his beautiful child, gazed at her with tenderly approving eye. But of a sudden his expression grew stern, and pointing to the silken apron, he broke out into a storm of bitter reproaches at her vanity for thus attiring herself in gear only suitable for the daughter of a prince. Hearing which, the bridegroom, aggrieved at the dishonor shown to his gift, gave his arm to his bride, and dispensing with the incensed father's blessing, led her off to church.

Most likely, too, it was the desire to repress all extravagance in dress which shaped itself into the following prophecy, still prevalent throughout Transylvania:

"When luxury and extravagance have so spread over the face of the earth that every one walks about in silken attire, and when sin is no longer shame, then, say the Saxons, the end of the world is not far off. There will come then an extraordinary fruitful year, and the ripening corn will stand so high that horse and rider will disappear in it; but no one will be there to cut and garner this corn, for a dreadful war will break out, in which all monarchs will fight against each other, and the war-horse will run up to its fetlocks in blood, with saddle beneath the belly, all the way from Cronstadt to Broos, without drawing breath. At last, however, will come from the East a mighty king, who will restore peace to the world. But few men will then remain alive in Transylvania—not more than can find place in the shade of a big oak-tree."

However, not all the authority of stern fathers and eloquent preachers was able to preserve the old custom intact in the towns, where, little by little, it dropped into disuse, being but seldom seen after the beginning of this century. What costumes there remain are now locked away in dark presses, only to see the light of day at costumed processions or fancy balls, while many of the accompanying ornaments have found their way into jewellers' show-windows or museums. Only in the villages the details of dress are still as rigidly controlled as ever, and show no sign of degeneration just yet. Each village, forming, as it does, a little colony by itself, and being isolated from all outward influences, is enabled to retain its characteristics in a manner impossible to the town. No etiquette is so rigid as Saxon village etiquette, and there are countless little forms and observances which to neglect or transgress would be here as grave as it would be for a lady to go to Court without plumes in England, or to reverse the order of champagne and claret at a fashionable dinner-party. The laws of exact precedence are here every whit as clearly defined as among our upper ten thousand, and the punctilio of a spinning-chamber quite as formal as the ordering of her Majesty's drawing-room.

These spinning meetings take place on winter evenings, the young girls usually coming together at different houses alternately, the young men being permitted to visit them the while, provided they do not interfere with the work. There are often two different spinning meetings in each village, the half-grown girls taking part in the one, while the other assembles the full-fledged maidens of marriageable age. It is not allowed for any man to enter a spinning-room in workday attire, but each must be carefully dressed in his Sunday's clothes. The eldest member of the Brotherhood present keeps watch over the decorum of the younger members, and assures himself that no unbecoming liberties are taken with the other sex.

There is a whole code of penalties drawn up for those who pre-sume to outstep the limits of proper familiarity, and the exact dis-tance a youth is allowed to approach the spinning-wheel of any girl is in some villages regulated by inches. A fine of ten kreuzers is attached to the touching of a maiden's breastpin, while stealing a kiss always proves a still more expensive amusement. As we see by ancient chronicles, these spinning meetings (which formerly used to be held in the towns as well) had sometimes to be prohibited by the clergy when threatening to degenerate into indecorous romps in any particular place; but this custom, so deeply inrooted in Saxon village life, was always resumed after an interval, and, thanks to the vigilant watch kept up by the heads of the Brotherhood, it is seldom that any-thing really objectionable takes place. The men are allowed to join the girls in singing the Rockenlieder (spinning songs), of which there are a great number.

No man may accompany a girl to her home when the meeting breaks up, but each must go singly, or along with her companions.

Many superstitions are attached to the spinning-wheel in Saxon households besides the one which is mentioned in the chapter on wed-dings. So on Saturday evening the work must be desisted with the first stroke of the evening bell, and there are many old pagan festivals which demand that the reel be spun empty the day before.

The girl who sits up spinning on Saturday night is considered as sinning against both sun and moon, and will only produce a coarse, unequal thread, which refuses to let itself be bleached white. The woman who spins on Ash-Wednesday will cause her pigs to suffer from worms throughout the year.

An amulet which preserves against accidents and brings luck in love matters may be produced by two young girls spinning a thread together in silence on St. John's Day after the evening bell has rung. It must be spun walking, one girl holding the distaff while the other twirls the thread, which is afterwards divided between the two. Each piece of this thread, if worn against the body, will bring luck to its wearer, but only so long as her companion likewise retains her por-tion of the charm.

For the twelve days following St. Thomas's Day (21st of December) spinning is prohibited, and the young men visiting the spinning-room during that period have the right to break and burn all the distaffs they find; so it has become usual for the maidens to appear on the feast of St. Thomas with a stick dressed up with tow or wool to represent the distaff in place of a real spinning-wheel.

The married women have also their own spinning meetings, which are principally held in the six weeks following Christmas; and she is considered to be a dilatory housewife who has not spun all her flax by the first week in February. Sometimes she receives a little covert assistance from her lord and master, who, when he has no other work to do in field or barn, may be seen half-shamefacedly plying the distaff, like Hercules at the feet of Omphale. On certain occasions the women hold what they call *Gainzelnocht* (whole-night)—that is, they sit up all through the long winter night, spinning into the gray dawn of the morning.

Dancing takes place either at the village inn on Sunday afternoons, or in summer in the open air, in some roomy court-yard or under a group of old trees, the permission to dance having been each time formally requested of the pastor by the head of the Brotherhood. The Alt-knecht also sometimes settles the couples beforehand, so as to insure each girl against the humiliating contingency of remaining partnerless, and no youth durst, under pain of penalty, refuse the hand of any partner thus assigned to him. Also, each man can stay near his partner only while the music is playing; he may not sit near or walk about with her during the pauses, but with the last note of the valse or *ländler* he drops her like a hot potato, the girls retiring to one side of the room and the men remaining at the other, till the renewed strains of music permit the sexes again to mingle.

Only girls and youths take part in these village dances as a rule, though in some districts it is usual for young couples to dance for a period of six months after their marriage. Also, there are some villages where the custom prevails of the married women dancing every fourth year, but more usually dancing ceases altogether with matrimony.

The usual dance which I have seen performed by Saxon peasants is a sort of valse executed with perfect propriety in a slow, ponderous style, and absolutely unaccompanied by any expression of enjoyment on the part of the dancers. In some villages, however, the amusement seems to be of a livelier kind, for there I am told that certain dances require that the men should noisily slap the calves of their legs at particular parts of the music. A curious explanation is given of this. In olden times it seems their dress was somewhat different from what it is now. Instead of wearing high boots, they had shoes and short breeches; and as the stockings did not reach up to the knee, a naked strip of skin was visible between, as in the Styrian and Tyrolese dress. In summer, therefore, when dancing in a barn or in the open air, the dancers were often sorely tormented by gnats and horse-flies settling on the exposed parts; and seeking occasional relief by vigorous slaps, these gradually took the form of a regular rhythm which has survived the change of costume.

The music used on these occasions is mostly execrable, both out of time and tune, unless indeed they have been lucky enough to secure the services of gypsy musicians; but this is rarely the case, for, bad as it is, the Saxon prefers his own music.

However, it is an interesting sight to look on at one of these village dances, as the girls' costume is both rich and quaint. Particularly interesting is this sight at the village of Hammersdorf, whose inhabitants, as I before remarked, are celebrated for their opulence. Only on the highest festivals, three or four times a year, is it customary for the girls to don their richest attire for the dance, and display all their ornaments — often an exceedingly handsome show of jewellery, descended from mother to daughter through many generations. Thus Pentecost, when there is dancing two days in succession in the open air, is a good time for assisting at one of these rustic balls.

Each girl wears on her head the high stiff *borten*, which in shape resembles nothing so much as a chimney-pot hat, without either crown or brim, though this is perhaps rather an Irish way of putting it. It is formed of pasteboard covered with black velvet, and from it depend numerous ribbons three or four fingers in breadth, hanging down almost to the hem of the skirt. In some villages these ribbons are blue; in others, as at Hammersdorf, mostly scarlet and silver. The skirt at Hammersdorf on Pentecost Monday was of black stuff, very full and wide, and above it a large white muslin apron covered with embroidery, with the name of the wearer introduced in the pattern. The wide bulging black skirt was confined at the waist by a broad girdle of massive gold braid set with round clumps of jewels at regular intervals; these were sometimes garnets, turquoises, pearls, or emeralds. Another ornament is the *patzel*, worn by some on the chest, as large as a tea-saucer, silver gilt, and likewise richly incrusted with two or three sorts of gems; some of these were of very beautiful and intricate workmanship. Altogether, when thus seen collectively, the costume presents a quaint and pretty appearance, with something martial about the general effect, suggesting a troop of sturdy young Amazons—the silver and scarlet touches, relieving the simplicity of the black and white attire, being particularly effective.

On Pentecost Tuesday the dance was repeated, with the difference that this time all wore white muslin skirts and black silk aprons.

DRESSING FOR THE DANCE.

None of them could tell me the reason of this precise ordering of the costume; it had always been so, they said, in their mothers' and grandmothers' time as well, to wear the black skirts on the Pentecost Monday and the white ones on the Tuesday.

Each girl carries in her hand a little nosegay of flowers, and has a large flowered silk handkerchief stuck in her waistband. Every youth is, of course, attired in his Sunday clothes; and however hot the weather, it is *de rigueur* that he keep on the heavy cloth jacket during the first two dances. Only then, when the Alt-knecht gives the signal, is it allowed to lay aside the coat and dance in shirt-sleeves, while the girls divest themselves of their uncomfortable head-dress—how uncomfortable being only too apparent from the dark red mark which it has left across the forehead of each wearer.

But if the young people are thus elegantly got up, the same cannot be said of their chaperons the mothers, who in their common week-day clothes have likewise come here to enjoy the fun. They have certainly made none of those concessions to society which reduce the lives of unfortunate dowagers to a perpetual martyrdom in the ball-room, but are as dirty and comfortable as though they were at home, each woman squatting on the low three-legged stool which she has brought with her.

The reason for this simplicity—not to say slovenliness—of attire presently becomes obvious, as the lowing of kine and a cloud of dust in the distance announce the return of the herd, and in a body the matrons rise and desert the festive scene, stool in hand, for it is milking-time, and the buffaloes, whose temper is proverbially short, durst not be kept waiting; only when this important duty has been accomplished do the mammas return to the ball-room.

CHAPTER XIII.

THE SAXONS: BETROTHAL.

OATS have been defined by Dr. Johnson as a grain serving to nourish horses in England and men in Scotland; and in spite of this contemptuous definition, its name, to us Caledonian born, must always awaken pleasant recollections of the porridge and bannocks of our childhood. It is, however, a new experience to find a country where this often unappreciated grain occupies a still prouder position, and where its name is associated with memories yet more pregnant and tender; for autumn, not spring, is the season of Saxon love, and oats, not myrtle, are here emblematic of courtship and betrothal.

In proportion as the waving surface of the green oat-fields begins to assume a golden tint, so also does curiosity awaken and gossip grow rife in the village. Well-informed people may have hinted before that such and such a youth had been seen more than once stepping in at the gate of the big red house in the long street, and more than one chatterer had been ready to identify the speckled carnations which on Sundays adorned the hat of some youthful Conrad or Thomas, as having been grown in the garden of a certain Anna or Maria; but after all these had been but mere conjectures, for nothing positive can be known as yet, and ill-natured people were apt to console themselves with the reflection that St. Catherine's Day was yet a long way off, and that "there is many a slip 'twixt cup and lip."

But now the great day which is to dispel all doubt and put an end to conjecture is approaching—that day which will destroy so many illusions and fulfil so few; for now the sun has given the final touch to the ripening grain, and soon the golden sheaves are lying piled together on the clean-shorn stubble-field, only waiting to be carted away. Then one evening when the sun is sinking low on the horizon, and no breath of air is there to lift the white powdery dust from off the hedge-rows, the sound of a drum is heard in the village street, and a voice proclaims aloud that "to-morrow the oats are to be fetched home."

Like wildfire the news has spread throughout the village; the cry is taken up and repeated with various intonations of hope, curiosity, anticipation, or triumph, "To-morrow the oats will be fetched."

A stranger probably fails to perceive anything particularly thrilling about this intelligence, having no reason to suppose the garnering of oats to be in any way more interesting than the carting of potatoes or wheat; and, no doubt, to the majority of land-owners the thought of to-morrow's work is chiefly connected with dry prosaic details, such as repairing the harness and oiling the cart-wheels. But there are others in the village on whom the announcement has had an electrifying effect, and for whom the words are synonymous with love and wedding-bells. Five or six of the young village swains, or maybe as many as eight or ten, spend that evening in a state of pleasurable bustle and excitement, busying themselves in cleaning and decking out the cart for the morrow, furbishing up the best harness, grooming the work-horses till their coats are made to shine like satin, and plaiting up their manes with bright-colored ribbons.

Early next morning the sound of harness-bells and the loud crack-

ing of whips cause all curious folk to rush to their doors; and as
every one is curious, the whole population is soon assembled in the
street to gaze at the sight of young Hans N——, attired in his bravest
clothes and wearing in his cap a monstrous bouquet, riding postilion
fashion on the left-hand horse, and cracking his whip with ostentatious
triumph, while behind, on the gayly decorated cart, is seated a blushing
maiden, who lowers her eyes in confusion at thus seeing herself the
object of general attention—at least this is what she is supposed to
do, for every well-brought-up girl ought surely to blush and hang her
head in graceful embarrassment when she first appears in the character of a bride; and although no formal proposal has yet taken place,
by consenting to assist the young man to bring in his oats she has
virtually confessed her willingness to become his wife.

Her appearance on this occasion will doubtless cause much envy
and disappointment among her less fortunate companions, who gaze
out furtively through the chinks of the wooden boarding at the
spectacle of a triumph they had perhaps hoped for themselves. "So
it is the red-haired Susanna after all, and not the miller's Agnes, as
every one made sure," the gossips are saying. "And who has young
Martin got on his cart, I wonder? May I never spin flax again if it is
not that saucy wench, the black-eyed Lisi, who was all but promised
to small-pox Peter of the green corner house"—and so on, and so on,
in endless variety, as the decorated carts go by in procession, each one
giving rise to manifold remarks and comments, and not one of them
failing to leave disappointment and heart-burning in its rear.

This custom of the maiden helping the young man to bring in his
oats, and thereby signifying her willingness to marry him, is prevalent only in a certain district to the north of Transylvania called the
Haferland, or country of oats—a broad expanse of country covered
at harvest-time by a billowy sea of golden grain, the whole fortune
of the land-owners. In other parts various other betrothal customs
are prevalent, as for instance in Neppendorf, a large village close to
Hermanstadt, inhabited partly by Saxons, partly by Austrians, or
Ländlers, as they call themselves. This latter race is of far more
recent introduction in the country than the Saxons, having only come
hither (last century) in the time of Maria Theresa, who had summoned
them to replenish some of the Saxon colonies in danger of becoming
extinct. If it is strange to note how rigidly the Saxons have kept
themselves from mingling with the surrounding Magyars and Rou-

manians, it is yet more curious to see how these two German races
have existed side by side for over a hundred years without amalgamat-
ing; and this for no sort of antagonistic reason, for they live together
in perfect harmony, attending the same church, and conforming to
the same regulations, but each people preserving its own individual

SAXON BETROTHED COUPLE.

costume and customs. The Saxons and the Ländlers have each their
different parts of the church assigned to them; no Saxon woman
would ever think of donning the fur cap of a Ländler matron, while
as little would the latter exchange her tight-fitting fur coat for the
wide hanging mantle worn by the other.

7

Until quite lately unions have very seldom taken place between members of these different races. Only within the last twenty years or so have some of the Saxon youths awoke to the consciousness that the Austrian girls make better and more active housewives than their own phlegmatic countrywomen, and have consequently sought them in marriage. Even then, when both parties are willing, many a projected union makes shipwreck upon the stiff-neckedness of the two *paterfamilias*, who neither of them will concede anything to the other. Thus, for instance, when the Saxon father of the bridegroom demands that his future daughter-in-law should adopt Saxon attire when she becomes the wife of his son, the Ländler father will probably take offence and withdraw his consent at the last moment; not a cap nor a jacket, not even a pin or an inch of ribbon, will either of the two concede to the wishes of the young people. Thus many hopeful alliances are nipped in the bud, and those which have been accomplished are almost invariably based on the understanding that each party retains its own attire, and that the daughters born of such union follow the mother, the sons the father, in the matter of costume.

Among the Ländlers the marriage proposal takes place in a way which deserves to be mentioned. The youth who has secretly cast his eye on the girl he fain would make his wife prepares a new silver thaler (about 2s. 6d.) by winding round it a piece of bright-colored ribbon, and wrapping the whole in a clean sheet of white letter-paper. With this coin in his pocket he repairs to the next village dance, and takes the opportunity of slipping it unobserved into the girl's hand while they are dancing. By no word or look does she betray any consciousness of his actions, and only when back at home she produces the gift, and acquaints her parents with what has taken place. A family council is then held as to the merits of the suitor, and the expediency of accepting or rejecting the proposal. Should the latter be decided upon, the maiden must take an early opportunity of intrusting the silver coin to a near relation of the young man, who in receiving it back is thereby informed that he has nothing further to hope in that direction; but if three days have elapsed without his thaler returning to him, he is entitled to regard this as encouragement, and may commence to visit in the house of his sweetheart on the footing of an official wooer.

In cases of rejection, it is considered a point of honor on the part of all concerned that no word should betray the state of the case to the outer world—a delicate reticence one is surprised to meet with in these simple people.

This giving of the silver coin is probably a remnant of the old custom of "buying the bride," and in many villages it is customary still to talk of the *brautkaufen*.

In some places it is usual for the lad who is courting to adorn the window of his fair one with a flowering branch of hawthorn at Pentecost, and at Christmas to fasten a sprig of mistletoe or a fir-branch to the gable-end of her house.

To return, however, to the land of oats, where, after the harvest has been successfully garnered, the bridegroom proceeds to make fast the matter, or, in other words, officially to demand the girl's hand of her parents.

It is not consistent with village etiquette that the bridegroom *in spe* should apply directly to the father of his intended, but he must depute some near relation or intimate friend to bring forward his request. The girl's parents, on their side, likewise appoint a representative to transmit the answer. These two ambassadors are called the *wortmacher* (word-makers)—sometimes also the *hochzeitsväter* (wedding-fathers). Much talking and speechifying are required correctly to transact a wedding from beginning to end, and a fluent and eloquent wortmacher is a much-prized individual.

Each village has its own set formulas for each of the like occasions —long-winded pompous speeches, rigorously adhered to, and admitting neither of alteration nor curtailment. The following fragment of one of these speeches will give a correct notion of the general style of Saxon oration. It is the hochzeitsvater who, in the name of the young man's parents, speaks as follows:

"A good-morning to you herewith, dear neighbors, and I further wish to hear that you have rested softly this night, and been enabled to rise in health and strength. And if such be the case I shall be rejoiced to hear the same, and shall thank the Almighty for his mercies towards you; and should your health and the peace of your household not be as good as might be desired in every respect, so at least will I thank the Almighty that he has made your lot to be endurable, and beg him further in future only to send you so much trouble and affliction as you are enabled patiently to bear at a time.

"Furthermore, I crave your forgiveness that I have made bold to

enter your house thus early this morning, and trust that my presence
therein may in no way inconvenience you, but that I may always
comport myself with honor and propriety, so that you may in nowise
be ashamed of me, and that you may be pleased to listen to the few
words I have come hither to say.

"God the Almighty having instituted the holy state of matrimony
in order to provide for the propagation of the human race, it is not
unknown to me, dearest neighbor, that many years ago you were
pleased to enter this holy state, taking to yourself a beloved wife,
with whom ever since you have lived in peace and happiness; and
that, furthermore, the Almighty, not wishing to leave you alone in
your union, was pleased to bless you, not only with temporal goods
and riches, but likewise with numerous offspring, with dearly beloved
children, to be your joy and solace. And among these beloved children is a daughter, who has prospered and grown up in the fear of
the Lord to be a comely and virtuous maiden.

"And as likewise it may not be unknown to you that years ago
we too thought fit to enter the holy state of matrimony, and that the
Lord was pleased to bless our union, not with temporal goods and
riches, but with numerous offspring, with various beloved children,
among whom is a son, who has grown up, not in a garden of roses,
but in care and toil, and in the fear of the Lord.

"And now this same son, having grown to be a man, has likewise
bethought himself of entering the holy state of matrimony; and he
has prayed the Lord to guide him wisely in his choice, and to give
him a virtuous and God-fearing companion.

"Therefore he has been led over mountains and valleys, through
forests and rivers, over rocks and precipices, until he came to your
house and cast his eyes on the virtuous maiden your daughter. And
the Lord has been pleased to touch his heart with a mighty love for
her, so that he has been moved to ask you to give her hand to him in
holy wedlock."

Probably the young couple have grown up in sight of each other,
the garden of the one father very likely adjoining the pigsty of the
other; but the formula must be adhered to notwithstanding, and
neither rocks nor precipices omitted from the programme; and even
though the parents of the bride be a byword in the village for their
noisy domestic quarrels, yet the little fiction of conjugal happiness
must be kept up all the same, with a truly magnificent sacrifice of

veracity to etiquette worthy of any Court journal discussing a royal alliance.

And in point of fact a disinterested love-match between Saxon peasants is about as rare a thing as a genuine courtship between reigning princes. Most often it is a simple business contract arranged between the family heads, who each of them hopes to reap advantage from the bargain.

When the answer has been a consent, then the compact is sealed by a feast called the *brautvertrinken* (drinking the bride), to which are invited only the nearest relations on either side, the places of honor at the head of the table being given to the two ambassadors who have transacted the business. A second banquet, of a more solemn nature, is held some four weeks later, when rings have been exchanged in presence of the pastor. The state of the weather at the moment the rings are exchanged is regarded as prophetic for the married life of the young couple, according as it may be fair or stormy.

Putting the ring on his bride's finger, the young man says,

"I give thee here my ring so true;
God grant thou may it never rue!"

CHAPTER XIV.

THE SAXONS: MARRIAGE.

THE 25th of November, feast of St. Catherine,* is in many districts the day selected for tying all these matrimonial knots. When this is not the case, then the weddings take place in Carnival, oftenest in the week following the Sunday when the gospel of the marriage at Cana has been read in church; and Wednesday is considered the most lucky day for the purpose.

The preparations for the great day occupy the best part of a week in every house which counts either a bride or bridegroom among its inmates. There are loaves and cakes of various sorts and shapes to be

---

* St. Catherine is throughout Germany the patroness of old maids — likewise in France, "coiffer la Sainte Catherine."

baked, fowls and pigs to be slaughtered; in wealthier houses even the sacrifice of a calf or an ox is considered necessary for the wedding-feast; and when this is the case the tongue is carefully removed, and, placed upon the best china plate, with a few laurel leaves by way of decoration, is carried to the parsonage as the customary offering to the reverend Herr Vater.

The other needful provisions for the banquet are collected in the following simple manner: On the afternoon of the Sunday preceding the wedding, six young men belonging to the Brotherhood are de-spatched by the Alt-knecht from house to house, where, striking a re-sounding knock on each door, they make the village street re-echo with their cry, " Bringt rahm !" (bring cream). This is a summons which none may refuse, all those who belong to that neighborhood being bound to send contributions in the shape of milk, cream, eggs, butter, lard, or bacon, to those wedding-houses within their quarter; and every gift, even the smallest one of a couple of eggs, is received with thanks, and the messenger rewarded by a glass of wine.

Next day the women of both families assemble to bake the wedding-feast, the future mother-in-law of the bride keeping a sharp lookout on the girl, to note whether she acquits herself creditably of her household duties. This day is in fact a sort of final examination the bride has to pass through in order to prove herself worthy of her new dignity; so woe to the maiden who is dilatory in mixing the dough or awkward at kneading the loaves.

While this is going on the young men have been to the forest to fetch firing - wood, for it is a necessary condition that the wood for heating the oven where the wedding-loaves are baked should be brought in expressly for the occasion, even though there be small wood in plenty lying ready for use in the shed.

The cart is gayly decorated with flowers and streamers, and the wood brought home with much noise and merriment, much in the old English style of bringing in the yule-log. On their return from the forest, the gate of the court-yard is found to be closed; or else a rope, from which are suspended straw bunches and bundles, is stretched across the entrance. The women now advance, with much clatter of pots and pans, and pretend to defend the yard against the besiegers; but the men tear down the rope, and drive in triumphantly, each one catching at a straw bundle in passing. Some of these are found to contain cakes or apples, others only broken crockery or egg-shells.

The young men sit up late splitting the logs into suitable size for burning. Their duties further consist in lighting the fire, drawing water from the well, and putting it to boil on the hearth. Thus they work till into the small hours of the morning, now and then refreshing themselves with a hearty draught of home-made wine. When all is prepared, it is then the turn of the men to take some rest, and they wake the girls with an old song running somewhat as follows:

> "All in the early morning gray,
> A lass would rise at break of day.
>> Arise, arise,
>> Fair lass, arise,
>> And ope your eyes,
>> For darkness flies,
> And your true-love he comes to-day.

> "So, lassie, would you early fill
> Your pitcher at the running rill,
>> Awake, awake,
>> Fair maid, awake,
>> Your pitcher take,
>> For dawn doth break,
> And come to-day your true-love will."

Another song of equally ancient origin is sung the evening before the marriage, when the bride takes leave of her friends and relations.*

> "I walked beside the old church wall;
> My love stood there, but weeping all.
> I greeted her, and thus she spake:
> 'My heart is sore, dear love, alack!
>> I must depart, I must be gone;
>> When to return, God knows alone!
>> When to return?—when the black crow
>> Bears on his wing plumes white as snow.

> "'I set two roses in my father's land—
> O father, dearest father, give me once more thy hand!
> I set two roses in my mother's land—
> O mother, dearest mother, give me again thy hand!
>> I must depart, I must be gone;
>> When to return, God knows alone!
>> When to return?—when the black crow
>> Bears on his wing plumes white as snow.

---

* Out of the several slightly different versions of this song to be found in different districts I have selected those verses which seemed most intelligible.

" 'I set two roses in my brother's land—
O brother, dearest brother, give me again thy hand!
I set two roses in my sister's land—
O sister, dearest sister, give me again thy hand!
　　　I must away, I must be gone;
　　　When to return, God knows alone!
　　　When to return ?—when the black crow
　　　Bears on his wing plumes white as snow.

" 'I set again two roses under a bush of yew—
O comrades, dearest comrades, I say my last adieu!
No roses shall I set more in this my native land—
O parents, brother, sister, comrades, give me once more your hand!
　　　I must away, I must be gone;
　　　When to return, God knows alone!
　　　When to return ?—when the black crow
　　　Bears on his wing plumes white as snow.

" 'And when I came to the dark fir-tree,*
An iron kettle my father gave me;
And when I came unto the willow,
My mother gave a cap and a pillow.
　　　Woe's me ! 'tis only those who part
　　　Can tell how parting tears the heart!

" 'And when unto the bridge I came,
I turned me round and looked back again;
I saw no mother nor father more,
And I bitterly wept, for my heart was sore.
　　　Woe's me ! 'tis only those who part
　　　Can tell how parting tears the heart!

" 'And when I came before the gate,
The bolt was drawn, and I must wait;
And when I came to the wooden bench,
They said, " She's but a peevish wench!"
　　　Woe's me ! 'tis only those who part
　　　Can tell how parting tears the heart!

" 'And when I came to the strangers' hearth,
They whispered, "She is little worth;"
And when I came before the bed,
I sighed, "Would I were yet a maid!"
　　　Woe's me ! 'tis only those who part
　　　Can tell how parting tears the heart!

" 'My house is built of goodly stone,
But in its walls I feel so lone!

---

* Two fir-trees were often planted before Saxon peasant houses.

A mantle of finest cloth I wear,
But 'neath it an aching heart I bear.
Loud howls the wind, wild drives the snow,
Parting, oh, parting is bitterest woe!
On the belfry tower is a trumpet shrill,
But down the kirkyard the dead lie still.' "

Very precise are the formalities to be observed in inviting the wedding - guests. A member of the bride's family is deputed as *einlader* (inviter), and, invested with a brightly painted staff as insignia of his office, he goes the round of the friends and relations to be asked.

It is customary to invite all kinsfolk within the sixth degree of relationship, though many of these are not expected to comply with the summons, the invitations in such cases being simply a matter of form, politely tendered on the one side and graciously received on the other, but not meant to be taken literally, as being but honorary invitations.

Unless particular arrangements have been made to the contrary, it is imperative that the invitations, in order to be valid, should be repeated with all due formalities as often as three times, the slightest divergence from this rule being severely judged and commented upon; and mortal offence has often been taken by a guest who bitterly complains that he was only twice invited. In some villages it is, moreover, customary to invite anew for each one of the separate meals which take place during the three or four days of the wedding festivities.

Early on the wedding morning the bridegroom despatches his *wortmann* with the *morgengabe* (morning gift) to the bride. This consists in a pair of new shoes, to which are sometimes added other small articles, such as handkerchiefs, ribbons, a cap, apples, nuts, cakes, etc. An ancient superstition requires that the young matron should carefully treasure up these shoes if she would assure herself of kind treatment on the part of her husband, who "will not begin to beat her till the wedding-shoes are worn out." The ambassador, in delivering over the gifts to the *wortmann* of the other party, speaks as follows:

" Good-morning to you, Herr Wortmann, and to all worthy friends here assembled. The friends on our side have charged me to wish you all a very good morning. I have further come hither to remind you of the laudable custom of our fathers and grandfathers, who bethought themselves of presenting their brides with a small morning gift. So in the same way our young master the bridegroom, not wishing to neglect this goodly patriarchal custom, has likewise sent me here with a trifling offering to his bride, trusting that this small gift may be agreeable and pleasing to you."

The bride, on her side, sends to the bridegroom a new linen shirt, spun, woven, sewed, and embroidered by her own hands. This shirt he wears but twice—once on his wedding-day for going to church, the second time when he is carried to the grave.

Before proceeding to church the men assemble at the house of the bridegroom, and the women at that of the bride. The young people only accompany the bridal pair to church, the elder members of both families remaining at home until the third invitation has been delivered, after which all proceed together to the house of the bride, where the first day's festivities are held.

In some villages it is customary for the young couple returning from church to the house of the bridegroom to have their two right hands tied together before stepping over the threshold. A glass of wine and a piece of bread are given to them ere they enter, of which they must both partake together, the bridegroom then throwing the glass away over the house-roof.

There is much speechifying and drinking of healths, and various meals are served up at intervals of three or four hours, each guest being provided with a covered jug, which must always be kept replenished with wine.

It is usual for each guest to bring a small gift as contribution to the newly set-up household of the young couple, and these are deposited on a table decked for the purpose in the centre of the court-yard, or, if the weather be unfavorable, inside the house—bride and bridegroom standing on either side to receive the gifts. First it is the bridegroom's father, who, approaching the table, deposits thereon a new shining ploughshare, as symbol that his son must earn his bread by the sweat of his brow; then the mother advances with a new pillow adorned with bows of colored ribbon, and silver head-pins stuck at the four corners. These gay ornaments are meant to represent the pleasures and joys of matrimony, but two long streamers of black ribbon, which hang down to the ground on either side, are placed there likewise to remind the young couple of the crosses and misfortunes which must inevitably fall to their share. The other relations of the bridegroom follow in due precedence, each with a gift. Sometimes it is a piece of homespun linen, a colored handkerchief, or some such article of dress or decoration; sometimes a roll of sheet-iron, a packet of nails, a knife and fork, or a farming or gardening implement, each one laying down his or her gift with the words, " May it be pleasing to you."

Then follow the kinsfolk of the bride with similar offerings, her father presenting her with a copper caldron or kettle, her mother with a second pillow decorated in the same manner as the first one.

Playful allusions are not unfrequently concealed in these gifts—a doll's cradle, or a young puppy-dog wrapped in swaddling-clothes, often figuring among the presents ranged on the table.

Various games and dances fill up the pauses between the meals—songs and speeches, often of a somewhat coarse and cynical nature, forming part of the usual programme. Among the games occasionally enacted at Saxon peasant weddings there is one which deserves a special mention, affording, as it does, a curious proof of the tenacity of old pagan rites and customs transmitted by verbal tradition from one generation to the other. This is the *rössel-tanz*, or dance of the horses, evidently founded on an ancient Scandinavian legend, to be found in Snorri's "Edda." In this tale the gods Thor and Loki came at nightfall to a peasant's house in a carriage drawn by two goats or rams, and asked for a night's lodging. Thor killed the two rams, and with the peasant and his family consumed the flesh for supper. The bones were then ordered to be thrown in a heap on to the hides of the animals; but one of the peasant's sons had, in eating, broken open a bone in order to suck the marrow within, and next morning, when the god commanded the goats to get up, one of them limped on the hind-leg because of the broken bone, on seeing which Thor was in a great rage, and threatened to destroy the peasant and his whole family, but finally allowed himself to be pacified, and accepted the two sons as hostages.

In the peasant drama here alluded to, the gods Thor and Loki are replaced by a colonel and a lieutenant-colonel, while instead of two goats there are two horses and one goat; also, the two sons of the peasant are here designated as Wallachians. Everything is, of course, much distorted and changed, but yet all the principal features of the drama are clearly to be recognized — the killing of the goat and its subsequent resurrection, the colonel's rage, and the transferment of the two Wallachians into his service, all being part of the performance.

At midnight, or sometimes later, when the guests are about to depart, there prevails in some villages a custom which goes by the name of *den borten abtanzen*, dancing down the bride's crown. This head-covering, which I have already described, is the sign of her maiden-hood, which she must lay aside now that she has become a wife, and it is danced off in the following manner: All the married women pres-ent, except the very oldest and most decrepit, join hands—two of them, appointed as brideswomen, taking the bride between them. Thus forming a wide circle, they dance backward and forward round and round the room, sometimes forming a knot in the centre, sometimes far apart, till suddenly, either by accident or on purpose, the chain is broken through at one place, which is the signal for all to rush out into the court-yard, still holding hands. From some dark corner there now springs unexpectedly a stealthy robber, one of the bridesmen, who has been lying there in ambush to rob the bride of her crown. Sometimes she is defended by two brothers or relations, who, dealing out blows with twisted up handkerchiefs or towels, endeavor to keep the thief at a distance; but the struggle always ends with the loss of the head-dress, which the young matron bewails with many tears and sobs. The brideswomen now solemnly invest her with her new head-gear, which consists of a snowy cap and veil, held together by silver or jewelled pins, sometimes of considerable value. This head-dress, which fits close to the face, concealing all the hair, has a nun-like effect, but is not unbecoming to fresh young faces.

Sometimes, after the bride is invested in her matronly head-gear, she, along with two other married women (in some villages old, in others young), is concealed behind a curtain or sheet, and the husband is made to guess which is his wife, all three trying to mislead him by grotesque gestures from beneath the sheet.

On the morning after the wedding bridesmen and brideswomen early repair to the room of the newly married couple, presenting them with a cake in which hairs of cows and buffaloes, swine's bristles, feathers, and egg-shells are baked. Both husband and wife must at least swallow a bite of this unsavory compound, to insure the welfare of cattle and poultry during their married life.*

After the morning meal the young wife goes to church to be

---

* So in the Altmark the newly married couple used to be served with a soup com-posed of cattle-fodder, hay, beans, oats, etc., to cause the farm animals to thrive.

blessed by the priest, escorted by the two brideswomen, walking one on either side. While she is praying within, her husband meanwhile waits at the church-door, but no sooner does she reappear at the threshold than the young couple are surrounded by a group of masked figures, who playfully endeavor to separate the wife from her husband. If they succeed in so doing, then he must win her back in a hand-to-hand fight with his adversaries, or else give money as ransom. It is considered a bad omen for the married life of the young couple if they be separated on this occasion; therefore the young husband takes his stand close against the church-door, to be ready to clutch his wife as soon as she steps outside—for greater precaution, often holding her round the waist with both hands during the dance which immediately ensues in front of the church, and at which the newly married couple merely assist as spectators.

As several couples are usually married at the same time, it is customary for each separate wedding-party to bring its own band of music, and dance thus independently of the others. On the occasion of a triple wedding I once witnessed, it was very amusing to watch the three wedding-parties coming down the street, each accelerating its pace till it came to be a sort of race between them up to the church-door, in order to secure the best dancing-place. The ground being rough and slanting, there was only one spot where anything like a flat dancing-floor could be obtained; and the winning party at once securing this enviable position, the others had to put up with an inclined plane, with a few hillocks obstructing their ball-room *parquet*.

The eight to ten couples belonging to each wedding-party are enclosed in a ring of by-standers, each rival band of music playing away with heroic disregard for the scorched ears of the audience. "Walser!" calls out the first group; "Polka!" roars the second—for it is a point of honor that each party display a noble independence in taking its own line of action; and if, out of mere coincidence, two of the bands happen to strike up the self-same tune, one of them will be sure to change abruptly to something totally different, as soon as aware of the unfortunate mistake—the caterwauling effect produced by this system baffling all description. "This is nothing at all," said the pastor, from whose garden I was overlooking the scene, laughing at the dismay with which I endeavored to stop my ears. "Sometimes we have eight or ten weddings at a time, each with its own fiddlers—that is something worth hearing indeed!"

The rest of this second day is spent much in the same way as the former one, only this time it is at the house of the bridegroom's parents.

In some places it is usual on this day for the young couple, accompanied by the wedding-party, to drive back to the house of the bride's parents in order to fetch her *truhe*—viz., the painted wooden coffer in which her trousseau has been stored. The young wife remains sitting on the cart, while her husband goes in and fetches the coffer. Then he returns once more, and addresses the following speech to his mother-in-law : "It is not unknown to me, dearest mother, that you have prepared various articles, at the toil of your hands, for your dearest child, for which may you be heartily thanked ; and may God in future continue to bless your labor, and give you health and strength to accomplish the same.

" But as it has become known to me that the coffer containing your dear child's effects has got a lock, and as to every lock there must needs be a key, so have I come to beg you to give me this key, in order that we may be enabled to take what we require from out the coffer." *

Among the customs attached to this first day of wedded life is that of breaking the distaff. If the young matron can succeed in doing so at one stroke across her knee, she will be sure to have strong and healthy sons born of her wedlock; if not, then she has but girls to expect.

The third day is called the finishing-up day, each family assembling its own friends and relations to consume the provisions remaining over from the former banquets, and at the same time to wash up the cooking utensils and crockery, restoring whatever has been borrowed from neighbors in the shape of plates, jugs, etc.—the newly married couple joining the entertainment, now at the one, now at the other house. This day is the close of the wedding festivities, which have kept both families in a state of bustle and turmoil for fully a week. Everything now returns to every-day order and regularity, the young couple usually taking up their abode in a small back room of the house of the young man's parents, putting off till the following spring the important business of building their own house. Dancing

---

* In Sweden the mother takes her seat on the coffer containing her daughter's effects, and refuses to part with it till the son-in-law has ransomed it with money.

and feasting are now at an end, and henceforth the earnest of life begins, though it is usual to say that "only after they have licked a stone of salt together" can a proper understanding exist between husband and wife.

CHAPTER XV.

THE SAXONS: BIRTH AND INFANCY.

BY-AND-BY, when a few months have passed over the heads of the newly married couple, and the young matron becomes aware that the prophecies pointed at by the broken distaff and the doll's cradle are likely to come true, she is carefully instructed as to the conduct she must observe in order to insure the well-being of herself and her child.

In the first place, she must never conceal her state nor deny it, when interrogated on the subject; for if she do so, her child will have difficulty in learning to speak; nor may she wear beads round her neck, for that would cause the infant to be strangled at its birth. Carrying pease or beans in her apron will produce malignant eruptions, and sweeping a chimney makes the child narrow-breasted.

On no account must she be suffered to pull off her husband's boots, nor to hand him a glowing coal to light his pipe, both these actions entailing misfortune. In driving to market she may not sit with her back to the horses, nor ever drink at the well out of a wooden bucket. Likewise, her intercourse with the pigsty must be carefully regulated; for should she, at any time, listen over-attentively to the grunting of pigs, her child will have a deep grunting voice; and if she kick the swine or push one of them away with her foot, the infant will have bristly hair on its back. Hairs on the face will be the result of beating a dog or cat, and twins the consequence of eating double cherries or sitting at the corner of the table.

During this time she may not stand godmother to any other child, or else she will lose her own baby, which will equally be sure to die if she walk round a new-made grave.

If any one unexpectedly throw a flower at the woman who expects to become a mother, and hit her with it on the face, her child will have a mole at the same place touched by the flower.

Should, however, the young matron imprudently have neglected any of these rules, and have cause to fear that an evil spell has been cast on her child, she has several very efficacious recipes for undoing the harm.   Thus if she sit on the door-step, with her feet resting on a broom, for at least five minutes at a time, on several consecutive Fri- days, thinking the while of her unborn babe, it will be released from the impending doom; or else let her sit there on Sundays, when the bells are ringing, with her hair hanging unplaited down her back; or climb up the stair of the belfry tower and look down at the sinking sun.

When the moment of the birth is approaching, the windows must be carefully hung over with sheets or cloths, to prevent witches from entering; but all locks and bolts should, on the contrary, be opened, else the event will be retarded.

If the new-born infant be weakly, it is usual to put yolks of eggs, bran, sawdust, or a glass of old wine into its first bath.

Very important for the future luck and prosperity of the child is the day of the week and month on which it happens to have been born.

Sunday is, of course, the luckiest day, and twelve o'clock at noon, when the bells are ringing, the most favorable hour for beginning life.

Wednesday children are *schlabberkinder* — that is, chatterboxes. Friday bairns are unfortunate, but in some districts those born on Saturday are considered yet more unlucky; while again, in other places Saturday's children are merely supposed to grow up dirty.

Whoever is born on a stormy night will die of a violent death.

The full or growing moon is favorable; but the decreasing moon produces weakly, unhealthy babes.

All children born between Easter and Pentecost are more or less lucky, unless they happen to have come on one of the distinctly un- lucky days, of which I here give a list:

> January 1st, 2d, 6th, 11th, 17th, 18th.
> February 8th, 14th, 17th.
> March 1st, 3d, 13th, 15th.
> April 1st, 3d, 15th, 17th, 18th.
> May 8th, 10th, 17th, 30th.
> June 1st, 17th.
> July 1st, 5th, 6th, 14th.
> August 1st, 3d, 17th, 18th.
> September 2d, 15th, 18th, 30th.
> October 15th, 17th.
> November 1st, 7th, 11th.
> December 1st, 6th, 11th, 15th.

I leave it to more penetrating spirits to decide whether these seemingly capricious figures are regulated on some occult cabalistic system, the secret workings of which have baffled my understanding, so that I am at a loss to explain why January and April have the greatest, June and October the least, proportion of unlucky days allotted to them; and why the 1st and 17th of each month are mostly pernicious, while, barring the 30th of May and September, no date after the 18th is ever in bad odor.

Both mother and child must be carefully watched over during the first few days after the birth, and all evil influences averted. The visit of another woman who has herself a babe at the breast may deprive the young mother of her milk; and whosoever enters the house without sitting down will assuredly carry off the infant's sleep.

If the child be subject to frequent and apparently groundless fits of crying, that is proof positive that it has been bewitched—either by some one whose eyebrows are grown together, and who consequently has the evil eye, or else by one of the invisible evil spirits whose power is great before the child has been taken to church. But even a person with quite insignificant eyebrows may convey injury by unduly praising the child's good looks, unless the mother recollect to spit on the ground as soon as the words are spoken.

Here are a few specimens of the recipes *en vogue* for counteracting such evil spells:

"Place nine straws, which must be counted backward from nine to one, in a jug of water drawn from the river *with* the current, not *against* it; throw into the water some wood-parings from off the cradle, the door-step, and the four corners of the room in which the child was born, and add nine pinches of ashes, likewise counted backward. Boil up together, and pour into a large basin, leaving the pot upside down in it. If the boiling water draws itself up into the jug" (as of course it will), "that is proof positive that the child is bewitched. Now moisten the child's forehead with some of the water before it has time to cool, and give it (still counting backward) nine drops to drink."

The child that has been bewitched may likewise be held above a red-hot ploughshare, on which a glass of wine has been poured; or else a glass of water, in which a red-hot horseshoe has been placed, given to drink in spoonfuls.

In every village there used to be (and may still occasionally be found) old women who made a regular and profitable trade out of preparing the water which is to undo such evil spells.

The Saxon mother is careful not to leave her child alone till it has been baptized, for fear of malignant spirits, who may steal it away, leaving an uncouth elf in its place. Whenever a child grows up clumsy and heavy, with large head, wide mouth, stump nose, and crooked legs, the gossips are ready to swear that it has been changed in the cradle—more especially if it prove awkward and slow in learning to speak. To guard against such an accident, it is recommended to mothers obliged to leave their infants alone to place beneath the pillow either a prayer-book, a broom, a loaf of bread, or a knife stuck point upward.

Very cruel remedies have sometimes been resorted to in order to force the evil spirits to restore the child they have stolen and take back their own changeling. For instance, the unfortunate little creature suspected of being an elf was beaten with a thorny branch until quite bloody, and then left sitting astride on a hedge for an hour. It was then supposed that the spirits would secretly bring back the stolen child.

The infant must not be suffered to look at itself in the glass till after the baptism, nor should it be held near an open window. A very efficacious preservative against all sorts of evil spells is to hang round the child's neck a little triangular bag stuffed with grains of incense, wormwood, and various aromatic herbs, and with an adder's head embroidered outside. A gold coin sewed into the cap is also much recommended.

Two godfathers and two godmothers are generally appointed at Saxon peasant christenings, and it is customary that the one couple should be old and the other young; but in no case should a husband and wife figure as godparents at the same baptism, but each one of the quartette must belong to a different family. This is the general custom, but in some districts the rule demands two godfathers and one godmother for a boy, two godmothers and one godfather for a girl.

If the parents have previously lost other children, then the infant should not be carried out by the door in going to church, but handed out by the window and brought back in the same way. It should be carried through the broadest street, never by narrow lanes or by-ways, else it will learn thieving.

The godparents must on no account look round on their way to church, and the first person met by the christening procession will decide the sex of the next child to be born—a boy if it be a man.

If two children are baptized out of the same water, one of them is sure to die; and if several boys are christened in succession in the same church without the line being broken by a girl, there will be war in the land as soon as they are grown up. Many girls christened in succession denotes fruitful vintages for the country when they shall have attained a marriageable age.

If the child sleep through the christening ceremony, it will be pious and good-tempered—but if it cries, bad-tempered or unlucky; therefore the first question asked by the parents on the party's return from church is generally, "Was it a quiet baptism?" and if such has not been the case, the sponsors are apt to conceal the truth.

In some places the christening procession returning to the house finds the door closed. After knocking for some time in vain, a voice from within summons the godfather to name seven bald men of the parish. This having been answered, a further question is asked as to the gospel read in church, and only on receiving this reply, "Let the little children come to me," is the door flung open, saying, "Come in; you have hearkened attentively to the words of the Lord."

The sponsors next inquiring, "Where shall we put the child?" receive this answer:

> "On the bunker let it be,
> It will jump then like a flea,
> Put it next upon the hearth,
> Heavy gold it will be worth.
> On the floor then let it sleep,
> That it once may learn to sweep.
> On the table in a dish,
> Grow it will then like a fish."

After holding it successively in each of the places named, the baby is finally put back into the cradle, while the guests prepare to enjoy the *tauf schmaus*, or christening banquet, to which each person has been careful to bring a small contribution in the shape of eggs, bacon, fruit, or cakes; the godparents do not fail to come, each laden with a bottle of good wine besides some other small gift for the child.

The feast is noisy and merry, and many are the games and jokes practised on these occasions. One of these, called the *badspringen* (jumping the bath), consists in placing a washing trough or bath up-side down on the ground with a lighted candle upon it. All the young women present are then invited to jump over without upsetting or putting out the light. Those successful in this evolution will be mothers of healthy boys. If they are bashful and refuse to jump, or awkward enough to upset and put out the candle, they will be child-less or have only girls.

The *spiesstanz*, or spit dance, is also usual at christening feasts. Two roasting-spits are laid on the ground crosswise, as in the sword-dance, and the movements executed much in the same manner. Some-times it is the grandfather of the new-born infant, who, proud of his agility, opens the performance singing :

> "Purple plum so sweet,
> See my nimble feet,
> How I jump and slide,
> How I hop and glide.
> Look how well I dance,
> See how high I prance.
> Purple plum so sweet,
> See my nimble feet."

But if the grandfather be old and feeble, and the godfathers unwilling to exert themselves, then it is usually the midwife who, for a small consideration, undertakes the dancing.

It is not customary for the young mother to be seated at table along with the guests; and even though she be well and hearty enough to have baked the cakes and milked the cows on that same day, etiquette demands that she should play the interesting invalid and lie abed till the feasting is over.

Full four weeks after the birth of her child must she stay at home, and durst not step over the threshold of her court-yard, even though she has resumed all her daily occupations within the first week of the event. "I may not go outside till my time is out; the Herr Vater would be sorely angered if he saw me," is the answer I have often received from a woman who declined to come out on the road. Neither may she spin during these four weeks, lest her child should suffer from dizziness.

When the time of this enforced retirement has elapsed, the young mother repairs to church to be blessed by the pastor; but before so doing she is careful to seek out the nearest well and throw down a piece of bread into its depths, probably as an offering to the *brunnen-frau* who resides in every well, and is fond of luring little children down to her.

With these first four weeks the greatest perils of infancy are considered to be at an end, but no careful mother will fail to observe the many little customs and regulations which alone will insure the further health and well-being of her child. Thus she will always remember that the baby may only be washed between sunrise and sunset, and that the bath water should not be poured out into the yard at a place where any one can step over it, which would entail death or sickness, or at the very least deprive the infant of its sleep.

Two children which cannot yet talk must never be suffered to kiss each other, or both will be backward in speech.

A book laid under the child's pillow will make it an apt scholar; and the water in which a puppy dog has been washed, if used for the bath, will cure all skin diseases.

Whoever steps over a child as it lies on the ground will cause it to die within a month. Other prognostics of death are to rock an empty cradle, to make the baby dance in its bath, or to measure it with a yard measure before it can walk.

CHAPTER XVI.

THE SAXONS: DEATH AND BURIAL.

In olden times, when the Almighty used still to show himself on earth, the people say that every one knew beforehand exactly the day and hour of his death.

Thus one day the Creator in the course of his wanderings came across a peasant who was mending his garden paling in a careless, slovenly manner.

"Why workest thou so carelessly?" asked the Lord, and received this answer:

"Why should I make it any better? I have got only one year left to live, and it will last till then."

Hearing which God grew angry, and said,

"Henceforward no man shall know the day or hour of his death;

thou art the last one who has known it." And since that time we are all kept in ignorance of our death-hour; therefore should every man live as though he were to die in the next hour, and work as if he were to live forever.

Death to the Saxon peasant appears in the light of a treacherous enemy who must be met with open resistance, and may either be conquered by courageous opposition or conciliated with a bribe. "He has put off death with a slice of bread" is said of a man who has survived some great danger.

When the first signs of an approaching illness declare themselves in a man, all his friends are strenuous in advising him to hold out against it—not to let himself go, but to grapple with this foe which has seized him unawares. Even though all the symptoms of typhus-fever be already upon him, though his head be burning like fire and his limbs heavy as lead, he is yet exhorted to bear up against it, and on no account to lie down, for that would be a concession to the enemy.

In this way many a man goes about with death upon his face, determined not to give in, till at last he drops down senseless in the field or yard where he has been working. Even then his family are not disposed to let him rest. With well-meant but mistaken kindness they endeavor to rouse him by shouting in his ear. He must be made to wake up and walk about, or it will be all over with him; and not for the world would they send for a doctor, who can only be regarded as an omen of approaching death.*

Some old woman, versed in magic formulas and learned in the decoction of herbs and potions, is hastily summoned to the bedside, and the unfortunate man would probably be left to perish without intelligent advice, unless the pastor, hearing of his illness, takes upon himself to send for the nearest physician.

By the time the doctor arrives the illness has made rapid strides, and most likely the assistance comes too late. The first care of the doctor on entering the room will be to remove the warm fur cap and

---

* On the rare occasions when the Saxon peasant consults a physician, he is determined to reap the utmost advantage from the situation. An amusing instance of this was related to me by a doctor to whom a peasant had come for the purpose of being bled. Deeming that the patient had lost sufficient blood, the doctor was about to close the wound, when the Saxon interposed. "Since I have come this long way to be bled, doctor," he remonstrated, "you might as well let ten kreuzers' worth more blood flow!"

the heavy blankets, which are wellnigh stifling the patient, and order
him to be undressed and comfortably laid in his bed. He prescribes
cooling compresses and a medicine to be taken at regular intervals,
but shakes his head and gives little hope of recóvery.

Already this death is regarded as a settled thing in the village; for
many of the gossips now remember to have heard the owl shriek in
the preceding night, or there has been an unusual howling of dogs
just about midnight. Some remember how a flight of crows flew
cawing over the village but yesterday, which means a death, for it is
meat that the crows are crying for; or else the cock has been heard to
crow after six in the evening; or the loaves were cracked in the oven
on last baking-day. Others call to mind how over-merry the old man
had been four weeks ago, when his youngest grandchild was christened,
and that is ever a sign of approaching decease. "And only a week
ago," says another village authority, "when we buried old N——
N——, there was an amazing power of dust round the grave, and the
Herr Vater sneezed twice during his sermon; and that, as every one
knows, infallibly means another funeral before long. Mark my words,
ere eight days have passed he will be lying under the nettles!"

"So it is," chimes in another gossip. "He will hear the cuckoo
cry no more."

The village carpenter, who has long been out of work, now hangs
about the street in hopes of a job. "How is the old man?" he anxiously inquires of a neighbor.

"The preacher has just gone in to knock off the old sinner's irons,"
is the irreverent reply, at which the carpenter brightens up, hoping
that he may soon be called in to make the "fir-wood coat," for he has
a heap of damaged boards lying by which he fain would get rid of.

Sometimes, however, it is the thrifty peasant himself, who, knowing
the ways of village carpenters, and foreseeing this inevitable contingency, has taken care to provide himself with a well-made solid coffin
years before there was any probability of its coming into use. He
has himself chosen out the boards, tested their soundness, and driven
a hard bargain for his purchase, laying himself down in the coffin to
assure himself of the length being sufficient. For many years this
useless piece of furniture has been standing in the loft covered with
dust and cobwebs, and serving, perhaps, as a receptacle for old iron
or discarded boots; and now it is the dying man himself who, during
a passing interval of consciousness, directs that his coffin should be

brought down and cleaned out; his glassy eye recovering a momentary brightness as he congratulates himself on his wise forethought.

Death is indeed approaching with rapid strides. Only two spoonfuls of the prescribed medicine has the patient swallowed. "Take it away," he says, when he has realized his situation—"take it away, and keep it carefully for the next person who falls ill. It can do me no good, and it is a pity to waste it on me, for I feel that my time has come. Send for the preacher, that I may make my peace with the Almighty."

The last dispositions as to house and property have been made in the presence of the pastor or preacher. The house and yard are to belong to the youngest son, as is the general custom among the Saxons; the eldest son or daughter is to be otherwise provided for. The small back room belongs to the widow, as jointure lodging for the rest of her life; likewise a certain proportion of grain and fruit is assured to her. The exact spot of the grave is indicated, and two ducats are to be given to the Herr Vater if he will undertake to preach a handsome funeral oration, and to compose a suitable epitaph for the tombstone.

When it becomes evident that the last death-struggle is approaching, the mattress is withdrawn from under the dying man, for, as every one knows, he will expire more gently if laid upon straw.

Scarcely has the breath left his body than all the last clothes he has worn are taken off and given to a gypsy. The corpse, after being washed and shaved, is dressed in bridal attire—the self-same clothes once donned on the wedding-morning long ago, and which ever since have been lying by, carefully folded and strewn with sprigs of lavender, in the large painted *truhe* (bunker), waiting for the day when their turn must come round again. Possibly they now prove a somewhat tight fit; for the man of sixty has considerably developed his proportions since he wore these same clothes forty years ago, and no doubt it will be necessary to make various slits in the garments in order to enable them to fulfil their office.

The coffin is prepared to receive the body by a sheet being spread over a layer of wood-shavings; for the head a little pillow, stuffed with dried flowers and aromatic herbs, which in most houses are kept ready prepared for such contingencies. In sewing this pillow great care must be taken not to make any knot upon the thread, which would hinder the dead man from resting in his grave, and likewise prevent his widow from marrying again ; also, no one should be suffered to smell at the funeral wreaths, or else they will irretrievably lose their sense of smell.

A new-dug grave should not if possible stand open overnight, but only be dug on the day of the funeral itself.

An hour before the funeral, the ringer begins to toll the *seelenpuls* (soul's pulse), as it is called ; but the sexton is careful to pause in the ringing when the clock is about to strike, for "if the hour should strike into the bell" another death will be the consequence.

Standing before the open grave, the mourners give vent to their grief, which, even when true and heartfelt, is often expressed with such quaint realism as to provoke a smile :

"My dearest husband," wails a disconsolate widow, "why hast thou gone away? I had need of thee to look after the farm, and there was plenty room for thee at our fireside. My God, is it right of thee to take my support away? On whom shall I now lean?"

The children near their dead mother.—"Mother, mother, who will care for us now? Shall we live within strange doors?"

A mother bewailing her only son.—"O God, thou hast had no pity! Even the Emperor did not take my son away to be a soldier. Thou art less merciful than the Emperor!"

Another mother weeping over two dead children.—"What a misfortune is mine, O God! If I had lost two young foals, at least their hides would have been left to me!" And the children, standing by the open grave of their father, cry out, "Oh, father, we shall never forget thee! Take our thanks for all the good thou hast done to us during thy lifetime, as well as for the earthly goods thou hast left behind!"

The banquet succeeding the obsequies is in some places still called the *tor*—perhaps in reference to the old god Thor, who with his hammer presides alike over marriages and funerals.

CHAPTER XVII.

THE ROUMANIANS: THEIR ORIGIN.

"It is a fine country, but there are dreadfully many Roumanians," was the verdict of a respectable Saxon, who accompanied his words with a deep sigh and a mournful shake of the head. Evidently the worthy man thought necessary to adopt a deprecatory tone in alluding to these objectionable people, as though the presence of Roumanians in a landscape were matter for apology, like the admission of rats in a stable, or bugs in a bedstead. To an unprejudiced outsider, it is certainly somewhat amusing to observe the feelings with which the three principal races inhabiting this country regard each other : thus, to the Hungarian and the Saxon the Roumanian is but simple, unqualified vermin; while the Saxon regards the Magyar as a barbarian, which compliment the latter returns by considering the Saxon a boor ; and the poor Roumanian, even while cringing before his Saxon and Hungarian masters, is taught by his religion to regard as unclean all those who stand outside his faith.

Briefly to sum up the respective merits of these three races, it may be allowable to define them as representing manhood in the past, present, and future tenses.

The Saxons *have been* men, and right good men, too, in their day ; but that day has gone by, and they are now rapidly degenerating into mere fossil antiquities, physically deteriorated from constant intermarriage, and morally opposed to any sort of progress involving amalgamation with the surrounding races.

The Hungarians *are* men in the full sense of the word, perhaps all the more so that they are a nation of soldiers rather than men of science and letters.

The Roumanians *will be* men a few generations hence, when they have had time to shake off the habits of slavery and have learned to recognize their own value. There is a wealth of unraised treasure, of abilities in the raw block, of uncultured talent, lying dormant in this ignorant peasantry, who seem but lately to have begun to understand that they need not always bend their neck beneath the yoke of other masters, nor are necessarily born to slavery and humiliation. In face of their rapidly increasing population, of the thirst for knowledge and the powerful spirit of progress which have arisen among them of late years, it is scarcely hazardous to prophesy that this people have a great future before them, and that a day will come when, other nations having degenerated and spent their strength, these descendants of the ancient Romans, rising phœnix-like from their ashes, will step forward with a whole fund of latent power and virgin material to rule as masters where formerly they have crouched as slaves.

Two popular legends current in Transylvania may here find a place, as somewhat humorously defining the national characteristics of the three races just alluded to.

" When God had decreed to banish Adam and Eve from Paradise because they had sinned against his laws, he first deputed his Hungarian angel Gabor (Gabriel) to chase them out of the garden of Eden. But Adam and Eve were already wise, for they had eaten of the fruit of knowledge; so they resolved to conciliate the angel by putting good cheer before him, and inviting him to partake of it. In truth, the angel ate and drank heartily of the good things on the table, and, after having eaten, he had not the heart to repay his kind hosts for their hospitality by chasing them out of Paradise, so he returned to heaven without having executed his commission, and begged the Lord to send another in his place, for he could not do it.

" Then God sent the Wallachian angel Florian, thinking he was less fine-feeling and would execute the mission better. Adam and Eve were sitting at table when the servant of the Lord entered, shod in leather *opintschen* (sandals) and with fur cap under his arm. After humbly saluting, he told his errand. But Adam, on seeing the appearance of this messenger, felt no more fear, and asked roughly, ' Hast brought no written warrant with thee?' At this the angel Florian began to tremble, turned round on the spot, and went back to heaven.

" Then the Lord became angry, and sent down the German Archangel Michael. Adam and Eve were mightily terrified on seeing him, but resolved to do their best to soften his heart; so they prepared for him a sumptuous meal of his favorite dishes—ham-sausage, pickled sauerkraut, beer, wine, and sweet mead. The German angel was highly pleased, and played such a good knife and fork that Adam and Eve began to feel light of heart again. But hardly had the archangel eaten his fill when, rising from the table, he swung his flaming sword overhead and thundered forth to his terrified hosts, ' Now pack yourselves off !'   In vain did our first parents beg and sue for mercy; nothing served to touch the heart of the inflexible German angel, who, without further ado, drove them both out of Paradise."

The second legend relates to the Holy Sepulchre, and tells us how a deputation, consisting of a Hungarian, a Saxon, and a Wallachian, was once sent by the Transylvanian Diet to Palestine in order to recover the Saviour's body from the infidels.   "They started on their journey full of hope, but when they had reached Jerusalem they found the sepulchre guarded by a strong enforcement of Roman sol- diers.   What was now to be done ?   was the question debated between them.   The Hungarian was for cutting into the soldiers at once with his sword, but the canny Saxon held him back and said, ' They are stronger than we, and we might receive blows; let us rather attempt to barter.'   The Wallachian only winked with one eye and whispered, ' Let us wait till nightfall, and then we can steal the body.' "

There has been of late years so much learned discussion about the origin of this Roumanian people that it were presumption, in face of the erudite authorities enlisted on either side, to advance any inde- pendent opinion on the subject.   German writers, especially Saxons, have been strenuous in sneering down all claims to Roman extraction, and contending that whatever Roman elements remained over after their evacuation of the territory must long since have been swallowed up in the great rush of successive nations which passed over the land in the early part of the Middle Ages.   Roumanian writers, on the contrary, are fond of laying great stress on the direct Roman line- age which it is their pride to believe in, sometimes, however, injuring their own cause by over-anxiety to claim too much—laying too little stress on the admixture of Slave blood, which is as surely a funda- mental ingredient of the race.   One of the most enlightened Rouma- nian authors, Joan Slavici, states the case more accurately in saying that the ethnographical importance of the Roumanians does not lie in the fact of their being descendants of the ancient Romans, nor in that of the long-vanished Dacian race having been Romanized by the conquerors, but solely and entirely therein; that this people, placed between two sharply contrasting races, form an important connecting link in the chain of European tribes,

The classical type of feature so often to be met with among Roumanian peasants of both sexes pleads strongly in favor of the theory of Roman origin ; and if in a former chapter I compared the features of Saxon peasants to those of Noah's-ark figures, rudely cut out of the very coarsest wood, the Roumanians as often remind me of a type of face chiefly to be met with on cameo ornaments or ancient signet-rings. If we take at random a score of individuals from any Roumanian village, we cannot fail to find a goodly choice of classical profiles, worthy to be immortalized on agate, onyx, or jasper, like a handful of antique gems which have been strewn broadcast over the land.

Wallack, or Wlach, by which name this people was generally designated up to the year '48, points equally to Roman extraction—Wallack being but another version of the appellations Welsh, Welch, Wallon, etc., given by Germans to all people native of Italy. It may, however, not be superfluous here to mention that at no period whatever did these people describe themselves otherwise than as "Romāns," Roumanians, and would have been as little likely to speak of themselves as Wallacks as would be an American to call himself a Yankee, or a Londoner to designate himself as a cockney. As far as I can make out, a certain sense of opprobrium seems to be attached to this word Wallack as applied by strangers, explainable perhaps by the fact that the appellation Wlach was formerly used to describe all people subjugated by the Romans.

CHAPTER XVIII.

THE ROUMANIANS: THEIR RELIGION, POPAS, AND CHURCHES.

In order at all to understand the Roumanian peasant, we must first of all begin by understanding his religion, which alone gives us the clew to the curiously contrasting shades of his complicated character. Monsieur De Gerando, writing of the Wallacks some forty years ago, says,

"Aujourd'hui leur seul mobile est la religion, si on peut donner ce nom à l'ensemble de leurs pratiques superstitieuses ;" and another author, with equal accuracy, remarks that "the whole life of a Wallack is taken up in devising talismans against the devil."

Historians are very much divided as to the date of the Roumanians' conversion to Christianity, for while some consider this to have only taken place in the time of Patriarch Photius (in the ninth century), others are of opinion that they embraced Christianity as early as the third century. It is not improbable that during the Roman occupation of Transylvania in the second and third centuries Christians may have come hither, and so imparted their religion to the ancient inhabitants with whom they intermingled.

Up to the end of the seventeenth century all the Transylvanian Roumanians belonged to the Greek Schismatic Church. In the year 1698, however, the Austrian Government succeeded in inducing a great portion of the people to embrace the Greek united faith, and acknowledge the supremacy of the Pope; and at the present day the numbers of the two confessions in Transylvania are pretty equally balanced, with only a small proportion in favor of the Schismatic Church.

The united Roumanians in Transylvania are subject to an archbishop residing at Blasendorf, while those of the Greek Schismatic Church stand under another archbishop, whose seat is at Hermanstadt.

Old chronicles of the thirteenth century make mention of the Wallacks as a people " which, though professing the Christian faith, is yet given to the practice of manifold pagan rites and customs wholly at variance with Christianity ;" and even to-day the Roumanians are best described by the paradoxical definition of Christian-pagans, or pagan-Christians.

True, the Roumanian peasant will never fail to uncover his head whenever he passes by a way-side cross, but his salutation to the rising sun will be at least equally profound; and if he goes to church and abstains from work on the Lord's Day, it is by no means certain whether he does not regard the Friday (Vinere), dedicated to Paraschiva (Venus), as the holier day of the two. The list of other unchristian feast-days is lengthy, and still lengthier that of Christian festivals, in whose celebration pagan rites may yet be traced.

Whoever buries his dead without placing a coin in the hand of the corpse is regarded as a pagan by the orthodox Roumanian. "*Nu-i-de-legea-noastra*" — he is not of our law — he says of such a one ; and whosoever stands outside the Roumanian religion, be he Christian, pagan, Jew, or Mohammedan, is invariably regarded as unclean, and consequently whatever comes in contact with any such individual is unclean likewise.

The Roumanian language has a special word to define this uncleanness—*spurcat*—which corresponds somewhat to the *koscher* and *unkoscher* of the Jews.

If any animal fall into a well of drinking-water, then the well forthwith becomes *spurcat*, and *spurcat* likewise whoever drinks of this water. If it be a large animal, such as a calf or goat, which has fallen into the well, then the whole water must be bailed out; and should this fail to satisfy the conscience of any ultra-orthodox proprietor, then the popa must be called in to read a mass over the spot where perhaps a donkey has found a watery grave. But when it is a man who has been drowned there, no further rehabilitation is possible for the unlucky well, which must therefore be filled up and discarded as quite too hopelessly *spurcat*.

Every orthodox Roumanian household possesses three different classes of cooking and eating utensils: unclean, clean for the meat-days, and the cleanest of all for fast-days.

The cleansing of a vessel which has, through some accident, become *spurcat* is only conceded in the case of very large and expensive articles, such as barrels and tubs; copious ablutions of holy-water, besides thorough scouring, scraping, and rubbing, being resorted to in such cases. All other utensils which do not come under this denomination must simply be thrown away, or at best employed for feeding the domestic animals. The Roumanian who does not strictly observe all these regulations is himself *spurcat*.

This same measure he applies to all individuals whom he considers to be clean or unclean, according to their observance of these rules. The uncleanliness, according to him, does not lie in the individual, but in his laws, which fail to enforce cleanliness; the law it is, therefore, which is unclean, *lege spurcat*, which, for the Roumanian, is synonymous with unchristian. For instance, a man who eats horse-flesh is by him regarded as a pagan.

This recognition of the uncleanliness of most of his fellow-creatures is, however, wholly independent of either hatred or contempt on the part of the Roumanian, who, on the contrary, shows much interest in foreign countries and habits; and when he wishes to affirm the high character of a stranger, he says of him that he is a man who keeps his own law—*tine la legea lui*—spite of which the Roumanian will refuse to wear the coat or eat off the plate of this honorable stranger, and would regard any such familiarity as a deadly sin.

The idea so strongly rooted in the Roumanian mind, that they alone are Christians, and that, consequently, no man can be a Christian without being also a Roumaniau, seems to imply that there was a time when the two words were identical for them, and that, surrounded for long by pagans with whom they could hold no sort of community, they lacked all knowledge of other existing Christian races.

On the other hand, these people are curiously liberal towards strangers in the matter of religion, allowing each one, whatsoever be his confession, to enter their churches and receive their sacraments. No Roumanian popa durst refuse to administer a sacrament to whosoever may apply to him, be he Catholic, Protestant, Jew, or pagan, provided he submits to receive it in the manner prescribed by the Oriental Church. So to-day, as six hundred years ago, the popa cannot, without incurring scandal, refuse to bury a Jew, or administer the sacrament to a dying infidel; his church must be open to all mankind, and all are welcome to avail themselves of its blessings and privileges.

This liberality in religious matters cannot, however, be reversed, and no true Roumanian ever consents to receive a sacrament from a priest of a different confession; and though he may occasionally assist at a Protestant or Catholic service, he conforms himself to no foreign forms of worship, but is careful to comport himself precisely as though he were in his own church. He does not mind joining a Catholic procession on occasion, but no power on earth can induce him to take part in a strange funeral.

The position occupied by the Roumanian clergyman towards his flock is such a peculiar one that it deserves a special notice. Though his influence over his people is unlimited, it is in nowise dependent on his personal character. Unlike the Saxon pastor, it is quite superfluous for the popa to present in his person a model of the virtues he is in the habit of describing from the altar. He may, for his part, be drunken, dishonest, and profligate to his heart's content, without thereby losing his prestige as spiritual head. Like the Indian Bramins, his official character is absolutely intangible, and not to be shaken by any private misdemeanors; and the Roumanian proverb which says, "*face zice popa dar unce face el*"—that is to say, "do as the popa tells you, but do not act as he does"—describes his attitude with perfect accuracy. Only the popa has the privilege of wearing a beard, as he alone is privileged to indulge in certain pet vices which it is his mission officially to condemn, and, like the virtue of charity, this beard may often be said literally to cover a very great multitude of sins.

These Roumanian popas, with their thick curly beards, long flowing garments, and wide-brimmed hats, used to give me the impression of a set of jolly apostles, such as we sometimes see depicted on old church-windows; not infrequently the extreme joviality of their appearance threatening to overpower the apostolic character altogether, and completing the simile by suggesting further ideas of glorious crimson sunsets deepening each tint of the mellow-stained glass.

Mr. Boner, in his work on Transylvania, mentions an instance of a group of Roumanian villagers who were seen on a Saturday afternoon dragging their sorely resisting spiritual head in the direction of the church. On being asked what they were about, the peasants explained that they were going to lock him up till Sunday morning, else he would be too drunk to say mass for the congregation. "When church is over we shall let him out again." From personal observation I have no doubt of the veracity of this story, having come across more than one Roumanian village popa who would have been none the worse for a little such judicious confinement.

Although of late years, thanks chiefly to the enlightened efforts of the late Archbishop Schaguna, much has been done to raise the moral standard of the Roumanian clergy, yet there remains still much to do before the prevailing coarseness, brutality, and ignorance too often characterizing this class can be removed. At present the average village popa is simply a peasant with a beard, and is not necessarily a particularly respected or respectable individual. Many well-authenticated cases are told of popas who could not write or read, and who betrayed their ignorance by holding the book of Gospels upside down.

On week-days the popa goes about his agricultural duties like any other peasant, digging in the garden or going behind the plough as a matter of course; his wife is a simple peasant woman, and her children run about as dirty and unkempt as any other brats in the village.

On one occasion when I had visited a Roumanian church I dropped twenty kreuzers (about fourpence) into the hand of the peasant lass who had unlocked the door for me. She accepted the coin with humble gratitude, but I felt myself to have been guilty of a terrible *gaucherie* when I subsequently discovered the young lady to be no other than Madame Popa herself!

Towards any one of the higher classes the popa, as a rule, is
crouching and obsequious, humbly uncovering his head, and hardly
daring to take a seat when offered. An old Hungarian gentleman
told me of a Roumanian popa who, when requested to be seated, declined so doing, as he considerately observed that he should not like
to distress the noble gentleman by leaving vermin on his furniture.

The Roumanian churches offer a pleasant contrast to the bleak,
uncompromising appearance of the Saxon ones. Even when archi-
tecturally not remarkable, they are invariably covered with a profusion
of ornament and decoration of extremely artistic effect. Few places
of worship appeal so strongly to the imagination as these Oriental
buildings, which, without as well as within, are one mass of warm
soft coloring. The belfry tower is encircled by a procession of celestial beings, and the walls divided off into little arched niches beneath
the roof, each of which harbors some quaint Byzantine saint, with
pale golden aureole and shadowy palm-branch. Though the outlines
may be somewhat primitive, and the laws of perspective but imper-
fectly understood, nature, the greatest artist of all, has here stepped
in to complete the picture: summer showers and winter snows have
mellowed each tint, and blended together the color into perfect
harmony.

The same style of ornament is repeated inside with increased
effect; for here the saintly legions which adorn the walls are brighter
and more vivid, stronger and fiercer looking, because in better preservation. They seem to be the living originals of which those others
outside are but the pale ghosts, and appear to rush at us from all
sides as we enter the place, increasing in numbers as our eyesight
gets used to the dim, mysterious twilight let in by the narrow windows. Not a corner but from which starts up some grinning devil,
not a nook but reveals some choleric-looking saint, till we feel ourselves to be surrounded by a whole pageant of celestial and diabolical
beings, only distinguishable from one another by the respective fashions of their head-gear—horns or halos, as the case may be.

These horned devils play a very important part in each Roumanian church, where usually a large portion of the walls is given up to
representations of the place of eternal punishment. The poor Roumanian peasant, whose daily life is often so wretched and struggling
as hardly to deserve that name, seems to derive considerable consola-

tion from anticipations of the day when the tables are to be turned, and the hitherto despised poor shall receive an eternal crown. Thus the hapless victims depicted as being marched off to the infernal regions under the escort of several ferocious-looking demons armed with terrific pitchforks, are invariably recruited from the ranks of the

ARCHBISHOP SCHAGUNA.

upper ten thousand. They are all being conducted to their destination with due regard for etiquette, and rigid observance of the laws of exact precedence. First comes a row of kings, easily to be distinguished by their golden crowns; then a procession of mitred bishops, followed by a line of noblemen booted and spurred; while on the other side of the wall a crowd of simple peasants and a group of shaven friars are being warmly invited by St. Peter, key in hand, to step over the threshold of the golden gate which leads to Paradise.

Each of these churches is divided into three sections: first, there is the sanctuary, partitioned off by trellised gates, painted and gilt, behind which the priest disappears at certain parts of the ceremony; then, in the body of the church, up to the step approaching the sanctuary, stand the men, and behind them, in a sort of outer department connected by an archway, are the women, next to the door, and close to the pictures of hell.

In the more primitive buildings there are rarely benches for the congregation, but a curious sort of prong may be sometimes seen, constructed out of the forked branch of a tree, and which, placed at intervals along the walls, is intended to give support to feeble old people unable to stand upright during a lengthy service.

It is a pretty sight to look on at the celebration of mass in any Roumanian church, more especially in summer, when every matron and maiden carries a bunch of sweet-scented flowers in her hand, and each man has a similar nosegay stuck in the cap which he holds beneath his arm. These flowers bestow an additional sprinkling of bright color over the scene, and counteract any closeness in the atmosphere by their pungent aromatic scent.

CHAPTER XIX.

THE ROUMANIANS: THEIR CHARACTER.

The Roumanian is very obstinate in character, and does not let himself be easily persuaded. He does nothing without reflection, and often he reflects so long that the time for action has passed. This slowness has become proverbial, for the Saxon says, " God grant me the enlightenment which the Roumanian always gets too late." In the same proportion as he is slow to make up his mind, he is also slow to change it. Frankness is not regarded as a virtue, and the Roumanian language has no word which directly expresses this quality. The Hungarians, on the contrary, regard frankness and truth-speaking as a duty, and are therefore often laughed at by their Roumanian neighbors, who consider as a fool any man who injures himself by speaking the truth.

Of pride the Roumanian has little idea as yet; he has been too long treated as a degraded and serf-like being, and the only word approaching this characteristic would rather seem to express the vanity of a handsome man who sees himself admired. Also for dignity the epithet is wanting, and the nearest approach to it is to say that a man is sensible and composed if you would express that he is dignified.

Revenge is cultivated as a virtue, and whoever would be considered a respectable man must keep in mind the injuries done to him, and show resentment thereof on fitting occasions. Reconciliation is regarded as opprobrious, and forgiveness of wrongs degrading. But the Roumanian's rage is stealthy and disguised, and while the Hungarian lets his anger openly explode, the Roumanian will dissemble and mutter between his teeth, "*Tine mente*" ("Thou shalt remember this"); and his memory is good, for he does not suffer himself to forget. When an injury has been done to him henceforward it becomes his sacred duty to brood over his vengeance. He must not say a good word more to his enemy nor do him a service, and must strive to injure his foe to the best of his ability—with, however, this nice distinction, that he himself do not profit by the injury done. Thus, it would not be consistent with the Roumanian's code of honor were he to steal the horse or ox of his enemy, but there can be no reasonable objection to his advising or inducing another man to do so. Such behavior is considered only right and just, and by so acting he will only be fulfilling his duty as an honest and honorable man.

The Roumanian does not seem to be courageous by nature—at least not as we understand courage — nor does courage exactly take rank as a virtue in his estimation, for courage implies a certain recklessness of consequences, and, according to his way of thinking, every action should be circumscribed, and only performed after due deliberation. When, however, driven to it by circumstances, and brought to recognize the necessity, he can fight bravely and is a good soldier. In the same way, he will never expose his life without necessity, and will coolly watch a house burning down without offering assistance; but when compelled to action under military orders, he will go blindly into the fire, even knowing death to be inevitable.

What is commonly understood by military enthusiasm is wanting in the Roumanian (at least on this side of the frontier), for he is too ignorant to perceive the advantage of letting himself be shot in the service of a foreign master, for a cause of which he understands nothing and cares less. He is extremely sorry for himself when forced to enlist, and sometimes becomes most poetically plaintive on the subject, as in the following verses translated from a popular song:

"To the battle-field I go,
  There to fight the country's foe.
  Wash my linen, mother mine,
  All my linen white and fine.*
  Rinse it in thy tears, and then
  Dry on burning breast again.
  Send it, mother, to me there
  Where you hear the trumpet's blare.
  Where the banners droop o'erhead,
  There shall I be lying dead,
  Stricken by the musket's lead,
  Seamed by gashes rosy red,
  Trampled by the charger's tread."

Something of the spirit of the ancient Spartans lies in the Roumanian's idea of virtue and vice. Stealing and drunkenness are not considered to be intrinsically wrong, only the publicity which may attend these proceedings conveying any sense of shame to the offender. Thus a man is not yet a thief because he has stolen; and whoever becomes accidentally aware of the theft should, if he have no personal interest in the matter, hold his peace, on the Shakespearian principle that

"He that filches from me my good name
Robs me of that which not enriches him,
And makes me poor indeed."

Even the injured party whose property has been abstracted is advised if possible to reckon alone with the thief, without drawing general attention to his fault.

Neither is drunkenness necessarily degrading. On the contrary, every decent man should get drunk on suitable occasions, such as weddings, christenings, etc., and then go quietly to a barn or loft and sleep off his tipsiness. *Bea cat vrei apoi te calcu si dormi* (drink thy fill and then lie down and sleep) says their proverb; but any man who has been seen reeling drunk in the open street, hooted at by children and barked at by dogs, were it but once, is henceforward branded as a drunkard. It is therefore the duty of each Roumanian who sees a drunken man to conduct him quietly to the nearest barn or loft.

There are some few villages where even the noblest inhabitants

---

* The Roumanian peasant has a passion for white snowy linen. Usually it is his sweetheart on whom devolves the duty of keeping it clean, or, when he has no sweetheart, then his mother or sister.

are not ashamed to be seen drunk in the open street, but in such villages the moral standard is a low one throughout.

Another curious side of the Roumanian's morality is the point of view from which he regards personal property, such as grain and fruit. In general, whatever grows plentifully in the fields, or, as they term it, "whatever God has given," may be taken with impunity by whoever passes that way, but with this restriction, that he merely take so much as he can consume at the moment. This is but right and just, and the proprietor who makes complaint at having his vineyard or his plum-trees rifled in this manner only exposes himself to ridicule. Whoever carries away of the fruits with him is a thief, but, strictly speaking, only when he sells the stolen goods, not when he shares them quietly with his own family.

With regard to fowls, geese, lambs, and sucking-pigs, the rule is more or less the same. Whoever steals only in order to treat himself to a good dinner is not blamed, and may even boast of the feat on the sly; but the man caught in the act is punished by having the stolen goods tied round his neck, and being led round the village to the sound of the drum to proclaim his shame to the people. If, however, he has stolen from a stranger—that is, some one of another village—the culprit does not usually lose his good reputation; and he who robs a rich stranger is never considered base, but simply awkward to have exposed himself to the odium of discovery.

The Roumanian only looks at deeds and results, motives being absolutely indifferent to him. So the word passion he translates as *pâtima*, which really expresses weakness. Thus an *om pâtima*—a weak man—may be either a consumptive invalid, a love-sick youth, or a furious drunkard. Passion is a misfortune which should excite compassion, but not resentment; and whoever commits a bad action is above all foolish, because it is sure to be found out sooner or later.

An anecdote which aptly characterizes the Roumanian's moral sense is told by Mr. Patterson. Three peasants waylaid and murdered a traveller, dividing his spoils between them. Among his provisions they discovered a cold roast fowl, which they did not eat, however, but gave to their dog, as, being a fast-day, they feared to commit sin by tasting flesh. This was related by the murderers themselves when caught and driven to confess the crime before justice.

While on the subject of fasts, I may as well here mention that those prescribed by the Greek Church are numerous and severe; and it is a well-ascertained fact that the largest average of crimes committed by Roumanians occurs during the seasons of Advent and Lent, when the people are in a feverish and over-excited state from the unnatural deprivation of food—just as the Saxon peasants are most quarrelsome immediately after the vintage.

Another English traveller, speaking disparagingly of the serf-like, crouching demeanor of the Roumanians, remarked that " perhaps nothing else could be expected of people who are required to fast two hundred and twenty-six days in the year."

The inhabitants of each Roumanian village are divided into three classes:

First, the distinguished villagers—front-men—called *fruntasi,* or *oameni de frunta.*

Second, the middle-men—*mylocasi,* or *oameni de mana adona*—men of second-hand.

Third, the hind-men, or *codas* (tail-men).

Each man, according to his family, personal gifts, reputation, and fortune, is ranged into one or other of these three classes, which have each their separate customs, rights, and privileges, which no member of another class durst infringe upon.

Thus the codas may do much which would not be suitable for the other two classes. The mylocasi have, on the whole, the most difficult position of the three, and are most severely judged, being alternately accused of presumption in imitating the behavior of the fruntas, and blamed for demeaning themselves by copying the irregular habits of the codas. In short, it would seem to be all but impossible for an unfortunate middle-man to hit off the *juste milieu,* and succeed in combining in his person the precise proportions of dignity and deference required of his state.

Nor is the position of the front-men entirely an easy one. Each one of these has a separate party of hangers-on, friends and admirers, who profess a blind faith and admiration for him—endorsing his opinion on all occasions, and recognizing his authority in matters of dispute. His dress, his words, his actions are all strictly regulated on the axiom *noblesse oblige;* but woe to him if he be caught erring himself — for only in the case of the popa is it allowable for the practice to differ from the preaching. A fruntas may sit down to table with the codas of his own village, whenever they are in his service helping him to bring in the harvest or to build a house; but he durst not, under pain of losing caste, be equally familiar with any strange codas.

There are, moreover, whole districts which are reckoned as distinguished, and whose codas take rank along with the mylocasi, or even the front-men, of less aristocratic villages. A single woman, coming from one of these distinguished neighborhoods, may in a short time transform the whole village into which she marries, the inhabitants eagerly studying and imitating her dress, manners, and gestures, down to the most insignificant details.

A distinctive quality of the Roumanian race is the touching affection which mostly unites all members of one family. Unlike the Saxon, who seeks to limit the number of his offspring, the poor Roumanian, even when plunged into the direst poverty, yet regards each addition to his family as another gift of God; while to be a childless wife is considered as the greatest of misfortunes.

Numerous instances are recorded of children of other nationalities, who, deserted by their unnatural parents, have been taken in by poor Roumanians, themselves already burdened with a numerous family.

There is an ancient Roumanian legend which tells us how in olden times there used to prevail the custom of killing off all old men and useless encumbrances, on the same principle as in Mr. Trollope's "Fixed Period." One young man, however, being much attached to his parent, could not resign himself to executing this cruel order; but fearing the anger of his country-people, he concealed his father in an empty barrel in the cellar, where every day he secretly brought him food and drink.

But it came to pass that all arms-bearing men were summoned together to sally forth in quest of a terrible dragon which was devastating the land. The pious son, sorely puzzled to know how to provide his father with nourishment during his absence, carried together all the victuals in the house, lamenting to him that possibly he might never return from the expedition, in which case his beloved parent would be obliged to die of hunger. The old man answered,

"If in truth thou returnest not, then life has no more charms for me, and gladly will I let my weak body sink into the grave. But wouldst thou come back victorious out of the conflict with the dragon, listen to my words. The cavern inhabited by the monster has over a hundred subterraneous passages and galleries which run like a labyrinth in every direction, so that even if the enemy be killed the victors, unable to find the outlet, will perish miserably. Therefore take with thee our black mare which goes to pasture with a foal, and lead them both to the mouth of the cavern. There kill and bury the foal, but take the mother with thee, and when the struggle with the dragon is over, she will safely lead thee back to the light of day."

The son then took leave of his father with many tears, and marched away with his comrades, and when he reached the cavern he obeyed the given directions, without, however, revealing the secret to any one.

After a desperate struggle, the monster in the cavern was slain; but terror and dismay took possession of the warriors when it proved impossible to find the outlet from this dreadful labyrinth. Then stepped forward the pious son with his black mare, and called upon the others to follow him. The mare began to neigh for her foal, and, seeking the daylight, soon hit on the right track, which brought them safely to the mouth of the cavern.

The warriors, seeing how their comrade had saved them all from certain death, now besought him to reveal to them how he chanced to have hit on this cunning device. But he now took fright that if he spoke the truth, not only his own life but that of his old father would be forfeited for having thus dared to disobey the law of the land. Only at last, when all had sworn to do him no injury, did he consent to unseal his lips and tell them how, in his cellar, there lived his father, an old and experienced man, who, at parting, had given him this advice with regard to the mare.

On hearing this the warriors were mightily astonished, and one of them called out, "Our ancestors did not do wisely in teaching us to kill the old ones, for these are more experienced than we, and can often help the people with their sage counsels when mere strength of arm is powerless to conquer."

All applauded this sentiment, and the cruel law which demanded the death of the aged was henceforth abolished.

CHAPTER XX.

ROUMANIAN LIFE.

THE Roumanians seem to be a long-lived race, and it is no uncommon thing to come across peasants of ninety and upwards, in full possession of all their faculties. In 1882 an old Roumanian peasant, being called as witness in a court of justice in Transylvania, and desired to state his age, was, like many people of his class, unable to name the year of his birth, and could only designate it approximately by saying, "I remember that, when I was a boy, our emperor was a woman," which, as Maria Theresa died in 1780, could not have made him less than one hundred and ten years of age.

Many people have supposed the Roumanians to be more productive than other races, but the truth will more likely be found to be that although the births are not more numerous than among many other races, the mortality among infants is considerably less; the children inheriting the hardy resisting nature of the parents, and so to say, coming into the world ready seasoned to endure the hardships in store for them.

Perhaps it is because the Roumanian has himself so few wants that he feels no anxiety about the future of his children, and therefore the rapid increase of his family occasions him no uneasiness. Having little personal property, he is a stranger to the cares which accompany their possession. Like the lilies of the field, he neither sows nor reaps, and the whole programme of his life, of an admirable simplicity, may be thus summed up:

In early infancy the Roumanian babe is treated as a bundle, often packed in a little wooden oval box, and slung on its mother's back, thus carried about wherever she goes. If to work in the field, she attaches the box to the branch of a tree; and when sitting at market it can be stowed on the ground between a basket of eggs and a pair of cackling fowls. When after a very few months it outgrows the box, and crawls out of its cocoon, the baby begins to share its parents' food, and soon learns to manage for itself. The food of both children and adults chiefly consists of maize - corn flour, which, cooked with milk, forms a sort of porridge called balmosch, or, if boiled with water, becomes mamaliga — first-cousin to the polenta of the Italians. This latter preparation is eaten principally in Lent, when milk is prohibited altogether; and there are many families who, during the whole Lenten season, nourish themselves exclusively on dried beans.

When the Roumanian child has reached a reasonable age, it is old enough to be a help and comfort to its parents, and assist them in gaining an honest livelihood. By a reasonable age may be understood five or six, and an honest livelihood, translated—helping them to steal wood in the forest. Later on the boy is often bound over as swine or cow herd to some Saxon landholder for a period of several years, on quitting whose service he is entitled to the gift of a calf or pig from the master he is leaving.

Once in actual possession of a calf the Roumanian lad considers himself to be a made man. He has no ground of his own; but such petty considerations not affecting him, he proceeds to build himself a domicile, wherever best suits his purpose, on some waste piece of land. Stone hardly ever enters into the fabrication of his building; the framework is roughly put together of wooden beams, and the walls clay-plastered and wattled, while the roof is covered with thatch of reeds or wooden shingles, according as he may happen to live nearest to a marsh or a forest. Yet, such as it is, the Roumanian's hut is his castle, and he is as proud of its possession as the King can be of his finest palace. Each man's hut is regarded as his own special sanctuary, and however intimate a man may be with his neighbor, it is not customary for him to step over the threshold, or even enter the courtyard, after dusk. Only in special and very pressing cases does this rule admit of any exception.

The inside of a Roumanian hut is by no means so miserable as its outward appearance would lead us to suppose. The walls are all hung with a profusion of holy pictures, mostly painted on glass and framed in wood; while the furniture is brightly painted in rough but not inartistic designs—the passion these people have for ornamenting all their wood-work in this fashion leading them even to paint the yoke of their oxen and the handles of their tools. There is always a weaving-loom set up at one end of the room, and mostly a new-born baby swinging in a basket suspended from the rafters.

The products of the loom—consisting in stuffs striped, chiefly blue, scarlet, and white, in Oriental designs, sometimes with gold or silver threads introduced in the weaving—are hung upon ropes or displayed along the walls. These usually belong to the trousseau of the daughter (perhaps the self-same infant we see suspended from the ceiling), but can occasionally be purchased after a little bargaining.

Every Roumanian woman spins, dyes, and weaves as a matter of course ; and almost each village has its own set of colors and patterns, according to its particular costume, which varies with the different localities, though all partake alike of the same general character, which,

in the case of the women, is chiefly represented by a long alb-like under-garment of linen reaching to the feet, and above two straight-cut Roman aprons front and back, which have the effect of a tunic slit up at the sides. The subject of Roumanian dress offers a most bewildering field for description, and the *nuances* and varieties to be found would lead one on *ad infinitum* were I to attempt to enumerate all those I have come across.

Thus in one village the costume is all black and white, the cut and make of an almost conventual simplicity, forming a *piquante* contrast to the blooming faces and seductive glances of the beautiful wear-

ROUMANIAN COSTUMES.

ers, who thus give the impression of a band of light-hearted maidens masquerading in nun's attire. In other hamlets I have visited blue or scarlet was the prevailing color; and a few steps over the Roumanian frontier will show us glittering costumes covered with embroidery and spangles, rich and gaudy as the attire of some Oriental princess stepped straight out of the "Arabian Nights."

The Roman aprons, here called *câtrinte*, are in some districts—as, for instance, in the Banat — composed of long scarlet fringes, fully three-quarters of a yard in length, and depending from a very few inches of solid stuff at the top. The *résumé* of this attire—a linen shirt and a little fringe as sole covering for a full-grown woman—may, in theory, be startling to our English sense of propriety, but in practice the effect has nothing objectionable about it. Dress, after all, is merely a matter of comparison, as we are told by a witty French writer. A Wallachian woman considers herself fully dressed with a *chemise*, while a Hungarian thinks herself naked with only three skirts.

The head-dress varies much with the different districts; sometimes it is a brightly colored shawl or handkerchief, oftener a creamy filmy veil, embroidered or spangled, and worn with ever-varied effect; occasionally it is wound round the head turban fashion, now floating down the back like a Spanish mantilla, or coquettishly drawn forward and concealing the lower part of the face, or again twisted up in Satanella-like horns, which give the wearer a slightly demoniacal appearance.

Whatever is tight or strained-looking about the dress is considered unbeautiful; the folds must always flow downward in soft easy lines, the sleeves should be full and bulging, and the skirt long enough to conceal the feet, so that in dancing only the toes are visible.

The men have also much variety in their dress for grand occasions, but for ordinary wear they confine themselves to a plain coarse linen shirt, which hangs down over the trousers like a workman's blouse, confined at the waist by a broad red or black leather belt, which contains various receptacles for holding money, pistols, knife and fork, etc. The trousers, which fit rather tightly to the leg, are in summer of linen, in winter of a coarse sort of white cloth. Of the same cloth is made the large overcoat which he wears in winter, sometimes replaced by a sheepskin pelisse.

Both sexes wear on the feet a sort of sandal called *opintschen*, which consists of an oval-shaped piece of leather drawn together by leather thongs, beneath which the feet are swaddled in wrappings of linen or woollen rags.

Dress makes the man, according to the Roumanian's estimate, and rather than want for handsome clothes a man should deprive himself of food and drink. *Stomacul nu are oglinda* (the stomach has no mirror), says their proverb; therefore the man who has no fitting costume to wear on Easter Sunday should hide himself rather than appear at church shabbily attired.

ROUMANIAN WOMEN,

To be consistent with the Roumanian's notion of cleanliness, his clothes should by rights be spun, woven, and made at home. Sometimes he may be obliged to purchase a cap or coat of a stranger, but in such cases he is careful to select a dealer of his own nationality.

Roumanian women are very industrious, and they make far better domestic servants than either Hungarians or Saxons, the Germans living in towns often selecting them in preference to their own country-women. In some places you never see a Roumanian woman without her distaff; she even takes it with her to market, and may frequently be seen trudging along the high-road twirling the spindle as she goes.

The men do not seem to share this love of labor, having, on the contrary, much of the Italian *lazzarone* in their composition, and not taking to any kind of manual labor unless driven to it by necessity. The life of a shepherd is the only calling which the Roumanian embraces *con amore*, and his love for his sheep may truly be likened to the Arab's love of his horse. A real Roumanian shepherd, bred and brought up to the life, has so completely identified himself with his calling that everything about him—food and dress, mind and matter—has, so to say, become completely "sheepified." Sheep's milk and cheese (called *brindza*) form the staple of his nourishment. His dress consists principally of sheepskin, four sheep furnishing him with the cloak which lasts him through life, one new-born lamb giving him the cap he wears; and when he dies the shepherd's grave is marked by a tuft of snowy wool attached to the wooden cross above the mound. His whole mental faculties are concentrated on the study of his sheep, and so sharpened have his perceptions become in this one respect that he is able to divine and foretell to a nicety every change of the weather, merely from observing the demeanor of his flock.

Forests have no charm for the shepherd, who, regarding everything from a pastoral point of view, sees in each tree an insolent intruder depriving his sheep of their rightful nourishment; and he covertly seeks to increase his pasture by setting fire to the woods whenever he can hope to do so with impunity. Whole tracts of noble forest have thus been laid waste, and it is much to be feared that half a century hence the country will present a bleak and desolate appearance, unless some means can be discovered in order to prevent this abuse.

10

CHAPTER XXI.

ROUMANIAN MARRIAGE AND MORALITY.

MARRIAGEABLE Roumanian girls often wear a head-dress richly embroidered with pearls and coins; this is a sign that their trousseaus are ready, and that they only wait for a suitor. The preparation of the trousseau, involving as it does much spinning, weaving, and embroidering, in order to get ready the requisite number of shirts, towels, pillow-covers, etc., considered indispensable, often keeps the girl and her family employed for years beforehand. In some districts we are told that it is customary for the young man who is seeking a girl in marriage to make straight for the painted wooden chest containing her dowry; and only when satisfied, by the appearance of the contents, of the skill and industry of his intended, does he proceed to the formal demand of her hand. If, on the contrary, the coffer prove to be ill-furnished, he is at liberty to beat a retreat, and back out of the affair. The matter has been still further simplified in one village, for there, during the carnival-time, the mother of each marriageable daughter is in the habit of organizing a sort of standing exhibition of the maiden's effects in the dwelling-room, where each article is displayed to the best advantage, hung against the walls or spread out upon the benches. The would-be suitor is thus enabled to review the situation merely by pushing the door ajar, and need not even cross the threshold if the display falls short of his expectations.

In some districts a pretty little piece of acting is still kept up on the wedding-morning. The bridegroom, accompanied by his friends, arrives on horseback at full gallop before the house of his intended, and roughly calls upon the father to give him his daughter. The old man denies having any daughter; but after some mock wrangling he goes into the house and leads out an old toothless hag, who is received with shouts and clamors. Then, after a little more fencing, he goes in again and leads out the true bride dressed in her best clothes, and with his blessing gives her over to the bridegroom.*

---

* In Sweden, when the guests sit down to the bridal banquet, an old woman decked in a wreath of birch-bark, in which straw and goose-feathers are interwoven,

An orthodox Roumanian wedding should last seven days and seven nights, neither less nor more; but as there are many who cannot afford this sacrifice of time, they circumvent the difficulty by interrupting the festivities after the first day, and resuming them on the seventh.

The ceremony itself is accomplished with much gayety and rejoicing. The parents of the bridegroom go to fetch the bride, in a cart harnessed with four oxen whose horns are wreathed with flower garlands; the village musicians march in front, and the chest containing the trousseau is placed on the cart. One of the bride's relations carries her dowry tied up in a handkerchief attached to the point of a long pole.

Whoever is invited to a Roumanian wedding is expected to bring not only a cake and a bottle of wine, but also some other gift of less transitory nature—a piece of linen, an embroidered towel, a handkerchief, or such-like.

In some villages it is customary for the bride, after the wedding-feast, to step over the banqueting-table and upset a bucket of water placed there for the purpose.* After this begins the dancing, at which it is usual for each guest to take a turn with the bride, and receive from her a kiss in return for the civility.

An ancient custom, now fast dying out, was the *tergul de fete*—the maidens' market—celebrated each year at the top of the Gaina mountain, at a height of nearly six thousand feet above the level of the sea, and where all the marriageable girls for miles around used to assemble to be courted on the 29th of June, Feast of St. Peter and St. Paul. The trousseau, packed in a gayly decorated chest, was placed in a cart harnessed with the finest horses or the fattest oxen, and thus the girl and her whole family proceeded to the place of rendezvous. Sheep, calves, poultry, and even beehives, were likewise brought by way of decoration; and many people went the length of borrowing strange cattle or furniture, in order to cut a better figure and lure on the suitors—although it was an understood thing that only a part of what was thus displayed really belonged to the maiden's dowry. The

and grotesquely dressed up with jingling harness, is led in and presented to the bridegroom as his consort, while in a pompous speech her charms are expatiated upon. She is chased away with clamorous hooting, whereupon the bridesmen go out again, and after a mock search they lead in the bride.

* Supposed to denote fruitfulness.

destination being reached, each family having a girl to dispose of erected its tent, with the objects grouped around, and seated in front was the head of the family, smoking his pipe and awaiting the suitors.

The young men on their side came also accompanied by their families, bringing part of their property with them, notably a broad leather belt well stocked with gold and silver coins.

When an agreement had been effected, then the betrothal took place on the spot, with music, dancing, and singing, and it hardly ever happened that a girl returned home unbetrothed from this meeting. But, to say the truth, this was, latterly, only because each girl attending the fair went there virtually betrothed to some youth with whom all the preliminaries of courtship had already been gone through, and this was merely the official way of celebrating the betrothal, the Roumanians in these parts believing that good-luck will attend only such couples as are affianced in this manner. Any girl who had not got a bridegroom *in spe* rarely went there at all, or, if she went, did not take her trousseau, but considered herself as a mere spectator.

In former days, however, this assemblage had a real signification, and was, moreover, dictated by a real necessity. There were fewer villages, and a far larger proportion than now of the population led the wandering, nomadic life of mountain shepherds, cut off from intercourse with their fellow-creatures during the greater part of the year, and with no opportunity of making choice of a consort. The couples thus betrothed on the 29th of June could not be married till the following spring, for immediately after this date the shepherds remove their flocks to higher pasturages, and, proceeding southward as the year advances, do not return to that neighborhood till the Feast of St. George.

Another curious custom in connection with the maidens' market was, that on Holy Saturday each girl who had been betrothed on the preceding 29th of June on the Gaina mountain came to a village of that district called Halmagy, dressed in her best clothes, and there offered a kiss to each respectable person of either sex she happened to meet on her way. The individual thus saluted was bound to give a present in return, even were it but a copper coin; and to decline or resist the embrace was regarded as the greatest affront. This custom, known as the kiss market, seems to have originated at the time when

all the newly married young shepherdesses used to leave the neighborhood to follow their husbands in their roving life, and this was
their mode of bidding farewell to all friends and relations. This custom has now likewise become almost extinct, for the conditions of
daily life have been considerably modified during the last fifty years,
and nowadays the newly married shepherd, after a very brief honey-
moon, goes away alone with his flock, leaving his wife established in
the village, even though his absence may extend over a year. Many
Roumanian villages are thus virtually inhabited solely by women, and
to a population of several thousand females we not unfrequently find
but twenty or thirty men, and these mostly old and decrepit, the real
lords and masters only appearing from time to time on a short and
flying visit. Szeliste, one of the largest Roumanian villages in the
neighborhood of Hermanstadt, and celebrated for the good looks of
its inhabitants, presents thus, during the greater part of the year, a
touching array of desolate Penelopes; and it is much to be feared that
the score of feeble old men left them as guardians are altogether
insufficient to defend the wholesale amount of female virtue intrusted
to their charge.

The Roumanian always regards marriage with a stranger as something opprobrious. The man who marries other than a Roumanian
woman ceases to be a Roumanian in his people's eyes, and is henceforward regarded as unclean; and a popa whose wife was not a Roumanian would not be accepted by any congregation. Yet more
severely condemned is the woman who marries a stranger; the marriage itself is considered invalid, and no Roumanians who respect
themselves would keep up acquaintance with such a person.

According to their views a girl should remain in her own village,
but a man may, without losing caste, marry into another neighborhood. Any father will consider it an honor to take a strange son-in-
law into his house, and the greater the distance this latter has come,
in the same proportion does the honor increase. But a man who
gives his daughter in marriage out of the village loses his prestige in
exact proportion as she goes farther away from home. "He has
given his daughter away from home" is a reproach to which no man
cares to expose himself.

In districts where Roumanians live together with other races professing the Greek faith, these marriage laws have been somewhat
modified. So unions in the Bukowina with Ruthenians and in the

Banat with Serbs, though still regarded as objectionable, are not so rare as they used to be.

No respectable girl should leave her parents' house unless driven to it by necessity; and if she be obliged to go into service, it should only be in the house of the popa, or in that of some particularly distinguished native of the place. The Roumanian girls serving in the towns are mostly such as have been obliged to leave their native village in consequence of a moral slip.

Much has been said about the lightness of behavior characterizing Roumanian girls—Saxons in particular being fond of drawing attention to the comparative statistics of the two races, which show, it is true, a very large balance of legitimate births in their own favor. If, however, we look at the matter somewhat more closely, we are forced to acknowledge that the words legitimate and illegitimate can only here be taken in a very modified sense; for while the Saxon peasant marries and divorces with such culpable lightness as to render the marriage tie of little real value, the Roumanian, has introduced a sort of regularity even into his irregular connections which goes far to excuse them. Whatever, also, may be said of the loose conduct of many of the Roumanian married women, the same reproach cannot be applied to the girls.

It happens frequently that among the Roumanians, who, like most Southern races, attain manhood early, there are many young men who have chosen a partner for life long before the time they are called for military conscription; and as it is here illegal for all such to marry before they have accomplished their three years' service as soldiers, and no parents could therefore be induced to give them their daughter, a curious sort of elopement takes place. Two or more of the lover's friends carry off the girl, after a mock resistance on her part, to some other village, where he himself awaits her with his witnesses. These latter receive the reciprocal declaration of the young couple that they wish to be man and wife. The girl is then solemnly invested with a head-kerchief, veil, or comb, whichever happens to be the sign of matronhood in her village; and from that moment she takes rank as a married woman, the lad as her husband, and their children are considered as legitimate as those born in regular wedlock. Three or four years later, when the young man has served his time as a soldier, the union is formally blessed by the priest in church; but in that case none of the usual marriage festivities take place.

It is very rare that a man deserts the girl to whom he has been wedded in this irregular fashion; and in cases where he has been known to do so and take another wife, both he and she are tabooed by the neighbors, and the first wife is regarded as the real one.

As, however, all children originating from such unions are officially classified as illegitimate, the barren figures would give an erroneously unfavorable idea of the Roumanian state of morality to those unacquainted with these details; and it is therefore really no anomaly to say that illegitimate here is tantamount to three-quarters legitimate, while the Saxons' legitimacy does not always quite deserve that name.

A jilted lover will revenge himself on his mistress by ostentatiously dancing with some other lass; and in order to do her some material injury as well, he goes secretly at night and cuts down with a sickle the unripe hemp and flax which were to have served for spinning her wedding-clothes. It is always an understood thing that the hemp belongs to the female members of the family, and there is a certain poetry in the idea of thus cutting off the faithless one's thread. Thus the father, finding his hemp prematurely cut down, is at once aware that something has gone wrong about his daughter's love-affair.

CHAPTER XXII.

THE ROUMANIANS: DANCING, SONGS, MUSIC, STORIES, AND PROVERBS.

THE dances habitual among the Roumanians may briefly be divided into three sorts:

1. *Caluseri* and *Batuta*, ancient traditional dances performed by men only, and often executed at fairs and public festivals. For these a fixed number of dancers is required, and a leader called the *vatav.* Each dancer is provided with a long staff, which he occasionally strikes on the ground in time to the music.

2. *Hora* and *Breül*, round dances executed either by both sexes or by men only.

3. *Ardeleana, Lugojana, Marnteana, Pe-picior,* and *Hategeana,* danced by both sexes together, and in which each man may have two or more female partners.

These last-named dances rather resemble a minuet or quadrille, and

are chiefly made up of a sort of swaying, balancing movement, alternately advancing and retreating, with varied modes of expression and
different rates of velocity. Thus the Ardeleana is slow, the Marnteana
rather quicker but still dignified, and the Pe-picior is fastest of all.
Also, each separate dance has two distinct measures, as in the Scotch
reel or the Hungarian *csardas*—the slow rhythm being called *domol*,
or reflectively, and the fast one being danced *cu foc*, with fire.

All these dances are found in different districts with varied appellations.

There is also a very singular dance which I have not myself witnessed, but which is said to be sometimes performed in front of the
church in order to insure a good harvest—one necessary condition of
which is that the people should dance till in a state of violent perspiration, figurative of the rain which is required to make the corn grow;
then the arms must be held on high for the hops to grow, wild jumps
in the air for the vines, and so on, each grain and fruit having a special
movement attributed to it, the dance being kept up till the dancers
have to give in from sheer fatigue.

The Roumanian does not say that a man is dancing with a girl,
but that "he dances her," as you would talk of spinning a top. This
conveys the right impression—namely, that the man directs her dancing and disposes her attitudes, so as to show off her grace and charms
to the best advantage. Thus a good dancer here does not imply a
man who dances well himself, but rather one skilful at showing off
two or three partners at a time. He acts, in fact, as a sort of showman
to the assortment of graces under his charge, to which he calls attention by appropriate rhymes and verses. Therefore the sharpest wit
rather than the nimblest legs is required for the post of *vatav flacailor*,
or director of dances in the village.

Dancing usually takes place in the open air; and in villages where
ball-room etiquette is duly observed, the fair ones can only be conducted to the dance by the director himself, or by one of his appointed
aides-de-camp. It is so arranged that after the leader has for a time
shown off several girls in the manner described—so to say, set them
agoing—he makes a sign to other young men to take them off his
hands, while he himself repeats the proceeding with other *débutantes*.

The music usually consists of bagpipes and violin, the latter sometimes replaced by one or two flutes. The musicians, who are frequently blind men or cripples, stand in the centre, the dancers revolving

around them. Tzigane-players are rarely made use of for Roumanian dances, as they do not interpret the Roumanian music correctly, and are accused of imparting a bold, licentious character to it.

There are many occasions on which music is prescribed, and on all such it should not be wanting; but it is considered unseemly for music to play without special motive, and when the Roumanian hears music he invariably asks, "La ce cântà ?"—for whom do they play?

Fully as many matrons as maidens figure at the village merry-makings, for, unlike the Saxon, the Roumanian woman does not dream of giving up dancing at her marriage. Wedlock is to her an emancipation, not a bondage, and she only begins really to enjoy her life from the moment she becomes a wife. For instance, it is considered quite correct for a married woman, especially if she has got children, to suffer herself to be publicly kissed and embraced by her dancer, and no one present would think of taking umbrage at such harmless liberties.

In reciting or making a speech, the Roumanian is careful to speak slowly and distinctly, with dignity and deliberation, and to avoid much gesticulation, which is regarded as ridiculous. It is also considered distinguished to speak rather obscurely, and veil the meaning under figures of speech—a man who says his meaning plainly in so many words being considered as wanting in breeding.

As in Italy, the *recitatore* (story-teller), called here *provestitore*, holds an important place among the Roumanians. The stories recited usually belong to the class of ogre and fairy tale, and would seem rather adapted to a nursery audience than to a circle of full-grown men and women. Sometimes in verse, sometimes in prose, these stories oftenest set forth the adventures of some prince subjected to the cruel persecutions of a giant or sorcerer. The hero has usually a series of tasks allotted to him, or difficulties to be overcome, before he is permitted to enjoy his father's throne in peace and lead home the beautiful princess to whom he is attached. The tasks dealt out to him must be three at least, sometimes six, seven, nine, or twelve; but never more than this last number, which indeed is quite sufficient for the endurance even of a fairy prince. When the tasks are nine or twelve in number they are then grouped together in batches of three, each batch being finished off with some stereotyped phrase, such as, "But our hero's trials were not yet over by any means, and much remains still to be told." As a matter of course, these trials must always be arranged *crescendo*, advancing in horror and difficulty towards the end.

The story invariably opens with the words,

"A fost ce a fost; dacà n'ar fi fost nici nu s'ar povesti," which, corresponding to our "once upon a time," may be thus translated: "It was what once took place, and if it had never been, it would not now be related;" and the concluding phrase is often this one, "And if they have not died, they are all yet alive."

It is not every one who can relate a story correctly according to the Roumanian's mode of thinking. He is most particular as to the precise inflections of voice, which must alternately be slow and impressive, or impetuous and hurried, according to the requirements of the narrative. If the story winds up with a wedding, the narrator is careful to observe that he also was present on the occasion, in proof of which he enumerates at great length the names of the guests invited and the dishes which formed part of the banquet; and according to the fertility of imagination he displays in describing these details he will be classed by his audience as a *provestitore* of first, second, or third rank.

The Roumanians have a vast *répertoire* of songs and rhymes for particular occasions, and many of these people seem to possess great natural fluency for expressing themselves in verse, assisted, no doubt, by the rich choice of rhymes offered by their language. Some people would seem to talk as easily in verse as in prose, and there are districts where it is not considered seemly to court a girl otherwise than in rhymed speech. All these rhymes, as well as most of their songs and ballads, are moulded in four feet verse, which best adapts itself to the fundamental measure of Roumanian music. Among the principal forms of song prevalent in the country are the *Doina*, the *Ballad*, the *Kolinda*, the *Cantece de Irogi*, the *Cantece de Stea*, the *Plugul*, the *Cantece de Paparuga*, the *Cantece de Nunta*, the *Descantece*, and the *Bocete*.

1. The *Doina* is a lyrical poem, mostly of a mournful, monotonous character, much resembling the gloomy *Dumkas* of the Ruthenians, and from which, perhaps, its name is derived; and this is all the more probable, as many of the songs sung by the Roumanians of the Bukowina are identical with those to be heard sung by their countrymen living in the Hungarian Banat. Thus it is of curious effect to hear

the celebrated song of the Dniester, "Nistrule riu blestemal" (Dniester, cursed river), in which lament is made over the women carried off by the Tartars, sung on the plains of Hungary, so many hundred miles away from the scenes which originated it.

2. The *Ballad*, also called *Cantece*, or song proper, its title usually specifying whose particular song it is; for instance, "Cantecul lui Horia"—the song of Hora, or more literally, Hora, his song—lui Jancu, lui Marko, etc.

These ballads are sung to the accompaniment of a shepherd's pipe or flute, but are oftener merely recited, it not being considered good form to have them sung except by blind or crippled beggars, such as go about at markets or fairs.*

3. The *Kolinda*, or Christmas song, the name derived from a heathen goddess, Lada.† These consist of songs and dialogues, oftenest of a mythological character, and bearing no sort of allusion to the Christian festival. The performers go about from house to house knocking at each door, with the usual formula, "Florile s'dalbe, buna sara lui Cracinim"—white is the flower, a happy Christmas-night to you.

The *Turca*, or *Brezaia*, also belongs to the same category as the *Kolinda*, but is of a somewhat more boisterous character, and is performed by young men, who, all following a leader grotesquely attired

---

* There is a story told of a village (but whether Hungarian or Roumanian I am unable to say) which, up to the year 1536, used to be inhabited by cripples, hunchbacks, lame, maimed, and blind men only, and which went by the name of the "Republic of Cripples." No well-grown and healthy persons were ever suffered to settle here, for fear of spoiling the deformity of their race, and all new-born children unlucky enough to enter the world with normally organized frames were instantly mutilated.

The inhabitants of this village, turning these infirmities to account, made a play of wandering over the country begging and singing at all fairs and markets, and trading on the compassion excited by their wretched appearance. They had also their own language, called the language of the blind, and were in so far privileged above the useful and industrious citizens as to be exempted from all taxes.

† The Council of Constantinople, 869, forbade the members of the Oriental Church to keep the feast of the pagan goddess Kolinda, or Lada, occurring on the shortest day. These Kolinda songs appear to be of Slav origin, since we find the Koleda among the Bohemians, Serbs, and Slavonians, the Koleda among Poles, and the Kolad with the Russians. Yet further proof of this would seem to be that unmistakable resemblance to the Slav words *Kaulo, Kul, Kolo*, a round dance—applying, no doubt, to the rotation of the sun, which on this day begins afresh. Grimm, however, in his Mythology, makes out the name to be derived from the Latin *Calendæ*.

in a long cloak and mask (oftenest representing the long beak of a stork, or a bull's head, hence the name), go about the villages night and day as long as the Christmas festivities last, pursuing the girls and terrifying the children. A certain amount of odium is attached to the personification of the Turca himself, and the man who has acted this part is regarded as unclean or bewitched by the devil during a period of six weeks, and may not enter a church nor approach a sacrament till this time has elapsed.

In the Bukowina the Turca, or *Tur*, goes by the name of the *Capra*, and is called *Cleampa* in the east of Transylvania.

4. The *Cantece de Irogi* is the name given to the text of many carnival games and dialogues in which *Rahula* (Rachel) and her child, a shepherd, a Jew, a Roumanian popa, and the devil appear in somewhat unintelligible companionship.

5. The *Cantece de Stea*—songs of the star—are likewise sung at this period by children, who go about with a tinsel star at the end of a stick.

6. The *Plugul*—song of the plough—a set of verses sung on New-year's Day by young men fantastically dressed up, and with manifold little bells attached to feet and legs. They proceed noisily through the streets of towns and villages, cracking long whips as though urging on a team of oxen at the plough.

7. The *Cantece de Paparuga* are songs which are sung on the third Sunday after Easter, or in cases of prolonged drought.

8. The *Cantece de Nunta* are the wedding songs, of which there are a great number. These are, however, rarely sung, but oftener recited. They take various forms, such as that of invitation, health-drinking, congratulations, etc. To these may be added the *Cantece de Cumetrie* and the *Cantecul ursitelor*, which express rejoicings over a new-born infant.

9. The *Descantece*, or descantations, are very numerous. They consist in secret charms or spells expressed in rhyme, which, in order to be efficacious, must be imparted to children or grandchildren only when the parent is lying on his death-bed. These oftenest relate to illnesses of man or beast, to love or to life; and each separate contingency has its own set formula, which is thus transmitted from generation to generation.

10. The *Bocete* are songs of mourning, usually sung over the corpse by paid mourners.

On the principle that the character of a people is best demonstrated by its proverbs, a few specimens of those most current among Roumanians may be here quoted :

"A man without enemies is of little value."

"It is easier to keep guard over a bush full of live hares than over one woman."

"A hen which cackles overnight lays no egg in the morning."

"A wise enemy is better than a foolish friend."

"In the daytime he runs away from the buffalo, but in the night he seizes the devil by the horn." *

"Carry your wife your whole life on your back, but, if once you set her down, she will say, 'I am tired.'"

"The just man always goes about with a bruised head."

"Sit crooked, but speak straight."

"Father and mother you will never find again, but wives as many as you list."

"The blessing of many children has broken no man's roof as yet."

"Better an egg to-day than an ox next year."

"No one throws a stone at a fruitless tree."

"Patience and silence give the grapes time to grow sweet."

"If you seek for a faultless friend you will be friendless all your life."

"There where you cannot catch anything, do not stretch out your hand."

"Who runs after two hares will not even catch one."

"The dog does not run away from a whole forest of trees, but a single stick will make him run."

"A real Jew will never pause to eat until he has cheated you."

"You cannot carry two melons in one hand."

"Who has been bitten by a snake is afraid of a lizard."

---

* The meaning of this I take to be, that the dangers we recognize and run away from are smaller than those we encounter without knowing it.

CHAPTER XXIII.

ROUMANIAN POETRY.

It is hardly necessary to remark that the history of Roumanian literature must needs be a scanty one as yet. Considering the past history of these people on either side of the frontier, and the manner in which they have been oppressed and persecuted, the wonder is rather to find them to-day so far advanced on the road that leads to immortality.

The first Roumanian book (a collection of psalms, probably translated from the Greek) was printed at Kronstadt in 1577, and was succeeded by many other similar works, all printed in Cyrillian characters.

As historians and chroniclers, the names of Ureki, Miron Kostin, Dosithei, and of Prince Dimetrie Kantemir, all hold honorable positions between the end of the sixteenth and the beginning of the eighteenth century. Political events then stemmed the current of progress for a time, and made of the rest of the eighteenth century a period of intellectual stagnation for all Roumanians, whether of Wallachia, Moldavia, or Transylvania. It was from the latter country that about the year 1820 was given the first impulse towards resurrection, connected with which we read the names of Lazar, Majorescu, Assaki, Mikul, Petru Major, Cipariu, Bolinteanu, Balcescu, Constantin Negruzzi, and Cogalnitscheanu.

It was only after the middle of the present century that Latin characters began to be adopted in place of Cyrillian ones, and indeed it is not easy to understand why the Cyrillian alphabet ever came to be used at all. On this subject Stanley, writing in 1856, speaks as follows:

"The Latinity of Rouman is, however, sadly disguised under the Cyrillic alphabet, in which it has hitherto been habited. This alphabet was adopted about 1400 A.D., after an attempt by one of the popes to unite the Roumans to the Catholic Church. The priests then burned the books in the Roman or European letters, and the Russians have opposed all the attempts made latterly to cast off the Slavonic alphabet, by which the Rouman language is enchained and bound to the Slavonic dialects. . . . The difficulty of coming to an agreement among the men of letters, as to the system to be adopted for rendering the Cyrillic letters by Roman type, has retarded this movement as much, perhaps, as political opposition."

The first Roumanian political newspaper was issued by Georg Baritin in 1838. At present several Roumanian newspapers appear in Transylvania, of which the *Observatorul* and the *Telegraful Roman* are the principal ones. There are in the country two Greek Catholic seminaries for priests, and one Greek Oriental one, a commercial school at Kronstadt, four upper gymnasiums, and numerous primary schools, all of which are self-supporting, and receive no assistance from the Hungarian Government.

Some portion of the rich store of folk songs which from time immemorial have been sung in the country by wandering minstrels, called *cantari*, has been rescued from oblivion by the efforts of Alexandri, and after him Torceanu, who, going about from village to village, have written down all they could learn from the lips of the peasants. One of the most beautiful and pathetic of the ballads thus collected by Alexandri is that of Curte d'Arghisch, an ancient and well-known Roumanian legend, the greater part of which I have here endeavored to reproduce in an English version. These ballads are, however, exceedingly difficult to translate at all characteristically, our language neither possessing that abundant choice of rhyme, so apt to drive a translator to envious despair, nor yet the harmonious current of sound which lends a peculiar charm to the loose and rambling metre in which these songs are mostly written.

CLOISTER ARGHISCH.

I.

By the Arghisch river.
By the bonny brim,
Goes the Voyvod Negru,*
Other ten with him.

---

* The Hospodar Negru, or Nyagon as he is sometimes called, reigned from 1513 to 1521. Long detained as hostage at the Court of Sultan Selim I., he had the opportunity of studying Oriental architecture, and himself directed the building of a cele-

Nine of these his comrades,
Master masons be,
And the tenth is Manoll,
Masters' master he.
And the ten are questing,
Where along the tide
They shall build the minster,
And their fame beside.
Then as on they stray,
Meets them on the way
A shepherd lad, that ditty sad
Upon his pipe doth play.

"Shepherd lad, dear shepherd lad,
Mournful ditty playing,
Up the river has thy flock
And hast thou been straying?
Down have strayed both thou and they,
Down along the river?
In thy wanderings where hast been,
Say, hast thou a building seen
Standing by the river,
Built of moss-grown ancient stone,
All unfinished and alone,
Where the hazels, green and lank,
Shoot amid the copsewood dank?"

"Ay, my master, that have I
Sighted as I wandered by;
Sooth, a wall doth on the strand
Lonely and unfinished stand,
At whose sight my hounds in haste
Howling fled across the waste!"

When this word the prince had heard,
Joyful man was he:
"Haste away! come, no delay,
Haste thee instantly;
These, my master masons nine,
Lead unto yon wall,
And Manoll the tenth, that is
Master of them all."

---

brated mosque which had, we are told, no less than 999 windows and 366 minarets. This edifice so delighted the Sultan that he set Nyagon at liberty, presenting him with all the rich materials remaining over from the building of the mosque, in order to erect a church in his native country. Returning thither, he is said to have brought with him the celebrated architect Manoll, or Manolli, by birth a Phanariot, who, with his wife Annika, is immortalized in this ballad.

" See ye yonder wall of mine?
Know that here the spot I name
For the sacred cloister's shrine,
For my everlasting fame.
Now, ye mighty masters all,
Fellows of the builder's craft,
Haste away! night and day
Raise ye, build ye, roof and wall.
Build a cloister worthy me,
Such as never men did see;
Fail to build it as I say,
I will build you instantly,
Build you living, every one,
'Neath the pile's foundation-stone."

II.

Hastily with line and rule
Work they out the cloister's plan :
Hastily with eager tool
Delve foundations in the sod,
Where shall stand the house of God.
Never resting night or day,
Building, ever building, they
Hurry on the work alway.
But what in the day has grown,
In the night is overthrown.
Next day, next, and next again,
What within the hours of light
They have reared with toil and pain,
Falls to ruin in the night,
And all labor is in vain ;
For the pile will not remain,
Falling nightly down again.

Wondering and wrathful then
Doth the prince the builders call,
Raging, threatens once again
He will build them, build them all,
Build them in beneath the wall.
And the master builders nine,
Thus, their wretched lives at stake,
Quaking toil, and toiling quake,
All throughout the summer light,
Till the day gives way to night.

But Manoll upon a day
Puts the irksome task away,
Lays him down to sleep, and thus
Dream he dreameth marvellous,

Which, awak'ning from repose,
Straightway doth he then disclose:

"Hear my story, masters mine,
Ye my fellow-craftsmen nine;
Hearken to me while I tell
Dream in sleep that me befell:
From the height of heaven clear
Was it borne upon my ear.
Ever we shall build in vain,
Crumbling still our work again,
Till together swear we all
To immure within the wall
Her who at the peep of day
Chances first to come this way
Hither, who is sent by fate,
Bearing food for swain or mate,
Wife or sweetheart though it be,
Maid or matron equally.
Therefore listen, comrades mine:
Would you build this holy shrine—
Would you to enduring fame
Evermore transmit your name—
Vow we all a solemn vow,
As we stand together now,
Whosoever it shall be
That his lovèd one shall see,
Chancing here her way to take
When the morrow's light doth break,
Will as victim bid her fall,
Buried living in the wall!"

III.

Smiling doth the morning break;
With the dawn Manoll, awake,
Scaling the enclosure's bound,
Mounts the scaffold; all around,
Hill and dale, with glance of fear,
Anxious searcheth far and near.
What is this that greets his eyes?
Who is it that hither hies?
'Tis his wife he doth behold,
Sweetest blossom of the wold;
She it is that hasteth here,
Bringing for her husband dear
Meat and wine his heart to cheer.

Sure too awful is the sight!
Can his senses witness right?

Leaps his heart and reels his brain
In an agony of pain.
Then on bended knees he falls,
Desperate on Heaven calls:

"O Lord my God,
    That rul'st on high,
Ope thou the flood-gates
    Of the sky;
Down upon earth
    Thy torrents pour,
Till brook and river
    Rise and roar,
Till raging floods
    My wife shall stay,
Shall turn her back
    The homeward way!"

Lo! in pity God has hearkened—
That which he has asked is done:
Clouds the heaven's face have darkened,
They have blotted out the sun;
Down the rains in torrents pour,
Brook and river rage and roar.
But nor storm nor flood can stay
Manoll's wife upon her way;
Pressing onward, halting never,
Plunging through the foaming river,
Knowing naught of doubt or fear,
Near she hasteth, and more near.

The poem goes on to say how Manoll a second time implores the Creator to send a hurricane which shall ravage the face of nature and impede her progress. Once more his prayer is granted, and a mighty wind, which,

Sighing loud and moaning,
Thundering and droning,
Down the plane-trees bending,
And the pines uprending,

rages over the land.

But no earthly force
Checks her steady course,
And all vainly passed
By the furious blast,
In the storm she quavers,
But yet never wavers,
And, oh, hapless lot!
Soon has reached the spot.

The fourth canto relates how the nine master masons are filled with joy at sight of this heaven-sent victim. Manoll alone is sad, as, kissing his wife, he takes her in his arms and carries her up the scaffolding. There he places her in a niche, explaining that they are going to pretend to build her in merely as a joke; while the poor young wife, scenting no danger, claps her hands in childish pleasure at the idea.

> But her spouse, with gloomy face,
> Speaks no word, and works apace;
> Of his dream he thinks alone,
> As they pile up stone on stone.
> And the church walls upward shoot,
> Cover soon her dainty foot,
> Reaching then above the knee;
> Where is vanished all her glee?
> As, becoming deadly pale,
> Thus the wife begins to wail:

> "Manolli, dear Manolli!
> Master, master Manolli!
> Prithee, now this joking cease,
> And thy wife from here release;
> See, the wall is closing fast,
> In its grip am I compassed.
> Manolli, dear Manolli!
> Master, master Manolli!"

> But Manoll makes no reply,
> Works with restless energy.
> Higher and yet higher
> Grows the wall entire,
> Grows with lightning haste,
> Reaches soon her waist,
> Reaches soon her breast;
> She no more can jest,
> Hardly can she speak,
> With voice faint and weak:

> "Manolli, dear Manolli!
> Master, master Manolli!
> Stop this joke and set me free—
> Soon a mother shall I be;
> See, the wall is crushing me,
> These hard stones my babe will kill;
> With salt tears my bosom fill."

> But Manoll makes no reply,
> Works with restless energy.

Higher and yet higher
Grows the wall entire;
O'er her dainty foot
Fast the church walls shoot;
Fair Annika's knee
Soon no more they see,
Building on in haste
To her lithesome waist;
Hidden is her breast,
By the stones compressed;
Hidden now her eye,
As the wall grows high;
Building on apace,
Hidden soon her face!
And the hapless woman, she
Laughs no longer now in glee,
But from out the cruel wall
Still the feeble voice doth call:

"Manolli, dear Manolli!
Master, master Manolli!
See the wall is closing quite,
Vanished the last ray of light."

There is still a fifth canto to this ballad, but of such decidedly inferior merit as to suggest the idea that it is a piece of patchwork added on at a later period. The prince, delighted at the success of the building, asks the master masons whether they could undertake to raise a second church of yet nobler, loftier proportions than the first. This question being answered in the affirmative, the tyrannical Voyvod, probably afraid of their embellishing some other country with the work of their genius, orders the ladders and scaffolding to be removed from the building, so that the ten illustrious architects are left standing on the roof, there to perish of starvation. Hoping to escape this doom, each of the master masons constructs for himself a pair of artificial wings, or rather a sort of parachute, out of light wooden shingles, and by means of which he hopes safely to reach the ground. But the parachutes are a miserable failure, and crashing down with violence, the nine master masons are turned into as many stones. Manoll, the last to descend, and distracted at hearing the wailing voice of his dying wife calling upon him, falls likewise; but the tears welling up from his breast cause him to be transformed into a spring of crystal water flowing near the church, and to this day known by the name of Manolli's well.

"Miora," or "The Lamb," is another popular ballad, which, sung and recited throughout Roumania and Transylvania, is gracefully illustrative of the idyllic bond by which shepherd and flock are united:

MIORA.

Where the mountains open, there
Runs a path-way passing fair,
And along this flowery way
Shepherds came one summer day.
    Snowy flocks were three,
    Led by shepherds three.
One from Magyarland had come,
Wrantscha was another's home,
From Moldavia one had come;
But the one from Magyarland,
And from Wrantscha—hand in hand,

Council held they secretly,
And resolved deceitfully,
    When behind the hill
    Sank the sun, to kill
The Moldavian herd, for he
Was the richest of the three.
    Strongest were his rams,
    Fattest were his dams,
    Whitest were his lambs,
And his dogs the fiercest,
And his horse the fleetest.

But a lambkin white,
With eyes soft and bright,
Since the break of day
Bleats so piteously,
Does not cease to bleat,
No more grass will eat.

"Little lambkin white,
Thou my favorite,
Why since break of day
Bleat so piteously?
Never cease to bleat,
No more grass wiltst eat.
O my lambkin sweet,
Wherefore dost complain?
Say, dost suffer pain?"

"Gentle shepherd, master dear,
Prithee but my warning hear;
Lead away thy flock of sheep
Where the woodland shades are deep:

There in peace can we abide—
Forests dense there are to hide.
Shepherd, shepherd! list to me;
Call thy dog to follow thee;
Choose the fiercest one of all,
Ear most watchful to thy call,
For the other herds have sworn
Thou shalt die before the morn!'

"Little lamb, if true dost say,
Hast the gift to prophesy,
And if it must come to pass
That I thus shall die, alas!
Is it written that my life
Thus shall end a cruel knife,
Tell the shepherds where to lay
My cold body in the clay.
    Near unto my sheep
    Would I wish to sleep,
    From the grave to hark
    When the sheep-dogs bark.
    On the mound I pray
    Three new flutes to lay:
One of beech-wood fine be made,
Sings of love that cannot fade;
One carved out of whitest bone,
For my broken heart makes moan;
One of elder-wood let be,
For its tones are proud and free.
    When at evenfall
    'Gin the winds to call,
    List'ning to the sound,
    Gather then around
    All my faithful sheep,
    Bloody tears to weep.
    But that I am dead
    Let no word be said:
    Tell them that a queen
    Passing fair was seen,
    Took me for her mate;
    That we sit in state
    On a lofty throne;
    That the sun and moon
    Held the golden crown,
    And a star fell down
    Straight above my head.
    Say, when I was wed,
    Oak-tree, beech, and pine,
    All were guests of mine

At the wedding-feast;
And the holy priest
Was a mountain high.
Made sweet melody
Thousand birds from near and far,
Every torch a golden star.
But if thou shouldst meet,
Oh, if thou shouldst meet,
A poor haggard matron,
Torn her scarlet apron,
Wet with tears her eyes,
Hoarse with choking sighs,
'Tis my mother old,
Running o'er the wold,
Asking every one,
'Have you seen my son?
In the whole land none
Other was so fair,
With such raven hair,
Soft to feel as silk;
Like the purest milk,
None had skin so white;
None had eyes so bright,
As a pair of sloes.
And where'er he goes,
Shepherd none there be
Half so fair as he!'
Lamb, oh pity take,
Else her heart will break.
Tell her that a queen
Passing fair was seen,
Took me for her mate;
That we sit in state
On a lofty throne;
That the sun and moon
Held the golden crown,
And a star fell down
Straight above my head.
Say, when I was wed,
Oak-tree, beech, and pine,
All were guests of mine
At the wedding-feast;
And the holy priest
Was a mountain high.
Made sweet melody
Thousand birds from near and far,
Every torch a golden star."*

---

* A prose translation of this poem appeared in Stanley's "Rouman Anthology," 1856.

The third and last of those folk songs which limited space permits me here to quote is one I have selected as being peculiarly characteristic of the tender and clinging affection these people bear to their progeny. Devoid of poetical merit it may perhaps be, but surely the unsatisfied yearnings of a childless woman have seldom been more pathetically rendered.

THE ROUMANIAN'S DESIRE.

Would it but th' Almighty please
This my yearning heart to ease,
But to send a little son,
Little cherub for mine own.

All the day and all the night
Would I rock my angel bright;
Gently shielded it should rest
Ever on my happy breast.

I would feed it, I would tend it,
From each peril I'd defend it;
Whisp'ring with the voice of love,
Suck, my chick, my lamb, my dove.

Did but Heaven hear my voice,
Evermore would I rejoice;
Golden gifts so bright and rare,
Little baby soft and fair.

Love that on him I'd bestow,
Other child did never know;
Such his loveliness and worth,
Ne'er was like him child on earth.

Lips like coral, skin like snow,
Eyes like those of mountain roe;
And the roses on his cheek
Elsewhere you in vain would seek.

Mouth so sweet, and eyes so bright,
Would I kiss from morn to night;
Kiss his cheek and kiss his hair,
Singing, "How my child is fair!"

Every holy prayer I know
Should secure my child from woe;
Every magic herb I'd pluck,
For to bring him endless luck.*

---

* This allusion to prayer and magic in the same breath is thoroughly characteristic of the Roumanian's religion.

> Surely, then, he'd grow apace,
> Strong of limb and fair of face,
> And a hero such as he
> Earth before did never see!

It is not easy to classify the cultivated Roumanian writers of the present day, still less so is it to select appropriate specimens from their works. Roumanian literature is in a transition state at present, and, despite much talent and energy on the part of its representatives, has not as yet regained any fixed national character. Perhaps, indeed, it would be more correct to say that precisely the talent and energy of some of the most gifted writers have harmed Roumanian literature more than they have assisted it, by dragging into fashion a dozen different modes utterly incongruous with one another, and with the mainsprings of Roumanian thought and feeling. No doubt the custom of sending their children to be educated outside the country is much to blame for this; and, naturally enough, French poets have been imported into the land along with Parisian fashions.

Béranger and Musset, along with Shakespeare, Goethe, Byron, and Heine, have all been abused in this manner by men who should have understood that the strength of any literature does not lie in the successful imitation of foreign models, however excellent, but rather in the intelligent exploitation of its own historical and artistic treasures. Even Basil Alexandri, the first and most national of Roumanian poets, sometimes falls unconsciously into this error, still more perceptible in the works of Rosetti, Negruzzi, and Cornea.

Odobescu, Gane, Alexi, and Dunca have acquired some fame as writers of fiction; and Joan Slavici in particular may here be cited for his charming sketches of rural life, which have something of the force and delicacy of Turguenief's hand.

FET LOGOFET * (*literally*, YOUNG FOOLHARDY).

> Thou radiant young knight,
> With glance full of light,
>   With golden-locked hair,
> Oh, turn thy proud steed;
> Of the forest take heed—
>   The dragon lies there.
>
> Thou fairest of maids,
> With silken-like braids,
>   So slender thy zone,

* By B. Alexandri.

My good sword will pierce
The monster so fierce,
   And fear I have none.

Thou wrestler, thou ranger,
Thou seeker of danger,
   With eyes flashing fire;
Thy fate will be dolesome;
The dragon is loathsome,
   And fearful his ire.

Thou coaxer, thou pleader,
Thou sweet interceder,
   My star silver bright!
Both dragon and drake,
Before me they quake,
   And fly at my sight.

Thou stealer of hearts,
With golden-tipped darts,
   Yet list to my cry!
Thou canst not escape,
His open jaws gape,
   Turn water to sky!

Thou angel-like child,
With blue eyes so mild,
   Yet needst not to sigh;
For this my good steed
The wind can outspeed,
   And rear heaven-high!

Oh, radiant young knight,
With eyes full of light,
   That masterful shine;
Oh, hark to my prayer,
And do not go there—
   My heart it is thine!

Yet needs I must ride
To win as my bride
   Thou, maiden most sweet;
I must gain renown—
Either death or a crown—
   To lay at thy feet.

THE FAULT IS NOT THINE.*

Full oft hast thou sworn that on this side the grave
Thy love and thy heart should forever be mine;

---

* By K. A. Rosetti.

But thou hast forgotten, and I—I forgave,
For such is the world, and the fault is not thine.

And again was thy cry, "Thou beloved of my heart,
In heaven itself, without thee I'd pine!"
On earth still we dwell—yet dwell we apart;
'Tis the fault of our age, and the fault is not thine.

My arms they embraced thee, I drank with delight
The dew from thy lips like a nectar divine;
But the dew turned to venom, its freshness to blight,
For such is thy sex, and the fault is not thine.

Thy love and thine honor, thy virtue and troth,
Given now to another, were yesterday mine;
Thou knowest not Love! then why should I be wroth?
'Tis the fault of thy race, and the fault is not thine.

Far stronger than Love were both riches and pride,
And swiftly and surely thy faith did decline;
Thy wounds they are healed, thy tears they are dried,
Thou couldst not remember—the fault is not thine.

Yet though thou art faithless, and falsely hast left me,
My eyes can see naught but an angel divine;
My heart flutters wildly whenever I see thee—
'Tis the fault of my love, and the fault is not mine!

I do not suppose that any one with the slightest knowledge of
Roumania and Roumanians can fail to detect an alien note in both
these compositions, despite the grace of the originals; nor can one
help feeling that these authors should have been capable of far better
things.

And surely far better and grander things will come ere long from
this nation, at once so old and so young! when, having regained its
lost self-confidence, it comes to understand that more evil than good
is engendered by a blind conformity to foreign fashions.

Already a step in the right direction has been taken in the matter
of national dress, which, thanks to the praiseworthy example of the
Roumanian queen, has lately received much attention. And as in
dress, so in literature, does Carmen Sylva take the lead, and endeavor
to teach her people to value national productions above foreign impor-
tations.

When, therefore, Roumanian writers begin to see that their force
lies not in the servile imitation of Western models, but in working out

the rich vein of their own folk-lore, and in bridging over the space which takes them back to ancient pagan traditions, then, doubtless, a new era will set in for the literature of the country. Let Roumanian poets leave Béranger and Musset to moulder on their book-shelves, and consign to oblivion Heinrich Heine, whose exquisitely morbid sentimentality is far too fragile an article to bear importation; let them cease from wandering abroad, and assuredly they will discover in their own forests and mountains better and more vigorous material than Paris or Germany can offer: the old stones around them will begin to speak, and the old gods will let themselves be lured from out their hiding-places. Then will it be seen that Apollo's lyre has not ceased to vibrate, and the lays of ancient Rome will arise and develop to new life.

CHAPTER XXIV.

THE ROUMANIANS: NATIONALITY AND ATROCITIES.

The Roumanians have often been called slavish and cringing, but, considering their past history, it is not possible that they should be otherwise, oppressed and trampled on, persecuted, and treated as vermin by the surrounding races; and it should rather be matter for surprise that they have been able to continue existing at all under such a combination of adverse circumstances, which would assuredly have worn out a less powerful nature.

Until little more than a century ago, it was illegal for any Wallachian child to frequent a German or Hungarian school; while at that same period the Wallachian clergy were compelled to carry the Calvinistic bishop on their shoulders to and from his church, whenever he thought fit to exact their services. Still more inhuman was a law which continued in force up to the end of the sixteenth century, ordaining that each Wallachian out of the district of Poplaka, in the neighborhood of Hermanstadt, who injured a tree, if only by peeling off the bark, was to be forthwith hung up to the same tree. "Should, however, the culprit remain undiscovered," prescribes the law, "then shall the community of Poplaka be bound to deliver up for execution some other Wallachian in his place."

The faults of the Roumanians are the faults of all slaves. Like all serfs, they are lazy, not being yet accustomed to work for themselves, nor caring to work for a master; they have acquired cunning and deceit as the only weapons wherewith to meet tyranny and oppression. Sometimes, when goaded to passion, the Roumanian forgets himself, and his eyes flash fiercely on his tormentor; but the gaze is instantly corrected, and the eyes lowered again to their habitual expression of abject humility.

Occasionally they have cast off the yoke and taken cruel revenge on their real or imaginary oppressors, as in 1848, when, instigated and stirred up by Austrian agents, they rose against their masters the Hungarian noblemen, and perpetrated atrocities as numerous as disgusting. They pillaged the country houses, setting everything on fire, and put the nobles to death with many torturing devices, crucifying some and burying others up to the neck, cutting off tongues and plucking out eyes, as a diabolical fancy suggested.

This was all the more surprising, as the bond between serfs and masters had always been of a most peaceful and patriarchal character, and it was to his Hungarian landlord that the Wallachian had been always accustomed to turn for counsel or assistance. True, the serf was forced to pay certain tithes to his master; but in return, whenever the crops failed, the master himself was obliged to sustain the serf, and provide him with corn out of his own granaries.

A Hungarian lady related to me a very horrible instance of cruelty which had happened on the property of a near relation of her own in the revolution of 1848. This gentleman, one of the most generous and humane landlords, did not usually reside at his country place, but had spent much time in foreign travel, and was unknown to most of his people, which, however, did not prevent them from resolving on his death. Hearing of the riots which had broken out on his estate, the nobleman was hastening to the spot; and the excited peasantry, informed of his impending arrival, prepared to receive him with scythes and pickaxes.

The servants of the household had all fled the neighborhood at the first alarm; but there remained behind at the chateau the foster-daughter of the gentleman, a girl of sixteen, who, brought up with the family, was warmly attached to her benefactor, whom she called father. Shutting herself up in a turret-room, she tremblingly awaited the *dénouement* of the fearful drama which was being enacted around her. From her window she could overlook the road by which her foster-father was expected to arrive, and she stood thus all day at her post, straining her eyes for what she feared to see, and praying God to keep her benefactor away.

Twilight had set in, and the moon began to rise, when a solitary rider was at last descried coming down the neighboring hill. The poor girl's heart sank within her, for she knew that this could be no other than her father; and even had she doubted it, the wild-beast roar which broke from the peasants at the sight of their long-expected prey destroyed all remnant of hope. As in a horrible nightmare, she saw them advance towards the horseman in a black, heaving mass, like a crawling thunder-cloud, broken here and there by the sinister gleam of a sharpened scythe. Paralyzed with horror, she yet was unable to look away, and no merciful fainting-fit came to spare her the sight of any of the horrible details which followed: how the hapless rider was surrounded and speedily overpowered; how a dreadful scuffle ensued; and after an interval which seemed like an eternity, how something was hoisted up at the end of a long pole—something round in shape and ghastly in hue—the head of her beloved benefactor!

By-and-by she was roused from her grief by the loud voices of rioters approaching, and presently the front door being shaken and forced in with a resounding crash, the bloody wretches proceeded to overrun the house, and ransack the larders and cellar, laying hands on whatever viands they could discover. In the large vaulted hall they began the carouse, seated round the banqueting-table, and on a platter in the centre was placed the head of their victim.

Two of the peasants who had been searching the upper apartments now appeared on the scene, dragging between them a convulsively trembling girl, who looked ready to die with terror. "They had found her up-stairs in the turret," they explained, "sobbing like a fool, and calling out for her father, like a suckling whelp that has lost its dam."

"The old man's daughter!" shouted one of the revellers; "let us cut off her head as well—they will look fine together on the platter!"

"No," said another; "she is not worth killing, she is half dead already. Let her look at her dear father, since it is for him she is crying;" and raising the dish from the table, he held it in horrible proximity to her shrinking face.

The poor girl tightly closed her eyes in order to escape the dreadful sight, but her persecutors were not inclined to let her off so easily.

Maddened alike by blood and drink, they grasped her roughly, and seizing her long black eyelashes on either side, by main force they compelled her to raise her eyelids and fix her swimming eyes on the gory head.

At first she could distinguish nothing for the blinding tears which obscured her vision, but suddenly the mist cleared away, and the cry she then uttered was so sharp and piercing that it re-echoed again from the vaulted roof, and caused the drinkers to pause for a minute, glass in hand. Lucky it was for her and hers that the dull ear of the tipsy murderers had failed to distinguish the meaning of that cry aright; for in moments of intense emotion widely different feelings are apt to resemble each other in expression, so that joy may be mistaken for grief, and hope for despair—and it was hope, not despair, which had given that piercing sharpness to her voice, for the ghastly grinning head before her was the head of a stranger!

The joyful exclamation rising to her lips was checked just in time, as her dazed brain began to recognize the urgency of the situation. She must not undeceive these men, who were exulting over the death of their landlord. Her father was not dead, it is true, but neither was the danger yet past, and his safety might depend on keeping up the delusion a little longer. By good-luck her confusion passed unnoticed by the semi-tipsy revellers, who presently had no more thought but for their bumpers, so that the young girl, enabled to creep away unobserved, was ultimately the means of saving the nobleman's life by sending a messenger to warn him of his danger.

The man who had been executed in his place turned out to be a gentleman from some neighboring district, who in the dusk had taken a wrong turn on the road, thus occasioning the mistake which cost him his life.

Many such instances of cruelty, of which the Roumanians made themselves guilty in the year '48, have deprived them of the sympathy to which they might have laid claim as a suffering and oppressed race; but people who have a thorough knowledge of the Roumanian character, and are able to estimate correctly all the influences brought to bear on them at that time, do not hesitate to affirm that these people were far more sinned against than sinning, and cannot be held responsible for the atrocities they perpetrated. Even Hungarian nobles, themselves the greatest sufferers by all that occurred during

the revolution, are wont to speak of them with a sort of pitying com-
miseration, as of poor misguided creatures led astray by unscrupulous
agents, and wholly incapable of comprehending the heinousness of
their behavior.

An amusing illustration has been given of the ignorance of these
revolutionary peasants in 1848. Some of them, having broken into a
nobleman's mansion, discovered a packet of old letters in a drawer,
and believing these to be patents of nobility, they proceeded to burn
them in front of the portrait of one of the family ancestors, exclaiming, tauntingly, "See, proud lord, how thy family becomes once more
as ignoble as we ourselves are!"

Few races possess in such a marked degree the blind and immovable sense of nationality which characterizes the Roumanians: they
hardly ever mingle with the surrounding races, far less adopt manners
and customs foreign to their own; and it is a remarkable fact that the
seemingly stronger-minded and more manly Hungarians are absolutely powerless to influence them even in cases of intermarriage. Thus
the Hungarian woman who weds a Roumanian husband will necessarily adopt the dress and manners of his people, and her children
will be as good Roumanians as though they had no drop of Magyar
blood in their veins; while the Magyar who takes a Roumanian girl
for his wife will not only fail to convert her to his ideas, but himself,
subdued by her influence, will imperceptibly begin to lose his nationality. This is a fact well known and much lamented by the Hungarians themselves, who live in anticipated apprehension of seeing their
people ultimately dissolving into Roumanians. This singular tenacity
of the Roumanians to their own manners and customs is doubtless
due to the influence of their religion, which teaches them that any
deviation from their own established rules is sinful—which, as I have
said before, is the whole pivot of Roumanian thought and action.

In some districts where an attempt was made in the time of Maria
Theresa to replace the Greek popas by other clergymen belonging
to the united faith, the inhabitants simply absented themselves from
all church attendance or reception of the sacraments; and there are
instances on record of villages whose churches remained closed for
over thirty years, because the people could not be induced to accept
the change.

As to that portion of the Transylvanian Roumanians which in
1698 consented to embrace the united faith, their separation from

12

their schismatic brethren is but a skin-deep one after all, having no influence whatsoever on their customs and superstitions, or on the strong bond of nationality which holds them all together.

It is a notable fact that among all Oriental races the ideas of religion and nationality are inextricably bound together. So with the Roumanians, whose language has no other word wherewith to express religion or confession but *lege*, law—obviously derived from the Latin *lex*.

The deeply inrooted sense of Roumanian nationality has, moreover, received fresh stimulus in the comprehension which of late years has been slowly but surely dawning on the minds of these people— that they are a nation like other nations, with a right to be governed by a monarch of their own choice, instead of being bandied about, backward and forward, changing masters at each European treaty. There is no doubt that the bulk of Roumanians living to-day in Hungary and Transylvania consider themselves to be serving in bondage, and covertly gaze over the frontier for their real monarch; and who can blame them for so doing? In the many Roumanian hovels I have visited in Transylvania, I have frequently come across the portrait of the King of Roumania hung up in the place of honor, but never once that of his Austrian Majesty. Old wood-cuts representing Michel the Brave, the great hero of the Roumanians, and of the rebel Hora,* are also pretty sure to be found adorning the walls of many a hut. It is likewise by no means uncommon to see village taverns bearing such titles as, " To the King of Roumania," or " To the United Roumanian Kingdom," etc.

A little incident which, taking place under my eyes, impressed me very strongly at the time, helped me to understand this feeling more clearly than I had done before. Two Roumanian generals engaged in some business regarding the regulation of the frontier, being at Hermanstadt for a few days, paid visits to the principal Austrian

---

* The real name of this celebrated Wallachian rebel, born in 1740, was Nykulaj Urszu. Under the reign of the Emperor Joseph II. he became the chief instigator of a revolution among the sorely oppressed Transylvanian Wallachs, who, rising to the number of thirty thousand men, proceeded to murder the Hungarian nobles, and plunder, sack, and burn their possessions. Hora's project was to raise himself to the position of sovereign, and he had already adopted the title of King of Dacia when he was captured, and, together with his confederate Kloska, very cruelly put to death at Karlsburg in 1785.

military authorities, and were the object of much courteous attention. One evening the Austrian commanding general had ordered the military band to play in honor of his Roumanian *confrères*, and seated along with them on the promenade, we were listening to the music. Presently two or three private soldiers passing by stopped in front of us to stare at the foreign uniforms. Apparently their curiosity was not easily satisfied, for after five minutes had elapsed they still remained standing, as though rooted to the spot, and other soldiers had joined them as well, till the group soon numbered above a dozen heads.

Being engaged in conversation, I did not at the moment pay much attention to this circumstance, but happening to turn round again some minutes later, I was surprised to see that the spectators had become doubled and quadrupled in the mean time, and were steadily increasing every minute. Little short of a hundred soldiers were now standing in front of us, all gazing intently. Why were they staring thus strangely? what were they looking at? I asked myself confusedly, but luckily checked the question rising to my lips, when it suddenly struck me that *all* these men had swarthy complexions, and *each* one of them a pair of dark eyes, and simultaneously I remembered that the infantry regiment whose uniform they wore was recruited from Roumanian villages round Hermanstadt.

They were perfectly quiet and submissive-looking, betraying no sign of outward excitement or insubordination; but their expression was not to be mistaken, and no attentive observer could have failed to read its meaning aright. It was at *their own generals* they were gazing in that hungry, longing manner; and deep down in every dusky eye, piercing through a thick layer of patience, stupidity, apathy, and military discipline, there smouldered a spark of something vague and intangible, the germ of a sort of fire which has often kindled revolutions and sometimes overturned kingdoms.

Heaven alone knows what was passing in the clouded brain of these poor ignorant men as they stood thus gaping and staring, in the intensity of their rapt attention! Visions of glory and freedom perchance, dreams of peace and of prosperity; dim far-off pictures of unattainable happiness, of a golden age to come, and an Arcadian state of things no more to be found on the dull surface of this weary world!

The Austrian generals tried not to look annoyed, the Roumanian generals strove not to look elated, and the English looker-on endeavored (I trust somewhat more successfully) to conceal her amusement at the serio-comicality of the situation, which one and all we tacitly ignored with that exquisite hypocrisy characterizing well-bred persons of every nation.

CHAPTER XXV.

THE ROUMANIANS: DEATH AND BURIAL—VAMPIRES AND WERE-WOLVES.

Nowhere does the inherent superstition of the Roumanian peasant find stronger expression than in his mourning and funeral rites, which are based upon a totally original conception of death.

Among the various omens of approaching death are the groundless barking of a dog, the shriek of an owl, the falling down of a picture from the wall, and the crowing of a black hen. The influence of this latter may, however, be annulled, and the catastrophe averted, if the bird be put in a sack and carried sunwise thrice round the dwelling-house.

It is likewise prognostic of death to break off the smaller portion of a fowl's merry-thought, to dream of troubled water or of teeth falling out,* or to be merry without apparent reason.

A falling star always denotes that a soul is leaving the earth—for, according to Lithuanian mythology, to each star is attached the thread of some man's life, which, breaking at his death, causes the star to fall. In some places it is considered unsafe to point at a falling star.

A dying man may be restored to life if he be laid on Holy Saturday outside the church-door, where the priest passing with the procession may step over him; or else let him eat of a root which has been dug up from the church-yard on Good Friday; but if these and other remedies prove inefficient, then must the doomed man be given a burning candle into his hand, for it is considered to be the greatest of all misfortunes if a man die without a light—a favor the Roumanian durst not refuse to his deadliest enemy.

The corpse must be washed immediately after death, and the dirt, if necessary, scraped off with knives, because the dead man will be

---

* Both Greeks and Romans attached an ominous meaning to a dream of falling-out teeth.

more likely to find favor above if he appear in a clean state before the Creator. Then he is attired in his best clothes, in doing which great care must be taken not to tie anything in a knot, for that would disturb his rest by keeping him bound down to the earth. Nor must he be suffered to carry away any particle of iron about his person, such as buttons, boot-nails, etc., for that would assuredly prevent him from reaching Paradise, the road to which is long, and, moreover, divided off by several tolls or ferries. To enable the soul to pass through these a piece of money must be laid in the hand, under the pillow, or beneath the tongue of the corpse. In the neighborhood of Forgaras, where the ferries or toll-bars are supposed to amount to twenty-five, the hair of the defunct is divided into as many plaits, and a piece of money secured in each. Likewise a small provision of needles, thread, pins, etc., is put into the coffin, to enable the pilgrim to repair any damages his clothes may receive on the way.

The family must also be careful not to leave a knife lying with the sharpened edge uppermost as long as the corpse remains in the house, or else the soul will be forced to ride on the blade.

The mourning songs, called *Bocete*, usually performed by paid mourners, are directly addressed to the corpse, and sung into his ear on either side. This is the last attempt made by the survivors to wake the dead man to life by reminding him of all he is leaving, and urging him to make a final effort to arouse his dormant faculties—the thought which underlies these proceedings being that the dead man hears and sees all that goes on around him, and that it only requires the determined effort of a strong will in order to restore elasticity to the stiffened limbs, and cause the torpid blood to flow anew in the veins.

Here is a fragment of one of these mourning songs, which are often very pathetic and fanciful:

> "Mother dear, arise, arise,
> Dry the tearful household's eyes!
> Waken, waken from thy trance,
> Speak a word or cast a glance!
> Pity thou thy children's lot!
> Rise, O mother, leave us not!
> Death triumphant, woe is me,
> From thy children snatcheth thee!
> To the wall hast turned thee now,
> Son nor daughter heedest thou.

Laid the church-yard sod beneath,
Thou shalt feel no breeze's breath
On the surface of thy grave;
From thy brow shall grasses wave,
From those eyes so mild and true
Nodding harebells take their blue."

Women alone are allowed to take part in these lamentations, and all women related to the deceased by ties of blood or friendship are bound to assist as mourners; likewise, those whose families have been on unfriendly terms with the dead man now appear to ask his forgiveness.

The corpse must remain exposed a full day and night in the chamber of death, and during that time must never be left alone, nor should the lamentations be suffered to cease for a single moment. For this reason it is customary to have hired women to act the part of mourners, by relieving each other at intervals in singing the mourning songs. Often the deceased himself, in his last testamentary disposition, has ordered the details of his funeral, and fixed the payment—sometimes very considerable—which the mourning women are to receive.

The men related to the deceased are also bound to spend the night in the house, keeping watch over the corpse. This is called keeping the *privegghia*, which, however, has not necessarily a mournful character, as they mostly pass the time with various games, or else seated at table with food and wine.

Before the funeral the priest is called in, who, reciting the words of the fiftieth psalm, pours wine over the corpse. After this the coffin is closed, and must not be reopened unless the deceased be suspected to have died of a violent death, in which case the man accused of the crime is confronted with the corpse of his supposed victim, whose wounds will, at his sight, begin to bleed afresh.

In many places two openings corresponding to the ears of the deceased are cut in the wood of the coffin, to enable him to hear the songs of mourning which are sung on either side of him as he is carried to the grave. This singing into the ears has passed into a proverb, and when the Roumanian says, "*I-a-cantat la urechia*" (they have sung into his ear), it is tantamount to saying that prayer, advice, and remonstrance have all been used in vain.

Whoever dies unmarried must not be carried by married bearers to the grave: a married man or woman is carried by married men, and a youth by other youths, while a maiden is carried by other maidens with hanging, dishevelled hair. In every case the rank of the bearer should correspond to that of the deceased, and a fruntas can as little be carried by mylocasi as the bearers of a codas may be higher than himself in rank.

In many villages no funeral takes place in the forenoon, as the people believe that the soul will reach its destination more easily by following the march of the sinking sun.

The mass for the departed soul should, if possible, be said in the open air; and when the coffin is lowered into the grave, the earthen jar containing the water in which the corpse has been washed must be shattered to atoms on the spot.

A thunder-storm during the funeral denotes that another death will shortly follow.

It is often customary to place bread and wine on the fresh grave-mound; and in the case of young people, small fir-trees or gay-colored flags are placed beside the cross, to which in the case of a shepherd a tuft of wool is always attached.

Seven copper coins, and seven loaves of bread with a lighted candle sticking in each, are often distributed to seven poor people at the grave. This also is intended to signify the tolls to be cleared on the way to heaven.

In some places it is usual for the procession returning from a funeral to take its way through a river or stream of running water, sometimes going a mile or two out of their way to avoid all bridges, thus making sure that the vagrant soul of the beloved deceased will not follow them back to the house.

Earth taken from a fresh grave-mound and laid behind the neck at night will bring pleasant dreams; it may also serve as a cure for fever if made use of in the following manner: The person afflicted with fever repairs to the grave of some beloved relative, where, calling upon the defunct in the most tender terms, he begs of him or her the loan of a winding-sheet for a strange and unwelcome guest. Taking, then, from the grave a handful of earth, which he is careful to tie up tightly and place inside his shirt, the sick man goes away, and for three days and nights he carries this talisman about with him wherever he goes. On the fourth day he returns to the grave by a different route, and replacing the earth on the mound, thanks the dead man for the service rendered.

A still more efficacious remedy for fever is to lay a string or thread the exact length of your own body into the coffin of some one newly deceased, saying these words, " May I shiver only when this dead man shivers." Sore eyes may be cured by anointing them with the dew gathered off the grass of the grave of a just man on a fine evening in early spring; and a bone taken from the deceased's right arm will cure boils and sores by its touch. Whoever would keep sparrows off his field must between eleven o'clock and midnight collect earth from off seven different graves and scatter it over his field; while the same earth, if thrown over a dog addicted to hunting, will cure him of this defect.

The *pomeana,* or funeral feast, is invariably held after the funeral, for much of the peace of the defunct depends upon the strict observance of this ancient custom. All the favorite dishes of the dead man are served at this banquet, and each guest receives a cake, a jug of wine, and a wax candle in his memory. Similar pomeanas are repeated after a fortnight, six weeks, and on each anniversary of the death for the next seven years. On the first anniversary it is usual to bring bread and wine to the church-yard. The bread is distributed to the poor, and the wine poured down through the earth into the grave.

During six weeks after the funeral the women of the family let their hair hang uncombed and unplaited in sign of mourning. It is, moreover, no uncommon thing for Roumanians to bind themselves down to a mourning of ten or twenty years, or even for life, in memory of some beloved deceased one. Thus in one of the villages there still lived, two years ago, an old man who for the last forty years had worn no head-covering, summer or winter, in memory of his only son, who had died in early youth.

In the case of a man who has died a violent death, or in general of all such as have expired without a light, none of these ceremonies take place. Such a man has neither right to bocete, privegghia, mass, or pomeana, nor is his body laid in consecrated ground. He is buried wherever the body may be found, on the bleak hill-side or in the heart of the forest where he met his death, his last resting-place only marked by a heap of dry branches, to which each passer-by is expected to add by throwing a handful of twigs — usually a thorny branch — on the spot. This handful of thorns—*o mână de spini,* as the Roumanian calls it—being the only mark of attention to which the deceased can lay claim, therefore to the mind of this people no thought is so dreadful as that of dying deprived of light.

The attentions due to such as have received orthodox burial often extend even beyond the first seven years after death; for whenever the defunct appears in a dream to any of the family, this likewise calls for another pomeana, and when this condition is not complied with, the soul thus neglected is apt to wander complaining about the earth, unable to find rest.

This restlessness on the part of the defunct may either be caused by his having concealed treasures during his lifetime, in which case he is doomed to haunt the place where he has hidden his riches until they are discovered; or else he may have died with some secret sin on his conscience—such, for instance, as having removed the boundary stone from a neighbor's field in order to enlarge his own. He will then probably be compelled to pilger about with a sack of the stolen earth on his back until he has succeeded in selling the whole of it to the people he meets in his nightly wanderings.

These restless spirits, called *strigoi*, are not malicious, but their appearance bodes no good, and may be regarded as omens of sickness or misfortune.

More decidedly evil is the *nosferatu*, or vampire, in which every Roumanian peasant believes as firmly as he does in heaven or hell. There are two sorts of vampires, living and dead. The living vampire is generally the illegitimate offspring of two illegitimate persons; but even a flawless pedigree will not insure any one against the intrusion of a vampire into their family vault, since every person killed by a nosferatu becomes likewise a vampire after death, and will continue to suck the blood of other innocent persons till the spirit has been exorcised by opening the grave of the suspected person, and either driving a stake through the corpse, or else firing a pistol-shot into the coffin. To walk smoking round the grave on each anniversary of the death is also supposed to be effective in confining the vampire. In very obstinate cases of vampirism it is recommended to cut off the head, and replace it in the coffin with the mouth filled with garlic, or to extract the heart and burn it, strewing its ashes over the grave.

That such remedies are often resorted to even now is a well-attested fact, and there are probably few Roumanian villages where such have not taken place within memory of the inhabitants. There is likewise no Roumanian village which does not count among its inhabitants some old woman (usually a midwife) versed in the precautions to be taken in order to counteract vampires, and who makes of this science a flourishing trade. She is frequently called in by the family who has lost a member, and requested to "settle" the corpse securely in its coffin, so as to insure it against wandering. The means by which she endeavors to counteract any vampire-like instincts which may be lurking are various. Sometimes she drives a nail through the forehead of the deceased, or else rubs the body with the fat of a pig which has been killed on the Feast of St. Ignatius, five days before Christmas. It is also very usual to lay the thorny branch of a wild-rose bush across the body to prevent it leaving the coffin.

First-cousin to the vampire, the long-exploded were-wolf of the Germans, is here to be found lingering under the name of *prikolitsch.* Sometimes it is a dog instead of a wolf whose form a man has taken, or been compelled to take, as penance for his sins. In one village a story is still told—and believed—of such a man, who, driving home one Sunday with his wife, suddenly felt that the time for his transformation had come. He therefore gave over the reins to her and stepped aside into the bushes, where, murmuring the mystic formula, he turned three somersaults over a ditch. Soon after, the woman, waiting vainly for her husband, was attacked by a furious dog, which rushed barking out of the bushes and succeeded in biting her severely as well as tearing her dress. When, an hour or two later, the woman reached home after giving up her husband as lost, she was surprised to see him come smiling to meet her; but when between his teeth she caught sight of the shreds of her dress bitten out by the dog, the horror of this discovery caused her to faint away.

Another man used gravely to assert that for several years he had gone about in the form of a wolf, leading on a troop of these animals, till a hunter, in striking off his head, restored him to his natural shape.

This superstition once proved nearly fatal to a harmless botanist, who, while collecting plants on a hill-side many years ago, was observed by some peasants, and, in consequence of his crouching attitude, mistaken for a wolf. Before they had time to reach him, however, he had risen to his feet and disclosed himself in the form of a man; but this in the minds of the Roumanians, who now regarded him as an aggravated case of wolf, was but additional motive for attacking him. They were quite sure that he must be a prikolitsch, for only such could change his shape in this unaccountable manner; and in another minute they were all in full cry after the wretched victim of science, who might have fared badly indeed had he not succeeded in gaining a carriage on the high-road before his pursuers came up.

I once inquired of an old Saxon woman, whom I had visited with a view to extracting various pieces of superstitious information, whether she had ever come across a prikolitsch herself.

"Bless you!" she said, "when I was young there was no village without two or three of them at least, but now there seem to be fewer."

"So there is no prikolitsch in this village?" I asked, feeling particularly anxious to make the acquaintance of a real live were-wolf.

"No," she answered, doubtfully, "not that I know of for certain, though of course there is no saying with those Roumanians. But close by here in the next street, round the corner, there lives the widow of a prikolitsch whom I knew. She is still a young woman, and lost her husband five or six years ago. In ordinary life he was a quiet enough fellow, rather weak and sickly-looking; but sometimes he used to disappear for a week or ten days at a time, and though his wife tried to deceive people by telling them that her husband was lying drunk in the loft, of course we knew better, for those were the times when he used to be away *wolving* in the mountains."

Thinking that the relict of a were-wolf was the next best thing to the were-wolf himself, I determined on paying my respects to the interesting widow; but on reaching her house the door was closed, and I had the cruel disappointment of learning that Madame Prikolitsch was not at home.

We do not require to go far for the explanation of the extraordinary tenacity of the were-wolf legend in a country like Transylvania, where real wolves still abound. Every winter here brings fresh proof of the boldness and cunning of these terrible animals, whose attacks on flocks and farms are often conducted with a skill which would do honor to a human intellect. Sometimes a whole village is kept in trepidation for weeks together by some particularly audacious leader of a flock of wolves, to whom the peasants not unnaturally attribute a more than animal nature; and it is safe to prophesy that as long as the flesh-and-blood wolf continues to haunt the Transylvanian forests, so long will his spectre brother survive in the minds of the people.

CHAPTER XXVI.

ROUMANIAN SUPERSTITION : DAYS AND HOURS.

Grimm has said that "superstition in all its multifariousness constitutes a species of religion applicable to all the common household necessities of daily life;"* and if we view it as such, particular forms of superstition may very well serve as guide to the character and habits of the particular nation in which they are prevalent. In Transylvania, however, the task of classifying all the superstitions that come under our notice is a peculiarly hard one, for perhaps nowhere else does this curious crooked plant of delusion flourish so persistently and in such bewildering variety as in the land beyond the forest; and it would almost seem as though the whole species of demons, pixies, witches, and hobgoblins, driven from the rest of Europe by the wand of science, had taken refuge within this mountain rampart, aware that here they would find secure lurking-places whence to defy their persecutors yet a while.

There are many reasons why such fabulous beings should retain an abnormally firm hold on the soil of these parts, and looking at the matter closely, we find no less than three distinct sources of superstition :

First, there is what may be called the indigenous superstition of the country, the scenery of which is particularly adapted to serve as background to all sorts of supernatural beings. There are innumerable caverns whose depths seem made to harbor whole legions of evil spirits; forest glades, fit only for fairy folk on moonlight nights; solitary lakes, which instinctively call up visions of water-sprites; golden treasures lying hidden in mountain chasms—all of which things have gradually insinuated themselves into the minds of the oldest inhabitants, the Roumanians, so that these people, by nature imaginative and poetically inclined, have built up for themselves, out of the sur-

---

* "Der Aberglaube in seiner bunten Mannigfaltigkeit bildet gewissermassen eine Religion für den ganzen neideren Hausbedarf."

rounding materials, a whole code of fanciful superstition, to which they adhere as closely as to their religion itself.

Secondly, there is here the imported superstition—that is to say, the old German customs and beliefs brought hither by the Saxon colonists from their native land, and, like many other things, preserved here in greater perfection than in the original country.

Thirdly, there is the influence of the wandering superstition of the gypsy tribes, themselves a race of fortune-tellers and witches, whose ambulatory caravans cover the country as with a net-work, and whose less vagrant members fill up the suburbs of towns and villages.

All these kinds of superstition have twined and intermingled, acted and reacted upon each other, so that in many cases it becomes a difficult matter to determine the exact parentage of some particular belief or custom; but in a general way the three sources I have named may be admitted as a rough sort of classification in dealing with the principal superstitions here afloat.

Few races offer such an interesting field for research in their folk-lore as the Roumanians, in whose traditions we find side by side elements of Celtic, Slav, and Roman mythology—a subject well worth a closer attention than it has hitherto received. The existence of the Celtic element has been explained by the assumption (believed by many historians to be well founded), that as the present Roumanians are a mixed race originating in the fusion of Romans with Dacians, so were these latter themselves a complex nationality composed of Slav and Celtic ingredients.

The spirit of evil—or, not to put too fine a point on it, the devil—plays a conspicuous part in the Roumanian code of superstition, and such designations as *Gaura Draculuj** (devil's hole), *Gregyna Draculuj* (devil's garden), *Jadu Draculuj* (devil's abyss), frequently found attached to rocks, caverns, and heights, attest that these people believe themselves to be surrounded on all sides by whole legions of evil spirits. These devils are furthermore assisted by *ismejus* (another sort of dragon), witches, and goblins, and to each of these dangerous beings are ascribed particular powers on particular days and

---

* *Dracu*, which in Roumanian does duty for the word devil, really means dragon; as for devil proper the word is wanting.

One writer, speaking of the Roumanians, observes that they swear by the dragon, which gives their oaths a painful sense of unreality.

at certain places. Many and curious are therefore the means by which the Roumanians endeavor to counteract these baleful influences; and a whole complicated study, about as laborious as the mastering of an unknown language, is required in order to teach an unfortunate peasant to steer clear of the dangers by which he supposes himself to be beset on all sides. The bringing up of a common domestic cow is apparently as difficult a task as the rearing of any " dear gazelle," and even the well-doing of a simple turnip or potato about as precarious as that of the most tender exotic plant.

Of the seven days of the week, Wednesday (Miercuri) and Friday (Vinere) are considered suspicious days, on which it is not allowed to use needle or scissors, or to bake bread ; neither is it wise to sow flax on these days. No bargain should ever be concluded on a Friday; and Venus (here called Paraschiva), to whom the Friday is sacred, punishes all infractions of this rule by causing conflagrations.

Tuesday, however—or Marti, named from Mars, the bloody god of war — is a decidedly unlucky day, on which spinning is utterly prohibited; and even such seemingly harmless actions as washing the hands and combing the hair are not unattended by danger. About sunset on Tuesday the evil spirit of that day is at its fullest force, and many people refrain from leaving their huts between sunset and midnight. "May the *mar sara* (spirit of Tuesday evening) carry you off !" is here equivalent to saying, "May the devil take you !"

It must not, however, be supposed that Monday, Thursday, and Saturday are unconditionally lucky days, on which the Roumanian is at liberty to do as he pleases. Thus every well-informed Roumanian matron knows that she may wash on Thursday and spin on Saturday, but that it would be a fatal mistake to reverse the order of these proceedings; and though Thursday is a lucky day for marriage,* and is on that account mostly chosen for weddings, it is proportionately unfavorable to agriculture. In many places it is considered unsafe to work in the fields on all Thursdays between Easter and Pentecost, for it is believed that if these days be not kept as days of rest, ravaging hail-storms will be the inevitable consequence. Many of the more enlightened Roumanian popas have preached in vain against this belief; and some years ago the inhabitants of a village presented an

---

* This would seem to suggest a German or Scandinavian element—the thunder-god Donar, or Thor, who with his hammer confirms unions.

official complaint to the bishop, requesting the removal of their popa, on the ground that he not only gave scandal by working on the prohibited days, but had actually caused them serious material damage by the hail-storms his sinful behavior had provoked. This respect of the Thursday would seem to be the result of a deeply rooted, though now unconscious, worship of Jupiter (Joi), who gives his name to the day.

To different hours of the day are likewise ascribed different influences, favorable or the reverse. Thus it is always considered unlucky to look at one's self in the mirror after sunset; neither is it wise to sweep dust over the threshold in the evening, or to restore a whip borrowed of a neighbor. The exact hour of noon is precarious, because of the evil spirit *Pripolniza;** and so is midnight, because of the *miase nopte* (night spirit); and it is safer to remain in-doors at these hours. If, however, some misguided peasant does happen to leave his home at midnight, and espies (as very likely he may) a flaming dragon in the sky, he need not necessarily give himself up as lost, for if he have the presence of mind to stick a fork into the ground alongside of him, the fiery monster will thereby be prevented from carrying him off.

The advent of the new moon is always more or less fraught with danger, and nothing may be sown or planted at that time.

The Oriental Church has an abnormal number of feast-days, to each of which peculiar customs and superstitions are attached, a few of which may here find place.

On New-year's Day it is customary for the Roumanian to interrogate his fate by placing a leaf of evergreen on the freshly swept and heated hearth-stone. If the leaf takes a gyratory movement, he will be lucky; but if it shrivels up where it lies, then he may expect misfortune during the coming year.† To insure the welfare of the cattle, it is advisable to place a gold or silver piece in the water-trough out of which they drink for the first time on New-year's morning.

The Feast of the Epiphany, or Three Kings (*tre crai*), is one of the oldest festivals, and was solemnized by the Oriental Church as

---

* This spirit corresponds to the Poledniue of the Bohemians and the Poludnica of Poles and Russians. Grimm, in speaking of the Russians in his "German Mythology," quotes from Boschorn's "Resp. Moscov.:" "Dæmonem quoque meridianum Moscovitæ et colunt."

† Also practised by the Saxons.

early as the second century. On this day, which popular belief regards as the coldest in the winter, the blessing of the waters, known as the Feast of the *Jordan* or *Bobetasu* (baptism), takes place. The priests, attired in full vestments, proceed to the shore of the nearest river or lake, and there bless the waters, which have been unclosed by cutting a Greek cross, some six to eight feet long, in the ice. Every pious Roumanian is careful to fill a bottle with this consecrated water before the surface freezes over again, and keeps it tightly corked and sealed up, as a remedy in case of illness. On this day the principal food in most Roumanian houses consists of a sort of jelly; and in the evening the popa, coming to each house in order to bless the cattle, which he does by sprinkling holy-water with a bunch of wild basil-weed,* finds a table with food and drink awaiting him, from which a dish of boiled plums must never be wanting.

He who dies on that day is considered particularly lucky, for he will be sure to go straight to heaven, the gate of which is believed to stand open all day, in memory of the descent of the Holy Ghost at the baptism of Christ.

The Feast of St. Theodore, January 11th (corresponding to our 23d of January), is a day of rest for the girls, those transgressing this rule being liable to be carried off by the saint, who sometimes appears in the shape of a beautiful youth, sometimes in that of a terrible monster. No decent girl should leave her house unescorted on this day, for fear of the terrible Theodore.† In some districts youths and maidens choose this day for swearing friendship, which bonds are inaugurated by a tree being hung over with little circular cakes, and danced round with songs and music, after which each cake is broken in two and divided between a youth and a maiden.‡

On the Wednesday in Holy Week the Easter loaves and cakes are baked, which next day are blessed, and some of the hallowed crumbs mixed up with the cows' fodder. Woe to the woman who indulges in a nap to-day; for the whole year she will not be able to shake off her drowsiness. In the evening the young men bind as many wreaths as

---

* This plant, *Ocimum basilicum*, is much used by the Roumanians, who ascribe to it both medicinal and magic properties.

† The Serbs have also a corresponding day, called the Theodor Saturday (*Todoroma Sumbota*), on which no work is done, on account of the sintotere, a monster, half man half horse, who rides upon whoever falls in his power.

‡ Similar customs exist among the Hindoos, Slavs, and Serbs.

there are persons in their family, and each of these, marked with the name of an individual, is thrown up on the roof, the wreaths which fall to the ground indicating those who will die that year.

Skin diseases are cured by taking a bath on Good Friday in a stream or river which flows towards the east. This will not only cure the patient, but prevent the disease recurring within the year.*

In the night preceding Easter Sunday witches and demons are abroad, and hidden treasures are said to betray their site by a glowing flame. No God-fearing peasant will, however, allow himself to be tempted by the hope of such riches, which he cannot on that day appropriate without sin. He must not omit to attend the midnight church-service, and his devotion will be rewarded by the mystic qualities attached to the wax candle he has carried in his hand, and which, when lighted hereafter during a thunder-storm, will keep the lightning from striking his house.

The greatest luck which can befall a mortal is to be born on Easter Sunday, and this luck is increased if the birth take place at mid-day when the bells are ringing; but it is not lucky to die on that day.

Egg-shells are glued up against the doors in memory of the Israelites, who anointed the door-posts with the lambs' blood at their flight from Egypt; and the wooden spoon with which the Easter eggs have been removed from the boiling pot is carefully treasured up by each shepherd, for, worn in his belt, it gives him the power to distinguish the witches who seek to molest his flocks. Witches may also be descried by the man who on Easter Monday takes up his stand on a bridge above running water, remaining there from sunrise to sunset.

Perhaps the most important day in the Roumanian's year is that of St. George, April 24th (May 6th), the eve of which is said to be still frequently kept up by occult meetings taking place at night in lonely caverns or within ruined walls, and where all the ceremonies usual to the celebration of a witches' Sabbath are put into practice. This night is the great one to beware of witches, to counteract whose influence square-cut blocks of turf (to which are sometimes added thorny branches) are placed in front of each door and window.† This is supposed effectually to bar their entrance to house or stables; but for still greater precaution it is usual for the peasants to keep watch all night

---

* Also believed by most Slav races.

† Also usual in Moldavia.

13

near the sleeping cattle. This same night is likewise the best one for seeking treasures.

The Feast of St. George, being the day when most flocks are first driven out to pasture, is in a special manner the feast of all shepherds and cow-herds, and on this day only is it allowed for the Roumanian shepherd to count his flocks and assure himself of the exact number of sheep—these numbers being, in general, but approximately guessed at and vaguely described. Thus, when interrogated as to the number of his master's sheep, the Roumanian shepherd will probably inform you that they are as numerous as the stars of heaven, or as the daisies which dot the meadows.

The custom of throwing up wreaths on to the roof, as described above, is in some districts practised on the Feast of St. John the Baptist, June 24th (July 6th), instead of on the Wednesday in Holy Week. This is the day when the sun, having reached its zenith, begins its backward course (according to the people) with a trembling, dancing movement, in the same way as the sun is said to dance on Easter Sunday. The gate-way of each house is decorated with a wreath of field-flowers; and at night fires lighted on the mountain heights are supposed to keep away evil spirits from the flocks. This custom of the St. John fires is, however, to be found in many other countries, and is undoubtedly a remnant of the old sun-worship practised by Greeks, Romans, Scandinavians, Celts, Slavs, Indians, Parsees, etc.

The Feast of St. Elias, July 20th (August 1st), is a very unlucky day, on which the lightning may be expected to strike.* Every year —so we are told in an ancient legend—St. Elias appears in heaven before the throne of the Almighty, and humbly inquires when his feast-day is to be. He is invariably put off with divers excuses, being sometimes told that his feast-day has not yet come, sometimes that the date for it is already past. At this the saint grows angry, and wishing to punish the human race for thus forgetting him, he hurls down his thunderbolts upon the earth.

The Feast of St. Spiridion, December 13th (January 24th), is an ominous day, especially for housewives; and this saint often destroys those who desecrate his feast by manual labor.

---

* St. Elias is also known in Serbia as "Thunderer;" Bohemians and Russians have a thunder-god named Perum; the Poles, Piorun; the old Russians had Perkun, and the Lithuanians Perkunos—all of which may be assumed to be derived from the Indian sun-god, Surjar, or Mihirar, who, as personification of fire, is also named Perus.

That the cattle are endowed with speech during the Christmas night is a general belief, but it is not considered wise to pry upon them, or try to overhear what they say, as the listener will rarely overhear any good. This night is likewise favorable to the discovery of hidden treasures, and the man who has courage to conjure up the evil one will be sure to see him if he call upon him at midnight. Three burning coals placed on the threshold will prevent the devil from carrying him off.

A round cake baked at Christmas goes by the name of the *rota* (wheel), and is probably symbolic of the sun's rotation.

The girl whose thoughts are turned towards love and matrimony has many approved methods of testing her fate on the new-year's night. First of all, she may, by cracking her finger-joints, accurately ascertain the number of her admirers; also a fresh-laid egg broken into a glass of water will give much clew to the events in store for her by the shape it assumes; and a swine's bristle stuck in a straw and thrown on the heated hearth-stone is reliable as a talisman which disperses love or jealousy.* To form a conjecture as to the figure and build of her future husband, she is recommended to throw an armful of firewood as far as she can backward over her shoulder; the piece which has gone farthest will be the image of her intended, according as the stick happens to be long or short, broad or slender, straight or crooked.

Another such game is to place on the table a row of earthen pots upside down. Under each of these is concealed something different —as corn, salt, wool, coals, or money—and the girl is desired to make her choice; thus money stands for a rich husband, and wool for an old one; corn signifies an agriculturist, and salt connubial happiness; but coals are prophetic of misfortune.

If these general indications do not suffice, and the maiden desire to see the reflection of her bridegroom's face in the water, she has only to step naked at midnight into the nearest lake or river; or if she not unnaturally shrink from this chilly oracle, let her take her stand on the more congenial dunghill, with a piece of Christmas cake in her mouth, and, as the clock strikes twelve, listen attentively for

---

* Swine have been regarded as sacred animals by various people, which is probably the explanation of the German expression of *sauglück* (sow's luck), and of the *glückschweinchen* (little luck-pigs) which have lately become fashionable as charms to hang to the watch-chain.

the first sound of a dog's bark which reaches her ear. From whichever side it proceeds will also come the expected suitor.

It is likewise on the last day of the year that the agriculturist seeks a prognostic of the weather for the coming year, by making what is called the onion calendar, which consists in putting salt into twelve hollowed-out onions and giving to each the name of a month. Those onions in which the salt has melted by the following morning will be rainy months.*

CHAPTER XXVII.

ROUMANIAN SUPERSTITION—CONTINUED : ANIMALS, WEATHER, MIXED SUPERSTITIONS, SPIRITS, SHADOWS, ETC.

Of the household animals the sheep is the most highly prized by the Roumanian, who makes of it his companion, and frequently his oracle, as by its bearing it is often supposed to give warning when danger is near.

The swallows here, as elsewhere, are luck-bringing birds, and go by the name of *galinele lui Dieu* — fowls of the Lord. There is always a treasure to be found where the first swallow has been espied.

The crow, on the contrary, is a bird of evil omen, and is particularly ominous when it flies straight over the head of any man.†

The magpie, when perched on a roof, gives notice of the approach of guests,‡ but a shrieking magpie meeting or accompanying a traveller denotes death.

The cuckoo is an oracle to be consulted in manifold contingencies. This bird plays a great part in Roumanian poetry, and is frequently supposed to be the spirit of an unfortunate lover.

It is never permissible to kill a spider, but a toad taking up its residence in a cow-byre should be stoned to death, as assuredly standing in the service of a witch, and sent there to purloin the milk.

The same liberty must not, however, be taken with the equally pernicious weasel, and when these animals are found to inhabit a barn or stable, the peasant endeavors to render them harmless by diverting

---

* Also practised by the Saxons. † Likewise in Bavaria.
‡ Believed by most Slav races.

their thoughts into a safer channel. To this end a tiny thrashing-flail is prepared for the male weasel, and a distaff for his female partner, and these are laid at some place the animals are known to frequent.

Those houses which can boast of a house-snake are particularly lucky.* Food is regularly placed for it near the hole; and killing it would entail dire misfortune to the family.

The skull of a horse placed over the gate of the court-yard,† or the bones of fallen animals buried under the door-step, are preservatives against ghosts.

The place where a horse has rolled on the ground is unwholesome, and the man who steps upon it will be visited by eruptions, boils, or other skin diseases.

Black fowls are always viewed with suspicion, as possibly standing in the service of a witch; and the Brahmapootra fowl is, curiously enough, believed to be the offspring of the devil and a Jewish girl.

The best remedy for a murrain among the cattle is with an axe to behead a living pig, hoisting up its head on the end of a long pole at the village entrance. This, however, is only efficacious when it is the cattle or sheep which are thus afflicted; and should an illness have broken out among the swine themselves, the only remedy for it will be for the herd, divested of his clothes, to lead his drove to pasture in the early morning.‡

The skull of a ram is often stuck up at the boundary of a parish, and if turned towards the east is supposed to be efficacious in keeping off cattle diseases.

A cow that has wandered can be insured against wolves if the owner recollect to stick a pair of scissors in the centre cross-beam of the dwelling-room.

A whirlwind always denotes that the devil is dancing with a witch, and whoever approaches too near to the dangerous circle may be carried off bodily to hell, and sometimes only barely escapes by losing his cap.

As a matter of course, such places as church-yards, gallows-trees,

---

* Likewise in Poland.
† The original signification of this seems to have gone astray, but was probably based on some former worship of the horse, long regarded as a sacred animal by Indians, Parsees, Arabs, and Germans.
‡ See "Saxon Superstition," chap. xxix.

and cross-roads are to be avoided; but even the left bank of a river may, under circumstances, become equally dangerous.

The finger which points at a rainbow will be seized by a gnawing disease, and a rainbow appearing in December always bodes misfortune. Pointing at an approaching thunder-storm is also considered unsafe, and whoever stands over-long gazing at the summer lightning will go mad.

If a house struck by lightning begins to burn, it is not allowed to put out the flames, because God has lit the fire, and it were presumption for man to dare meddle with his work.* In some places it is supposed that a fire kindled by lightning can only be extinguished with milk.

An approved method for averting the lightning from striking a house is to form a top by sticking a knife through a loaf of bread, and spin it on the floor of the loft while the storm lasts. The ringing of bells is also efficacious in dispersing a storm, provided, however, that the bell in question has been cast under a perfectly cloudless sky.

As I am on the subject of thunder-storms, I may as well here mention the *scholomance*, or school, supposed to exist somewhere in the heart of the mountains, and where the secrets of nature, the language of animals, and all magic spells are taught by the devil in person. Only ten scholars are admitted at a time, and when the course of learning has expired, and nine of them are released to return to their homes, the tenth scholar is detained by the devil as payment, and, mounted upon an *ismeju*, or dragon, becomes henceforward the devil's aide-de-camp, and assists him in "making the weather"—that is, preparing the thunder-bolts.

A small lake, immeasurably deep, and lying high up in the mountains to the south of Hermanstadt, is supposed to be the caldron where is brewed the thunder, under whose water the dragon lies sleeping in fair weather. Roumanian peasants anxiously warn the traveller to beware of throwing a stone into this lake, lest it should wake the dragon and provoke a thunder-storm. It is, however, no mere superstition that in summer there occur almost daily thunder-storms at this spot, and numerous stone cairns on the shores attest the fact that many people have here found their death by lightning. On this account

---

* Also believed by most Slav races.

the place is shunned, and no true Roumanian will venture to rest here at the hour of noon.

Whoever turns three somersaults the first time he hears the thunder will be free from pains in the back during a twelvemonth; and the man who wishes to be insured against headache has only to rub his forehead with a piece of iron or stone on that same occasion.

A comet is sign of war; and an earthquake denotes that the fish on which the earth is supposed to rest has moved. Another version informs us that originally the world was balanced on the backs of four fishes, one of which was drowned in the flood, so that the earth, now lacking support at one corner, has sunk down and is covered by the sea.

The Slàv custom of decking out a girl at harvest-time with a wreath of corn-ears, and leading her in procession to the house of the priest or the landed proprietor, is likewise practised here, with the difference that, instead of the songs customary in Poland, the girl is here followed by loud shouts of *Prihu! Prihu!* or else *Priku!** and that whoever meets her on the way is bound to sprinkle her with water. If this detail be neglected, the next year's crops will assuredly fail. It is also customary to keep the wreaths till next sowing-time, when the corn, if shaken out and mingled with the grain to be sown afresh, will insure a rich harvest.

Every fresh-baked loaf of wheaten bread is sacred, and should a piece inadvertently fall to the ground, it is hastily picked up, carefully wiped and kissed, and if soiled thrown into the fire—partly as an offering to the dead, and partly because it were a heavy sin to throw away or tread upon any particle of it.

It is unfortunate to meet an old woman or a Roumanian popa, but the meeting of a Catholic or Protestant clergyman is indifferent, and brings neither good nor evil.

To be met by a gypsy the first thing in the morning is particularly lucky.

It is bad-luck if your path be traversed by a hare, but a fox or wolf crossing the way is a good omen.

Likewise, it is lucky to meet a woman with a jugful of water,

---

* Archæologists have derived this word from *Pri*, which in Sanscrit means fruitful, and *Hu*, the god of the Celtic deluge tradition, and likewise regarded as the personification of fruitful nature.

while an empty jug or pail is unlucky; therefore the Roumanian maiden meeting you on the way back from the well will smilingly display her brimming pitcher as she passes, with a pleased consciousness of bringing good-luck; while the girl whose pitcher is empty will slink past shamefacedly, as though she had a crime to conceal.

The Roumanian is always very particular about the exact way he meets any one. If he happens to be placed to the right of the comer, he will be careful not to cross over to the left, or *vice versa.* Should, however, his way lead him straight across the path of another higher in rank, he will stop and wait till the latter has passed. These precautions are taken in order not to cut or disturb the thread of a person's good-luck.

Every orthodox Roumanian woman is careful to do homage to the *wodna zena,* or *zona,* residing in each spring, by spilling a few drops on the ground after she has filled her jug, and it is regarded as an insult to offer drink to a Roumanian without observing this ceremony. She will never venture to draw water against the current, for that would strike the spirit home and provoke her anger, nor is it allowable, without very special necessity, to draw water in the night-time; and whoever is obliged to do so should nowise neglect to blow three times over the brimming jug to undo all evil spells, as well as to pour a few drops on to the glowing embers.

The vicinity of deep pools of water, more especially whirlpools, is to be avoided, for here resides the dreadful *balaur,* or the *wodna muz* —the cruel waterman who lies in wait for human victims.

Each forest has likewise its own particular spirit, its *mama padura,** or forest mother. This fairy is generally supposed to be good-natured, especially towards children who have lost their way in the wood.

Less to be trusted is *Panusch,†* who haunts the forest glades and lies in wait for helpless maidens.

In deep forests and wild mountain-gorges there wanders about a wild huntsman of superhuman size and mysterious personality, but rarely seen by living eyes. Oftenest he is met by huntsmen, to whom he has frequently given good advice. He once appeared to a peasant

---

* So in India the Matris, known also among Egyptians, Chaldeans, and Mexicans. A corresponding spirit is likewise found in Scandinavian and Lithuanian mythology; in the latter, under the name of the *medziajna.*

† Surely a corruption of "great Pan," who, it would seem, is not dead after all, but merely banished to the land beyond the forest.

who had already shot ninety-nine bears, and warned him now to desist, for no man can shoot the hundredth bear. But the passion for sport was too strong within the peasant ; so, disregarding the advice, he shot at the next bear he met, and missing his aim, was torn to pieces by the infuriated animal. Another hunter to whom he appeared learned from him the secret that if he loaded his gun on New-year's night with a live adder, the whole of that year he would never miss a shot.

Another and more malevolent forest-spectre is the wild man—or, as the Roumanian calls him, the *om ren*—usually seen in winter, when he is the terror of all hunters and shepherds. Whoever may be found dead in the forest is supposed to have fallen a prey to his vengeance, which pursues all such as venture to chase his deer and wild-boar, or approach too near the cavern where he resides. His rage sometimes takes the form of uprooting pine-trees, with which to strike dead the intruder ; or else he throws his victims down a precipice, or rolls down massive rocks on the top of them.

Oameni micuti (small men), as the Roumanian calls them, are gray-bearded dwarfs, who, attired like miners, with axe and lantern, haunt the Transylvanian gold and silver mines. They seldom do harm to a miner, but give warning to his wife when he has perished by three knocks on her door. They are, however, very quarrelsome among themselves, and may often be heard hitting at one another with their sharp axes, or blowing their horns as signal of battle.

Also the mountain monk plays a great part in mining districts, but is to be classed among the malevolent spirits. He delights in kicking over water-pails, putting out lamps, and breaking tools, and will sometimes even strangle or suffocate workmen to whom he has taken aversion. Occasionally, but rarely, he has been known to help distressed miners in replenishing the oil in their lamps, or guiding those who have lost their way ; but woe to the man who relates these circumstances, for he will be sure to suffer for it.

The *gana* is the name of a beautiful but malicious witch who presides over the evil spirits holding their meetings on the eve of the first of May. Gana is said to have been the mistress of Transylvania before the Christian era. Her beauty bewitched many ; but whoever succumbed to her charms, and let himself be lured into quaffing mead from her ure-ox drinking-horn, was doomed. Once the handsome Maldovan, the Roumanian national hero, when riding home from visiting his bride, waylaid by the siren, and beguiled into drinking from the horn, reached his mountain fortress a sick and dying man, and was a corpse before next morning.

Ravaging diseases like the pest, cholera, etc., are attributed to a spirit called the *dschuma*, to whom is sometimes given the shape of a toothless old hag, sometimes that of a fierce virgin, only to be appeased by the gift of clothing of some sort. Oftenest the spirit is supposed to be naked and suffering from cold, and its complaining voice may be heard at night crying out for clothing whenever the disease is at its highest. When this voice is heard, the inhabitants of a village hasten to comply with its summons by preparing the required clothing. Sometimes it is seven old women who are to spin, weave, and sew a scarlet shirt all in one night, and without breaking silence; sometimes the maidens are to make garments and hang them out at the entrance of the afflicted village. Mr. Paget mentions having once seen a coarse linen pair of trousers suspended by means of a rope straight across the road where he was driving, and on inquiring being informed that this was to pacify the cholera spirit.

Some places, moreover, can boast of a perpetually naked spirit, who requires a new suit of clothes every year. These are furnished by the inhabitants, who on each New-year's night lay them out in readiness near some place supposed to be haunted by the spirit.

In a Wallachian village in the county of Bihar, during the prevalence of the cholera in 1866, the following precautions were taken to protect the village from the epidemic : six maidens and six unmarried youths, having first laid aside their clothes, with a new ploughshare traced a furrow round the village, thus forming a charmed circle, over which the cholera demon was supposed to be unable to pass.

When the land is suffering from protracted and obstinate droughts, the Roumanian not unfrequently ascribes the evil to the Tziganes, who by occult means procure the dry weather in order to favor their own trade of brickmaking. In such cases, when the necessary rain has not been produced by soundly beating the guilty Tziganes, the peasants sometimes resort to the *papaluga*, or rain-maiden. This is done by stripping a young Tzigane girl quite naked, and dressing her up with garlands of flowers and leaves, which entirely cover her, leaving only the head visible. Thus adorned, the papaluga is conducted round the village to the sound of music, each person hastening to pour water over her as she passes. The part of the papaluga may also be enacted by Roumanian maidens, when there is no particular reason to suspect the Tziganes of being concerned in the drought. The custom of the rain-maiden is also to be found in Serbia, and I believe in Croatia.

Killing a frog is sometimes effectual in bringing on rain; but if this also fails in the desired effect, then the evil must evidently be of deeper nature, and is to be attributed to a vampire, who must be sought out and destroyed, as before described.

The body of a drowned man can be recovered only by sticking a lighted candle into a hollowed-out loaf of bread, and setting it afloat at night on the lake or river: there, where the light comes to a stand-still, the corpse will be found. Till this has been done the water will continue to rise and the rain to fall.

At the birth of a child each one present takes a stone and throws it behind him, saying, "This into the jaws of the strigoi"—a custom which would seem to suggest Saturn and the swaddled-up stones. As long as the child is unbaptized it must be carefully watched over for fear of being changed or harmed by a witch. A piece of iron or a broom laid beneath the pillow will keep spirits away.

Even the Roumanian's wedding-day is darkened by the shadow of superstition. He can never be sure of his affection for his bride being a natural, spontaneous feeling, since it may just as well have been caused by the influence of a witch; and he lives in anticipated dread lest the devil, in shape of a fiery comet, may appear any day to make love to his wife. Likewise at church, when the priest offers the blessed bread to the new-made couple, he will tremblingly compare the relative sizes of the two pieces, for whoever chances to get the smaller one will inevitably be the first to die.

Although it has been said of the Roumanian that his whole life is taken up in devising talismans against the devil, yet he does not always endeavor to keep the evil one at arm's-length—sometimes, on the contrary, directly invoking his aid, and entering into a regular compact with him.

Supposing, for instance, that a man wishes to insure a flock, garden, or field against thieves, wild beasts, or bad weather, the matter is very simple. He has only to repair to a cross-road, at the junction of which he takes his stand in the centre of a circle traced on the ground. Here, after depositing a copper coin as payment, he summons the demon with the following words:

"Satan, I give thee over my flock [garden, or field] to keep till——

[such and such a term], that thou mayst defend and protect it for me, and be my servant till this time has expired."

He must, however, be careful to keep within the circle traced until the devil, who may very likely have chosen to appear in the shape of a goat, crow, toad, or serpent, has completely disappeared, otherwise the unfortunate man is irretrievably lost. He is equally sure to lose his soul if he die before the time of the contract has elapsed.

As long as the contract lasts, the peasant may be sure of the devil's services, who for the time being will put a particular spirit—*spiridusui*—at his disposal. This spirit will serve him faithfully in every contingency; but in return he expects to be given the first mouthful of every dish partaken of by his master.*

Apothecaries in the towns say that they are often applied to for an unknown magic potion called *spiridusch* (that is, I suppose, a potion compelling the services of the demon *spiridusui*), said to have the property of disclosing hidden treasures to its lucky possessor. While I was at Hermanstadt, an apothecary there received the following letter, published in a local paper, and which I here give as literally as possible:

Worthy Sir,—I wish to ask you of something I have been told by others—that is, that you have got for sale a thing they call *spiridusch*, but which, to speak more plainly, is the devil himself; and if this be true, I beg you to tell me if it be really true, and how much it costs, for my poverty is so great that I must ask the devil himself to help me. Those who told me were weak, silly fellows, and were afraid; but I have no fear, and have seen many things in my life—therefore I pray you to write me this, and to take the greeting of an unknown and unhappy man. N. N.

Besides the tale of the Arghisch monastery which I have quoted in a former chapter, there are many other Roumanian legends which tell us how every new church, or otherwise important building, became a human grave, as it was thought indispensable to its stability to wall in a living man or woman, whose spirit henceforth haunted the place. In later times, people having become less cruel, or more prob-

---

* The ancients used likewise to cook for their household demons (*cœna dæmonum*).—Plaut. Pseudol. Also, the Hindoos prepared food for the house-spirit.

ably because murder is now attended with greater inconvenience to those concerned, this custom underwent some modifications, and it became usual, in place of a living man, to wall in his shadow. This is done by measuring the shadow of a person with a long piece of cord, or a tape made of strips of reed fastened together, and interring this measure instead of the person himself, who, unconscious victim of the spell thus cast upon him, will pine away and die within forty days. It is, however, an indispensable condition to the success of this proceeding that the chosen victim be ignorant of the part he is playing, wherefore careless passers-by near a building in process of erection may chance to hear the warning cry, " Beware lest they take thy shadow !" So deeply ingrained is this superstition that not long ago there were still professional shadow-traders, who made it their business to provide architects with the victims necessary for securing their walls. " Of course the man whose shadow is thus interred must die," argues the Roumanian, "but being unaware of his doom, he feels neither pain nor anxiety, so it is less cruel than to wall in a living man."

Similar to the legend of the Arghisch monastery is that told of the fortress of Deva, in Transylvania, which twelve architects had undertaken to build for the price of half a quarter of silver and half a quarter of gold. They set to work, but what they built each morning fell in before sunset, and what they built overnight was in ruins by next morning. Then they held counsel as to what was to be done in order to give strength to the building; and so it was resolved to seize the first of their wives who should come to visit her husband, and, burning her alive, mix up her ashes with the mortar to be used in building.

Soon after this the wife of Kelemen, the architect, resolving to visit her husband, ordered the carriage to be got ready. On the way she is overtaken by a heavy thunder-storm, and the coachman, an old family servant, warns her against proceeding, for he has had an ominous dream regarding her. She, however, persists in her resolve, and soon comes in sight of the building. Her husband, on seeing her, prays to God that the carriage might break down or the horses fall lame, in order to hinder her arrival; but all is in vain, and the carriage soon reaches its destination. The sorrowing husband now reveals to his wife the terrible fate in store for her, to which she resigns herself, only begging leave to say farewell to her little son and her friends. This favor is granted, and returning the following day, she is burned.

Her ashes mixed with the mortar give solidity to the walls; the building is completed, and the architects obtain the high price for which they had contracted.

Meanwhile the unhappy widower, returning home, is questioned by his little son as to where his mother stays so long. At first the father is evasive, but subsequently confesses the truth, on learning which the child falls dead of a broken heart.

Also, at Hermanstadt we are shown a point in the old town wall where a live student, dressed in *ampel* and *toga*, the costume of those days, was walled in, in order to "make fast" the fortified wall.

If we compare these legends with the traditions of other countries we find many instances of a like belief: so at Arta, in Albania, where, according to Grimm, a thousand masons labored in vain at a bridge, whose walls invariably crumbled away overnight. There was heard the voice of an archangel saying, "If ye do not wall in a living person the bridge will never stand; neither an orphan nor yet a stranger shall it be, but the own wife of the master builder." The master loves his wife, but yet stronger is his ambition to see his name made famous by the bridge; so when his wife comes to the spot he pretends to have dropped a ring in the foundations, and asks her to seek for it, in doing which she is seized upon and walled up. In dying she speaks a curse upon the bridge, that it may ever tremble like the head of a flower on its stalk.

In Serbia there is a similar legend of the fortress Skoda; and at Magdeburg, in Germany, the same is told of Margaretha, bondwoman of the Empress Editha, wife of the Emperor Otto, who voluntarily gave up her illegitimate child to be walled up in the gate-way of the newly fortified town. Fifty years later, devoured by remorse, Margaretha appears before the judges to confess her crime, and crave Christian burial for the bones of her child. The wall being now opened at the place she indicates, there steps forth a small wizened figure with long, tangled gray beard and shrunken limbs—no other than the child who, walled up here for half a century, had been miraculously kept alive by the birds of the air bringing him food through an opening in his narrow prison.

Sometimes, indeed, the Roumanian seeks covertly to compass the death of a fellow-creature without the excuse of public benefit, and merely from motives of personal revenge. In such cases it is recommended to send gifts of unleavened bread to nine different churches to be used simultaneously on the same Sunday at mass. This will insure the death of the victim.

To the hand of a man who has committed murder from revenge is ascribed the virtue of healing pains in the side.

CHAPTER XXVIII.

SAXON SUPERSTITION: REMEDIES, WITCHES, WEATHER-MAKERS.

THE superstitions afloat among Saxon peasants are of less poetical character than those *en vogue* with the Roumanians; there is more of the quack and less of the romantic element here to be found, and the invisible spiritual world plays less part in their beliefs, which oftenest relate to household matters, such as the well-being of cattle and poultry, the cure of diseases, and the success of harvest and vintage.

Innumerable are the recipes for curing the ague, or *frir* as it is termed in Saxon dialect. So, for instance:

1. To cover up the patient during his shivering-fit with nine articles of clothing, each of a different color and material.

2. To go into an inn or public-house, and after having drunk a glass of wine go out again without breaking silence or paying, but leaving behind some article of clothing which is of greater value than the wine taken.

3. Drinking in turn out of nine different wells.

4. To go into the garden when no one is looking, shake a young tree, and return to the house without glancing back. The fever will then have passed into the tree.

5. Any article of clothing purposely dropped on the ground will convey the fever to whoever finds it. This method is, however, to be distrusted, we are told by village authorities, for the finder may avert the spell by thrice spitting on the article in question. According to Saxon notions, you can apparently never go wrong in spitting on each and every occasion, this being a prime recipe for averting evil of all sorts. "When in doubt, play trumps," we are told in the rules for whist; and in the same way the Saxon would seem to say, "When in doubt, spit."

6. A spoonful of mortar taken from three different corner houses in the village, and, dissolved in vinegar, given to the patient to drink before the paroxysm.

7. If it be a child that is suffering from the fever, it may be rolled at sunrise over the grave-mounds in the church-yard, particular formulas being murmured the while.

8. The first three corn-ears seen in spring will, if gathered and eaten, keep off the ague during that whole year.

9. Take a kreuzer (farthing), an egg, and a handful of salt, and with these walk backward to the nearest cross-way, without looking back or breaking silence, and laying them down at the place where the roads join, speak the following words: "When these three things return to me, then may likewise the fever come back."

10. Or else go to a stream or river, and throw something into it over the shoulder without looking back.

The intermittent fever recurring on every third day is here called the *schweins-fieber* (swine-fever), and for recovery it is recommended to eat with the pigs out of their trough, and to lie down on the threshold of the pigsty, where the swine may walk over the prostrate body.

To shake off drowsiness, it is advised to swallow some drops of the water which falls back from the horses' mouths when they drink at the trough.

A person afflicted with warts can take as many dried peas as there are warts, and, standing before the fire, count backward, thus: "Five, four, three, two, one, none," and with the last word throw all the peas on to the glowing embers, running away quickly, so as not to hear the crackling sound of the bursting peas, which would counteract the spell.

Another method is to lay a piece of bacon on the top of a hedge or paling, saying these words:

> "This meat I give to the crow,
> That away the warts may go."

Rheumatism is cured by wearing a little bag filled with garlic and incense, or putting a knife under the pillow; and water taken from the spot where two ditches cross is good for sore eyes.

An approved love-charm is to take the two hind-legs of a green tree-frog, bury these in an ant-hill till all the flesh is removed, then securely tie up the bones in a linen cloth. Whoever then touches this cloth will be at once seized with love for its owner.

Still more infallible is it to procure a piece of stocking or shoe-lace of the person you desire to captivate, boil it in water, and wear this token night and day against your heart. This recipe has passed into a proverb, for it is here said of any man known to be desperately in love, that "she must have secretly boiled his stockings."

It is usually considered lucky to dream of pigs, except in some villages, where there is a prevalent belief that such a dream is prognostic of a death in the family.

To avert any illnesses which may occur to the pigs, it is still customary in some places for the swine-herd to dispense with his clothes the first time he drives out his pigs to pasture in spring. A newly elected Saxon pastor, regarding this practice as immoral, tried to prohibit it in his parish, but was sternly asked by the village Hann whether he were prepared to pay for all the pigs which would assuredly die that year in consequence of the omission.

The same absence of costume is recommended to women assisting a cow to calve for the first time.

When the cows are first driven to pasture in spring they should be made to step over a ploughshare placed across the threshold of the byre. Three new-laid eggs, deposited each at the junction of a different cross-road, will likewise bring luck to the herd.

If a swallow flies under a cow feeding in the meadow it is believed that the milk will turn bloody. In some villages the skin of a weasel is kept in every byre, with which to rub the udder when the milk is bloody.

The ancient belief that certain old village matrons have the power surreptitiously to purloin their neighbors' milk is prevalent throughout Transylvania, as I have had occasion over and over again to learn. "They mostly do it out of revenge," I was informed by a village oracle, to whom I owe much information on this and other subjects, "and are apt to molest those houses whose children have mocked at or played tricks upon them; but just leave them alone, and they are not likely to do you any harm."

In former days, however, people in Transylvania were by no means inclined to "leave alone" those suspected of such occult proficiency, and witch-burning was a thing of quite every-day occurrence. In the neighborhood of Reps alone, in the seventeenth century, the number of unfortunates who thus perished in the flames was upwards of twenty-five; and in 1697, Michael Hirling, member of the Schäsburg

14

Council, has, with significant brevity, noted down in his diary under such and such a date, "Went to Keisd, burned a witch," just as a sportsman of to-day might note down in his game-book that he shot a hare or a pheasant.

The widow of the Saxon Comes and Royal Judge Valentin Seraphim had a similar fate in 1659 at Hermanstadt, and there is mention of another witch destroyed in 1669 in the same town. The very last witch-burning in Transylvania took place at Maros-Varshahely in 1752.

The following is an extract from the account of a witch's trial at Mühlbach in the last century:

"A woman had engaged two laborers by the day to assist her in working in the vineyard. After the mid-day meal all three lay down to rest a little, as is customary. An hour later the workmen got up and wanted to wake the woman, who lay there immovable on her back, with open mouth; but their efforts to rouse her were all in vain, for she neither seemed to feel them when they shook her, nor to hear them shouting in her ear. So the men let her lie, and went about their work. Coming back to the spot about sunset, they found the woman still lying as they had left her, like a corpse. And as they gazed at her wonderingly, a big fly came buzzing past, which one of the men caught and shut up in his leathern pouch. Then they renewed their attempts to awake the woman, but with no better success than before. After about an hour they released the fly, which straightway flew into the mouth of the sleeping woman, who immediately woke up and opened her eyes. On seeing this the two workmen had no further doubt that she was a witch."

Also, in the year 1734, an Austrian officer who had been in Transylvania related the following story as authentic: Once when the roll was called on Sunday morning a soldier was missing. The corporal being sent to fetch him, the soldier called down from the window of the house where he was billeted, "I cannot go to church, for I have only one boot." Hereupon the corporal went up-stairs, and the soldier explained how, seeking for something wherewith to grease his boots in the absence of the Saxon housewife, he had found some ointment in an old broken pot concealed in a corner; but scarcely had he rubbed the first boot with it, when the boot flew out of his hand and straight up the chimney. In the corporal's presence the soldier now proceeded to grease the second boot, which disappeared in the same way as the first.

The corporal reported these circumstances to his officer, "who had no difficulty in discerning the Saxon housewife to be a dangerous and malignant witch, of whom there are but too many in the land."

The woman, called to account, consented to pay for new boots for the soldier, but warned the officer against prosecuting her, "else he should repent it."

Another class of sorcerers, the *wettermacher* (weather-makers), are those who have power to conjure up thunder and hail storms at will or to disperse them.

My old village oracle told me many stories about a man she had known, who used to go about the country with a small black bag in which were a book, a little stick, and a bunch of herbs. Whenever a storm was brewing he was to be seen standing on some rising piece of ground, and repeating his formulas against the gathering clouds. "People used to abuse him," she said, "and to say that he was in league with the devil; but I never saw him do any harm, and now that he is dead there are many who regret him, for since then we have had heavier hail-storms than ever were known in his time." *

We are also told that many years ago, in the village of Wermesch, there lived a peasant who, whenever a thunder-storm was seen approaching, used to take his stand in front of it armed with an axe, by which means he always turned the storm aside. One day, when an unusually heavy storm was seen approaching, the weather-maker, as usual, placed himself in front of it, and hurled the axe up into the clouds. The storm passed by, but the axe did not fall down to the earth again. Many years later, the same peasant, taking a journey farther into the land, entered the hut of a Wallachian, and there to his astonishment found the axe he had thrown into the thunder-clouds several years previously. This Wallachian was a still greater sorcerer in weather-making than the Wermesch peasant, and had therefore succeeded in getting the axe down again from the sky.

There are many old formulas and incantations bearing on this sub-

---

* Instances of weather-makers are also common in Germany. We are told that there used to live in Suabia long ago a pastor renowned for his proficiency in exorcising the weather, and whenever a thunder-storm came on he would stand at the open window invoking the clouds till they had all dispersed. But the work was heavy and difficult to do, and the pastor used frequently to be so exhausted after dispersing a storm that large drops of perspiration would trickle down his face.

ject to be found in ancient chronicles, of which the following one
bears a date of the sixteenth century:

FORMULA.

And the Lord went forth down a long and ancient road, and there
was met by an exceeding large black cloud; and the Lord spoke thus
to it, "Where goest thou, thou large black cloud? Where dost thou
go?" Then spoke the cloud, "I am sent to do an injury to the poor
man—to wash away the roots of his corn and to throw down the corn-
ears; also to wash away the roots of his vines, and to overthrow the
grapes." But the Lord spoke, "Turn back, turn back, thou big black
cloud, and do not wander forth to do an injury to the poor man, but
go to the wild forest and wash away the roots of the big oak-tree and
overthrow its leaves. St. Peter, do thou draw thy sharp sword and
cut in twain the big black cloud, that it may not go forth to do an injury to the poor men."

Underneath this incantation the writer has put the following mem-
orandum, "Probatum an sit me latet probet quicunque vult."

In many houses it is still customary to burn juniper-berries during
a thunder-storm, or to stick a knife in the ground before the house.
Like the Roumanian, the Saxon also considers it unsafe to point at an
approaching thunder-storm; but this is a belief shared by many people, I understand.

CHAPTER XXIX.

SAXON SUPERSTITION—CONTINUED: ANIMALS, PLANTS, DAYS.

THE cat, dedicated to Frouma, Frezja, or Holda, in old German
times, still plays a considerable part in Saxon superstition. Thus, to
render fruitful a tree which refuses to bear, it will suffice to bury a
cat among its roots.* Epileptic people may be cured by cutting off
the ears of a cat and anointing them with the blood; and an eruption
at the mouth is healed by passing the cat's tail between the lips.

---

* An old German saying, "Hier liegt der Hund begraben"—and which is equivalent to saying, That now we penetrate the true meaning of something not previously
understood—has been explained in the same way in Büchner's "Geflügelte Worte:"
There the dog lies buried; that is why the tree bears fruit.

When the cat washes its face visitors may be expected, and as long as the cat is healthy and in good looks the cattle will likewise prosper.

A runaway cat, when recovered, must be swung three times round the hearth to attach it to the dwelling; and the same is done to a stolen cat by the thief who would retain it. In entering a new house, it is recommended to throw in a cat (sometimes also a dog) before any member of the family step over the threshold, else one of them will die.

The dog is of less importance than the cat, except for its power of giving warning of approaching death by unnatural howling.

Here are some other Saxon superstitions of mixed character:

1. Who can blow back the flame into a candle will become pastor.

2. New servants must be suffered to eat freely the first day they enter service, else their hunger will never be stilled.

3. Who visits a neighbor's house must sit down, even were it but for a moment, or he will deprive the inhabitants of their sleep. (Why, then, do Saxon peasants never offer one a chair? or is a stranger too insignificant to have the power of destroying sleep?)

4. It is dangerous to stare down long into a well, for the well-dame who dwells at the bottom of each is easily offended. But children are often curious, and, hoping to get a look at her face, they bend over the edge, calling out mockingly, " Brannefrà, Brannefrà, zieh mich än de Brännen " (Dame of the well, pull me down into the well); but quickly they draw back their heads, afraid of their own audacity, lest their wish be in truth realized.

5. It is not good to count the beehives, or the loaves when they are put in the oven.

6. Neither is it good to whitewash the house when the moon is decreasing, for that produces bugs.

7. Who eats mouldy bread will live long.

8. Licking the platter clean at table brings fine weather.

9. On the occasion of each merrymaking, such as weddings, christenings, etc., some piece of glass or crockery must be broken to avert misfortune.*

10. Salt thrown on the back of a departing guest will prevent him from carrying away the luck of the house. Neither salt nor garlic should ever be given away, as with them the luck goes.

---

* The Greeks also observed this at their banquets in order to appease the gods.

11. A broom put upside down behind the door will keep off the witches.

12. It is bad-luck to lay a loaf on the table upside down.

13. When foxes and wolves meet in the market-place, their prices will rise (of course, as these animals could only be thus bold during the severest cold, when prices of eggs, butter, etc., are at their highest).

14. A piece of bread found lying in the field or road should never be eaten by the finder; nor should he untie a knotted-up cloth or a rag he chances to discover, for the knot perhaps contains an illness.

15. Whoever has been robbed of anything, and wishes to discover the thief, must select a black hen, and for nine consecutive Fridays must, together with his hen, abstain from all food. The thief will then either die or bring back the stolen goods. This is called taking up the black fast against a person.

On this last subject an anecdote is told of a peasant of the village of Petersdorf, who returned one day from the town of Bistritz, bearing two hundred florins, which he had received as the price for a team of oxen. Reaching home in a somewhat inebriated state, he wished to sleep off his tipsiness, and laid himself down behind the stove, but took the precaution of first hiding the money in a hole in the kitchen wall. Next morning, on waking up, the peasant searched for his money, but was unable to find it, having completely forgotten where he had put it in his intoxication; so, in the firm belief that some one had stolen the two hundred florins, he went to consult an old Wallachian versed in magic, and begged him to take up the black fast against the man who had abstracted the money. Before long people began to notice how the peasant himself grew daily weaker and seemed to pine away. At last, by some chance, he hit upon the place where the money was hidden, and joyfully hurried to the Wallachian to counter-order the black fast. But it was now too late, for the charm had already worked, and before long the man was dead.

There is also a whole set of rhymes and formulas for exorcising thieves, and forcing them to return whatever they have taken; but these would be too lengthy to record here.

Of the plants which play a part in Saxon superstition, first and foremost is the fulsome garlic—not only employed against witches, but likewise regarded as a remedy in manifold illnesses and as an antidote against poison. Garlic put into the money-bag will prevent the witches from getting at it, and in the stables will keep the milk from being abstracted, while rubbed over the body it will defend a person against the pest.

To the lime-tree are also attached magic qualities, and in some villages it is usual to plant a lime-tree before the house to keep witches from entering.

Much prized is the lilac-bush. Its blossoms, made into tea, are good for the fever; and the bush itself is often reverently saluted with bent knee and uncovered head. Many of the formulas against sickness are directed to be recited while walking thrice round a bush of lilac.

The first strawberry-blossom, if swallowed by whoever finds it, will keep him free from sickness during that year.

The four-leaved shamrock here, as elsewhere, is considered to confer particular luck on the finder, but only when he carries it home without having to cross over water of any sort. Laid in the prayer-book, a four-leaved shamrock will enable its possessor to distinguish witches in church.

The common houseleek, here called *donnerkraut* (thunder-herb), will protect from lightning the roof on which it grows.

Animals beaten with a switch of privet or dog-wood will die or fall sick.

Larkspur hung over the stable door will keep witches from entering.

The *Atropa belladonna* (called here *buchert*) renders mad whoever tastes of it, and in his madness he will be compelled blindly to obey the will of whoever has given him of this herb to eat; therefore it is here said of a man who behaves insanely that "he must have eaten buchert."

Whoever kills an adder under a white-hazel bush, plants a pea in the head of this adder, and then buries it in the earth so that the pea can strike root, has only to gather the first flower which grows from the pea and wear it in his cap in order henceforward to have power over all witches in the neighborhood. But let him beware of the witches, who, knowing this, are ever on the lookout to catch him without the pea-flower and to do him an injury.

A particular growth of vine-leaf, whose exact definition I have not succeeded in rightly ascertaining, is eagerly sought for by Saxon girls in some villages. Whoever finds it sticks it in her hair, and thus decorated she has the right to kiss the first man she meets on her homeward way. This will insure her speedy marriage. A story is related of a girl who, meeting a nobleman driving in a handsome four-in-hand carriage, stopped the horses, and begged leave to kiss him, to the gentleman's no small astonishment. He resigned himself, however, with a good grace when he had grasped the situation, and gave the kiss as well as a golden piece to the fair suppliant. The proper romantic *dénouement* of this episode would have been for the gentleman to lead home as bride the maiden thus cast in his path by fate, but we are not told that he pushed his complacence quite so far.

A whole volume might be written on the subject of agrarian superstition, of which let a few examples here suffice.

In many villages it is customary for the ploughman, going to work for the first time that year in the field, to drive his plough over a broomstick laid on the threshold of the court-yard.

The first person who sows each year will have meagre crops. During the whole sowing-time no one should give a kindling out of the house. It is never allowable to sow in Holy Week.

To insure the wheat against being eaten by birds, the sowing should be done in silence before sunrise, and without looking over the shoulder. Also earth taken from the church-yard will keep birds off the field.

Whoever lies down to sleep in a new-ploughed furrow will fall ill; nor must the women be allowed to sew or spin in the cornfield, for that would occasion thunder-storms; while washing the hands in the field will cause the house to burn.

In obstinate droughts it is customary in some places for several girls, led by an old woman, and all of them absolutely naked, to repair at midnight to the court-yard of some neighboring peasant, whose harrow they must steal, and with it proceed across the field to the nearest stream, where the harrow is put afloat with a burning light on each corner.

The harvest will be bad if the cuckoo comes into the village and cries there.

In bringing in the corn a few heads of garlic bound up in the first sheaf will keep off witches.

The most important days in Saxon superstition are Sunday, Tuesday, and Friday.

Whoever wears a shirt sewed by his mother on a Sunday will die. According to another version, however, a shirt which has been spun, woven, and sewed entirely on Sundays is a powerful talisman, which will render all enemies powerless against the wearer, and bring him safely through every battle.

Wood cut on a Sunday serves to heat the fire of hell. Sunday children are lucky, and can discover hidden treasures.

In some districts no cow or swine herd would lead his animals to pasture on any other day but a Tuesday.*

Thursday is in many places the luckiest day for marriages, also for markets.

On Friday the weather is apt to change. It is a good day for sowing and for making vinegar, but a bad one for baking, or for starting on a journey. In some places it is considered unsafe to comb the hair on a Friday—therefore the village school on that day presents a somewhat rough and unkempt appearance.

Rain upon Good Friday is a favorable omen.

On Easter Monday the lads run about the towns and villages sprinkling with water all the girls and women they meet. This is supposed to insure the flax growing well. On the following day the girls return the attention by watering the boys.†

On Easter Monday the cruel sport of cock-shooting is still kept up in many Saxon villages. The cock is tied to a post and shot at till it dies a horrible lingering death. Sometimes the sport is diversified by blindfolding the actors, who strike at their victim with wooden clubs.

Between Easter and Pentecost none should either marry or change their domicile.

On Pentecost Monday it is sometimes customary to elect three of the girls as queens, who, dressed up in their finest clothes, preside at church and at the afternoon dance.

In one village it is usual on Pentecost Sunday at mid-day, when the bells are ringing, to encircle each fruit-tree with a rope made of twisted straw.

---

* In the Harz and Westphalia Tuesday is considered the luckiest day for entering on a new service.

† This custom, which appears to be a very old one, is also prevalent among various Slav peoples, Poles, Serbs, etc. In Poland it used to be *de rigueur* that the water be poured over a girl who was still asleep; so in each house a victim, usually a servant-maid, was selected, who had to feign sleep, and patiently receive the cold shower-bath which was to insure the luck of the family during that year. The custom has now become modified to suit a more delicate age, and instead of formidable horse-buckets of water, dainty little perfume-squirts have come to be used in many places,

The fires on St. John's Day, and the belief that hidden treasures are to be found, are also prevalent among the Saxons.

No one should bathe or wade into a river on the 29th of June, Feast of SS. Peter and Paul, for fear of drowning, it being supposed that this day requires the sacrifice of a human victim.

Before the 24th of August no corn should be garnered, because only after that date do the thunder-storms cease, or as the people say, "the thunder-clouds go home."

The night of St. Thomas (December 21st), popularly considered to be the longest night in the year, is the date consecrated by Saxon superstition to the celebration of the games which elsewhere are usual on All-Halloween. Every girl puts her fate to the test on that evening, and there are various ways of so doing, with onions, flowers, shoes, etc.

One way of interrogating Fate is with a sharp knife to cut an apple in two. If in doing so no seed has been split, then the wish of your heart will be fulfilled.

Similar games are also practised on Sylvester night (December 31st), which night is also otherwise prophetic of what is to happen during the coming year. If it be clear, then the fowls will lay many eggs that year, and bright moonlight means full granaries. A red dawn on New-year's Day means war, and wind is significant of the pest or cholera.

CHAPTER XXX.

SAXON CUSTOMS AND DRAMAS.

Some of the Saxon customs are peculiarly interesting, as being obviously remnants of paganism, and offer curious proof of the force of verbal tradition, which in this case has not only borne transmigration from a distant country, but likewise weathered the storm of two successive changes of religion.

It speaks strongly for the tenacity of pagan habits and trains of thought, that although at the time these Saxon colonists appeared in Transylvania they had already belonged to the Christian Church for over three hundred years, yet many points of the landscape in their new country received from them pagan appellations. Thus we find the *Götzenberg,* or mountain of the gods,* which rises above the village of Heltau; and the *Wodesch* and *Wolenk* applied to woods and plains, both evidently derived from Woden.

Another remnant of paganism is the *feurix* or *feuriswolf,* which yet lingers in the minds of these people. According to ancient German mythology, the feuriswolf is a monster which on the last day is to open his mouth so wide that the upper jaw will touch the sky and the lower one the earth; and not long ago a Saxon woman bitterly complained in a court of justice that her husband had cursed her over-strongly in saying, " Der Wärlthangd saul dich frieszen !"— literally, " May the world-dog swallow thee !"

Many old pagan ceremonies are likewise still clearly to be distinguished through the flimsy shrouding of a later period—their origin piercing unmistakably through the surface - varnish of Christianity, thought necessary to adapt them to newer circumstances, and, like a clumsily remodelled garment, the original cut asserting itself despite the fashionable trimmings now adorning it. Thus, for instance, in many popular rhymes and dialogues it has been clearly proved that those parts now assigned to the Saviour and St. Peter originally belonged to the old gods Thor and Loki, while the faithless apostle Judas has had thrust upon him the personification of a whole horde of German demons. As to St. Elias, who in some parts of Hungary, as well as in Roumania, Serbia, and Croatia, is supposed to have the working of the thunder-bolts, there can be little doubt that he is verily no other than the old thunder-god Thor under a Christian mask.

One of the most striking of the aforementioned Christianized dramas is the *Tod-Austragen,* or throwing out the Death—a custom still extant in several Transylvanian villages, and which may likewise still be found existing in some remote parts of Germany.

The Feast of the Ascension is the day on which this ceremony takes place in a village near Hermanstadt, and it is conducted in the following manner:

After forenoon church on that day all the school-girls repair to the house of one of their companions, and there proceed to dress up the "Death." This is done by tying up a thrashed-out corn-sheaf into the rough semblance of a head and body, while the arms are simulated by a broomstick stuck horizontally. This being done, the

---

* The word *Götzen* in German is exclusively used to express pagan gods,

figure is dressed in the Sunday clothes of a young village matron, and the head adorned with the customary cap and veil, fastened by silver pins.   Two large black beads or black-headed pins represent the eyes; and thus equipped the figure is displayed at the open window, in order that all people may see it on their way to afternoon church. The conclusion of the vespers is the signal for the girls to seize on the figure and open the procession round the village.   Two of the eldest school-girls hold the "Death" between them; the others follow in regular order, two and two, singing a Church hymn.   The boys are excluded from the procession, and must content themselves with ad- miring the *Schöner Tod* (beautiful Death) from a distance.   When the whole village has been traversed in this manner from end to end, the girls repair to another house, whose door is locked against the be- sieging troop of boys.   The figure of Death is here stripped of its gaudy attire, and the naked straw bundle thrown out of the window, whereupon it is seized by the boys and carried off in triumph, to be thrown into the nearest stream or river.

This is the first part of the drama; while the second consists in one of the girls being solemnly invested with the clothes and orna- ments previously worn by the figure, and, like it, being led in proces- sion round the village to the singing of the same hymns as before. The ceremony terminates by a feast at the house of the parents whose daughter has acted the principal part, and from which, as before, the boys are excluded.

According to popular belief, it is allowed to eat fruit only after this day, as now the "Death"—that is, the unwholesomeness—has been expelled from them.   Also, the river in which the Death has been drowned may now be considered fit for public bathing.

If this ceremony be ever neglected in the village where it is cus- tomary, such neglect is supposed to entail death to one of the young people, or loss of virtue to a girl.

This same custom may, as I have said, be found still lingering in various other parts, everywhere with slight variations.   Thus there are places where the figure is burned instead of drowned; and Passion Sunday (often called the Dead Sunday), or else the 25th of March, is the day sometimes fixed for its accomplishment.

In some places it was usual for the figure to be attired in the shirt of the last person who had died, and with the veil of the most recent bride on its head.   Also, the figure is occasionally pelted with stones

SAXON GIRL IN FULL DRESS.

by the youths of both sexes—those who succeed in hitting it being secured against death for the coming year.

At Nuremberg little girls dressed in white used to go in procession through the town, carrying a small open coffin in which a doll was laid out in state, or sometimes only a stick dressed up, and with an apple to represent the head.

In most of these places the rhymes sung apply to the departure of winter and the advent of summer, such as the following:

> " And now we have chased the Death away,
> And brought in the summer so warm and gay—
> The summer and the month of May.
> We bring sweet flowers full many a one,
> We bring the rays of the golden sun,
> For the dreary Death at last is gone."

Or else :

> "Come all of you and do not tarry,
> The evil Death away to carry;
> Come, spring, once more, with us to dwell—
> Welcome, O spring, in wood and dell!"

And there is no doubt that similar rhymes used also to be sung in Transylvania, until they were replaced by Lutheran hymns after the Reformation.

Some German archæologists have attempted to prove the Death in these games to be of more recent introduction, and to have replaced the winter of former times, so as to give the ceremony a more Christian coloring by the allusion to the triumph of Christ over death on his resurrection and ascension into heaven. Without presuming to contradict the many well-known authorities who have taken this view of the question, I cannot help thinking that it hardly requires such explanation to account for the presence of Death in these dramas. Nowadays, when civilization and luxury have done so much towards equalizing all seasons, so that we can never be deprived of flowers in winter nor want for ice in summer, it is difficult to realize the enormous gulf which in olden times separated winter from summer. In winter not only were all means of communication cut off for a large proportion of people, but their very existence was, so to say, frozen up ; and when the granaries were scantily filled, or the inclement season prolonged by some weeks, death was literally standing at the door of millions of poor wretches. No wonder, then, that winter and death became identical in their minds, and that they hailed the advent of

spring with delirious joy, dancing round the first violet, and following
about the first cockchafer in solemn procession. It was the feast of
Nature which they celebrated then as now—Nature mighty and eternal, always essentially the same, whether decked out in pagan or in
Christian garb.

Another drama of somewhat more precise form is the *Königslied*,
or *Todtentanz* (King's Song, or Dance of Death), a rhymed dialogue
still often represented in Saxon villages all over Transylvania.

Dramatic representations of the Dance of Death were first introduced into Germany before the fifteenth century by the Dominican
order, but do not seem there to have taken any very firm root, since
we hear no more mention of such performance existing after the middle of the fifteenth century. It is therefore probable that this drama
was transmitted, as long as five hundred years ago at least, to the
Transylvanian Saxons, who thus have retained it intact long after it
had elsewhere fallen into disuse.

The personages consist of an Angel, robed in white, and with a
golden wand; the King, attired in purple or scarlet cloak, crown, and
sceptre, and followed by a train of courtiers; then Death, who is sometimes clothed in black, sometimes in a white sheet, and who either
bears a scythe or a bow and arrows in his hand. On either side of
him, by way of adjutants, stand two mute personages, a doctor and an
apothecary—the first with powdered head, hanging plait, tricorn hat,
and snuffbox in his hand; the latter bearing a basket containing medicine phials. The whole is sung, and the Angel opens the performance
with these lines:

> *Angel*. Good people all, come list to me—
> New tidings to you will I sing;
> 'Tis of a mighty King
> Who on the open market-place
> With Death met face to face.

> *Death*. All hail, thou rich and mighty King!
> Great news to thee this day I bring;
> Thy death-hour it has struck,
> 'Tis time for thee to join my band—
> I wander thus from land to land.

> *King*. Thou haughty man, who mayest be,
> That I should have to follow thee?

What is thy land, thy name?
Art thou a lord? thy rank proclaim,
Else shaltst be put to shame.

Death 'Twere well for thee my name to know;
Thy pride soon will I overthrow.
The people here they call me Death;
Of young or old I take no heed,
Alike they wither at my breath.

King. Of Death I oft have heard, indeed,
But cannot of thee now take heed.
Quick from my land begone!
Or shaltst be fettered foot and hand,
And in a dungeon thrown.

Angel. Then Death he shot a deadly dart,
And pierced the King unto the heart.
Death. O foolish mortal, proud and blind!
See now, where is thy vaunted power
In iron fetters Death to bind?

Angel. The King he turneth deadly pale,
And feels his strength about to fail.
King. Lord, mercif'ly my life prolong,
Thus wofully not let me die;
Hast plenty poor to choose among.

Death. More than I list of poor I have;
But rich men also do I crave
My ranks to ornament,
As bishops, princes, mighty kings—
These fill me with content.

King. Great is thy power—
Angel.   The King did say,
Out-stretched as on his bed he lay—
King. O Death, unto thy power I bow;
But still one hope I cherish yet,
A favor last grant to me now.

Death. Then speak—
Angel.   Said Death unto the King—
Death. Let's hear what is this mighty thing.
King. But twelve years longer let me iive;
Twelve thousand pounds of heaviest gold
In payment to thee will I give.

Death. For all thy gold I little care;
Do thou at once for death prepare.

'Tis vain to pray, 'tis vain to grieve;
Come in my ranks, for thou art mine—
Thy gold behind to others leave.

King. But give to me—
Angel. The King did say—
King. But half a year and yet a day;
I fain would build a castle new
Of massive stone, with lofty tower,
From which my kingdom I may view.

Death. Leave those to build who list to build;
For thee thy span of life is filled.
Come in my ranks and tarry not,
We must to-day a measure tread;
'Twill cause thee small delight, I wot.

King. Yet will I yet for something pray;
This only wish do not gainsay:
If only thou wiltst let me live,
A beggar humble will I be;
My royal crown to thee I give.

Death. O King, why useless words thus waste?
Prepare to go, and make thee haste,
Nor seek me idly to detain;
Still many thousand men must I
To-day invite to join my train.

King. Oh, hurry not—
Angel. The King did say—
King. But grant me yet another day.
To make my will still let me bide;
My silver, gold, and jewels rare,
I fain would righteously divide.

Angel. But Death then spoke.
Death. It cannot be;
Conform must thou to my decree.
Prepare to start without reprieve;
Thy silver, gold, and jewels rare,
Must be content behind to leave.

King. Then is it all in vain I pray?
Death. Lament and prayer all useless be.
King. Shall I not see another day?
Death. Not one. To judgment come with me.
King. Oh, grant me but one little hour!
Death. To grant aught is not in my power.

King. Have patience but three words to hear.
Death. Patience 's an herb* which grows not here.

Angel. The King upon his couch down sinks:
His haughty form all helpless shrinks;
To ashy white has turned his lip.
Both rich and poor the strangler thus
With iron hand alike doth grip.
Thus stealthy Death will oft appear,
When no one deems that he is near,
With deadly aim to shoot his dart.
So live in God, his laws observe,
That mayst in peace depart.

> [*The* KING *sinks down lifeless, and* DEATH *disappears.*
> *The soldiers raise up the dead body and lay it on a*
> *bier, singing—*

Soldiers. Why value crown or power,
Since neither can we own
But for a passing hour?
No sceptre and no throne
Grim Death away can scare,
Nor gold nor jewels rare.

Angel [*reappearing*]. By Providence as herald sent,
Touched by the sound of dire lament;
The monarch to his land restore
Will I, in pity for your grief.
King, for thy kingdom live once more.

> [*The* ANGEL *touches the* KING's *breast, who, waking*
> *apparently from a deep slumber, sits up and sings—*

King. How is't I feel? and can it be
That once again the earth I see?
What miracle of grace!
Who art thou, Lord? I knew thee not;
Deign to reveal thy face.

Angel. The Lord who sent me to this land,
He is a Lord of mighty hand.
He gives, he taketh life,
As thou hast seen, O King, this day;
To do his will must strive alway.

> [*The* KING, *now standing up, takes the crown from*
> *his head, and accompanied by the chorus, sings—*

---

* In the original the phrase runs:
    "This grows not in my garden."

King. Lord of the world, the crown is thine,
Who rulest us with power divine.
Oh, what is man! He is but dust,
And fall a prey to death he must.
Let none be proud of lofty rank,
For 'tis indeed but idle prank.
Guide thou us, Lord, upon our way;
Our souls receive in grace some day.

Grimm is of opinion that this drama is also allegorical of the triumph of spring over winter, which opinion he chiefly supports by the incident of the King's resurrection, and of the allusion to the garden. This view has, however, been strongly combated by other authorities, who remind us that in many old pictures Death is often represented as a gardener, and armed with bow and arrows.

"Herodes" is the name of a Christmas drama acted by the Transylvanian Saxons; but as, though undoubtedly ancient, it is totally wanting in humor and originality, I do not here reproduce it. Most probably such qualities as this drama may once have possessed have been pruned away by the over-vigorous knife of some ruthless reformer.

The Song of the Three Kings, beginning,

"Through storm and wind, through weather wild,
We come to seek the new-born child,"

is sung by little boys, who at Christmas-time go about from house to house with tinsel crowns on their heads, one of them having his face blackened to represent the negro king, and who expect a few coins and some victuals as reward for their performance.

At Hermanstadt these three kings threatened to become somewhat of a nuisance in Christmas-week, there being several sets of them who were continually walking uninvited into our rooms. At last one day when we had already received the visit of several such royal parties, our footman opened the door and inquired in a tone of mild exasperation, "Please, madam, the holy three kings are there again; had I not better kick them down-stairs?"

CHAPTER XXXI. ·

BURIED TREASURES.

FEW things possess such powerful attraction as the thought of buried treasures which may be lying unsuspected around us. To think that the golden buttercups which dot a meadow are, perchance, but the reflections of other golden pieces lying beneath the surface; to suppose the crumbling gray walls of some ancient tower to be the dingy casket enshrouding priceless gems, there secreted by long-vanished hands—is surely enough to set imagination on fire, and engender the wild, delirious hope that to you alone, favored among ten thousand other mortals who have passed by the spot unknowing, may be destined the triumph of finding that golden key.

Vain and futile as such researches mostly are, yet they have in Transylvania a somewhat greater semblance of reason than in most other countries, for nowhere else, perhaps, have so many successive nations been forced to secrete their riches in flying from an enemy, to say nothing of the numerous, yet undiscovered, veins of gold and silver which must be seaming the country in all directions. Not a year passes without bringing to light some earthen jar containing old Dacian coins, or golden ornaments of Roman origin—which discoveries all serve to feed and keep up the national superstitions connected with treasures and treasure-finders.

The night of St. George, the 24th of April (corresponding to our 6th of May), is of all others the most favorable in the year for such researches, and many Roumanian peasants spend these hours in wandering about the hills, trying to probe the earth for the gold it contains; for in this night (so say the legends) all these treasures begin to burn, or, to speak in technical, mystic language, "to bloom," in the bosom of the earth, and the light they give forth, described as a bluish flame, resembling the color of burning spirits of wine, serves to guide favored mortals to their place of concealment.

The conditions to the successful raising of a treasure are manifold and difficult of accomplishment. In the first place, it is by no means easy for a common mortal who has not been born on a Sunday, nor even at mid-day when the bells are ringing, to hit upon a treasure at all. If he does, however, chance to catch sight of a flame such as I have described, he must quickly pierce through the swaddling rags of his right foot with a knife, and then throw it in the direction of the flame seen. If two people are together during this discovery, they must on no account break silence till the treasure is raised; neither is it allowed to fill up the hole from which anything has been taken, for that would entail the death of one of the finders. Another important feature to be noted is that the lights seen before midnight on St. George's Day denote treasures kept by good spirits, while those which appear at a later hour are unquestionably of a pernicious nature.

For the comfort of less favored mortals who do not happen to have been born either on a Sunday nor to the sound of bells, I must here mention that these deficiencies may to some extent be condoned for and the mental vision sharpened by the consumption of mouldy bread; so that whoever has, during the preceding year, been careful to feed upon decayed loaves only, may (if he survive this trying diet) become the fortunate discoverer of hidden treasures.

Sometimes the power of finding a particular treasure is supposed only to be possessed by members of some particular family. A curious instance of this was lately recorded in Roumania, relating to an old ruined convent, where, according to a popular legend, a large sum of gold is concealed. A deputation of peasants, at considerable trouble and expense, found out the last surviving member of the family supposed to possess the mystic power, and offered him unconditionally a very handsome sum merely for the benefit of his personal attendance on the spot. The gentleman in question being old, and probably sceptical, declined the offer, to the peasants' great disappointment.

There is hardly a ruin, mountain, or forest in Transylvania which has not got some legend of a hidden treasure attached to it. These are often supposed to be guarded by some animal, as a serpent, turkey, dog, or pig; or sometimes the devil himself, in the shape of a black buffalo, haunts the place at night and carries off those who attempt to raise the treasure. Out of the many such tales there afloat I shall here quote only a few, which have been collected and written down from the words of old villagers in different places:

THE TREASURE OF DARIUS

is one of the principal treasures supposed to be somewhere concealed on Transylvanian ground. It is said to be of immense value, and is believed to have been secreted when the Persian king was compelled to fly before the Scythian forces; but opinions are divided as to the exact locality where it lies. One version, which places the treasure in a forest in the neighborhood of Hamlesch, relates of it that fifty years ago a poor German workman, sleeping in the forest one night, discovered the treasure, and being versed in the formalities to be observed on such occasions, laid upon it some article of clothing marked with his name in token of taking possession. Then, as he did not trust the country people, he went off to Germany to fetch his relations to assist him in raising the treasure. But, hardly arrived at his house, he fell ill and died; and though on his death-bed he exactly described the place where he had seen the gold, and gave directions for finding it, his relations were never able to hit upon the place.

Another story declares the treasure to have been hidden in the Sacsorer Burg, an old ruined fortress, where some centuries ago it was discovered by six Hungarian burghers, who swore to keep the secret among themselves; and once in each year they went and carried off a sack of gold and silver pieces, which they divided. Only after five of them had died did the last survivor in his testament leave directions how to reach the place. To approach the treasure (so runs the legend), one must pass through a strong iron door lying towards the west. This door can be opened from the outside, but whoever is not in possession of the secret is sure to fall down through a trap-door into a terrible abyss, where he will be cut to pieces by a thousand swords set in motion by machinery; therefore it is necessary to bridge over the trap-door with several stout planks before entering. After this a second iron door is reached, in front of which are lying two life-sized lions of massive silver. This second door leads into a large hall, where round a long table are sitting the figures of King Darius, and of twelve other kings whom he had vanquished in battle. King Darius himself, who sits at the head of the table, is formed of purest gold, while the other monarchs, six on either side, are of silver. This hall leads into a cellar, where are ranged twenty-four barrels bound with hoops of silver; half of these barrels contain gold, the other half silver pieces.

It is likewise asserted that towards the end of the last century a Wallachian hermit was known to reside in those same ruins, in whose possession were often seen gold and silver coins stamped with the image of King Darius, but that when questioned on the subject he would never reveal how he had come by them.

Finally, it is said that within the memory of people still living there came hither from Switzerland three men with an ancient parchment document, out of which they professed to have deciphered the directions for finding the treasure of Darius, but after spending several days in digging about the place they had to go empty-handed away.

After writing these lines I have unexpectedly come across a new version of the treasure of Darius, as I read in a current newspaper, dated November 24, 1886, that only a few weeks ago an old Roumanian peasant woman formally applied to the Government at Klausenburg for leave to dig for the treasure of Darius, which, as a sorcerer had revealed to her, lay buried at Hideg Szamos.

The directions she had received were to dig, at the spot indicated, as deep as the height of the Klausenburg church steeple, when stone steps and an iron door would be disclosed. The latter can be opened by a blow from an axe which had been dipped in holy-water. A large stone vault with twelve more iron doors will then appear. Twelve golden keys hang on the wall, and each door being opened will lead to a chamber filled to overflowing with solid gold-pieces. Three people only were permitted to dig simultaneously for the treasure, the sorcerer himself disinterestedly disclaiming any part in the matter, as he professes to have renounced all earthly goods.

The prosaic Klausenburg officials could not, however, be induced to share the woman's enthusiasm, and tried to convince her of the folly of such search; but all in vain, for, dispensing with the permission she had failed to obtain, she has now engaged three day-laborers, who since the 15th of November, 1886, are said to be engaged on this stupendous task.

Perhaps we shall some day hear the result of their labors.

THE TREASURE OF DECEBALUS

is also among those to which Transylvania lays claim. When Trajan went forth for the second time against the Dacian king, Decebalus, vanquished in the fight near his capital, Zarmiszegthusa, retired to a stronghold in the mountains, where he was again pursued by the conqueror, and, after a second defeat, perished by his own hand, in order to escape the ignominy of captivity. But before these reverses Decebalus had taken care to secure his immense riches. For this purpose he caused the river Sargetia,* which flowed past his residence, to be diverted from its course at great toil and expense; in the dry river-bed strong vaulted cellars were constructed, in which all the gold, silver, and precious stones were stowed away, the whole being then covered up with earth and gravel, and the river brought back to its original course.

The work had been executed by prisoners, who were all either massacred or deprived of their eyesight to avoid betrayal. But a confidant of the Dacian king, Bicilis, or Biculus, who afterwards fell into Roman captivity, revealed to the Emperor what he knew of it, and Trajan thus succeeded in appropriating a considerable portion of the secreted treasure, but not the whole, it is said.

In the year 1543 some Wallachian fishermen, when mooring their boat on the banks of the river Strell, became aware of something shining in the water at the place where a tree had lately been uprooted. Pursuing the search, they brought to light more than forty thousand gold-pieces, each of them as heavy as three ducats, and stamped with the image of King Decebalus on one side, and that of the Goddess of Victory on the other. This treasure was delivered up to the monk Martinuzzi, the counsellor of Queen Isabella, and the most powerful man in Transylvania of that time. Part of the money was sent to the Roman emperor, Ferdinand I.; but many people declare the treasure of Decebalus not to be exhausted even now, and prophesy that we have not yet heard the last of it.

THE TREASURE ON THE KOND.

The Kond is a gloomy wooded plain near to the town of Regen. Great riches are said to be here concealed, but they are difficult to obtain, for the place is haunted by coal-black buffaloes, which may be seen running backward and forward at night, especially about the time of St. George and St. Thomas. A citizen named Simon Hill, who once caught sight of the subterraneous fire, marked the place, resolving

---

* The present river Strell.

to raise the treasure the following night. But distrusting his own strength and courage, he confided his purpose to a neighbor called Martin Rosenau, asking him to come to the place that night at twelve o'clock.

This neighbor, however, was faithless, being one of those who pray against the Catechism; so he resolved to cheat his friend. Instead, therefore, of waking his neighbor, as had been agreed, at ten o'clock, he repaired alone to the spot, where, digging, he found nothing but a horse's skull filled with dead frogs. Full of anger at his bad-luck, he took the skull and flung it along with the frogs in at the open window of his sleeping friend. But what was the surprise of this latter when, waking in the morning, he found the whole room strewn with golden ducats, and in the midst the horse's skull, likewise half full of gold. Happy beyond measure, Simon Hill ran to his neighbor to tell him the joyful news how God had sent him the gold in his sleep; but the faithless Martin, on hearing the tale, was so seized with grief and anger that a stroke of apoplexy put an end to his life.

GOLD-DUST.

An old man at Nadesch relates how in his youth he missed a chance of becoming a rich man for life. Going once to the forest, he saw on the steep bank near a stream the handle of some sort of earthen-ware jar peeping out of the soil. Curious to investigate it, he climbed up the steep bank; but hardly had he seized the handle and drawn the heavy jar out of the earth, when, the ground giving way under his feet, he rolled to the bottom of the incline still holding the jar in his hand. But finding that it contained nothing but a dull yellow dust, which had partly been spilled in falling, he threw it as worthless into the stream. Often in later days did he regret this rash act, for, as he was told by others, this yellow powder could have been nothing else but gold-dust.

Other ancient vessels which have been sometimes discovered filled with ashes* are believed by the people to have contained golden treasures, thus changed by the devil to ashes.

There is a plant which is believed by both Saxons and Roumanians to possess the virtue of opening every lock and breaking iron fetters, as well as helping to the discovery of hidden treasures. The Rou-

---

* Evidently funeral urns.

manians call it *jarbe cherului* (iron grass or herb), and it is only efficacious when it has sprouted at the spot where a rainbow has touched
the earth. The rainbow is the bridge on which the angels go backward and forward between earth and heaven, and the flower grows
there where an angel has dropped his golden key of Paradise on to
the earth. The Germans call the flower *schlüssel blume* (key-flower),
and it may be recognized by having a heart-shaped leaf on which
is a spot like a drop of gold or blood. There are several places in
Transylvania where the plant is supposed to grow, but he who walks
over it unheeding will be sure to lose his way. In order to find it, it
is recommended to go out at daybreak and creep on all fours over the
grass. Who finds it should cut open the ball of his left hand and let
the leaf grow into the wound; he will then have power to break fetters and open locks. The celebrated robber F—— is said to have been
in possession of such a leaf, till the police destroyed his powers by
cutting it out of his hand. Horses whose fore-legs are tethered together by chains are sometimes set free when they happen to tread on
the jarbe cherului; and in the village of Heltau a Saxon peasant once
hit upon the device of putting his wife in chains and thus driving
her over the fields, expecting to find the flower where the fetters
should fall off.

Whoever sells land in certain parts of the country where gold is
supposed to be buried is always careful to indorse the reservation of
eventual treasures to be found on the spot.

But the people say that it is rarely good to seek for hidden treasures, for much of the gold buried in the country has been secured by
a heavy curse, so that he who raises it will be pursued by illness or
misfortune to himself and his family, unless he is descended in direct
line from the man who buried the treasure. Only such treasures as
lie above-ground exposed to the light of day may be appropriated
without misgiving. Many men have lost their reason, or have become
crippled or blind, but few indeed were ever made happy by gold dug
out of the earth.

CHAPTER XXXII.

THE TZIGANES; LISZT AND LENAU.

AMONG the many writers who have made of this singular race their special study, none, to my thinking, has succeeded in understanding them so perfectly as Liszt. Other authors have analyzed and described the gypsies with scientific accuracy, but their opinions are mostly tinged by prejudice or enthusiasm; for while Grellnan approaches the subject with evident repugnance, like a naturalist dissecting some nauseous reptile in the interest of science, Borrow, on the contrary, idealizes his figures almost beyond recognition. Perhaps it needed a Hungarian to do justice to this subject, for the Hungarian is the only man who, to some extent, is united by sympathetic bonds to the Tzigane; he alone has succeeded in identifying himself with the gypsy mind, and comprehending all the strange contradictions of this living paradox.

I cannot, therefore, do better than quote (in somewhat free translation) some passages from Liszt's valuable work on gypsy music, which, far more vividly than any words of mine, will serve to sketch the portrait of the Hungarian Tzigane.

"There started up one day betwixt the European nations an unknown tribe, a strange people of whom none was able to say who they were nor whence they had come. They spread themselves over our continent, manifesting, however, neither desire of conquest nor ambition to acquire the right of a fixed domicile; not attempting to lay claim to so much as an inch of land, but not suffering themselves to be deprived of a single hour of their time: not caring to command, they neither chose to obey. They had nothing to give of their own, and were content to owe nothing to others. They never spoke of their native land, and gave no clew as to from which Asiatic or African plains they had wandered, nor what troubles or persecutions had necessitated their expatriation. Strangers alike to memory as to hope, they kept aloof from the benefits of colonization; and too proud of their melancholy race to suffer admixture with other nations, they lived on, satisfied with the rejection of every foreign element. Deriving no advantage from the Christian civilization around them, they regarded with equal repugnance every other form of religion.

"This singular race, so strange as to resemble no other—possessing neither country, history, religion, nor any sort of codex—seems only to continue to exist because it does not choose to cease to be, and only cares to exist such as it has always been.

"Instruction, authority, persuasion, and persecution have alike been powerless to reform, modify, or exterminate the gypsies. Broken up into wandering tribes and hordes, roving hither and thither as chance

GYPSY TYPE.

or fancy directs, without means of communication, and mostly ignoring one another's existence, they nevertheless betray their common relationship by unmistakable signs—the self-same type of feature, the same language, the identical habits and customs.

"With a senseless or sublime contempt for whatever binds or hampers, the Tziganes ask nothing from the earth but life, and preserve their individuality from constant intercourse with nature, as well as by absolute indifference to all those not belonging to their race, with whom they commune only as far as requisite for obtaining the common necessities of life.

"Like the Jews they have natural taste and ability for fraud; but, unlike them, it is without systematic hatred or malice. Hatred and revenge are with them only personal and accidental feelings, never premeditated ones. Harmless when their immediate wants are satisfied, they are incapable of preconceived intention of injuring, only wishing to preserve a freedom akin to that of the wild horse of the plains, and not comprehending how any one can prefer a roof, be it ever so fine, to the shelter of the forest canopy.

"Authority, rules, laws, principles, duties, and obligations are alike incomprehensible ideas to this singular race—partly from indolence of spirit, partly from indifference to the evils engendered by their irregular mode of life.

"Such only as it is, the Tzigane loves his life, and would exchange it for no other. He loves his life when slumbering in a copse of young birch-trees: he fancies himself surrounded by a group of slender maidens, their long floating hair bestrewed with shining sapphire stones, their graceful figures swayed by the breeze into voluptuous and coquettish gestures, as though each were trembling and thrilling under the kiss of an invisible lover. The Tzigane loves his life when for hours together his eyes idly follow the geometrical figures described in the sky overhead by the strategical evolutions of a flight of rooks; when he gauges his cunning against that of the wary bustard, or overcomes the silvery trout in a trial of lightning-like agility. He loves his life when, shaking the wild crab-apple-tree, he causes a hailstorm of ruddy fruit to come pouring down upon him; when he picks the unripe berries from off a thorny branch, leaving the sandy earth flecked with drops of gory red, like a deserted battle-field; when bending over a murmuring woodland spring, whose grateful coolness refreshes his parched throat as its gurgling music delights his ear; when he hears the woodpecker tapping a hollow stem, or can distinguish the faint sound of a distant mill-wheel. He loves his life when, gazing on the gray-green waters of some lonely mountain lake, its surface spellbound in the dawning presentiment of approaching frost, he lets his vagrant fancy float hither and thither unchecked; when reclining high up on the branch of some lofty forest-tree, hammock-like he is rocked to and fro, while each leaf around him seems quivering with ecstasy at the song of the nightingale. He loves his life when, out of the myriads of ever-twinkling stars in the illimitable space overhead, he chooses out one to be his own particular sweetheart;

when he falls in love, to-day with a gorgeous lilac-bush of overwhelming perfume, to-morrow with a slender hawthorn or graceful eglantine, to be as quickly forgotten at sight of a brilliant peacock-feather, with which, as with a victorious war-trophy, he adorns his cap; when he sits by the smouldering camp-fire under ancient oaks or massive beeches; when, lying awake at night, he hears the call of the stag and the lowing of the respondent doe; when he has no other society but the forest animals, with whom he forms friendships and enmities—caressing or tormenting them, depriving them of liberty or setting them free, revelling in the treasures of Nature like a wanton child despoiling his parent's riches, but well knowing their wealth to be inexhaustible.

"What he calls life is to inhale the breath of Nature with every pore of his body; to surfeit his eye with all her forms and colors; with his ear greedily to absorb all her chords and harmonies. Life for him is to multiply the possession of all these things by the kaleidoscopic and phantasmagorial effects of alcohol, then to sing and play, shout, laugh, and dance, till utter exhaustion.

"Having neither Bible nor Gospels to go by, the Tziganes do not see the necessity of fatiguing their brain by the contemplation of abstract ideas; and obeying their instincts only, their intelligence naturally grows rusty. Conscious of their harmlessness they bask in the rays of the sun, content in the satisfaction of a few primitive and elementary passions—the *sans-gêne* of their soul fettered by no conventional virtues.

"What strength of indolence! what utter want of all social instinct must these people possess in order to live as they have done for centuries, like that strange plant, native of the sandy desert, so aptly termed the wind's bride, which, by nature devoid of root, and blown from side to side by every breeze, yet bears flower and fruit wherever it goes, continuing to put out shoots under the most unlikely conditions!

"And whenever the Tziganes have endeavored to bring themselves to a settled mode of life and to adopt domestic habits, have they not invariably sooner or later returned to their hard couch on the cold ground, to their miserable rags, to their rough comrades, and the brown beauty of their women?—to the sombre shades of the virgin forests, to the murmur of unknown fountains, to their glowing camp-fires and their improvised concerts under a starlit sky?—to their intoxicating dances in the lighting of a forest glade, to the merry knavery of their thievish pranks—in a word, to the hundred excitements they cannot do without?

"Nature, when once indulged in to the extent of becoming a necessity, becomes tyrannical like any other passion; and the charms of such an existence can neither be explained nor coldly analyzed—only he who has tasted of them can value their power aright. He must needs have slumbered often beneath the canopy of the starry heavens; have been oft awakened by the darts of the rising sun shooting like fiery arrows between his eyelids; have felt, without horror, the glossy serpent coil itself caressingly round a naked limb; must have spent full many a long summer day reclining immovable on the sward, overlapped by billowy waves of flowery grasses which have never felt the mower's scythe; he must often have listened to the rich orchestral effects and tempestuous melodies which the hurricane loves to draw from vibrating pine-stems, or slender quaking reeds; he must be able to recognize each tree by its perfume, be initiated into all the varied languages of the feathered tribes, of merry finches, and of chattering grasshoppers; full often must he have ridden at close of day over the barren wold, when the rays of the setting sun cast a golden glamour over the atmosphere, and all around is plunged in a bath of living fire; he must have watched the red-hot moon rise out of the sable night over lonely plains whence all life seems to have fled away; he must, in short, have lived like the Tzigane in order to comprehend that it is impossible to exist without the balmy perfumes exhaled by the forests; that one cannot find rest within stone-built prisons; that a breast accustomed to draw full draughts of the purest ozone feels weighed down and crushed beneath a sheltering roof; that the eye which has daily looked on the rising sun breaking out through pearly clouds must weep, forsooth, when met on all sides by dull, opaque walls; that the ear hungers when deprived of the loud modulations, of the exquisite harmonies, of which the mountain breeze alone has the secret.

"What have our cities to offer to senses surfeited with such ever-varied effects and emotions? What in such eyes can ever equal the bloody drama of a dying sun? What can rival in voluptuous sweetness the rosy halo of early dawn? What other voice can equal in majesty the thunder-roll of a midsummer storm, to which the woodland echoes respond as the voice of a mighty chorus? What elegy so exquisite as the autumn wind stripping the foliage from the blighted forest? What power can equal the frigid majesty of the cruel frost, like an implacable tyrant bidding the sap of trees to stand still, and rendering silent the voices of singing birds and babbling streams? To those accustomed to quaff of this bottomless tankard, must not all other pleasures by comparison appear empty and meaningless?

"Indifferent to the minute and complicated passions by which educated mankind is swayed, callous to the panting, gasping effects of such microscopic and supercultured vices as vanity, ambition, intrigue, and avarice, the Tzigane only comprehends the simplest requirements of a primitive nature. Music, dancing, drinking, and love, diversified by a childish and humorous delight in petty thieving and cheating, constitute his whole *répertoire* of passions, beyond whose limited horizon he does not care to look."

Having begun this chapter with the words of Liszt, let me finish it with those of the German poet Lenau, who, in his short poem, "Die Drei Zigeuner" ("The Three Gypsies"), traces a perfect picture of the indolent enjoyment of the gypsy's existence:

"One day, in the shade of a willow-tree laid,
    I came upon gypsies three,
As through the sand of wild moorland
    My cart toiled wearily.

"Giving to naught but himself a thought,
    His fiddle the first did hold,
While 'mid the blaze of the evening rays
    A fiery lay he trolled.

"His pipe with the lip the second did grip,
    A-watching the smoke that curled,
As void of care as nothing there were
    Could better him in the world.

"The third in sleep lay slumbering deep,
    On a branch swung his guitar;
Through its strings did stray the winds at play,
    His soul was 'mid dreams afar.

"With a patch or two of rainbow hue,
    Tattered their garb and torn;
But little recked they what the world might say,
    Repaying its scorn with scorn,

16

" And they taught to me, these gypsies three,
　When life is saddened and cold,
How to dream or play or puff it away,
　Despising it threefold!

" And oft on my track I would fain cast back
　A glance behind me there—
A glance at that crew of tawny hue,
　With their swarthy shocks of hair."

CHAPTER XXXIII.

THE TZIGANES: THEIR LIFE AND OCCUPATIONS.

In every other country where the gypsies made their appearance they were oppressed and persecuted — treated as slaves or hunted down like wild beasts. So in Prussia in 1725 an edict was issued ordering that each gypsy found within the confines of the country should be forthwith executed; and in Wallachia, until quite lately, they were regarded as slaves or beasts of burden, and bought and sold like any other marketable animal. Thus a Bucharest newspaper of 1845 advertises for sale two hundred gypsy families, to be disposed of in batches of five families—a handsome deduction being offered to wholesale purchasers. In Moldavia, up to 1825, a master who killed one of his own gypsies was never punished by law, but only if he killed one which was the property of another man—the crime in that case not being considered to be murder, but merely injury to another man's property.

In Hungary alone these wanderers found themselves neither oppressed nor repulsed, and if the gypsy can be said to feel at home anywhere on the face of the globe it is surely here; and although Hungarians are apt to resent the designation, Tissot was not far wrong when he named their country " Le pays des Tziganes," for the Tziganes are in Hungary a picturesque feature—a decorative adjunct inseparable alike from the solitude of its plains as from the dissipation of its cities. Like a gleam of dusky gems they serve to set off every picture of Hungarian life, and to play to it a running accompaniment in plaintive minor chords. No one can travel many days in Hungary without becoming familiar with the strains of the gypsy bands. And who has journeyed by night without noting the ruddy light of their myriad camp-fires, which, like so many gigantic glowworms, dot the country in all directions?

At the present time there are in Hungary above one hundred and fifty thousand Tziganes, of which about eighty thousand fall to the share of Transylvania, which therefore in still more special degree may be termed the land of gypsies.

The Transylvanian gypsies used to stand under the nominal authority of a nobleman bearing the title of a Gypsy Count, chosen by the reigning prince; as also in Hungary proper the Palatine had the right of naming four gypsy Woywods. To this Gypsy Count the chieftains of the separate hordes or bands were bound to submit, besides paying to him a yearly tribute of one florin per head of each member of the band; and every seventh year they assembled round him to receive his orders. The minor chieftains were elected by the votes of the separate communities; and to this day every wandering troop has its own self-elected leader, although these have no longer any recognized position in the eyes of the law.

The election usually takes place in the open field, often on the occasion of some public fair; and the successful candidate is thrice raised in the air on the shoulders of the people, presented with gifts, and invested with a silver-headed staff as badge of his dignity. Also, his wife or partner receives similar honors, and the festivities conclude with much heavy drinking.

Strictly speaking, only such Tziganes are supposed to be eligible as are descended from a Woywod family; but in point of fact the gypsies mostly choose whoever happens to be best dressed on the occasion. Being of handsome build, and not over-young, are likewise points in a candidate's favor; but such superfluous qualities as goodness or wisdom are not taken into account.

This leader—who is sometimes called the Captain, sometimes the *Vagda*, or else the *Gako*, or uncle—governs his band, confirms marriages and divorces, dictates punishments, and settles disputes; and as the gypsies are a very quarrelsome race the chief of a large band has got his hands pretty full. He has likewise the power to excommunicate a member of the band, as well as to reinstate him in honor and confidence by letting him drink out of his own tankard.

Certain taxes are paid to the Gako; also, he is entitled to percentages on all booty and theft. In return it is his duty to protect and defend his people to the best of his ability, whenever their irregularities have brought them within reach of the law.

Whether, besides the chieftains of the separate hordes, there yet exists in Hungary a chief judge or monarch of the Tziganes, cannot be positively asserted ; but many people aver such to be the case, and designate either Mikolcz or Schemnitz as the seat of his residence. In his hands are said to be deposited large sums of money for secret purposes, and he alone has the right to condemn to death, and with his own hands to put his sentence into execution.

No Tzigane durst ever accept the position of a gendarme or policeman, for fear of being obliged to punish his own folk ; and only very rarely is it allowed for one of them to become a game-keeper or wood-ranger.

Only the necessity of obtaining a piece of bread to still his hunger, or of providing himself with a rag to cover his nakedness, occasionally obliges the Tzigane to turn his hand to labor of some kind. Most sorts of work are distasteful to him—more especially all work of a calm, monotonous character. For that reason the idyllic calm of a shepherd's existence, which the Roumanian so dearly loves, could never satisfy the Tzigane ; and equally unpalatable he finds the sweating toils of the agriculturist. He requires some occupation which gives scope to the imagination and amuses the fancy while his hands are employed —conditions he finds united in the trade of a blacksmith, which he oftenest plies on the banks of a stream or river outside the village, where he has been driven by necessity. The snorting bellows seem to him like a companionable monster ; the equal cadence of the hammer against the anvil falls in with melodies floating in his brain ; the myriads of flying sparks, in which he loves to discern all sorts of fantastic figures, fill him with delight ; horses and oxen coming to be shod, and the varied incidents to which these operations give rise, are never-tiring sources of interest and amusement.

Instinctively expert at some sorts of work, the Tzigane will be found to be as curiously awkward and incapable with others. Thus he is always handy at throwing up earthworks, which he seems to do as naturally as a mole or rabbit digs its burrow ; but as carpenter or locksmith he is comparatively useless, and though an apt reaper with the sickle he is incapable of using the scythe.

All brickmaking in Hungary and Transylvania is in the hands of the Tziganes, and formerly they were charged with the gold-washing

GYPSY TINKER.

in the Transylvanian rivers, and were in return exempted from military service. They are also flayers, broom-binders, rat-catchers, basket-makers, tinkers, and occasionally tooth-pullers—dentist is too ambitious a denomination.

Up to the end of the sixteenth century in Transylvania the part of hangman was always enacted by a gypsy, usually taken on the spot. On one occasion the individual to be hanged happening to be himself a gypsy, there was some difficulty in finding an executioner, and the only one produced was a feeble old man, quite unequal to the job. A table placed under a tree was to serve as scaffold, and with trem-

BASKET-MAKER.

bling fingers the old man proceeded to attach the rope round the neck of his victim. All his efforts were, however, vain to fix this rope to the branch above, and the doomed man, at last losing patience at the protracted delay, gave a vigorous box on the ear to his would-be hangman, which knocked him off the table. Instantly all the spectators, terrified, took to their heels; whereon the culprit, securely fastening the rope to the branch above, proceeded unaided to hang himself in the most correct fashion.

When obliged to work under supervision, the Tzigane groans and moans piteously, as though he were enduring the most acute tortures;

and a single Tzigane locked up in jail will howl so despairingly as to deprive a whole village of sleep.

The Tzigane makes a bad soldier but a good spy; his cowardice has passed into a proverb, which says that "with a wet rag you can put to flight a whole village of gypsies."

The Tziganes are by no means dainty with regard to food, and have a decided leaning towards carrion, indiscriminately eating of the flesh of all fallen animals, or, as they term it, whatever has been killed by "God," and consider themselves much aggrieved when forced at the point of the bayonet to abandon the rotting carcass of a sheep or cow, over which they had been holding a harmless revelry.

A hedgehog divested of its spikes is considered a prime delicacy; likewise a fox baked under the ashes, after having been laid in running water for two days to reduce the flavor. Horse-flesh alone they do not touch.

The only animals whose training the gypsy cares to undertake are the horse and bear. For the first he entertains a sort of respectful veneration, while the second he regards as an amusing *bajazzo*. He teaches a young bear to dance by placing it on a sheet of heated iron, playing the while on his fiddle a strongly accentuated piece of dance music. The bear, lifting up its legs alternately to escape the heat, unconsciously observes the time marked by the music. Later on, the heated iron is suppressed when the animal has learned its lesson, and whenever the Tzigane begins to play on the fiddle the young bear lifts its legs in regular time to the music.

Of the tricks practised upon horses, in order to sell them at fairs, many stories are told of the gypsies. Sometimes, it is said, they will make an incision in the animal's skin, and blow in air with the bellows in order to make it appear fat; or else they introduce a living eel into its body under the tail, which serves to give an appearance of liveliness to the hind-quarters. For the same reason live toads are forced down a donkey's throat, which, moving about in the stomach, produce a sort of fever which keeps it lively for several days.

The gypsies are attached to their children, but in a senseless animal fashion, alternately devouring them with caresses and violently ill-treating them. I have seen a father throw large, heavy stones at his ten-year-old daughter for some trifling misdemeanor—stones as large as good-sized turnips, any one of which would have been sufficient to kill her if it had happened to hit; and only her agility in dodging these missiles—which she did, grinning and chuckling as though it were the best joke in the world—saved her from serious injury.

They are a singularly quarrelsome people, and the gypsy camp is the scene of many a pitched battle, in which men, women, children, and dogs indiscriminately take part with turbulent enjoyment. When in a passion all weapons are good that come to the gypsy's hand, and, *faute de mieux,* unfortunate infants are sometimes bandied backward and forward as *improvisé* cannon-balls. A German traveller mentions having been eye-witness to a quarrel between a Tzigane man and woman, the latter having a baby on the breast. Passing from words to blows, and seeing neither stick nor stone within handy reach, the man seized the baby by the feet, and with it belabored the woman so violently that when the by-standers were able to interpose the wretched infant had already given up the ghost.

BEAR-DRIVER.

The old-fashioned belief that gypsies are in the habit of stealing children has long since been proved to be utterly without foundation. Why, indeed, should gypsies, already endowed with a numerous progeny, seek to burden themselves with foreign elements which can bring them no sort of profit? That they frequently have beguiled children out of reach in order to strip them of their clothes and ornaments has probably given rise to this mistake; and when, as occasionally, we come across a light-complexioned child in a gypsy camp, it is more natural to suppose its mother to have been the passing fancy of some fair-haired stranger than itself to have been abstracted from wealthy parents.

Tzigane babies are at once inured to the utmost extremes of heat and cold. If they are born in winter they are rubbed with snow; if in summer, anointed with grease and laid in the burning sun. Though trained to resist all weathers, the Tzigane has a marked antipathy for wind, which seems for the time to weaken his physical and mental powers, and deprive him of all life and energy. Cold he patiently endures; but only in summer can he really be said to live and enjoy his life. There is a legend which tells how the gypsies, pining under the heavy frosts and snows with which the earth was visited, appealed to God to have pity on them, and to grant them always twice as many summers as winters. The Almighty, in answer to this request, spoke as follows: "Two summers shall you have to every winter; but as it would disturb the order of nature if both summers came one on the back of the other, I shall always give you two summers with a winter between to divide them." The gypsies humbly thanked the Almighty for the granted favor, and never again complained of the cold, for, as they say, they have now always two summers to every winter.

Another legend relates how the Tziganes once used to have corn-fields of their own, and how, when the green corn had grown high for the first time, the wind caused it to wave and shake like ripples on the water, which seeing, a gypsy boy came running in alarm to his parents, crying, "Father, father! quick, make haste! the corn is running away!" On hearing this the gypsies all hastened forth with knives and sickles to cut down the fugitive corn, which of course never ripened, and discouraged by their first agricultural essay the gypsies never attempted to sow or reap again.

Both Maria Theresa and her son Joseph II. did much to induce the Transylvanian gypsies to renounce their vagrant habits and settle down as respectable citizens, but their efforts did not meet with the success they deserved. The system of Maria Theresa was no less than to recast the whole gypsy nature in a new mould, and by fusion with other races to cause them by degrees to lose their own identity; the very name of gypsy was to be forgotten, and the Empress had ordained that henceforward they were to be known by the appellation of *Neubauer* (new peasants). With a view to this all marriages between gypsies were forbidden, and the Empress undertook to *dot* every young gypsy girl who married a person of another race. The Tziganes, however, too often accepted these favors, and took the earliest opportunity of deserting the partners thus forced upon them; while the houses built expressly for their use were frequently used for the pigs or cattle, the gypsies themselves preferring to sleep outside in the open air.

A gypsy girl, who had married a young Slovack peasant some years ago, used to run away and sleep in the woods whenever her husband was absent from home; while in another village, where the Saxon pastor had with difficulty induced a wandering Tzigane family to take up their residence in a vacant peasant house, he found them oddly enough established in their old ragged tent, which had been set up *inside* the empty dwelling-room. A story is also told of a gypsy man who, having attained a high military rank in the Austrian army, disappeared one day, and was later recognized with a strolling band.

There is, I am told, a certain method in the seemingly aimless roamings of each nomadic gypsy tribe, which always pursues its wanderings in a given circle, keeping to the self-same paths and the identical places of bivouac in plain or forest; so that it can mostly be calculated with tolerable accuracy in precisely how many years such and such a band will come round again to any particular neighborhood.

Nowadays the proportion of resident gypsies in towns and villages is, of course, considerably larger than it used to be, and nearly each Saxon or Hungarian town and village has a *faubourg* of miserable earth-hovels tacked on to it at one end. It is not uncommon, in these gypsy hovels, to find touches of luxury strangely out of keeping with the rest of the surroundings: pieces of rare old china, embroidered pillow-cases, sometimes even a silver goblet or platter of distinct value—to which things they often cling with a sort of blind superstition, always contriving to reclaim from the pawnbroker whatever of these articles they have been compelled to deposit there in a season of necessity. In the same way it is alleged that many of the wandering gypsy hordes in Hungary and Transylvania have in their possession valuable gold and silver vessels (some of these engraved in ancient Indian characters), which they carry about wherever they go, and bury in the earth wherever they pitch their temporary camp.

In order to count the treasures of one of the resident gypsies, it suffices to watch him when there is a fire in the village; ten to one it will be his fiddle which he first takes care to save, and next his bed and pillows—a soft swelling bed and numerous downy pillows being among the principal luxuries to which he is addicted.

Characteristic of the Tzigane's utter incomprehension of all social organization and privileges is an anecdote related by a Transylvanian proprietor. "In 1848," he told me, "when serfdom was abolished in Austria, and the gypsies residing in my village became aware that henceforward they were free, they were at first highly delighted at the news, and spent three days and nights in joyful carousing. On the fourth day, however, when the novelty of being free had worn off, they were at a loss what use to make of their novel dignity, and numbers of them came trooping to me begging to be taken back. They did not care to be free after all, they said, and would rather be serfs again."

Of their past history the only memory the Tziganes have preserved is that of the disastrous day of Nagy Ida, when a thousand of their people were slain. This was in 1557, when Perenyi, in want of soldiers, had intrusted to a thousand gypsies the fortress of Nagy Ida, which they defended so valiantly that the imperial troops beat a retreat. But, intoxicated with their triumph, the Tziganes called after the retreating enemy that but for the lack of gunpowder they would have served them still worse. On hearing this the army turned round again, and easily forcing an entrance into the castle cut down the gypsies to the last man.

All Hungarian gypsies keep the anniversary of this day as a day of mourning, and have a particular melody in which they bewail the loss of their heroes. This tune, or *nota*, they never play before a stranger, and the mere mention of it is sufficient to sadden them.

Only the higher class of Tzigane musicians (of which hereafter) are fond of calling themselves Hungarians, and of wearing the Hungarian national costume. This reminds me of a story I heard of a gypsy player who, brought to justice for a murder he had committed, obstinately persisted in denying his crime.

"Come, be a good fellow," said the judge at last, fixing on the weak side of the culprit; "show what a good Hungarian you are by speaking the truth. A true Hungarian never tells a lie."

The poor gypsy was so much flattered at being called a Hungarian that he instantly confessed the murder, and was, of course, hanged as the reward of his veracity.

Though without any regular social organization, the Hungarian gypsies may yet be loosely divided into five classes, which range as follows:

1. The musicians.
2. The gold-washers, who also make bricks and spoons.
3. The smiths.
4. The daily laborers, such as whitewashers, masons, etc.
5. The nomadic tent gypsies.

If, however, we reverse the order of things, and turn the social ladder upside down, these latter may well be ranked as the first, and so they deem themselves to be, for do they not enjoy privileges unknown to most respectable citizens?—free as the birds of the air, paying no taxes, acknowledging no laws, and making the whole world their own!

CHAPTER XXXIV.

THE TZIGANES: HUMOR, PROVERBS, RELIGION, AND MORALITY.

THE word Tzigane is used throughout Hungary and Transylvania as an opprobrious term by the other inhabitants whenever they want to designate anything as false, worthless, dirty, adulterated, etc.

"False as a Tzigane," "Dirty as a Tzigane," are common figures of speech. Likewise to describe a quarrelsome couple, "They live like the gypsies." And if some one is given to useless lamentation, it is said of him, "He moans like a guilty Tzigane."

Of a liar it is said that "he knows how to plough with the Tzigane," or that "he understands how to ride the Tzigane horse."

To call any one's behavior "gypsified" is to stamp it as dishonest. "He knows the Tzigane trade" is "he knows how to steal."

A showery April day is called "Tzigane weather;" adulterated honey, "Tzigane honey;" coriander-leaves, "Tzigane parsley;" a poor sort of wild-duck is the "Tzigane duck;" the *bromus scalinus* is the "Tzigane corn;" but why the little green burrs are called "Tzigane lice" is not very evident, for surely in this case the imitation has decidedly the advantage of the genuine article.

These phrases must not, however, be taken to express hatred, but rather a good-natured sort of contempt and indulgence for the Tzigane as a large, importunate, and troublesome child, who frequently requires to be chastised and pushed back, but whose vagaries cannot be taken seriously, or provoke anger.

The Tziganes are rarely wanting in a certain sense of humor and power of repartee, which often disarms the anger they have justly provoked. In a travelling menagerie the keeper, showing off his animals to a large audience, pointed to the cage where a furious lion was pawing the ground, and pompously announced that he was ready to give a thousand florins to whoever would enter that cage.

"I will," said a starved-looking gypsy, stepping forward.

"You will!" said the keeper, looking contemptuously at the small, puny figure. "Very well; please yourself, and walk in," and he made a feint of opening the door. "Step in; why are you not coming?"

"Certainly," said the Tzigane; "I have not the slightest objection, and am only waiting till you remove that very unpleasant-looking animal which occupies the cage at present."

Of course the laugh was turned against the showman, who, in his speech, had only spoken of the cage without mentioning the lion.

A peasant, accusing a Tzigane of having stolen his horse, declared that he could produce half a dozen witnesses who had seen him in the act.

"What are half a dozen witnesses?" said the gypsy. "I can produce a whole dozen who have not seen it!"

A starving and shivering Tzigane once, craving hospitality, was told to choose between food and warmth. Would he have something to eat; or did he prefer to warm himself at the hearth? "If you please," he answered, "I would like best to toast myself a piece of bacon at the fire."

When asked which was his favorite bird a Tzigane made reply, "The pig, if it had only wings."

Another gypsy, asked whether, for the remuneration of five florins, he would undertake the office of hangman on a single victim, answered, joyfully, "Oh, that is far too high a price! For five florins I would undertake to hang all the officials into the bargain!"

Some Tzigane proverbs are as follows:

"Better a donkey which lets you ride than a fine horse which throws you off."

"Those are the fattest fishes which fall back from the line into the water."

"It is not good to choose women or cloth by candlelight."

"What is the use of a kiss unless there be two to share it?"

" Who would steal potatoes must not forget the sack."

" Two hard stones do not grind smooth."

" Polite words cost little and do much."

" Who flatters you has either cheated you or hopes to do so."

" Who waits till another calls him to supper often remains hungry."

" If you have lost your horse, you had better throw away saddle and bridle as well."

" The best smith cannot make more than one ring at a time."

" A pleasant smile smooths away wrinkles."

" Nothing is so bad but it is good enough for some one."

" Do we keep the fast-days? Yes, when there is neither bread nor bacon in the cupboard."

" It is of no use to teach science to children, unless we explain it by means of the broomstick."

" Let nothing on earth sadden you as long as you still can love."

" It is easier to inherit than to earn."

" As long as there are poorer people than yourself in the world, thank God even if you go about with bare feet."

" When the bridge is gone, then even the narrowest plank becomes precious."

" Only the deaf and the blind are obliged to believe."

" Bacon makes bold."

" After misfortune comes fortune."

" Who has got luck need only sit at home with his mouth open."

" Never despair of your luck, for it needs only a moment to bring it."

There is no such thing as a gypsy church, and a legend current in Transylvania explains the reason of this:

" Once upon a time," so it runs, " the Tziganes had a right good church, solidly built of brick and stone like other churches. The Wallachs, who had neither stones nor bricks, had at that same time built themselves a church out of cheese and bacon, with sausage rafters and pancake roof.

" This building filled the greedy Tziganes with envy, causing them to lick their lips whenever they passed that way, and at last they proposed an exchange of churches to the Wallachs, who gladly accepted the bargain. But when the winter came the hungry Tziganes began to nibble at the pancake roof of their church; next they attacked the rafters, and there soon remained nothing more of the whole building. That is why since that time there has never been a Tzigane church, and why the gypsies, whenever they go to any place of worship at all, prefer to go to the Roumanian church, because, as they say, they like to remember that it once belonged to them."

This story has passed into a proverb, used to describe a man without religion, by saying, "He eats his faith, as the gypsies ate their church."

Their religion is of the vaguest description. They generally agree as to the existence of a God, but it is a God whom they fear without loving. "God cannot be good," they say, "or else he would not make us die." The devil they also believe in to a certain extent, but consider him to be a weak, silly fellow, incapable of doing much harm.

A Tzigane, questioned as to whether he believed in the immortality of the soul and the resurrection of the body, scoffed at the idea. "How could I be so foolish as to believe this?" he said, with unconscious philosophy. "We have been quite wretched enough and wicked enough in this world already. Why should we begin again in another?"

Sometimes their confused notions of Christianity take the form of believing in a God, and in his Son the young God; but while many are of opinion that the old God is dead, and that his Son now reigns in his place, others declare the old God to be not really dead, but merely to have abdicated in favor of his Son. Others, again, suppose this latter to be not really the Son of the old God, but only that of a poor carpenter, and are wont to say contemptuously that "the carpenter's son has usurped the throne."

The resident Tziganes often nominally adopt the religion of the landed proprietor—principally, it seems, because in former days they thus secured the privilege of being buried at his expense. Whenever they happen to have a quarrel with their landlord, they are fond of abruptly changing their religion, ostentatiously going to some other place of worship in order to mark their displeasure.

Two clergymen, the one Catholic, the other Protestant, visiting a Tzigane confined in prison, were each endeavoring with much eloquence to convert him to their respective religions. The gypsy appeared to be listening to their arguments with great attention, and when both had finished speaking he eagerly inquired, " Which of the two gentlemen can give me a cigar ?" One of these being in the advantageous position of gratifying this modest request, the scale was thereby turned in favor of the Church he recommended, and the other clergyman was sent away, doubtless with the bitter reflection that for lack of a pennyworth of tobacco he had failed to secure an immortal soul!

Another gypsy, in prison for having sworn falsely, was visited by a priest, who tried to convince him of the sinfulness of his conduct in swearing to what he had not seen.

" You are loading a heavy sin on your soul," said the priest.

" Have I got a soul ?" asked the Tzigane, innocently.

" Of course you have got a soul ; every man has one."

" Can your reverence swear that I have got a soul ?"

" To be sure I can."

" Yet your reverence cannot see my soul, so why should it be wrong to swear to what one has not seen ?"

A gypsy condemned to be hung bethought himself at the last moment of asking to be baptized. He wished to die a Christian, he said, having professed no religion all his life. His plan was successful, for the execution was suspended, and all sympathies enlisted in his favor. When, however, all was ready for the baptism, the gypsy occasioned much surprise by asking to be received into the Calvinistic faith. Why not choose the Catholic religion, which was that of the place, he was asked, since there was no apparent reason to the contrary. " No, no," returned the cautious Tzigane; "I will keep the Catholic religion for another time."

Though rarely believing in the immortality of the soul, the Tzigane usually holds with the doctrine of transmigration, and often supposes the spirit of some particular gypsy to have passed into a bat or a bird ; further believing that when that animal is killed, the spirit passes back to another new-born gypsy.

However miserable their lives, the Tziganes never commit suicide ; only one solitary instance is recorded by some traveller, whose name I forget, of an old gypsy woman, who, to escape her persecutors, begged a shepherd to bury her alive.

When a Tzigane dies, men and women assemble with loud howling, and the corpse, after having been prepared for burial, is carried on horseback to the grave, which is made in some lonely spot, often

17

deep in the forest. A chieftain is buried with much pomp, his people tearing their hair and scratching their faces in sign of mourning.

The abrupt transitions of joy to grief, and *vice versâ*, so characteristic of the Tzigane nature, are nowhere more apparent than in their rejoicings and their mournings. Thus each funeral ends with dancing and joyful songs, while every wedding terminates in howling and moaning.

The relations between the sexes are mostly free, and unrestrained by any attempt at morality. Unions oftenest take place without any attendant formalities, but in some hordes a sort of barbaric ceremony is kept up. The man, or rather boy—for he is often not more than fourteen or fifteen years of age — selects the girl happening to please him best, without any particular regard for relationship, and leads her before the Gako, where she breaks an earthen-ware jar or dish at the feet of the man to whom she gives herself. Each party collects a portion of the broken pieces and keeps them carefully. If these pieces are lost, either by accident or voluntarily, then both parties are free, and the

GYPSY GIRL.

union thus dissolved can only be renewed by the breaking of another vessel in the same manner.

The number of pieces into which the earthen-ware has been shattered is supposed to denote the number of years the couple will live together; and when the girl is anxious to pay a compliment to her bridegroom she stamps upon the fragments, in order to increase their number.

Sometimes, but rarely, the Tzigane is capable of violent and enduring love; and cases where lovers have killed their sweethearts out of jealousy are not unknown.

The Tziganes assimilate more easily with the Roumanians than with any of the neighboring races; and marriages between them, although not frequent, yet sometimes take place.

Some twelve or fifteen years ago, an Austrian officer, garrisoned in a small Transylvanian town, fell violently in love with a beautiful gypsy girl belonging to a wandering tribe. He carried his infatuation so far as to offer to marry her. The beautiful bohemian, however, refused to abandon her roving comrades; and at last the lover, seeing that he could not win her in any other way, and being convinced that he could not possibly exist without her, gave up his military rank, and for her sake became a gypsy himself, wandering about with the band, and sharing all their hardships and privations. How this peculiar union turned out in the end, and whether *à la longue* the gentleman remained of opinion that the world was well lost for love, is unknown; but several years later the *cidevant* officer was recognized as a member of a roving band of gypsies somewhere in northern Greece.

A touching instance of a young girl's devotion was related to me on good authority. Her lover had been confined in the village lock-up, presumably for some flagrant offence; and looking out of the small grated window, on a burning summer's day, he was bewailing his unhappy fate and the parching thirst which devoured him. Presently his dark slender sweetheart, attracted by the sound of his voice, drew near, and standing at the other side of a dried-up moat, she could see her lover at the grated window. She held in her hand a ripe juicy apple; but the only way to reach him lay through the moat. The girl was naked, not having the smallest rag to cover her brown and shining skin, and the moat was full of prickly thistles and tall stinging nettles. She hesitated for a moment, but only for one; then plunging bravely into the sea of fire, she handed up the precious apple through the close grating.

When she regained the opposite bank, the gypsy girl's skin was all blistered, and bleeding at places; but she did not seem to feel any pain, in the delight with which she watched her captive lover devour the apple.

CHAPTER XXXV.

THE GYPSY FORTUNE-TELLER.

THE ever-recurring excitements and excesses of which these people's life is made up cannot fail to have a deteriorating effect on mind
and body—early undermined constitutions and premature death or
dotage being the penalty paid by many for the unbridled and senseless gratification of their passions. This life, however, while it destroys many, sharpens the faculties of those whose stronger natures
have enabled them to defy these ravages, bestowing a singular power
of penetration in all matters relating to the senses and passions.

More especially is this the case with regard to the women, who,
already gifted by nature with keener perceptions, and prematurely
ripened in what may be termed a tropical atmosphere of passion, develop an almost supernatural power of clairvoyance, which enables
them with incredible celerity to unravel hitherto undisclosed secrets
by means only of intuitive deductions.

"The astounding vividness of their impressions" (again to quote
Liszt on the subject) "rarely fails to communicate itself like wildfire
to the hearers. As by the contagion of a deadly poison, the mere
touch of the gypsy fortune-teller is often sufficient to affect them with
the sensation of an electric shock or vibration.

"A few apt reflections strewed about in conversation, casual excla-
mations of apparent simplicity, some primitive rhymes and verses accentuated by passion, so to say hammered into relief like the raised
figures on a medal—such are the means which suffice to stir up in an
audience whatever elements may be there existing of secret wrath, of
latent rebellion, of characters bent but not broken, of affections discouraged but not despairing.

"The gypsy woman, herself well acquainted with all the signs and
workings of passion, distinguishes *à coup d'œil* the cause of the sallow
cheek and the fevered eye of such another woman ; she can feel instinctively whether the hand from which she is expected to decipher
a fate be stretched towards her with the hasty gesture of hope or with
the hesitation of fear. Without difficulty she reads in disdainfully

GYPSY MOTHER AND CHILD.

curled lips or ominously drawn brows whether the youth before her be chafing under a yoke or planning revenge; whether he craves love or has already lost it. She can further distinguish at a glance the delusive presumption of youth and beauty—the false security of possession which thinks to defy misfortune. She knows the annihilating blows of fate and the vulnerability of the human heart too well not to mistrust the smile of over-conscious happiness, and prophesy misfortune to those who refuse to believe in the instability of the future.

"She cannot be called a hypocrite, for she herself has faith in her own diagnosis; believing that each man carries within him the germ of his own fate, she is convinced that sooner or later her prognostics must be fulfilled. Her only care is therefore to clothe her predictions in a form which, easily captivating the imagination, and thereby impressed on the memory, will spring again to life, along with the image of the prophetess, whenever the latent emotions she has detected, having reached their culminating point, bring about the success or the catastrophe foreseen from the investigation of a hand and a heart.

"After all, why should we wonder that the secrets of the future can be deciphered by one so intimately acquainted with the inmost folds of the human soul, and the workings of different passions confined in the human breast like so many caged lions or torpid slumbering reptiles ?

"Passion always accompanied by a powerful sympathetic instinct quickly divines the presence of a kindred passion. Apt to decipher the symptoms inevitably betrayed in voice and gesture, and skilled to read in that mystic book whose characters are so plainly impressed on the leaves of a physiognomy which, betraying where it would fain conceal, becomes the more impressive in proportion as the heart within is agitated by tumultuous throbbings, the gypsy fortune-teller knows full well with whom she has to deal, and can justly estimate what sort of characters are those who seek her counsel."

It is, I think, Balzac who has said, " Si le passé a laissé des traces, il est à croire que l'avenir possède des racines ;" and on the principle that every man is master of his own fate, there is, after all, no reason why these roots, invisible to the rest of the world, should not be perceptible to such as have made of this subject the study of a lifetime. Why should not the seer be able to proclaim the fruits to be reaped from the recognition of germs which already exist?

The enlightened folk who sweepingly condemn the fortune-teller as a liar and cheat are probably no less mistaken than witless rustics, who blindly believe in her as an infallible oracle. Should not precisely the superior enlightenment of which we boast be argument for, rather than against, the fortune-teller? Why, if phrenology and graphology are permitted to take rank as acknowledged sciences, should not the gypsy woman's power of divination be equally allowed to count as a shrewd deciphering of character, coupled with logical deductions as to the events likely to be evoked by the passions she has recognized, when brought into combination with a given set of circumstances?

Ignorant people, surprised at the detection of secrets which they had believed to be securely locked up in their own breasts, and not understanding the process by which such conclusions were reached, are ready to attribute the fortune-teller's power of divination to supernatural agency, which opinion is strengthened and confirmed by the romantic conditions of the gypsy's existence, and the cabalistic glamour with which she contrives to invest herself.

But is not, in truth, this delicate and subtle perception in itself a secret and undeniable power—a sudden inspiration, a positive intuition of what will be from the rapid unveiling of what already is? And here, again, Liszt is probably right in asserting this gift of prophecy, so universally ascribed to the gypsies in all countries, to be a too deeply rooted belief in the minds of the people not to have some rational ground for its existence.

There is no doubt that the gypsy fortune-tellers in Transylvania exercise considerable influence on their Saxon and Roumanian neighbors, and it is a paradoxical fact that the self-same people who regard the Tziganes as undoubted thieves, liars, and cheats in all the common transactions of daily life, do not hesitate to confide in them blindly for charmed medicines and love-potions, and are ready to attribute to them unerring power in deciphering the mysteries of the future.

The Saxon peasant will, it is true, often drive away the fortune-teller with blows and curses from his door, but his wife will as often secretly beckon her in again by the back entrance, in order to be consulted as to the illness of the cows, or beg from her a remedy against the fever.

Wonderful potions and salves, composed of the fat of bears, dogs, snakes, and snails, along with the oil of rain-worms, the bodies of spiders and midges, rubbed into a paste, are concocted by these cunning bohemians, who thus sometimes contrive to make thrice as much money out of the carcass of a dead dog as another can realize from the sale of a healthy pig or calf. There is not a village in Transylvania which cannot boast of one or more such fortune-tellers, and living in the suburbs of each town are many old women who make an easy and comfortable livelihood out of the credulity of their fellow-creatures.

It has also been asserted that both Roumanian and Saxon mothers whose sickly infants are believed to be suffering from the effects of the evil eye, are often in the habit of giving the child to be nursed for a period of nine days to some Tzigane woman supposed to have power to undo the spell.

For my own part, I have seldom had inclination to confide the deciphering of my fate to one of these wandering sibyls, and can therefore only affirm that on the solitary occasion when, half in jest, I chose to interrogate the future, I was favored with a piece of intelligence so startling and improbable as could only be received with a laugh of derision ; yet before many days had elapsed this startling and improbable event had actually come to pass, and the gypsy's prophecy was accomplished in the most unlooked-for manner.

Chance, probably, or coincidence, most people will say ; and indeed I do not myself see how it could have been anything but the veriest coincidence. I merely state this fact as it occurred, and without attempting to draw any general conclusions from the isolated instance within my own personal range of observation.

CHAPTER XXXVI.

THE TZIGANE MUSICIAN.

THERE is a Transylvanian legend telling how a mother once pronounced on her son a curse, the effect of which should continue until he succeeded in giving a voice to a dry piece of wood.

The son left his mother, and went sorrowing into the pine forest, where he cut down a tree, and made a fiddle on which he played ; and his mother, hearing the sound, came running by and took the curse from off his head.

This story must surely have been written of a gypsy boy, for of none other could it have been equally appropriate; and if to the gypsy woman is given a certain power over the minds of her fellow-creatures, the male Tzigane—at least in Hungary—is not without his sceptre, and this sceptre is the bow with which he plies his fiddle.

Hungarian music and the Tzigane player are indispensable conditions of each other's existence. Hungarian music can only be rightly interpreted by the Tzigane musician, who for his part can play none other so well as the Hungarian music, into whose execution he throws all his heart and his soul, all his latent passion and unconscious poetry—the melancholy and dissatisfied yearnings of an outcast, the deep despondency of an exile who has never known a home, and the wild freedom of a savage who never owned a master.

Did the Tziganes bring their music ready-made into Hungary, or did they find it there and merely adopt it? is a question which has occasioned much learned controversy. Liszt inclines to the former opinion, which would mean that no Hungarian music existed previous to the Tziganes' arrival in the country in the fifteenth century. That this music is essentially of an Asiatic character is, however, no positive proof in favor of this theory, for are not the Hungarians themselves an out-wandered Asiatic race? and what more natural than the supposition that one Asiatic race should be the best interpreter of the music of a kindred people? More likely, however, this music is an unconscious joint production of the two, the Tzigane being the artist who has sounded the depths of the Hungarian nature and given expression to it.

I remember once asking a distinguished Polish lady—Princess C——, herself a notable musician and pupil of the great Chopin—whether she ever played Hungarian music. "No," she answered, "I cannot play it; there is something in that music which I have not got—something wanting in me."

What was here wanting I came to understand later, when I became familiar with Hungarian music as rendered by the Tzigane players. It was the training of several generations of gypsy life which was here wanting—a training which alone teaches the secret of deciphering those wild strains which seem borrowed from the voice of the tempest, or stolen from whispering reeds. In order to have played Hungarian music aright she would have required to have slept on mountain-tops during a score of years, to have been bathed over and

over again in falling dews, to have shared the food of eagles and squirrels, and have been on equally intimate terms with stags and snakes—
conditions which, unfortunately, lie quite out of the reach of delicate
Polish ladies!

Music was the only art within the Tzigane's reach, for despite his
vividness of imagination and the continual state of inspiration in
which he may be said to live, he could never have been a poet, painter, or sculptor to any eminent degree, because of the fitfulness of his
nature, and of his incapacity to clothe his inspirations in a precise image, or reduce them to a given form. Every man has the impulse to
manifest his feelings in some way or other, and music was the only
way open to the Tzigane, as being the one solitary art which, *à la
rigueur*, can dispense with a scientific training and be taught by instinct alone.

Devoid of printed notes the Tzigane is not forced to divide his
attention between a sheet of paper and his instrument, and there is
consequently nothing to detract from the utter abandonment with
which he absorbs himself in his playing. He seems to be sunk in an
inner world of his own; the instrument sobs and moans in his hands,
and is pressed tight against his heart as though it had grown and
taken root there. This is the true moment of inspiration, to which
he rarely gives way, and then only in the privacy of an intimate circle, never before a numerous and unsympathetic audience. Himself
spellbound by the power of the tones he evokes, his head gradually
sinking lower and lower over the instrument, the body bent forward in
an attitude of rapt attention, and his ear seeming to hearken to far-off
ghostly strains audible to himself alone, the untaught Tzigane achieves
a perfection of expression unattainable by mere professional training.

This power of identification with his music is the real secret of the
Tzigane's influence over his audience. Inspired and carried away by
his own strains, he must perforce carry his hearers with him as well;
and the Hungarian listener throws himself heart and soul into this
species of musical intoxication, which to him is the greatest delight on
earth. There is a proverb which says, "The Hungarian only requires
a gypsy fiddler and a glass of water in order to make him quite drunk;"
and indeed intoxication is the only word fittingly to describe the state
of exaltation into which I have seen a Hungarian audience thrown by
a gypsy band.

Sometimes, under the combined influence of music and wine, the

Tziganes become like creatures possessed; the wild cries and stamps of an equally excited audience only stimulate them to greater exertions. The whole atmosphere seems tossed by billows of passionate harmony; we seem to catch sight of the electric sparks of inspiration flying through the air. It is then that the Tzigane player gives forth everything that is secretly lurking within him—fierce anger, childish wailings, presumptuous exaltation, brooding melancholy, and passionate despair; and at such moments, as a Hungarian writer has said, one could readily believe in his power of drawing down the angels from heaven into hell!

Listen how another Hungarian has here described the effect of their music:

"How it rushes through the veins like electric fire! How it penetrates straight to the soul! In soft, plaintive minor tones the *adagio* opens with a slow, rhythmical movement: it is a sighing and longing of unsatisfied aspirations; a craving for undiscovered happiness; the lover's yearning for the object of his affection; the expression of mourning for lost joys, for happy days gone forever: then abruptly changing to a major key the tones get faster and more agitated; and from the whirlpool of harmony the melody gradually detaches itself, alternately drowned in the foam of over-breaking waves, to reappear floating on the surface with undulating motion—collecting as it were fresh power for a renewed burst of fury. But quickly as the storm came it is gone again, and the music relapses into the melancholy yearnings of heretofore."

These two extremes of fiercest passion and plaintive wailing characterize the nature of the Hungarian, of whom it is said that, "weeping, the Hungarian makes merry."

Under the influence of Tzigane music a Hungarian is capable of flinging about his money with the most reckless extravagance—fifty, a hundred, a thousand florins and more being often given for the performance of a single melody. Sometimes a gentleman will stick a large bank-note behind his ear, while the Tzigane proceeds to play his favorite tune, drawing nearer and nearer till he is almost touching; pouring the melody straight into the upturned ear of the enraptured auditor; dropping out the notes as though the music were some exquisitely flavored liquid flattering the palate of this superrefined *gourmet*, who, with half-closed eyes expressive of perfect beatitude, entirely abandons himself to the delirious ecstasy.

Not only do the people at rustic gatherings dance to the strains of these brown bohemians, but in no real Hungarian ball-room would other music be tolerated, and the Austrian military bands, so much prized elsewhere, are here at a discount and little appreciated.

Of course the gypsy bands in large towns are not composed of the ragged, unkempt individuals who haunt the village pothouses or the

GYPSY MUSICIANS.

lonely *csardas** on the *puszta*. Their constant intercourse with higher circles has given them a certain degree of polish, and they mostly appear in Hungarian costume; but intrinsically they are ever the same as their more vagabond brethren, and their eye never loses the semi-savage glitter reminding one of a half-tamed animal.

---

* The solitary inns standing on the wide *pusztas* are called *csardas*, and have given their name to the national dance.

The calling of musician has often become hereditary in certain families, who thus feel themselves to be interwoven with the fates of the nobility for whom they play ; and *vice versa,* for the youth of both sexes in Hungary the recollection of every pleasure they have enjoyed, the dawn of first love, and every alternation of hope, triumph, jealousy, or despair, is inextricably interwoven with the image of the Tzigane player. As Mr. Patterson says, "The Tzigane is a sort of retainer of the Magyar, who cannot well live without him—the insolent good-nature of the one just fitting in with the simple-hearted servility of the other; hence the Tzigane is most commonly found in those parts of the country where Hungarians and Roumanians are in the majority. He does not find the neighborhood of the hard-working, money-loving Suabians profitable to him." Those who are successful musicians gain a sort of abnormal social status far above their fellows. The proverb, "No entertainment without the gypsies," is acted upon by peasant and prince alike. Those nobles who have squandered their fortunes would, if they took the trouble to analyze the causes of their ruin, find the Tzigane player to form one of the heaviest items. As to the peasant there is a popular rhyme which says that if the Tzigane plays badly he gets his head broken with his own fiddle ; but should he succeed in touching the feelings of the excitable peasant, the latter will give him the shirt off his own back.

English people are apt to misunderstand the position of these Tzigane musicians, which is in every way a peculiar one—the intimacy with the upper classes thus brought about by their calling implying, however, no sort of equality. The Tzigane remains the gypsy fiddler, while the Magyar never forgets that he is a nobleman ; and the barrier between the two classes is as absolute as that between Jew and gentleman in Poland. Although it is no uncommon sight in the streets of any Hungarian town, towards the small hours of the morning, to see distinguished members of the *jeunesse dorée* (their spirits, no doubt, slightly raised by wine) going home affectionately linked arm-in-arm with these brown fiddlers, yet no Hungarian could fall into the amusing mistake of an English nobleman, who, making a point of lionizing all celebrities within reach, invited to dinner the first violin of a gypsy band starring in London some years ago. The flattering invitation occasioned the most intense surprise to the distinguished artist himself, who, though well used to many forms of enthusiasm called forth by his genius, was certainly not accustomed to be seriously taken in the sense of a civilized human being. It is said, however, that the gypsy's quickness of perception, doing duty for education on this occasion, enabled him to pass through the formidable ordeal of a London dinner-party without further breaches of our rigid etiquette than are quite permissible on the part of a barbarous grandee.

It is said that the Tziganes often perform the office of *postillon d'amour* in taking letters backward and forward between young people who have no other means of communication, their peculiar code of honor forbidding them to take any pecuniary remuneration in return. Thus many of them are able to show dainty pieces of handiwork and presents of valuable jewelled studs or amber mouth-pieces, received from their high-born patrons in token of gratitude for delicate services rendered.

The words "Tzigane" and "musician" have become almost synonymous in Hungary, and to say "I shall call in the Tziganes" is equivalent to saying "I shall send for the musicians."

When the dancers are limp and indolent the Tzigane musician loses interest as well, and plays carelessly and without spirit; but when he sees dancing *con amore*, and more especially if his playing be praised, then he knows neither hunger nor fatigue. He executes every sort of dance music with spirit, and his power of identifying himself with the dancers renders the gypsy's playing far superior to that of other professional musicians; but his real triumph is the *csardas*.

The band-master is fond of secretly selecting a couple from among the dancers, and at these directing his music—aiming it at them, if one may thus express it—following their every movement, and identifying himself with their every gesture. To watch a pair of lovers dancing is the gypsy player's greatest delight, and for them he exerts himself to the utmost, throwing his whole soul into the music, breathing the softest sighs and the most passionate rhapsodies of which his instrument is capable.

The Tzigane band-master—or, rather, the first violin, for the gypsies require no one to beat time for them—when playing in the ball-room, is wont to change the melody as fancy prompts, merely giving warning to his colleagues by two sharp raps of the bow that a change is impending. The other musicians do not know beforehand what tune is coming, but a note or two suffices to put them on the scent, and they fall in so smoothly that the transition is scarcely detected.

Almost every one of the dancers has his or her favorite air—their *nota*, as it is here called—and it is meant as a delicate attention when the Tzigane band-master, smiling or winking at a passing dancer, strikes into his air of predilection. The gypsy's memory in thus retaining (and never confounding) the favorite airs of each separate person in a large society is marvellous; and not only this, but he will likewise remember to a nicety which air was your favorite one three or four years ago, and all the attendant circumstances to which the former melody played accompaniment.

Thus, whirling past in the mazes of your favorite valse, with the girl you adore on your arm, you may catch the dark eye of the Tzigane player fixed expressively upon you, and in the next moment the music has changed; it is a long-forgotten melody they are playing now—a melody once familiar to your ears at a by-gone time, when you had other thoughts, other hopes, another partner on your arm ; when wood-violet, not patchouly, was perchance the scent you loved best, and fair ringlets had more charm than raven tresses.

For a moment the present scene has faded from your eyes, and in its place you see a vanished face and hear a voice grown strange to your ears. That valse, once to you the most entrancing music on earth, now sounds like the gibings of some tormenting spirit, and you breathe an involuntary sigh for a time that is no more!

Thus the Tzigane player, unlike the hired musicians in other countries, has an intimate and artistic connection with his dancers. In England or Germany the musician is simply the machine which plays, no more to be regarded than a barrel-organ or a musical-box; in Hungary alone he is something more, his power of directing being here not limited to the feet, but may almost be said to extend to the fancies and feelings of his audience—feelings which it is his delight to share and sway, with actual power to stimulate love or jealousy, and re-awaken grief and remorse, at the touch of his magic wand.

CHAPTER XXXVII.

GYPSY POETRY.

VERY little genuine Tzigane poetry has penetrated to the outer world, and many songs erroneously attributed to the gypsies (by Borrow among others) are proved to be adaptations of Spanish or Italian canzonets picked up in the course of their wanderings, while of those few which are undoubtedly their own productions hardly any exceed the length of six or eight lines.

" We sing only when we are drunk," was the answer given by an old gypsy to a collector of folk-songs, which pithy and concise definition of gypsy literature would seem to be a tolerably correct one—though, on the other hand, it might be urged with some show of reason that the gypsy, being often drunk, we might naturally expect his poetical effusions to be proportionately numerous.

And perhaps they are in fact more numerous than is generally supposed, only that for lack of a recording pen to take note of them as they arise their momentary inspirations pass by unheeded, leaving no more mark behind than does the song of some wild forest-bird when it has ceased to wake the woodland echoes. The conditions of the gypsy's life render all but impossible the task of a scribe, who has little chance of picking up anything of interest unless prepared for the time being to become almost a gypsy himself.

Nor have there been wanting ardent folk-lorists (if I may coin a word) who have gone this length; so, for instance, Dr. Heinrich von Wlislocki, who, in the summer of 1883, spent several months as member of a wandering troop of tent gypsies in Transylvania and Southern Hungary, and has lately published a volume of gypsy fairy tales, the fruit of his laborious expedition. Yet on the whole the harvest is a meagre one, if we take account of the time and trouble spent on its realization; and even this energetic collector has declared that he would hardly have the courage a second time to face the deceptions and fatigues of such an undertaking.

To his pen it is that we owe the first poem contained in this chapter; the second one, entitled, " The Black Voda," interesting as being an almost solitary instance of a consecutive gypsy ballad, was commu-

18

nicated to me by the courtesy of Professor Hugo von Meltzl, of Klausenburg, another Transylvanian authority in the matter of folk-lore,
who, in his "Acta Comparationis Literarum Universum," has given
many interesting details bearing on these subjects.

The other sixteen specimens of the Tzigane muse are so simple as
to call for no explanation, though in one or two cases not wholly devoid of poetical merit.

GYPSY BALLAD.

(From a German translation by Dr. H. von Wlislocki.)

O'er the meadow, o'er the wold,
Tracks a boy the wand'rer old,
Who a scarf wears by his side—
Follows him with stealthy stride.
Bleeding fells the wand'rer prone
In the forest dark and lone;
And the boy has ta'en the life
Of the man with murd'rous knife.
Throws the corse all stained with blood
In the river's rushing flood;
But, alas! not guessing he
Who this ancient wand'rer be.
Lightly running home then went,
Till he reached his mother's tent,
Held the scarf before her eyes;
She, long silent with surprise,
Cried at last with passion wild,
"Cursed be thou, my only child!
May the slayer of his sire
Branded be by Heaven's ire;
Hast thy father killed to-day,
And his scarf hast stolen away!"

THE BLACK VODA.*

"Rise, arise, my Velvet Georgie,†
Waken, set you to the bellows;
Forge and hammer nails of iron."

---

* This ballad, which in the original is called "Kalai Wodas," and begins thus:

"T'ushtyi, t'ushtyi, Barshon Gyuri,
Thai besh tuke pre tri vina,"

is, with slight variations, sung all over Transylvania, often by the gypsy smiths, who
mark the time on the anvil as they sing; the dialogue between husband and wife,
which forms the last part, being usually divided between two voices.

† Such names as "Velvet George," "Black Voda," etc., are very common among
the gypsies, and have probably had their origin in some peculiarity of costume or
complexion.

Said the husband, "I am coming;
Take the broom the dust out-sweeping."
And then Velvet Georgie rises,
Straightway on his feet is standing.
At the bellows quick down-sitting,
Nails of iron he is forging.
Then into the market going,
Roast-meat fresh and juicy bought he,
Roasted meat and white bread also.
And he walked into the tavern,
And he sat there eating, drinking,
Never thinking of his consort,
Nothing caring for her wishes—
No new dress for her is buying.
She to Voda ran complaining.
Voda thus his love did answer,
"To the merchant quickly hie thee,
Ask him what a dress will cost thee."
To the town she ran off smiling,
Chose a dress there for her wearing.
Quoth the merchant, "Not on credit;
Bring me cash before I sell it."
Voda paid him down the money;
Paid and went— But Velvet Georgie,
From the tavern soon returning,
Found his wife, and in his anger
Threw her in the glowing furnace,
Whence she, loud with cries of anguish,
Called upon her absent lover:

"Voda, Voda, O Black Voda,
See how both my feet are burning!"

"Let them burn, O faithless lassie,
Many pair of boots hast cost me."

"Voda, Voda, O Black Voda,
See now how my waist is burning!"

"Let it burn, thou brazen hussy,
Worn out hast thou many dresses."

"Voda, Voda, O Black Voda,
How my bosom burns and scorches!"

"Let it burn, O shameless harlot,
Many hands have oft caressed it."

"Voda, Voda, O Black Voda,
Both my hands are burning sorely!"

"Let them burn, O wanton lassie,
Many pair of gloves they cost me."

"Voda, Voda, O Black Voda,
Now my neck is burning also!"

"Let it burn, thou brazen hussy,
Many beads hast worn around it."

"Voda, Voda, O Black Voda,
Now my lips the fire is catching!"

"Let them burn, O shameless harlot,
Many kisses hast thou given."

"Voda, Voda, O Black Voda,
Now my head itself is burning!"

"Let it burn, thou worthless baggage,
Let the fire destroy thee wholly."

GYPSY RHYMES.

I.

The donkey is a lazy brute,
   That fact there is no hiding;
Yet those, methinks, the brute doth suit
   Who slow are fond of riding.

II.

Autumn glads the peasant's breast,
Sends the hunter on the quest;
Pines the gypsy's heart alone
For the sunshine that is gone!

III.

Since holds the tomb my mother dear,
My life is cheerless, bleak, and drear;
No sweetheart have on earth's wide face,
So is the grave my better place.

IV.

I my father never knew,
Friend to me was never true,
Dead the mother that I loved,
Faithless has my sweetheart proved,
Still alone with me you fare,
Faithful fiddle, everywhere!

v.

Of coin my purse is bare,
My heart is full of care;
Come here, my fiddle, 'tis for thee
To banish care and poverty.

vi.

Heaven grant the boon, I pray;
All I ask is but a gown—
But a gown with buttons gay,
Buttons jingling joyously,
Jingling to be heard in town!

vii.

God of vengeance! give to me
   That of wives the best;
Give me boot and give me spur,
   Give me scarlet vest.
Then though spite their visage darken
   In the market-place,
Fain must look and needs must hearken
   All my foemen's race.

viii.

Where soft the wee burn babbles down over there,
Full oft have I pressed these lips to my fair.
The burn it still babbles, will babble amain,
Shall lips to my fair be pressed never again!
The waves of the brook to the valley are flowing,
Where on grave of my fairest the blossoms are blowing.

ix.

Down there in the meadow they're mowing,
And looks at my sweetheart they're throwing;
Such looks at my sweetheart they're throwing,
That mad is this heart of mine going!

x.

Yonder strapping lass did bake,
Put no salt into the cake;
Lo! it sticks upon the pan—
Eat it, child, as best you can.

xi.

"Plainly, maiden, lov'st thou me?
Which thy true-love—I or he?"
"Thou, O thou, when thou art nigh;
But for love of him I die!"

XII.

Boots and shoes were never mine,
Seldom have I tasted wine;
But I once possessed a wife,
And she poisoned all my life!

XIII.

Hammer the iron! Deal thy blows
Heavy and hard, as a gypsy knows.
Poor, yet ever—how poor!—remain;
Heart full of bitterness, full of pain.
Ah, how well would it be if there
I could but in yon furnace glare,
Till soft it grew, my love's heart ply;
No man were then so rich as I.

XIV.

Underneath the greenwood-tree
Days I've waited three times three;
I would on my love set eyes,
Here I know her path-way lies.
Could I hope a kiss to earn,
Into weeks the days might turn;
Could I hope to win my dear,
Then each day might be a year!

XV.

Come, silvery moon, so silent and coy,
What does my brown sweetheart that dwells by the mere?
Say, was she not kissed by a flaxen-haired boy?
Or whispers a stranger soft words in her ear?

On second thoughts, better, moon, darling, be mute,
The odious trade of a telltale eschewing;
Or perhaps you might tell her—and that would not suit—
What yesterday evening myself I was doing!

XVI.

The bee ever makes for the flower,
And lads after lassies will go;
Was it otherwise, grandam so sour,
In the days of thy youth long ago?

For Nature her mould never varies,
To that can no wisdom say nay;
What the ancestor felt, that the heir is,
As inheritor, feeling to-day.

CHAPTER XXXVIII.

THE SZEKLERS AND ARMENIANS.

OF the Hungarians in general, who constitute something less than the third part of the total population of Transylvania, it is not my intention to speak in detail. Hungary and Hungarians have already been exhaustively described by abler pens, and I wish here to confine

myself chiefly to such points as are distinctively characteristic of the land beyond the forest. Under this head, therefore, come the Szeklers, as they are named—a branch of the Magyar race settled in the east and northeast of Transylvania, and numbering about one hundred and eighty thousand.

There are many versions to explain the origin of the Szeklers, and some historians have supposed them to be unrelated to the great body of Magyars living at the other side of the mountains. They are fond of describing themselves as being descended from the Huns. Indeed one very old family of Transylvanian nobles makes, I believe, a boast of proceeding in line direct from the Scourge

SZEKLER PEASANT.

of God himself, and there are many popular songs afloat among the people making mention of a like belief, as the following:

> A noble Szekler born and bred,
> Full loftily I hold my head.
> Great Attila my sire was he;
> As legacy he left to me
>
> A dagger, battle-axe, and spear;
> A heart, to whom unknown is fear;

A potent arm, which oft has slain
The Tartar foe in field and plain.

The Scourge of Attila the bold
Still hangs among us as of old;
And when this lash we swing on high,
Our enemies are forced to fly.

The Szekler proud then learn to know,
And strive not to become his foe,
For blood of Huns runs in him warm,
And well he knows to wield his arm.

There is also a popular legend telling us how Csaba, son of Attila, retreated eastward with the wreck of his army, after the last bloody battle, in which he had been vanquished. His purpose was to rejoin the rest of his tribe in Asia, and with their help once more to return and conquer.

On the extreme frontier of Transylvania, however, he left behind him a portion of his army, to serve as watch-post and be ready to support him on his return some day. Before parting the two divisions of troops took solemn oath ever to assist each other in hour of need, even though they had to traverse the whole world for that purpose. Accordingly, hardly had Csaba reached the foot of the hills, when the neighboring tribes rose up against the forlorn Szeklers; but the tree-tops rustling gently against one another soon brought news of their distress to their brethren, who, hurrying back, put the enemy to flight.

After a year the same thing was repeated, but the stream ran murmuring of it to the river, the river carried the news to the sea, the sea shouted it onward to the warriors, and again quickly returning on their paces they dispersed the foe.

Three years went by ere the Szeklers were again hard pressed by their enemies. This time their countrymen were already so far away that only the wind could reach them in the distant east, but they came again, and a third time delivered their brethren.

The Szeklers had now peace for many years; the nut-kernels they had planted in the land beyond the forest had meanwhile sprouted and developed to mighty trees with spreading branches and massive trunks; children had grown to be old men, and grandchildren to arms-bearing warriors; and the provisionary watch-post had become a well-organized settlement. But once again the neighbors, envying the strangers' welfare, and having forgotten the assistance which always came to them in hour of need, rose up against them. Bravely the Szeklers fought, but with such inferior numbers that they could not but perish; they had no longer any hope of assistance, for their brethren were long since dead, and gone where no messenger could reach them.

But the star of the Szeklers yet watched over them, and brought the tidings to another world.

The last battle was just being fought, and the defeat of the Szeklers seemed imminent, when suddenly the tramp of hoofs and the clank of arms is heard, and from the starlit vault of heaven phantom legions are seen approaching.

No mortal army can resist an immortal one. The sacred oath has been kept; once more the Szekler is saved, and silently as they came the phantoms wend back their way to heaven.

Since that time the Szekler has obtained a firm hold on the land, and enemies molest him no more; but as often as on a clear starry night he gazes aloft on the glittering track* left of yore by the passage of the delivering army, he thinks gratefully of the past, and calls it by the name of the *badak utja* (the way of the legions).

Recent historians have, however, swept away these theories regarding the Szeklers' origin, and explained it in different fashion. The most ancient records of the Magyars do not date farther back than the sixth century after Christ, when they are mentioned as a semi-nomadic race living on the vast plains between the Caucasian and Ural mountains. A portion of them quitted these regions in the eighth and ninth centuries to seek a new home in the territory between the rivers Dnieper and Szereth. From here a small fraction of them, pressed hard by the Bulgarians, traversed the chain of Moldavian Carpathians, and found a refuge on the rich fertile plains of Eastern Transylvania (895), where, living ever since cut off from their kinsfolk, they have formed a people by themselves. According to the most probable version, these fugitives would seem to have been the women, children, and old men, who, left unprotected at home in the absence of the fighting-men of the horde, had thus escaped the vengeance of Simeon, King of Bulgaria.

---

* The Milky Way.

"At the frontier," or "beyond," is the signification of the Hungarian word Szekler, which therefore does not imply a distinctive race, but merely those Hungarians who live beyond the forest—near the frontier, and cut off from the rest of their countrymen. One Hungarian authority tells us that the word Szekler, meaning frontier-keeper or watchman, was indiscriminately applied to all soldiers of whatever nationality who defended the frontier of the kingdom.

Later, when the greater body of Hungarians had established their authority over this portion of the territory as well, the two peoples fraternized with each other as kinsfolk, descended indeed from one common family tree, but who had acquired certain dissimilarities in speech, manner, and costume, brought about by their separation; and despite sympathy and resemblance on most points, they have never quite merged into one nationality, and the Szeklers have a proverb which says that there is the same difference between a Szekler and a Hungarian as there is between a man and his grandson—meaning that they themselves came in by a previous immigration.

The Szeklers had this advantage over their kinsfolk in Hungary proper, of never at any time having been reduced to the state of serfdom. They occupied the exceptional position of a peasant aristocracy, having, among other privileges, the right of hunting, also that of being exempted from infantry service and being enlisted as cavalry soldiers only; whereas the ordinary Hungarian peasant was, up to 1785, attached to the soil under conditions only somewhat lighter than those oppressing the Russian serf. Curiously enough, though the system of villanage had already been formally discarded by King Sigismond in 1405, it was taken up again some years later; and, in point of fact, up to 1848 there was scarcely any limit to the services which the Hungarian peasant was bound to render to his master.

Not so the Szeklers, who have always jealously defended their privileges and preserved their freedom, owing to which their bearing is prouder, freer, nobler than that of their kinsfolk. The Hungarian peasant, as a rule, is neither wanting in grace nor dignity. But freedom is just as much a habit as slavery; and as one writer has aptly remarked, "A people does not fully regain the stamp of manhood and its own self-respect in a single generation," so the man who can count back eight centuries of freeborn ancestors will always have an advantage over one whose fathers were still born in bondage.

Like the other Magyars, the Szeklers are an inborn nation of soldiers, and rank among the best of the Austrian army. It was principally on the Szeklers that the brunt fell of resisting attacks from the many barbarous hordes always infesting the eastern frontier. When the Wallachians fled to the mountains at the approach of an enemy, and the Saxons ensconced themselves within their well-built fortresses, the Szeklers advanced into the open plain and ranged themselves for battle, rarely abandoning the field till the ground was thickly strewn with their dead.

The Szekler, who has usually more children than his Hungarian brother, is well and strongly built, but rarely over middle size. His face is oval, the forehead flat, hands and feet rather small than large. With much natural intelligence, he cares little for art or science, and has but small comprehension of the beautiful. Even when living in easy circumstances, he does not care to surround himself with books like the Saxon, nor does he betray the latent taste for color and design so strongly characterizing the Roumanian. His inbred dignity seems to place him on a level with whoever he addresses. He is reserved in speech, with an almost Asiatic formality of manner, and it requires the stimulus of wine or music to rouse him to noisy merriment; but on occasions when speech is required of him, he displays inborn power of oration, speaking easily and without embarrassment, finding vigorous expressions and appropriate images wherewith to clothe his meaning. The Hungarian language has no dialect, and each peasant speaks it as purely as a prince.

The Hungarian's character is a singularly simple and open one; he is simple in his love, his hatred, his anger, and revenge, and though he may sometimes be accused of brutality, deceit can never be laid to his charge, while flattery he does not even understand. It is his inherent dignity and self-respect which makes him thus open, scorning to appear otherwise than he really is. You will never see a Hungarian bargaining for his money with clamorous avidity like the Saxon, nor will he accept an alms with humble gratitude like the Roumanian.

He uncovers his head courteously to the master of his village, but he will not think of uncovering for a strange gentleman, even were it the greatest in the land. Hospitality is with him not a virtue but an instinct, and he cannot even comprehend the want of it in another.

A Hungarian who had stopped to rest the horses in a Saxon village came wonderingly to his master. "What strange people are these?"

he said. "They were sitting round the table eating bread and onions, and not one of them asked me to join them !"

On another occasion a gentleman travelling with an invalid wife was overtaken by a storm near a Saxon village, and wanted to put up there for the night. There was no inn in the place, and not one of the families would consent to receive them. "You had better drive on to the next village but one," was the advice volunteered by one of the most good-natured Saxon householders. "Not to the next village, for there they are Saxons like us and will not take you in; but to the village after that, which is Hungarian. They are always hospitable, and will give you a bed."

The Szekler villages, of a formal simplicity, are as far removed from the Roumanian poverty as from Saxon opulence. The long double row of whitewashed houses, their narrow gable-ends all turned towards the road, have something camp-like in their appearance, and have been aptly compared to a line of snowy tents ready to be folded together at the approach of an enemy. The Magyar has a passion for whitewashing his dwelling-house, and several times a year, at the fixed dates of particular festivals, he is careful to restore to his walls the snowy garment of their lost innocence. This custom of whitewashing at stated periods is still said to be practised among the tribes dwelling in the Caucasian regions.

In the midst of the village stands the church, whitewashed like the other houses. It is slender and modest in shape, neither surrounded by fortified walls like the Saxon churches, nor made glorious with color like those of the Roumanians. Near to the entrance of the village is the church-yard, and in some places it is still customary to bury the dead with their faces turned towards the east.

There are few Roumanian villages in Szekler-land, neither do we find here the inevitable outgrowth of Roumanian hovels tacked on to each village, as is usual in Saxon colonies. The Roumanians do not thrive alongside of their Szekler neighbors, because these do not require their aid and will take no trouble to learn their language. The Szekler cultivates his own soil without help from strangers, whereas the Saxon, whose ground is usually larger than he can manage himself, and obliged to take Roumanian farm-servants, is compelled to learn their language; and it has often been remarked that a whole Saxon household has been brought to speak Roumanian merely on account of one single Roumanian cow-wench.

The greater number of Szeklers have remained Catholics, the population of the western district only having adopted the Reformed faith, while the Unitarian sect, which has made of Klausenburg its principal seat, and counts some fifty-four thousand members, is chiefly composed of Hungarians proper.

There are not above a dozen really wealthy Hungarian nobles in Transylvania, and of many a one it is jokingly said that his whole possessions consist of four horses, as many oxen, and a respectable amount of debts. The same sort of open-handed hospitality which has ruined so many Poles has also here undermined many fortunes.

The conjugal relations are somewhat Oriental among the lower classes, the position of the wife towards the husband involving a sense of social inferiority; for while she addresses him as *kend* (your grace), and speaks of him as *uram* (lord or master), he calls her thou, and speaks of her as *felsegem* (my consort). In walking along the road it is her place to walk behind her lord and master; and at weddings men and women are usually separated, and if the house have but a single room it is reserved for the men to banquet in, while the women, as inferior creatures, are relegated to the cellar or to a stable or byre cleared for the purpose. Bride and bridegroom must eat nothing at this banquet, and only in the evening is a separate meal served up for them, and, like the other guests, the new-married couple must spend this day apart.

If we are to believe popular songs, of which the following is a sample, the stick would seem to play no unimportant part in each Hungarian *ménage :*

> "O peacock fair, O peacock bright,
>   O peacock proud and high!
> I fool for though of lowly birth,
>   A noble wife took I;
> But nothing that I e'er could do
>   Would please my peacock high.
> To market once I went and bought
>   A pair of blood-red shoon.
> I placed my present on the bench—
>   'Twas at the hour of noon.
> 'Thy duty bids thee call me lord,
>   My darling wife,' quoth I.
> 'Nay, nevermore, that will I not,
>   And though I had to die,

For gentlemen of noble birth
    Sat round my father's board,
And if I said not "sir" to them,
    How should I call thee lord?'

"O peacock fair, O peacock bright,
    O peacock proud and high!
I fool! for though of lowly birth,
    A noble wife took I;
But nothing that I e'er could do
    Would please my peacock high.
Again to market did I go
    And bought a kirtle fine;
'Twas growing dark as on the bench
    I laid this gift of mine.
'Thy duty bids thee call me lord,
    My darling wife,' quoth I.
'Nay, nevermore, that will I not,
    And though I had to die,
For gentlemen of noble birth
    Sat round my father's board,
And if I said not "sir" to them,
    How should I call thee lord?'

"O peacock fair, O peacock bright,
    O peacock proud and high!
I fool! for though of lowly birth,
    A noble wife took I;
But nothing that I e'er could do
    Would please my peacock high.
The moon was shining in the skies
    When to the woods I sped;
I cut a hazel rod full long,
    And hid it 'neath the bed.
'Thy duty bids thee call me lord,
    My darling wife,' quoth I.
'Nay, nevermore, that will I not,
    And though I had to die.'
Then in my hand I took the rod
    And beat my bosom's wife,
Until she cried, 'Thou art my lord!
    My lord for death and life!'"

The Armenians deserve something more than a passing notice at the fag-end of a chapter; but having had little opportunity of being thrown together with these people, I am unable to furnish many details as to their life and manners.

Persecuted and oppressed in Moldavia during the seventeenth century, the Armenians were offered a refuge in Transylvania by the Prince Michael Apafi, and came hither about 1660, at first living dispersed all over the land, till in 1791 the Emperor Leopold granting them among other privileges the right to establish independent colonies, they founded the settlements of Szamos-Ujvar (Armenopolis) and Elisabethstadt, or Ebesfalva. This latter town, which counts to-day about twenty-five hundred Armenian inhabitants, is renowned for the good looks of its women—pale, dark-eyed beauties, with low foreheads and straight eyebrows, whose portraits might be taken in pen and ink only, without any help from the palette. They have the reputation— I know not with what reason—of being very immoral, but in a quiet, unostentatious fashion.

In the men the pure Asiatic type is yet more clearly marked—the fine-shaped oval head, arched yet not hooked nose, black eyes, jetty beard, and clean-cut profiles betraying their nationality at the first glance. In manner they are singularly calm and self-possessed, never evincing emotion or excitement. They are much addicted to card-playing. In many parts of Hungary the Armenians have so completely amalgamated with the Magyars as to have forgotten their own language, but where they live together in compact colonies it is still kept up. There are two languages—the popular idiom and the written tongue, the language of science and literature. Their religion is the Catholic one, but their services are conducted in their own language instead of Latin.

Like the Hebrews, the Armenians have great natural aptitude for trade; and it is chiefly due to their influence that the Jews have not here succeeded in getting the reins of commerce into their hands. The bankers and money-lenders in Transylvania are almost invariably Armenians.

A Saxon legend explains the origin of the Armenians by saying that when God had created all the different sorts of men, there remained over two little morsels of the clay of which he had respectively moulded the Jew and the gypsy; so, in order not to waste these, he kneaded them up together, and formed of them the Armenian.

CHAPTER XXXIX.

FRONTIER REGIMENTS.

THE south-west of Transylvania used to form part of the territory called the *Militär-Grenze* (military frontier) — a peculiar institution now extinct, which, interesting as being to some extent of Roman origin, may here claim a few lines of notice.

When the Roman conquerors had taken possession of the countries north of the Danube, they found it necessary to organize a sort of standing rampart of troops to be always at hand, ready to oppose unexpected attacks from the barbarian hordes on the other side. These soldiers, who might be designated as military agriculturists, found their sustenance in cultivating the ground assigned to each of them, and, being always ready on the spot, could be speedily formed in line at the slightest alarm of an enemy.

Similar circumstances caused the Hungarian kings to imitate these institutions, and organize the population of the southern frontier to that purpose, allotting to them the task of protecting the country against the frequent invasions of Turks. Not content, however, with resisting attacks from without, these troops often adopted an offensive line of action, making raids over the frontier to plunder, burn, and massacre in the enemy's country. The continual state of skirmishing warfare resulting from these arrangements kept up the martial spirit of the population, and many are the legends recorded of doughty deeds accomplished at that time.

After the fall of the Hungarian kingdom in 1526, the noblemen subscribed among themselves to keep up the frontier in the same fashion, often availing themselves of the assistance of these troops in their attempted insurrections against Austria.

But the Hungarian soldiers, who in this somewhat rough school of chivalry had acquired objectionable habits—such, for instance, as that of bringing back their enemies' heads attached to the saddle-bow whenever they returned from a skirmish—had, despite their evident utility, fallen into bad odor at Vienna; so when the Hungarian nobles themselves lost their independence, these frontier troops were suffered to fall into disorganization. Only after Maria Theresa had ascended the throne, and, having consolidated the Austrian power, obtained for herself and her descendants the irrevocable right to the Hungarian crown, was it thought necessary to reorganize in more regular fashion this living rampart along the frontier, with a view to keeping out the Turks, who were again showing signs of being troublesome. Accordingly, the population of the whole southern frontier, from Poland to the Adriatic, was classified in military companies and regiments, and the ground distributed to the peasants under condition that they and their children should live and die on the spot, their sons inheriting the obligation of serving in like manner as their fathers.

Of these frontier regiments, altogether fourteen in number, six were created in Transylvania. Of these two infantry and one dragoon regiment were recruited from the Wallachian population; the remaining three, two infantry and one hussar, from the Hungarians.

This system was carried out without trouble in the provinces recently reconquered from the Turks, which, being thinly populated, offered greater inducements for fresh settlers; but elsewhere, where there already existed a fixed population of Hungarians and Roumanians, there was much difficulty in establishing it. In former days the peasants had consented to pass their life on horseback in order to protect the frontier; but those days were long since gone by when people found such life to be congenial, and many of the novel conditions imposed by the Austrians were exceedingly distasteful. They did not care to be commanded by German officers, nor to feel themselves amalgamated with the Austrian regular troops, liable to be sent to fight on foreign territory.

Among the Wallachians whole villages emigrated in order to evade these new laws. Those who declined to serve, and were not inclined to leave their homes, were driven from their huts at the point of the bayonet, and replaced by other settlers brought from a distance. Much cruelty was resorted to in order to compel their obedience, the Austrians sparing neither fire nor sword to gain their ends; and the year 1784 in particular was most disastrous to those poor people, who, after all, were only trying to escape from unjustifiable tyranny. Also, a few years later, when some of these troops had risen in insurrection, declaring themselves only obliged to defend the frontier, not to espouse foreign quarrels in which Austria alone had a personal interest, whole regiments were decimated, shot down by the

19

cannon; and the place is still shown where the bodies of the victims of this wholesale butchery repose under two giant hillocks.

From an Austrian point of view, no doubt this institution was a most excellent and practical one; eighty thousand trained men, who cost but little in time of peace, were ready at a moment's notice for war. Before the officer's dwelling-house at each station stood a high pole, wound over with ropes of straw and other combustible matter, which was set fire to at the slightest alarm of an enemy. The signal being thus taken up and repeated from station to station, the whole frontier was speedily marked out in a fiery line, and the men collected and in arms in an incredibly short space of time.

When serving against an enemy their pay was equal to that of the regular troops, while in time of peace they received no pay except a few kreuzers per day whenever a soldier was on duty—that is, whenever he had frontier inspection.

On these troops devolved the duty of keeping in order all roads, buildings, etc., within their circuit, and nowhere in Hungary and Transylvania were to be found such excellent, well-kept roads, bridges, and buildings as those within the territory of the military frontier.

The men could not marry without permission of their superiors, their sons being, so to say, enrolled as soldiers before their birth; while daughters could only inherit their share of the father's land on condition of marrying a soldier.

The lot of those born and bred in this species of military bondage has been pathetically rendered in a Hungarian song, of which I offer a translation :

The wild wood was my native home,
Though born unto a soldier's doom.
  Amid the green leaves sighing,
  And gentle cushats crying,
  My father nurtured me.

But soon as I, a stripling grown,
Could sit a horse's back alone,
  I to the plough remaining,
  My sire must go campaigning
  Against the French afar.

Drive furrows deeper and more deep!
Outbursting tears in torrents leap!
  My father ne'er returning,
  My mother pining, yearning,
  Soon wore her life away.

Now we to war to-morrow go;
The Ruler's word has bid it so.
 Ah me! ye green leaves sighing,
 And gentle cushats crying,
 When shall I hear you more?

In former days, when the country was in a state of semi-barbarism, this system answered well enough; the military discipline was in itself an education, and the bribe of becoming landed proprietors induced many, no doubt, to accept the conditions involved. Later on, however, when all peasants obtained possession of the soil they tilled, the tables were turned, and the frontier soldier found himself to be

THE ROTHENTHURM PASS.

considerably worse off than his neighbor. Likewise, the original reason of these institutions no longer existed; the Ottoman power was rapidly decreasing, and surprises at the frontier were no more to be looked for. The spirit, the adventure, the poetry of warfare (which alone had caused these people to accept their lot) had departed, and they could no longer be induced to let themselves be led to butchery in distant climes to gratify a stranger's whim. Therefore, in the reorganization of the Austrian army after the disastrous campaign of

1866, these frontier regiments were, like other antiquated institutions, finally abolished, and have left no other trace behind but here and there a ruined watch-tower standing deserted in a mountain wilderness.

Many of the points selected for the erection of these military establishments lay amid the wildest and most beautiful mountain scenery, and for a keen sportsman, or an ardent lover of nature, the lot of an Austrian officer in one of these beautiful wildernesses must have been a very El Dorado.

One of the most beautiful, and from a military point of view, most important, of these military cordon stations was the Rothenthurm Pass (Pass of the Red Tower), so named from the color of a fortress-tower whose ruins may yet be seen beside the road.

This lovely mountain-gorge, traversed by the river Aluta, and to be reached in a pleasant two hours' drive from Hermanstadt, has been the scene of much cruel strife in by-gone days. Many a time have the wild devastation - bringing hordes poured into the land by this narrow defile; and here it was that in 1493 George Hecht, the burgomaster of Hermanstadt, obtained a signal victory over the Turks, whom he butchered in wholesale fashion, dyeing the river ruddy red, it is said, with the blood of the slain.

Nowadays the river Aluta flows by peaceably enough, and the primitive little inn which stands at the boundary of the two countries offers an inviting retreat to any solitary angler who cares to study the characters of Transylvanian *versus* Roumanian trout.

CHAPTER XL.

WOLVES, BEARS, AND OTHER ANIMALS.

TRANSYLVANIA has often been nicknamed the Bärenland, and though bears and wolves do not exactly walk about the high-roads in broad daylight, as unsophisticated travellers are apt to expect, yet they are common enough features in the landscape, and no one can be many weeks in the country without hearing them mentioned as familiarly as foxes or grouse are spoken of at home.

The number of bears shot in Transylvania in the course of the year 1885 was about sixty. Eight of these fell to the share of the

Crown-prince Rudolf of Austria, who for the last few years has rented a *chasse* at Gyergyó Szent Imre, in one of the most favorable bear-hunting neighborhoods.*

As to the wolves destroyed each year, they are not to be reckoned by dozens, nor even by scores, but by hundreds, and I was assured by a competent authority that between six and seven hundred is the number of those who last year perished by the hand of man.

It is the commonest thing in the world on market-days to see a group of shepherds in the ironmonger's shop (where a store of common fire-arms is kept), in deep consultation as to the merits of the pistol or revolver they are in want of for scaring the wolves so constantly molesting their flocks; and occasionally a snapping and snarling wolf, or a pair of bear cubs, are brought in a cart to the town in quest of an amateur of such fierce pets.

Even in the neighborhood of Hermanstadt it is not safe to walk far into the country alone in very cold weather for fear of wolves, which can easily approach the town under cover of the forest, which runs unbroken up to the hills; and while I was at Hermanstadt a large gray wolf was reported to have been seen several nights in succession prowling about within the actual precincts of the lower town.

At one of the toll-bars marking the limits of the town, and whence stretches off a lonely plain towards the south, a large fierce dog is kept chained up; but he never retains his situation two years running, because he is invariably destroyed by wolves before the winter is out. "The dog at the Poplaka toll-bar has been eaten again," is the matter-of-fact announcement one hears every year when the cold is rising, and which has long since lost all flavor of sensation or novelty; and one only wonders how any Hermanstadt dog can still be found infatuated enough to undertake this forlorn hope.

Up in the mountains, however, the wolves do not slink in stealthy groups of twos and threes, but assemble in such mighty packs that sometimes on the high pasturages the snow is found to be trampled down by the tread of many hundred feet, as though large droves of cattle had passed over the place. Officers who have been engaged in

---

* Since writing this, Crown-prince Rudolf has terminated another successful bear-hunting expedition in Transylvania (November, 1887), the booty on this occasion being a dozen head.

the work of going over the country, classifying all horses for purposes of national defence, have told me that in many out-of-the-way places up the hills they used to find the horses frequently bitten or scarred about the nose—as many keepsakes from the wolves, whose invariable habit it is first to spring at the horse's head.

Many are the ruses which the wolf employs in order to induce a horse or foal to detach itself from a drove of grazing animals. Sometimes he will roll himself up into a shapeless mass, and lie thus immovable for hours on the ground, till some young inexperienced colt, bitten with curiosity, wanders from its mother's side to investigate the strange bundle it espies at a distance. The wily murderer lets himself be approached without moving, and only then, when the hapless victim bends down to snuff the packet, he springs at the throat, and makes of it an easy prey.

The more experienced horses have long since learned that their only safety is in numbers; so at the approach of wolves they draw themselves together in a wheel, each head turned inward touching the others, their tails all pointing outward, and with their hind-hoofs dealing out such furious kicks as to enable them to keep at bay several enemies at a time.

The Transylvanian bears will rarely attack a man unless provoked, experiencing as much terror from a chance encounter as any they are likely to occasion. A Saxon peasant told me of such a meeting he had some years ago, when up in the mountains with some gentlemen who had come there in quest of deer. As they were to sleep in the open air, he had gone to collect firewood on the ground between a scattered group of fir-trees. When issuing from behind a tree-trunk he suddenly found himself face to face with a gigantic bear—not ten paces off. "We were both so taken aback," he said, "that for nearly a minute we stood staring at each other without moving. Then I called out, 'Der Teufel!' and took to my heels; and the bear, he just gave a grunt, which perhaps also meant 'Der Teufel' in his language, and he also turned to run; and when I looked back to see where he was, there, to be sure, he was still running down the hill as hard as ever he could go."

Only a couple of summers ago two Hungarian gendarmes were patrolling near Szent Mihaly where each of them, walking at a different side of a deep ravine, could see, without being able to reach, his comrade. As one of them came round a point of rock, he was suddenly confronted by a bear carrying a sheep in his mouth. In this case, also, man and bear stared at each other for some seconds; then the bear turned away in order to carry off his booty to a safe place. The gendarme, recovering from his surprise, fired at the retreating bear, which, wounded, gave a loud roar. A second shot likewise took effect, for now the bear, dropping the sheep, raised himself on his hind-legs, and advanced on his assailant. By the time a third shot was fired the bear had come up close and seized the muzzle of the gun. A fearful struggle now began between man and beast. The gendarme was holding on convulsively to his gun, when, his foot catching in a tree-root, he stumbled and fell to the ground. Already he saw the dreadful jaws of the bear close to his face, and gave himself up for lost. However, the bear was getting weaker, and let go its hold on the gun to seize the leg of the man, who, with a last desperate effort, struck the animal on the breast with the butt-end of his rifle. This turned the scale, and the animal fled down the ravine to hide itself in the stream. In the mean time the second gendarme, who from the other side had been spectator of the scene, arrived, along with some shepherds armed with clubs and pickaxes, and pursued the bear into his retreat. The animal received them with terrific roars, and began to pick up large stones, which he hurled at his adversaries with such correct aim as severely to wound one of the shepherds on the head. Finally the beast was killed, and his stomach discovered to be full of fresh ox-flesh. The wounded gendarme had to be conveyed home on horseback, and his gun was found to have been completely bent in the struggle.

At the costumed procession commemorating the arrival of the Saxons in Transylvania, which I have described in Chapter V., the most conspicuous object in the group of hunting-trophies was a gigantic stuffed bear, which, as a current newspaper announced, "had been shot expressly for the occasion." This paragraph excited considerable derision among non-Transylvanian sportsmen, who mockingly inquired whether a bear could be killed to order like an ox or a prize pig.

In this case, however, the newspapers said no more than the simple truth, the bear in question having been literally shot to order by Oberlieutenant Berger, a native of the place, and one of the most noteworthy Nimrods in the land.

It happened, namely, that about a fortnight before the day fixed for the procession, some of the gentlemen charged with its arrangement were lamenting that the only bear they had for figuring in the hunting-group was of somewhat shabby dimensions; on hearing which Oberlieutenant Berger volunteered to go into the mountains in quest of a better one. Chance favored his expedition, for within forty-eight hours he met and shot the magnificent animal which had the honor of figuring in the historical pageant.

Besides the two fresh bullets which had caused its death, no less than eleven old lead balls were found completely grown into the flesh and muscles of the animal.

Two young bear cubs captured alive by another sportsman earlier in the year had originally been destined to join the procession as well as their dead relative; but proving too unruly, they had to be discarded from the programme, as it was feared that their roaring might alarm the horses.

Though stocked by nature with a profusion of every sort of game, such as roe-deer, stags, chamois, etc., sportsmen generally find Transylvania to be an unsatisfactory country for hunting purposes. It is just sufficiently preserved in order to hamper an ardent sportsman who wishes, gun in hand, to roam unmolested about the hills; yet not enough protected to prevent the Roumanian peasants from calmly appropriating everything which happens to cross their path. They can hardly be called poachers either, because they are simply and utterly wanting in comprehension for this sort of personal property, and it would be as easy to persuade one of them that it is wrong to slake his thirst at a mountain spring as get him to believe that any of the animals he sees running wild in the forest can belong to any one man more than to another.

Even when regular hunting *battues* are organized, the Roumanians employed as beaters will not fail to put in a shot whenever they have the chance, nor will they hesitate to despoil your bag of half its booty whenever your back is turned.

In a large shooting-party in the neighborhood of Hermanstadt two years ago, two roe-deer had been shot down at the first drive. More than one of the gentlemen had distinctly marked the place where the animals fell, yet on coming up to it no trace of either was there to be seen save a little blood upon the grass, and the beaters who had first reached the spot loudly swore that the wounded animals had made their escape. All search was unavailing to discover where the carcasses had been hidden, and neither threat nor bribe could induce the peasants to disgorge the booty; but early next morning there were offered for sale at the Hermanstadt market-place two fine roe-deer, which, without rash judgment, may be safely asserted to be identical with those so mysteriously spirited away the day before.

On the occasion of this same shooting-party some of the beaters had formed the further ingenious project of stealing the gun from one of the gentlemen as he lay asleep near the camp-fire; but they had reckoned without their host, not having counted on the exceptional contingency of there being one honest man among them, who took upon himself to put his masters on their guard. The other beaters, enraged at this treachery on the part of a comrade, revenged themselves by destroying the saddle and cutting out the tongue of his horse.

Chamois are sometimes to be seen in numbers of thirty to forty heads at once. Roe and stags are common, but the lynx and marten are growing rare; while the ibex and urus have completely died out, the last urus known of in Transylvania having been killed near Udvarhely in 1775.

Small game, such as hares, partridges, etc., are rarely to be purchased in the market, and still more rarely to be met with in the stubble-fields. *Haselhühner** and capercailzie are, however, sufficiently numerous in the pine woods to reward more than a passing acquaintance; and whoever takes the trouble to approach the river Alt with anything resembling a civilized rod may be sure of a basketful of well-flavored trout.

The wild-cat, badger, fox, and otter are still plentiful, as well as almost every European variety of eagle and falcon. Vultures are likewise numerous; and a friend of ours who, to attract these birds of prey, lately invested in the unsavory purchase of five dead dogs, which were deposited on a sand-bank near the river, had presently the satisfaction of seeing nine well-grown vultures settle on the place.

Those same bear cubs which had shown themselves so unworthy of figuring in the historical procession were a great source of amusement to us. When they arrived they were tiny round balls of fur yelping

---

* The technical name of the *Haselhuhn* is *Tetrao bonasia.* They reside chiefly in pine woods.

piteously for their mother, and hardly able to walk, but soon got reconciled to their position, and became most intimate with the soldiers
at the barracks, where they were lodged. One day when we went to
visit them in the barrack-yard, accompanied by several terriers, one of
the cubs, happening to be in a playful mood, began making advances
to the dogs, which mostly took to their heels in terror at sight of this
formidable playmate. One white fox-terrier only stood his ground
and entered into the spirit of the thing, and in the wild game of gam-
bols which ensued the ponderous antics of the baby bear beside the
lightning-like movements of the wiry terrier, as they chased each other
round and round the barrack-yard, were a sight worth seeing.

In spite of their apparent awkwardness, however, it is wonderful
to see with what agility these young bears could run up and down a
tree-trunk, leading one to the uncomfortable conclusion that if pursued by one of their kinsfolk in a forest the hope of saving one's self
by climbing a tree would be a slender one.

These two cubs, which for some incomprehensible reason had been
christened Dick and John, grew warmly attached to the officer who
had brought them here, and would rush impetuously to meet him
whenever he was seen approaching. Both of them seemed likewise
to be much attracted by the sight of scarlet, and whenever they espied
a pair of red hussar breeches, or the scarlet stripe down a general's
legging, there was instantly a race to this brilliant goal, not always rel-
ished by the object of these attentions, who sometimes failed to see the
fun of being folded in their uncouth embrace.

Dick was apt to be sulky at times, and wont to misinterpret a
friendly poke from a parasol, but John had an angelic disposition, and
soon became the favorite. Dick had a bad habit of sucking his brother's ears, who used patiently to submit to the operation for an hour at
a time, which course of treatment soon transformed his beautiful bushy
ears into two limp fleshy flaps, devoid of the slightest appearance of
hair.

They both very soon learned to know the soldiers' dinner-hour,
and while the food was preparing used to push open the kitchen door
in hopes of a share, till their importunities were baffled by an order
to keep the kitchen locked in future. This much aggrieved the cubs,
which stood outside thumping the door for admittance; and one day
when the key had been merely turned, and left sticking on the outside,
Dick seized hold of it between his teeth, working it backward and for-

ward with such persistency that he finally forced the lock and marched triumphant into the kitchen.

Unfortunately the golden age of childish grace and innocence is but of short duration in the case of bears, and Dick and John proved no exception to this rule. After a very few months they began to grow large and gawky; the amount of butcher's meat required for their sustenance was something terrific, and Dick's temper was daily growing more precarious. Arrangements for their removal to more suitable quarters were therefore made, and finding their kennel empty one day, we received the mournful intelligence that the furry brothers had been transferred to the safer guardianship of a zoological establishment at Pesth.

CHAPTER XLI.

A ROUMANIAN VILLAGE.

In our intercourse with the Roumanian peasantry we are constantly reminded of the fact that only yesterday they were a barbarous race with whom murder and plunder were every-day habits, and in whom the precepts of respect for life and property have yet to be instilled. Not that the Roumanian is by nature murderously inclined—on the contrary, he is gentle and harmless enough as a general rule, and in nine cases out of ten the idea of harming you will not even occur to him; but should your life by any chance happen to stand between him and the object of his desire, no sentiment of religion or morality will be likely to restrain him from using his knife as freely as he would in the case of a hare or roe-deer. It is not that he takes life for the pleasure of shedding blood, but simply that he sets little value on it, and that he regards as far greater sin any infraction of his Church laws than the most flagrant attack on life and property.

The study of this people, gradually emerging from barbarism into civilization, is most curious and interesting. While eagerly grasping at the benefits held out to them by science, they are as yet unable to shake themselves clear of the cobwebs of paganism and superstition which often obscure their vision. It is the struggle between past and future, between darkness and light, between superstition and science; and who can doubt that the result will be a brilliant one, and that a glorious resurrection awaits these spirits, so long enchained in bondage.

But this hour has not yet struck, and the study of this people, however interesting, has its drawbacks, sometimes even perils; and especially for a lady, it is not always advisable to trust herself alone and unarmed in one of the out-of-the-way Roumanian villages, as I had occasion myself to discover in one of my expeditions to a hamlet lying south-east of Hermanstadt.

Some time previously I had "spotted" this place on the map; it seemed to be within easy walking distance—not more than two hours off—and, lying somewhat away from the high-road, was not likely to have been much visited, and might therefore be expected to possess a fair assortment of china jugs and embroidered towels.

"Take your revolver with you, mamma," suggested my youngest son, when I told him where I was going.

"Nonsense!" I replied; "the map and some sandwiches are all I shall require;" for my experience, which till then had lain entirely in Saxon villages, had shown me no ground for such precautions. I do not suppose that the child's warning had been dictated by any prophetic spirit; more likely he wondered how any one lucky enough to possess such a delightful toy as a real revolver could refuse themselves the pleasure of sporting it on every possible occasion. So, leaving the neat little fire-arm hanging on its customary nail, I started on my walk, accompanied by a young German maid, who, speaking both Hungarian and Roumanian fluently, was useful as an interpreter.

It was early in October, and a bright sunshiny day; the high-road was crowded with carts and peasants coming to town, for it was market-day; but after we had struck into a path across the fields the way lay solitary before us. The village, which nestled against a bare hillside, was neither very picturesque nor interesting-looking; and as we drew nearer I saw that it had a somewhat poverty-stricken aspect, which considerably depressed my hopes of ceramic treasures. I had not been aware that this hamlet, formerly a flourishing Saxon settlement, had by degrees become flooded by the Roumanian element, and that the Protestant church, for lack of a congregation, was now usually shut up. Many of the people had German names, while speaking the Roumanian language and wearing the Roumanian dress; and of all the inhabitants four families only still professed the Lutheran faith. Intermarriage with Roumanians, and the total extinction of many Saxon families, had been the causes which had thus metamorphosed the national character of the village.

Crossing a little bridge over the bed of a partially dried-up stream, we entered the hamlet, where I forthwith began operations, proceeding from house to house. At the very outset I found two pretty specimens of china jugs in a gypsy hovel, but this was a solitary instance of good-luck which had no sequel, for all the other huts could only produce coarse Roumanian ware, very much inferior to Saxon pottery.

Our appearance in the village made a considerable sensation, and at first we were slightly mobbed by all sorts of wild uncouth figures, mostly gypsies; but luckily by degrees the interest wore off, and we were left alone, but for one particularly villanous-looking man who kept following at a little distance. Already I had been rather provoked by several attempts to pick my pocket on the part of the gypsies, so was on my guard, when, standing still to reflect where next to go, the villanous-looking individual approached to accost me, and I could see that his eyes were riveted on my gold watch-chain, which imprudently I had left visible outside my jacket. These suspicions were presently strengthened by his asking me what o'clock it was. "Look at your own church clock," I answered, rather shortly, pointing to the tower close at hand; but he gave a roguish grin, and said, "Our clock is slow; I wanted to set it right."

I could not help laughing, though I did not feel quite easy in my mind, and gave him the information he professed to want, but which of course was only an excuse to look at my watch. I now tried to shake him off, but my villanous friend was anxious to improve the acquaintance, and would not leave me without having ascertained who I was, and what I wanted here.

"Old china jugs!" he exclaimed, when somewhat weakly I had admitted my errand. "I have got plenty such jugs, if the gracious lady will only condescend to come into my house close by."

I looked again more narrowly at the face of my villanous friend, and the result of my investigations was to answer with great decision, "Thank you, I have got enough china jugs for to-day—*quite* enough."

He tried to insist, till I found it expedient to lose my temper, telling him to go about his business and leave me in peace. He did leave me in peace, but only indirectly, for we saw him soon after speaking to a gypsy woman, who presently began to dog our footsteps in the same manner, trying to induce me to go into this or that one of the more disreputable-looking houses.

By this time I was thoroughly tired out. Any one who has had like experience will know how fatiguing it is to go into twenty or thirty houses in succession, with the invariable stereotyped questions, "Have you any jugs? and will you sell them?" and then to repeat over and over again the self-same process of persuasion and bargaining. Besides this, I had risen early, had a long walk, and was very hungry, so naturally wanted a quiet spot to sit down and eat my sandwiches. "There must surely be a village inn where we can get a glass of milk," I said, turning round to our persistent follower.

"There, there," said the woman, pointing in advance, and she disappeared running down the street.

We had no difficulty in finding the inn, as indicated by the usual sign all over Austria—a bunch of wood-shavings hung over the doorway. I was about to enter the room, when my German servant suddenly drew back and pulled my dress. "Come away, come away, madam," she whispered; "it is not safe to go in there," and as soon as we had regained the road and shaken ourselves clear of some loungers outside who tried to persuade us to re-enter, she explained the cause of her terror: she had caught sight of that same man who had asked to see the watch hiding behind the pothouse door, and evidently lying in wait for us.

This looked serious, and it was evident that some sort of trap was being laid for my unfortunate watch, so I resolved that nothing in the world should induce me to enter any such suspicious-looking house. My maid was nearly crying with fright by this time, and shaking like an aspen leaf, so I kindly advised her not to be a fool, pointing out that there was really no cause for alarm after all. "We need not enter any house unless we like, and they will hardly think of murdering us in the open street, so do not make a fuss about nothing."

"It is not for myself, but on account of the *gnädige frau*, that I am frightened," the girl now explained, apparently stung by the insinuation of cowardice. "If anything should happen to you, madam, what will the master say to me when I go home alone? He will say it was all my fault!"

"Make your mind quite easy," I said (perhaps rather cruelly, as it now strikes me). "If they should cut my throat to get the watch, they will for a certainty cut yours as well to prevent you telling tales of them, so you will never reach home to be scolded."

But the question of what to do was in truth becoming perplexing;

rest and food were now secondary considerations, my only thought being how safely to reach home. The long lonely way that separated this village from the town seemed doubly long and desolate in anticipation, and I hardly liked to start from here alone. I now thought with regretful longing of the handy little revolver I had left at home in its Russia-leather case. Not that I should ever have required to use it, of course, but its appearance alone would have served as antidote to the dangerous fascinations of the gold watch. If I had but followed my boy's advice I should not have found myself in this awkward predicament.

Taking a turn down the road to collect my ideas, a thought struck me. In the course of my peregrinations through the village earlier in the day, I had noted one house where the people appeared more respectable, though in nowise wealthier, than their neighbors. The man had a frank open face, in which I could hardly be mistaken; and, moreover, I had observed a few books lying on a shelf, in itself an unusual circumstance in any Roumanian house, which would seem to imply some degree of culture. To this man, therefore, I resolved to go for advice; perhaps he would himself accompany us part of the way, or else provide some other escort who would undertake not to cut our throats between this and Hermanstadt.

This plan seemed reasonable; but just as I was about to push open the gate of the little court-yard, the same gypsy woman who had been set on before to follow me came running up: "Don't go in there; there is a terrible bad dog." She warned so earnestly that for a moment I hesitated with my hand on the latch; for if in the whole world there is a thing which has the power to make my flesh creep and my blood run cold, it is a savage dog, and this woman, with the quickness of her race, had already had occasion to note my weak point. Her warning, however, missed its effect, for having been in that courtyard before, I distinctly remembered the absence of any dog whatever, whether good, bad, or indifferent, and her anxiety to prevent me from entering was in itself a sign that there was no danger.

So in I went: the man with the good face was not at home, I was told—he had gone to the field, but would presently return; only his wife, a sweet-faced young woman, and his aged mother, being alone in the house. Yes, I might sit down and welcome, said the young woman; and she hastened to bring me a chair and set some fresh milk before me; so I passed half an hour very pleasantly in examining the cottage and its inhabitants.

The young wife was seated at her loom weaving one of the red and blue towels which adorn each Roumanian cottage. Some of the pillow-cases and towels here hung up were of superior make to those usually seen, being both softer in color and richer in texture. " It is the old mother who made them," she explained. "She works far better than I can do, but now she is too old, and the weaving fatigues her; she was ninety-five this year."

"Was she in good health?" I asked by means of my interpreter.

"Quite good; but she cannot eat much—a little soup and a glass of wine every day is about all she takes."

"And where is your dog?" was my next inquiry, remembering the gypsy woman's caution.

"Dog?" she asked in surprise. "We never had a dog. What should we keep one for? We are too poor to be afraid of robbers."

When the husband came back I explained our errand. He smiled a little, and said he thought my fears were groundless. Those fellows would hardly dare to attempt any violence in daylight; but after all, it was just possible, he admitted. There certainly were several very bad characters in the village, and no doubt a gold watch was a great temptation; it would certainly be wiser not to start from here alone. After considering a little (apparently it *did* require consideration), he said that he knew of one respectable man in the village, and would come with us to look for him. I expressed my astonishment at seeing so many books in his house. "I began by being school-master in a neighboring village," he told me, "but it was only for a short time. Then my father died, and I had to return here to look after the fields. That was ten years ago. If I had remained there longer I should know more than I do." He showed me a volume of general history he was then studying. "I read a little of it every evening when I come back from work. I try to keep myself from forgetting everything—one is apt to get rusty and *verbauert* (peasantified) living here among peasants."

The sole other respectable man which the village could produce turning out to be absent, our host expressed his willingness to accompany us as far as I wished, though I knew that he was leaving his work to do so. Before quitting the village, however, I had a last encounter with my villanous friend of heretofore, whom I found waiting for me near the little bridge. He begged me so urgently to come in just for one minute to look at his china jugs, which he described in enthusiastic terms, that I gave an unwilling consent. He was apparently surprised and not over-pleased on recognizing my escort, and would have shaken him off on reaching his door, saying, " Well, good-by, neighbor ; you need not trouble yourself further."

Of course I refused to go into the house alone, and of course, too, when I did go in, the much-vaunted jugs turned out to be cracked and worthless specimens of the very commonest sort of ware, bearing no resemblance to what I was seeking.

I was fairly glad to turn my back on this horrid little village, fully resolved never again to set foot within its precincts ; and in conversation with our obliging protector, who spoke very tolerable German (an unusual thing in any Roumanian), three-quarters of an hour passed very quickly. He told me much about himself and his family ; also about the village, which twice had been burned down within fifteen years and reduced to the most abject poverty ; everything of value in the place had perished on the one or other of these occasions. His family life seemed happy, but for one source of grief, for his marriage was childless, and to any Roumanian this is a very great grief indeed. " It is sad for us to be alone," he said ; " but God has willed it so."

In the course of our talk he inquired, but with great delicacy, who I was, saying, "I do not know whether I should say madam or fräulein ; and perhaps I seem impolite if I am not giving the gracious lady her proper title." And when I had mentioned the name and position of my husband, I found him to be well informed as to all the military arrangements of the country, correctly naming off-hand all the ten or twelve cavalry stations in Transylvania. He recognized our name as being a Polish one, and began to talk of that nation. " Those Poles have sometimes very good heads," he remarked, " but they do not seem able to manage their own affairs. What a pity they were not able to keep their country together !" After this he inquired much about the state of commerce and agriculture in Poland, the influence of the Jews, etc., all he said indicating such a mixture of natural refinement and shrewd common-sense that I was quite sorry when, arriving within sight of the high-road, and there being no reason further to tax his good-nature, he took his leave with a bow which would not have disgraced any gentleman.

20

CHAPTER XLII.

A GYPSY CAMP.

WALKING across the country one breezy November day, I was attracted by the sight of a gypsy tent pitched on a piece of waste-land some hundred yards off my path — motive enough to cause me to change my direction and approach the little settlement; for these roving caravans have always had a peculiar fascination for me, and I rarely pass one by without nearer investigation.

This particular encampment turned out to be of the very poorest and most abject description: one miserable tent, riddled with holes, and patched with many-colored rags, was propped up against a neighboring bank. Alongside, a semi-starved donkey, laden with some tattered blankets and coverings, was standing immovable, and in the foreground a smoking camp-fire, over which was slung a battered kettle. There was very little fire and a great deal of smoke, which at first obscured the view, and prevented me from understanding why it was that the gypsies, usually so quick to mark a stranger, gazed at me with indifference: not a hand was stretched forth to beg, nor a voice raised in supplication. The men were standing or reclining on the turf in listless attitudes, while the women, crowded round the fire, were swaying their bodies to and fro, as though in bodily pain.

Soon, however, the shining point of a bayonet descried through the curling smoke gave me the clew to this abnormal behavior, and approaching nearer, I saw the figures of three Hungarian gendarmes dodging about between the ragged tent and the skeleton donkey; they were searching the camp, as they presently informed me, for a stolen purse. A peasant had had his pocket picked that morning at market, and as some of these gypsies had been seen in town, of course they must be guilty; and the speaker, with an oath, stuck his bayonet right into the depths of the little tent, bringing out to light a motley assortment of dirty rags, which he proceeded to turn over with scrutinizing investigation.

Any person with a well-balanced mind would, I suppose, have rejoiced at this improving spectacle of stern justice chastising degraded vice ; but I must confess that on this occasion my sympathies were all the wrong way, and I could not refrain from wishing that these poor hunted mortals might elude their punishment, whether deserved or not. Justice, as represented by these well-fed boorish gendarmes, who were turning over so ruthlessly the contents of the little camp, holding up to light each sorry rag with such pitiless scorn, and stripping the clothes from the half-naked backs of the gypsies with such needless brutality, appeared in the light of malicious and unnecessary persecution ; while vice, so poor, so wretched, so woe-begone, could surely inspire no harsher feeling than pity.

Among the females I remarked a young woman of about twenty-five, with splendid eyes, skin of mahogany brown, and straight-cut regular features like those of an Indian chieftainess. She wore a tattered scarlet cloak, and had on her breast a small baby as brown as herself, and naked, in spite of the sharp November air. One of the gendarmes approached her, and with a coarse gesture would have removed her cloak (apparently her sole upper garment) to search beneath for the missing purse ; but with the air of an outraged empress she waved him off, and raising full upon him her large black eyes, she broke into a torrent of speech. I could not understand her language, but the tenor of her discourse was easy to guess at from her expressive gestures and play of features. Her voice was of a rich contralto, as she poured forth what seemed to be the maledictions of an oppressed queen cursing a tyrant. Her gestures had an inbred majesty, and her attitude was that of an inspired sibyl. I thought what a glorious tragic actress she would have made—perfect as Lady Macbeth, and divine as Azucena in the "Trovatore." Even the brutal gendarme felt her influence, for he did not attempt to molest her further, but half shamefacedly withdrew, as though conscious of defeat, transferring his attentions to one of the men, whom he vigorously poked with the butt-end of his gun to force him to rise from his recumbent position.

The fruitless search had now come to an end ; the ragged tent had been demolished and the skeleton donkey unladen without so much as a single florin of the stolen money having come to light. In a prolonged discussion between gypsies and gendarmes, the word " Hinka, Hinka," was often repeated ; and Hinka, as it appeared, was the name of one of the gypsies who was at that moment missing from the camp. She was expected back by nightfall, they said.

Hearing this, the gendarmes proceeded to make themselves comfortable, awaiting Mrs. or Miss Hinka's return, lighting their pipes at the fire, and playfully upsetting the caldron containing the gypsies' supper. One gendarme walked up and down with fixed bayonet to see that no one attempted to leave the camp.

There being nothing more to see, I took my leave, for it was getting late, and I had still a long walk before me. I had almost forgotten the little episode with the gypsies, when, near the town, I met a small linen-covered cart drawn by a ghastly-looking white horse, worthy companion of the skeleton donkey. I should probably not have given a second thought or glance to this cart, for it was nearly dark, but as it passed me two or three curly black heads peeped out from under the linen awning, and instantaneously as many semi-naked children had bounded, India-rubber-like, on to the road, surrounding me with clamorous begging. While I was giving them some coppers, I saw that in the cart was sitting a somewhat pale and jaded-looking young woman, probably their mother, holding the reins and waiting for the children to get in. "Is your name Hinka?" I asked, as a thought struck me.

The woman stared at me in a bewildered manner without speaking, but her panic-struck face was answer sufficient.

"Do not go back to the camp to-night," I said, speaking on the impulse of the moment. "The gendarmes are there, and they are waiting for you."

My meaning was evidently plain, though I had spoken in German; probably the word gendarmes had a familiar ring in her ear, for she now gazed at me with positive terror in her wild, dilated eyes—the terror of a hunted animal which sees the huntsmen closing in on all sides; then, without a word of explanation, excuse, or thanks, she abruptly turned round the horse's head, and lashing it to its utmost speed, disappeared in the opposite direction.

Several very worthy friends of mine have since pronounced my behavior in this circumstance to have been highly reprehensible: I had sided with the malefactor, and possibly defeated the ends of justice by screening the culprit. Perhaps they are right, and it can only be owing to some vital defect in my moral constitution that I have never succeeded in feeling remorse for this action. On the contrary, it was with a feeling of peculiar satisfaction that I thought that evening of the three brutal gendarmes waiting in vain for the return of the guilty Hinka. I wondered how long they waited, and how many pipes they smoked, and to how many oaths they gave vent on finding that they had waited in vain, and their victim was not going to walk into the trap after all.

CHAPTER XLIII.

THE BRUCKENTHALS.

AMONG the crooked, irregular houses, low-storied and unpretentious, which form the streets of Hermanstadt, there is one which stands out conspicuous from its neighbors, resembling as it does nothing else in the town. This is the Bruckenthal palace, a stately building which might right well be placed by the side of some of the most aristocratic residences at Vienna, and of which even the Grand Canal at Venice need not be ashamed—but here absolutely out of place and incongruous. Looking like a nobleman amid a group of simple burghers, everything about this building has an air thoroughly aristocratic and *grand seignior:* the broad two-storied façade richly ornamented, the fantastically wrought iron gratings over the lower windows, the double escutcheon hanging above the stately entrance, even the very garret windows looking out of the high-pitched triple roof, have the appearance of old-fashioned picture-frames which only want to be filled up with appropriate rococo figures.

As we step through the roomy *porte-cochère* into a spacious court, we glance round half expecting to see a swelling porter or gorgeously attired Suisse prepared to challenge our entrance, and instinctively we fumble in our pocket for our card-case; but no one appears, and all is silent as death. Passing over the grass-grown stones which pave the court, we step through a capacious archway into a second court as large as the first, and surrounded in the same manner by the building running round to form another quadrangle. Here apparently are the stables, as a stone-carved horse's head above a door at the farther end apprises us, and hither we direct our steps in hopes of finding some stable-boy or groom to guide us, and tell us to whom this vast silent palace belongs.

The stable door is ajar, and we push it open, but pause in astonishment on the threshold, met by the stony stare of countless unseeing eyes. A stable it is undoubtedly, as testify the carved stone cribs and partitioned-off stalls—six stalls on the one side, six on the other, roomy and luxurious, fit only for the pampered stud of a monarch or of an English fox-hunter, but which now, deserted of its rightful occupants, has been usurped by a collection of plaster casts and terra-cotta copies of ancient statues. Where majestic Arabs used formerly to be stabled, now stands a naked simpering Venus, and the Dying Gladiator writhes on the flag-stones once pawed by impatient hoofs.

THE BRUCKENTHAL PALACE.*

By-and-by we come across some one, who in a few words gives us the history of the Bruckenthal palace.

Samuel Bruckenthal, of Saxon family, was raised alike to the rank of baron and to the position of governor of Transylvania by the Empress Maria Theresa, this being the first instance of a Saxon being thus distinguished. In this capacity he governed the land for fourteen years, from 1773 to 1787, and much good is recorded of the manner in which he filled his office, and of the benefits he conferred on the land. Baron Samuel Bruckenthal was a special favorite of the great empress, who seems to have overpowered both him and his

---

* Reprinted from a publication of the Transylvanian Carpathian Society.

family with riches and favors of all kinds. Besides this splendid palace (truly magnificent for the country and the time when it was built), and which boasted of a picture-gallery and an exceedingly valuable library, the Bruckenthal family became possessed of extensive landed property, some of which was to belong to them unconditionally, other estates being granted to the family for a period of ninety-nine years, afterwards reverting to the Crown. Likewise, villas and manufactories, summer and winter residences, gardens and hot-houses, which have belonged to them, are to be met with in all directions.

Baron Bruckenthal, who died in 1803, had decreed in his last will, dated 1802, that the gallery and museum he had formed were to be thrown open for the benefit of his Saxon townsmen; while his second heir, Baron Joseph Bruckenthal, further decreed, in a will dated 1867, that in the case of the male line of his family becoming extinct, the palace, inclusive of the picture-gallery, library, etc., should revert to the Evangelical Gymnasium at Hermanstadt, along with the interest of a capital of thirty-six thousand florins, to be expended in keeping up the edifice and adding to the collection. The contingency thus provided for having come to pass a dozen years ago, the directors have appropriated different suites of apartments for various purposes of public utility and instruction. Thus the lofty vaulted stables were found to be conveniently adapted for containing the models for a school of design; while up-stairs the gilded ball-room has been converted into a cabinet of natural history. Here rows of stuffed birds, as well as double-headed lambs, eight-legged puppies, and other such interesting deformities, are ranged on shelves against the crumbling gilt mouldings which run round the room; and tattered remnants of the rich crimson damask once clothing the walls hang rustling against glass jars, in which are displayed the horrid coils of many loathsome reptiles preserved in spirits of wine. Truly a sad downfall for these sumptuous apartments, where high-born dames were wont to glide in stately minuets over the polished floor!

The picture-gallery, opened to the public on appointed days, contains above a thousand pictures, which, filling fifteen rooms, are divided off into the three schools to which they belong—viz., Italian, Dutch, and German. The greater part of these pictures is said to have been purchased from French refugees at the time of the First Revolution, many families having then sought an asylum in Hungary and Transylvania.

Mr. Boner, in his work on Transylvania, has thought fit to condemn in a wholesale manner the contents of this gallery as "wretched daubs fit only for a broker's stall," a verdict as rash as unjust, and which has since been refuted by the opinion of competent judges. Of course, in a small provincial town like Hermanstadt, situated at the extreme east of the Austrian empire, it would be unreasonable to expect to find in a private gallery collected in the eighteenth century priceless *chefs-d'œuvres* of the kind we travel hundreds of miles to admire in the Louvre or at Dresden. No doubt, also, some of the paintings erroneously attributed to famous masters, such as Rubens or Titian, are but good copies of original works, while the parentage of a good number of others is unknown, or matter for guess-work. Granting all this, however, the wonder is rather, I think, to find such a very presentable collection of paintings of second and third rank in a small country town, among which no intelligent and straightforward connoisseur can fail to pass some hours without both pleasure and profit.

The best picture in the gallery, and the most celebrated, is the portrait of Charles I. of England, and of his wife, Henrietta Maria, by Vandyck, which has brought many Englishmen hither in hopes of purchasing it.

The library, now numbering about forty thousand volumes, is added to each year from part of the legacy attached to the Bruckenthal palace, and is a great boon to the town; for not only does it comprise a comfortable reading-room, to which any one may have gratuitous access, but all sorts of works are freely placed at the disposal of those who wish to study them at home, on condition of signing a voucher by which the party holds himself responsible for loss or damage to the work.

The Bruckenthal library is indeed a great and valuable resource to those banished to this remote corner of the globe, and it is only surprising that more people do not avail themselves of the advantages which permit one to enjoy at home, sometimes for two or three months at a time, several valuable works of history, biography, or science. Some of the editions of older classical authors are most beautifully bound and illustrated with fine copperplates—perfect *éditions de luxe*, such as one rarely sees nowadays.*

---

* It was to me a curious sensation in this out-of-the-way place to come across a copy of my great-grandfather's work, 'Gerard on Taste," translated into German. I had not been before aware of any such translation existing.

Many curious manuscripts, principally relating to the country, are also here to be found; but the gem of the collection, and by far its most interesting and precious object, is a prayer-book of the fifteenth century, which, written on finest vellum, contains six hundred and thirty pages in small quarto, each page being adorned with some of the finest specimens of the illuminated art to be met with anywhere.

The collection of coins is exceedingly remarkable, containing, as it does, abundant specimens of the ancient Greek, Dacian, and Roman coins, which are continually turning up in the soil, as well as of all the various branches of Transylvanian coinage in the Middle Ages. An assemblage of old Saxon ceramic objects, such as jugs and plates, may also be mentioned, as well as samples of old German embroidery, and some exceedingly beautiful pieces of jewellery belonging to the Saxon burgher, and peasant costumes.

The least interesting part of the museum is what is called the African and Japanese Cabinet, hardly deserving such a pompous designation, as the objects it mostly contains (savage weapons, dried alligators, etc., added to the collection some thirty years ago) are by no means more interesting or varied than what one is so tired of beholding in any well-furnished English drawing-room.

There is a legend attached to the Bruckenthal palace which tells us how an old soldier, who had served his emperor faithfully through many years, took his dismission at last, and, with only three coppers in his pocket, prepared to pilger homeward. On his way he was met by an old white-bearded man, who said, "Give me an alms, for all you have is mine." The soldier replied, "Your gain will not be great, for see, I have got but three kreuzers, but you are welcome to one of them." Hereupon the old man took one kreuzer, and the soldier proceeded on his way. Soon, however, he was met by another old man, who in like manner demanded an alms, and received a second copper; and this happened again a third time. But when the soldier had thus divested himself of his last coin the third old man thus spoke: "See, I am one and the same as the two old men who begged from you before, and am no other than Christ the Lord. As, therefore, you have been charitable, and have given of the little you had, so will I reward you by granting any boon you choose to ask."

After the soldier had reflected for a little, he begged for a sack which should have the virtue that, whenever he spoke the words, " Pack yourself in the sack," man or beast should equally be obliged to creep inside it. "I see," said the Lord, "that you are a wise man, and do not crave treasures and riches. The sack is yours."

With this magic sack on his back the soldier wandered on till he reached the town of Hermanstadt. Here he found all the population talking of a ghost in the Bruckenthal palace, which had lately been disturbing the place, and whosoever attempted to pass the night in those rooms was found as a corpse next morning.

On hearing this the veteran went with his sack to old Baron Bruckenthal, and begged for a night's lodging in those very rooms. In vain the old gentleman warned him of the danger, and prophesied that assuredly he would lose his life. The soldier persisted in his resolution, begging only for the loan of a Bible and two lighted candles. These were given to him, and likewise a copious supper, with wine and roast-meat. However, he ate and drank but sparingly, for he wished to remain wide-awake and sober; but he opened the Bible between the two candles, and read diligently therein.

Shortly before midnight the room began to be unquiet, but the soldier did but read the Bible all the more fervently as the noise increased. Then as twelve o'clock struck there was a sound like the report of a gun, and a leg was seen suspended from the ceiling.

The soldier remained quietly sitting, and said to himself, "Where there is one leg, there must be another too," and verily a second leg became soon visible beside the first. Quoth the soldier then, "Where there are two legs, there must perforce be body and arms as well," and without much delay these also made their appearance. Then he said, "A body cannot be without a head," but hardly had he said the words when the entire figure fell down from the ceiling, and rushing at the soldier, began to strangle him.

Quickly he cried, "Pack yourself in the sack," and in the self-same instant the ghost was imprisoned, and plaintively begging to be let out again. The soldier at first only permitted the ghost to put out its head, which was quite gray, but it went on begging to be released, and promising to reveal a mighty secret.

Hearing this the soldier opened the sack; but, hardly set free, the spectre again rushed at his throat, so that he had barely time to call out, "Pack yourself in the sack."

Now, being again in his power, the ghost was forced to confess to the soldier that in these walls there were concealed many barrels containing treasures, and over these it was his mission to watch. It promised to make over in writing a portion of this money to the veteran, and for this purpose begged to have its arms released from the sack in order to sign the document.

This being granted, the ghost a third time attempted the soldier's life, who, however, used the magic formula once more, and, determined to show no further mercy to his antagonist, cut off the head of the treacherous phantom.

BARON SAMUEL BRUCKENTHAL.

Next morning the inhabitants of Hermanstadt were greatly astonished to find the soldier still alive, and the praise of his valor was in every mouth. Under his directions the walls were now broken open, and within many little barrels were discovered, all containing heavy gold, of which the brave soldier received a handsome portion, sufficient to enable him to live in comfort to the end of his days.

It is to this discovery that many impute the great riches of the

Bruckenthal family, and were it not for the valiant soldier the fortune they left behind them would hardly have been so great.

Though the name of Bruckenthal is probably but little known outside Transylvania, and I have failed to find it in several German encyclopædias, yet here it is a word pregnant with meaning; and people at Hermanstadt are wont to swear by the Bruckenthal palace as the most stable and immutable object within their range of knowledge, just as an Egyptian might swear by the Pyramids or the Sphinx. "May you be lucky as long as the Bruckenthal palace stands," or "Sooner may the Bruckenthal palace fall down than such and such an event come to pass," are phrases I have frequently had occasion to hear.

But the memories of the Bruckenthals are not confined to the palace which bears their name. Every vestige of past grandeur or remnant of an extinct luxury, each work of art which comes to light in or about Hermanstadt, may be traced back to this once omnipotent family. If in your country walks you come upon a double row of massive lime-trees, twelve or sixteen perhaps, standing forlorn on the grass, with nothing to explain their presence on a lonely meadow, you are surely informed that these are the last survivors of a stately avenue leading to spacious orangeries in the Bruckenthal time. The orangeries have now disappeared, yet these few old trees linger on with senseless persistency—their snowy blossoms reminding one of powdered heads, their circling branches suggesting wide-hooped skirts setting to each other in the evening breeze, like an ancient quadrille party forgotten in the ball-room, long after the other guests have departed.

If you find an old statue chipped and moss-grown, dreaming away in the shade of a rose-bush which soon will stifle it in thorny embrace, you may take for granted that you are standing on the site of a former Bruckenthal garden.

If in a pawnbroker's shop you disinter a carved oak chair heavily wreathed in shrouding cobwebs, be sure that it has wandered hither from the old palace on the Ring; and should you chance to espy a rococo mirror, with curiously fretted gold frame, but tarnished and blurred, do not doubt that at some remote period gallant beaux and stately dames of the house of Bruckenthal have mirrored themselves complacently in its surface.

Look closer still in the miscellaneous heap of bric-a-brac which encumbers this same pawnbroker's back shop, and ten to one you will be able to recognize on some rotting canvas the grim features of old Samuel Bruckenthal himself, or those of his imperial mistress Maria Theresa.

Some of these old portraits, which I passed almost daily in my peregrinations about the town, seemed to look at me so plaintively with their canvas eyes, as though imploring me to release them from their ignoble position, that I had to take pity upon them at last and offer them an asylum in my house.

Few things ever gave me so vivid an impression of the transitory nature of earthly possessions, and the evanescence of power and grandeur, as these scattered relics of an extinct family meeting the eye at every turn ; and as the sea of chance was continually casting up some of these shipwrecked treasures, more than one of them happened to drift my way. Thus one day a poor woman brought to my door a delicate little piece of fancy porcelain, which I was glad to purchase for a small sum. About ten inches high, it represents a miniature citron-tree with blossoms and fruit, growing in a gold-hooped tub of exactly the same shape as the wooden cases in which real orange-trees are often planted. An old lady who recollects the vanished days of the Bruckenthal glory recognized this graceful trifle standing on my drawing-room *console,* and told me that she remembered a whole set of them, pomegranates and citron - trees alternately, with which the table used to be decked out on the occasion of large dinner-parties.

What has become of the many companions of my lonely citron-tree, I wonder? and where are now all the faces that used to meet round that festive board? *Tout passe, tout lasse, tout casse!*

CHAPTER XLIV.

STILL–LIFE AT HERMANSTADT—A TRANSYLVANIAN CRANFORD.

LIFE at Hermanstadt always gave me the impression of living inside one of those exquisitely minute Dutch paintings of still-life, in which the anatomy of a lobster or the veins on a vine - leaf are rendered with microscopic fidelity, and where such insignificant objects as half-lemons or mouldy cheese-rinds are exalted to the rank of centre-pieces,

During seven months of the year—from April till November—the idyllic quiet of Hermanstadt was certainly not without its charms. So long as the forest was green and the birds were singing, one did not feel the want of other society, and the *répertoire* of walks and rides furnished variety sufficient for an active body and a contented mind. It has often been remarked of Transylvania, that while resembling no other country precisely, it partakes of the character of many, and that within the space of half a dozen miles you may be reminded of as many different lands. Thus one day your road will take you through a little piece of Dutch scenery, a sluggish stream bordered by squat willow - trees, with at intervals a sprinkling of quaint old Flemish figures; another time it savors perhaps of Rhineland, as your path, leading upward to the top of a sandy hill, loses itself in a labyrinth of luxuriant vineyards; or else you may deem yourself on the Roman Campagna, when, issuing forth on the vast tracts of waste - land, you see shaggy buffaloes standing about in attitudes of lazy enjoyment, leisurely cropping the sunburnt grass or voluptuously steeping their bodies in the cooling bath of a green shining morass.

You may ride for hours in the shade of gnarled oak - trees, or, emerging on to an open glade, indulge in a long-stretched gallop over the velvety sward. In spring-time these grassy stretches are crowded thick with scented violets, whose purple heads are crushed by dozens at each stride of your horse; and in autumn, when the grass is close cropped, these meadows become one vast playing-ground for legions of brown field-mice, scampering away from under the horse's feet, or peeping at us with beady black eyes from out the porticos of their sheltering holes.

But once the winter has fairly set in, when those same frisky brown mice have retired to their strongholds in the bowels of the earth; when the last flower has withered on its stalk, and birds of passage have left the land; when streams have ceased babbling, and mill-wheels, made captive by chains of glittering icicles, are forced to stand still; when parasols have been exchanged for muffs, and the new toll-dog has already been eaten by the wolf—then indeed a season of desperate desolation settles down on the place. What is usually understood by the word amusement does not here exist. There is a theatre, it is true, but this is available in summer only; for as the crazy old tower which has been turned into a temple of the muses

cannot be heated, it remains closed till the return of spring brings
with the swallows some theatrical company of third or fourth class to
delight the population during a space of some weeks. Now and then
a shabby menagerie or still shabbier circus finds its way to the place;
and such minor attractions as an educated seal, a fat lady, or a family
of intelligent fleas, offer themselves for the delectation of a distinguished public. I have known persons who paid as many as six visits
to the seal and eight to the fat lady during this period of vital stagnation. Is not this bare statement wellnigh pathetic in its dreary sug-
gestiveness? What stronger proof can there be of the mournful state
of an intellect reduced to seek comfort from seals or fat women?

STREET AT HERMANSTADT.

Had it not been for the resources of the Bruckenthal library, life
would have hardly been endurable at this *saison morte;* but after all,
even reading has limits, and the question of what next to do was apt
to become puzzling to unfortunate mortals whose tastes did not happen to lie in the directions of music, love, or cookery.

About the liveliest thing to be done was to go often to the *place*
on market-days, and watch the endless succession of pictures always to

be found there. It is the sort of market-place which would be a perfect godsend to any artist in search of models for his studio. No difficulty here in collecting types of every sort: an amazing display of pretty dark-eyed women in rich Oriental costumes; a still greater assortment of shaggy, frowning figures armed with dagger and pistol, representing every possible gradation of the Italian bandit or the mediæval bravo. Here a sweet-faced young Roumanian woman, tenderly pressing a naked sucking-pig to her breast, might sit for a portrait of the Madonna; there a Saxon matron, prim and puritanical in her stiff old-fashioned dress, is offering cider for sale in a harsh metallic voice; yonder a row of old dames, who sit weaving funeral wreaths out of berries and evergreens, would offer famous models for the Parques, or the *Tricoteuses* under the guillotine (it was just about here, by-the-way, that the scaffold used to stand in olden times). Dishevelled gypsy women are trying to dispose of coarse wooden spoons, or baskets made out of shavings, no doubt combining their trade with a little profitable pocket-picking; and half-naked gypsy children are searching the mire for scraps of bread or vegetables which no well-bred dog would condescend to regard.

There is no great choice of delicacies to be found at this Hermanstadt market-place. Game is but rare, for reasons that I have mentioned before, and the finer sorts of vegetables are entirely wanting. The beef, veal, pork, and mutton, which form the whole *répertoire* of the butcher's stall, cannot be compared to English meat, but have the great advantage of being much cheaper—beef about 4*d*. and mutton 3*d*. per lb. Eggs and butter are good and plentiful; and as for the milk, let no one pretend to have tasted milk till he has been in Transylvania; so thick, so rich, so exquisitely flavored is the milk of those repulsive-looking and ferocious buffaloes, as good almost as cream elsewhere, and for the rest of your life putting you out of conceit of your vaunted Alderney or short-horn breeds, and making everything else taste like skim-milk by comparison. Some people indeed there are, of superdelicate digestions, who cannot stand buffaloes' milk, and are deterred by the delicate almond flavor usually considered to be its greatest attraction.

The Transylvanian wines have been described and extolled by other authors (Liebig, for instance), and deserve to be yet more widely known. There are, of course, many different sorts and gradations, those from the Kokel valley being the most highly prized. It is mostly white, and even the common *vin du pays* is distinguished by its rich amber hue, making one think of liquid topazes, if ever topazes could be melted down and sold at sixpence the gallon.

It is a noticeable and praiseworthy fact that at Hermanstadt there are no beggars. It is the pride of the Saxons to be absolutely without proletariat of the kind which seems as necessary an ingredient of other town populations as rats and mice. Even the Roumanians, though poor, are not addicted to begging, and, excepting the gypsies, I do not recollect one single instance of meeting a beggar in or about the town. Nor can the gypsies be called beggars by profession; no gypsy will in cold blood set himself to go begging from door to door, though he instinctively holds out his hand to any one who passes his tent.

Curious old legends occur to us while picking our way about the streets, and more than one old house is pointed out as being inhabited by ghosts. Also, Dr. Faust, of famous memory, is said to have long resided at Hermanstadt, and of him a very old woman who died not long ago used to relate as follows:

"My grandfather was serving as apprentice at the time when Dr. Faust lived here, and told me many tales of the wonderful things the great doctor used to do. Thus one day he played at bowls on the big Ring (*place*) with large round stones, which as they rolled were changed into human heads, and became stones again as soon as they stood still. Another time he assumed the shape of the town parson, and as such walked up and down the church roof, finally standing on his head at the top of the steeple, to the terror and amazement of the people below; then when the real parson made his appearance on the Ring, he jumped down among the crowd in guise of a large black cat with fiery eyes, which forthwith disappeared.

"Once, also, on occasion of a large cattle-fair, there was suddenly heard the sound of military music, and, lo and behold! in place of the sheep, calves, oxen, and horses, there marched past a regiment of soldiers with flying colors and resounding music. The people rubbed their eyes, scarce believing what they saw and heard; then, as still they stared and gaped, the band-master gave a signal, the music turned to a hundredfold bleating and bellowing, and the sheep, cattle, and horses stood there as before.

"At last, as every one knows, Dr. Faust was carried off to hell. Our Lord would gladly have saved him from this doom, for the doctor had always a kind heart, and had done much good to the poor;

21

but to save him was impossible, for he had sold himself by contract to the devil, who kept strict watch over him, and never let him out of sight."

Also, as architect Dr. Faust was renowned throughout Transylvania, but he often played tricks on the people, who grew to distrust him and decline his services. The numerous Roman roads still to be met with all over the country are attributed to Dr. Faust, who, it is said, constructed them with the assistance of the evil one.

The shops at Hermanstadt are such as might be expected from its geographical position and the sort of people inhabiting it; in fact, you are agreeably surprised to find here fashions no more ancient than of two years' date. Shopkeepers here still retain the antediluvian habit of eating their dinner as we hear of them doing some hundred years ago. When twelve o'clock strikes every shop is closed, and you would knock in vain against any of the barred-up doors; the streets become suddenly empty, and a stranger arriving at that hour would be prone to imagine himself to have stepped into a sleeping city. There are two fairly good German booksellers, several photographers, and sufficient choice of most other things to satisfy all reasonable wants. Yet there were people among our acquaintances who, scarcely more reasonable than children crying for the moon, used to fly into a passion, and consider themselves ill-used, because they had failed to procure some fashionable kind of note-paper, or the newest thing out in studs.

Sometimes, it is true, the narrow circle of Hermanstadt traffic showed its threadbare surface in the most amusing manner, as, for instance, when in an evil hour I bethought myself of ordering a winter jacket trimmed with otter-skin fur. Three skins would suffice for my purpose, as the tailor had calculated; so, accordingly, I went the round of all the fur-selling shops in the place. There were four of these who kept fur among other goods, and by a curious coincidence each of them confessed to possessing one otter only. Three out of the four could not show me their skin; they were unable to lay hand on it at that precise moment, it seemed, but if I would step round later in the day it should be produced. Returning, therefore, some hours later, I found, indeed, the promised otter in shop No. 2, but Nos. 3 and 4 were, for some mysterious reason, unable to keep their word, putting me off again to the following day; and by a strange accident the otter in shop No. 1 had now disappeared. Then ensued a wild-goose chase —or, I suppose, I should call it a wild-otter hunt—all round the shops again for several days, having glimpses of an otter now at one shop, now at another, but never by any chance in two shops simultaneously, till at last an energetic summons on my part to confront all four together, led to the melancholy revelation that there existed but one single otter in the whole town of Hermanstadt, the poor hard-worked animal alternately figuring among the goods of four different tradesmen.

In olden times, as we are told, the furrier guild of Hermanstadt was very illustrious. Its members once specially distinguished themselves in a fray with the Turks by delivering their Comes, in danger of being cut down. Since that time the guild enjoyed the distinction of executing the sword-dance on solemn occasions, particularly at the installation of each new Comes.

This anecdote occurred to my mind more than once in the course of my otter-hunt; and I sadly reflected that the Comes would probably be left to perish to-day, while the sword-dance would be apt to assume somewhat shabby proportions if executed by the four greasy Jews, with their solitary otter, which is all that remains of the once famous guild.*

Other provincial towns as small as or smaller than Hermanstadt can always show a certain amount of resident families whose hospitable houses are thrown open to strangers living there for a time. Here there is nothing of the sort, the wealthier class being entirely made up of Saxon burghers, who have no notions of friendly intercourse with strangers. It is difficult to explain the reason of this ungracious reserve, for they are neither wanting in intelligence nor in learning. Their education is unquestionably superior to that of Poles or Hungarians of the same class of life; but even when well informed in all

---

* Not only the furriers, but many other guilds, flourished here in a remarkable degree, the goldsmiths in particular taking rank along with Venetian and Genoese artists of the same period. After the middle of last century, the guilds began to fall into decadence; and finally, when the old restrictions on trade were abolished in 1860, they began to disappear. Yet the guild system, in all its essentials, was here kept up much longer than in any part of Germany; and even long after it had nominally exploded, many little customs relating to the guilds were still retained—as, for instance, that of all members sitting together in church, each corporation having its arms painted up above the seats. It is only within the last twenty years that this custom has fallen into disuse, for Mr. Boner, writing in 1865, makes mention of it as still extant. Also, to this day, in several of the Saxon towns it is quite usual to see signboards bearing such inscriptions as "lodging-house for joiners," tailors, etc.

branches of science, music, and literature, and on the most intimate terms with Goethe and Schiller, Mozart and Beethoven, they can rarely be classed as gentlefolk, from their total lack of outward polish and utter incomprehension of the commonest rules of social intercourse. Even persons occupying the very highest positions in Church and State are constantly giving offence by glaring breaches of every-day etiquette. This proceeds, no doubt, from ignorance, from want of natural tact, rather than from any intentional desire to slight; but the result is unquestionably that strangers, who might certainly derive much advantage from intercourse with some of these people, are deterred from the attempt by the lack of encouragement with which they are met.

I should, however, be ungrateful were I not to acknowledge that among the Transylvanian Saxons I learned to know several, to whose acquaintance I shall always look back as a pleasant reminiscence. First and foremost among these I should like to mention our worthy physician Dr. Pildner von Steinburg, to whom I am indebted for many interesting details of Saxon folk-lore. Also, I can count among the people I am glad to have known more than one of the school professors and several village pastors; and I am truly convinced that I might have extended my acquaintance with pleasure and profit considerably had circumstances so permitted. But precisely therein lies the difficulty. The Transylvanian Saxon burgher is a very hard nut indeed to crack, and in order to get at the sound kernel within, one has to encounter such a very tough outside that few people care to attempt it. No doubt much of the imposed code of etiquette of the civilized world is an empty sham which lofty spirits should be able to dispense with; but unfortunately we are so narrow-minded that we cannot entirely divest ourselves of the prejudices in which we were brought up.

In other parts of Transylvania the country-seats of the Hungarian nobility offer a pleasant diversion; but here there is nothing of the sort, all the land about the place being in the hands of Saxon village communities. Social life at Hermanstadt was therefore reduced to a few military families, who either might or might not happen to suit one another; and whoever has experience with this class will know that the cases of non-suitability are, alas! by far the most frequent.

"Small towns are so much nicer—don't you think so?" I heard a gushing creature remark to a gentleman she was endeavoring to captivate. "One gets to know people so much better than in large towns. Isn't it true?" "Very true," he replied, dryly; "one gets to know and to dislike people so much more thoroughly than in a large town."

Of course there were exceptions; but even if you do succeed in finding one or two friends whose society you care to cultivate, the case is not really much better—for whose feelings, what affection could stand the test of meeting their best friend six times a day in every possible combination of weather, locality, and costume?—in church, on the promenade, at the confectioner's, and in every second shop, till you have long exhausted your whole *répertoire* of smiles, nods, and ejaculatory salutations. What galvanized attempts were made at gayety only served to bring out the social barrenness into stronger relief; for how was it possible to get up interest in a ball when you knew exactly beforehand what every woman would wear, what each man would say, and which of them would dance together?

None of the military families then stationed at Hermanstadt happening to have grown-up daughters, the absence of girls from most social reunions gave them much of the effect of a third-class provincial theatre, where the part of *soubrette* is performed by a respectable matron of fifty, and where Juliets and Ophelias are apt to be *passée* and wrinkled. We hear so much about the corruption of large towns; but for a good, steady, infallible underminer of morals, commend me to the life of a dull little country town. People here began to flirt out of very *ennui* and desolation of spirit; beardless boys at a loss to dispose of their soft green hearts, desperately offered them to women twice their age; couples who had lived happily together in the whirl of a dissipated capital now drifted asunder under the deadening influence of this idyllic *tête-à-tête*, each seeking distraction in another direction—the result of all this being an amount of middle-aged flirtation exceedingly nauseous to behold. Each evening-party was thus broken up into duets of these elderly lovers, while by daytime every man walked with his neighbor's wife beneath the bare elm-trees which shaded the only dry walk near the town.

This is, perhaps, what Balzac means by saying that life in the provinces is far more intense than in a capital—so intense, indeed, as frequently to be entirely made up of unnatural dislikes and equally unnatural likings; while that serene indifference which, after all, is the only really comfortable feeling in life, has here no place.

Cranford-like, we all walked to and from the social meetings, which

took place at alternate houses. The distances were so short as not to
make it worth while getting in and out of a carriage, and people who
loved their horses did not care to drive them on a cold, dark night
over the slippery and uneven pavement of the town. Every party,
therefore, terminated by a Cinderella-like transformation scene—thick
wadded hoods, heavy fur cloaks, and monstrous clogs reducing us one
and all to shapeless bundles, as we walked home in the starlight over
the crisp, crunching snow.

As the winter advances the social gloom deepens, and the liveliest
spirits fall a prey to a sense of mild desperation. I began to realize
the possibility of paying endless visits to the seal or the fat lady, and
only wondered why no one had as yet hit upon the bright expedient
of buying the one or marrying the other, merely by way of bringing
some variety into his existence. Some women changed their cooks,
and others their lovers, merely for change's sake; and as there was far
greater choice of the latter than of the former article—there being
many men, but of cooks very few—any woman known to be capable
of roasting a hen or making a plain rice-pudding became the centre
of a dozen intrigues woven round her greasy person. A single roe-
deer appearing in the market infallibly gave birth to three or four
evening-parties within the week. You were invited to sup on its saddle at the general's, to partake of the right haunch at the colonel's
house, and the left at the major's, and might deem yourself exceptionally lucky indeed if not further compelled to study its anatomy at
some other house or houses—everywhere accompanied by the identical brown sauce, the same slices of lemon, the self-same dresses, cards,
and conversation !

Oh, roebuck, roebuck! why did you not remain in your own native forest? Much better would it have been for yourself—and for us !

CHAPTER XLV.

FIRE AND BLOOD—THE HERMANSTADT MURDER.

AT risk of dispelling the idea just given of the somnolent nature of
life at Hermanstadt, I am bound to mention that the quiet little town
was once distinguished by a murder as repulsive and cold-blooded as
any of which our most corrupted capitals can boast.

It came to pass, namely, that during the summer of 1883 the town was several times roused by the fire-alarm, and at short intervals more than one barn or stable was partially reduced to ashes. Nobody thought much of this at the time, for, thanks to the energetic conduct of the volunteer fire-brigade, assistance was promptly rendered, and though some few Saxon voices were heard to express a belief that their beloved compatriots the Roumanians were probably at the bottom of this, as of most other unexplained pieces of mischief, the majority of people were of opinion that the unusually dry summer, coupled with some chance acts of negligence, was quite sufficient to account for these conflagrations.

In the month of September, however, the entire garrison of Hermanstadt being absent at the military manœuvres, these fires began to assume an epidemic character, and by a strange coincidence they occurred invariably at night. During the week the troops were away there were no less than four or five fires.

Vague alarm now began to take possession of the population, and the uneasy feeling that something was wrong took shape in a dozen fantastic rumors, the one more startling than the other. The cook coming back from market brought news of a parcel of combustible materials found concealed in some barn or hay-loft; the boys returned from school full of some mysterious threatening letter, said to have been discovered posted up on a tree of the promenade; and the shopman, while tying up a parcel, sought to enliven us by dark allusions to sinister-looking individuals seen dodging about the scene of conflagration, and apparently regarding their handiwork with fiendish glee.

By daytime these rumors certainly tended to break the monotony of our solitude, and, proud of our superior common-sense, we, the bereaved grass-widows of the absent officers, could afford to laugh at the many ridiculous stories which were scaring our weaker-minded attendants.

Only when darkness had set in, when the children had gone to bed, and we ourselves prepared to spend a long, lonely evening, did these various reports begin to assume a somewhat more definite shape in our brain, and to appear infinitely less absurd than they had done in broad daylight. We nervously wondered whether again this night we should be roused from sleep by the horrid sound of the tocsin. Though it was autumn, not spring, we could not shake ourselves free from an atmosphere of vague April fools on a large and most unpleasant scale, and dimly began to realize what it must feel like to be a Russian emperor, as quaking we counted the days which must elapse before our natural protectors and the defenders of the town were restored to us.

One night, having, as usual, gone to bed with these sensations, I was just dropping into an uneasy sleep, when, sure enough, shortly before midnight the odiously familiar sound of the fire-alarm broke in upon my dream, and, hastily opening the window, I could see the sky all red with the fiery glare, at what appeared to be a very short distance from our house in the direction of the stables where, about a hundred paces farther up the street, our horses were lodged. My husband's chargers were, of course, away with him at the manœuvres, but the children's pony and one horse had remained behind; so, afraid of anything happening to them in case the orderly were asleep or absent, I resolved to go and assure myself of their safety. In a few minutes I was dressed, and, accompanied only by my faithful Brick, who was vastly delighted at the idea of a midnight walk, I left the house.

Before I had gone many steps I saw that my fears for the horses were groundless, the fire being ever so much farther away than had appeared from the window. However, having taken the trouble to rise and dress, I resolved to go on a little, and see whatever there was to be seen. It was a lovely moonlight night, almost as bright as day, only that the town had a much more lively aspect than I had ever seen it wear by daylight, for every one was afoot, and, like myself, hurrying towards the red glare visible over the high-pointed gables.

It proved impossible to get close to the fire raging in a narrow street at the beginning of the Untere Stadt, but any one standing at the top of the steep stone staircase by which this portion of the town is reached could command a good view of the scene, all the more striking from being seen from above. After I had stood there for nearly half an hour watching the tossing flames below me, and choked by occasional puffs of smoke, I began to feel both chilly and sleepy, and thought I might as well go back to bed, since it was nearly one o'clock, and the excitements of this night appeared to be exhausted. I left a large crowd still assembled round the scene of action, while the streets I passed on my homeward way were empty and deserted. Deserted, likewise, was our own street, the Fleischer Gasse, as it lay before me in the moonlight; but as I approached I became aware of the solitary dark-clad figure of a slender young man walking on the pavement just in front of our house. He seemed to me well dressed, and in appearance thoroughly respectable—an opinion which Brick, however, failed to share, for he advanced to meet the stranger with a low growl of suppressed but intense disapproval, which compliment the respectable young man returned by savagely hitting the dog with the tightly rolled-up umbrella he carried in his hand.

I should probably not have cast a second look at this stranger had not something in the needless brutality of his action attracted my attention, and caused me to scan his features. I thus noticed that he appeared to be little over twenty years of age, had a small sallow face, a sprouting mustache, and dark eyes set rather near together.

I rang the house-bell, and my maid came down to let me in, when, to my surprise, the stranger rudely attempted to force himself in behind me; but we slammed the door in his face, and then my servant told me that this same young man had been hanging about here for over half an hour, and had already once endeavored to effect an entrance behind some other person.

Two days later the troops came back from the manœuvres, and everything returned to accustomed order and quiet. The officers were, however, one and all far too much engrossed in recollection of those glorious imaginary laurels they had been winning on their bloodless battle-fields to take interest in anything so commonplace as a real fire; so the tale of the terrors we had undergone during their absence fell upon callous ears, and as no more conflagrations ensued to give color of semblance to our story, the matter soon lapsed into oblivion.

The usual winter torpor settled down upon the place, and the months wore slowly away towards spring without anything having occurred to disturb their peaceful current, when late on the evening of the 21st of February the almost forgotten sound of the tocsin was again heard in the streets, and simultaneously the news of a fourfold murder spread like wildfire through the town. The house inhabited by a retired military surgeon, Dr. Friedenwanger, had been discovered burning, and some members of the fire-brigade, on forcing an entrance, found his corpse, along with that of his wife, child, and maidservant, still reeking with warm blood, and mutilated in the most disgusting manner.

At first everybody was quite at sea as to where to look for the perpetrators of this crime, but by a curious chance, just while Dr. Friedenwanger was being buried, two days later, a bloody knife and some iron crowbars, found concealed in a drain near the cemetery, led to the identification of the murderers in the persons of Anton von Kleeberg and Rudolf Marlin,* two young men of respectable burgher families, aged about nineteen and twenty-one. The photographs of these youthful criminals being soon after exhibited in several shop-windows, neither I nor my maid had any difficulty in recognizing that of Kleeberg as the portrait of the mysterious stranger who had tried to enter our house on the night of the fire.

Many interesting details, too lengthy to be here recorded, came out at the trial, and a long list of misdeeds was brought home to the culprits, who, among other things, confessed to having laid every one of the fires the previous summer, thus diverting public attention while they proceeded to rob some particular house known to be ill-guarded, or inhabited by women only. There is therefore every reason to suppose that Messrs. Kleeberg and Marlin, well aware of the temporary absence of all masculine element from the household, had selected our house for a visit of this description; and I am likewise firmly convinced that my beloved and sagacious dog Brick, with that delicate sense of perception which so favorably distinguishes the canine from the coarser human race, had instantaneously detected the guilty intentions of the very respectable-looking young man we met in the moonlight before our house that September night. The victim, Dr. Friedenwanger, enjoyed a bad reputation as a usurer, and his murder had been undertaken for the sake of stealing the watches and jewellery he kept in pawn; while by subsequently setting fire to the premises the murderers had hoped to annihilate all traces of their crime. Some of the horrible disclosures at the trial brought, nevertheless, moments of intense satisfaction to more than one female breast, as being so many triumphant vindications of those terrors so cavalierly treated by the other sex a few months before. Did they now realize in what danger we had been last autumn, when they were all away engrossed in their miserable sham-fights? Did they know that their homes might have been reduced to ashes while they were complacently toying with blank-cartridges? or that their helpless progeny could easily have been made

---

* In justice to Saxon national feeling, I have been specially requested to mention the fact that neither of these two young German murderers was of Saxon extraction.

mince-meat of while they were slaying their legions of visionary Russians or Turks?

Such the self-evident arguments with which we were now able to clear ourselves from the base imputation of cowardice, and surely no woman worthy her sex forbore to make use of these handy weapons, or missed such glorious opportunity of turning the tables on her lord and master.

Characteristic of Magyar legislation was the circumstance of the whole trial being conducted in Hungarian, though this language was absolutely unknown to the two German prisoners, who were thus debarred the doubtful privilege of comprehending their own death-sentence when finally pronounced about a year after their crime. Like enough, though, its meaning was subsequently made clear to them, for Anton von Kleeberg and Rudolf Marlin were executed at Hermanstadt on the 16th of June, 1885.*

CHAPTER XLVI.

THE KLAUSENBURG CARNIVAL.

READERS of the foregoing pages will have had occasion to remark that, except when diversified by fire or bloodshed, life at Hermanstadt was *not* a lively one; therefore an invitation which I received during my second winter in Transylvania to spend some weeks at Klausenburg during the carnival season was very welcome. It was a decided relief to get away from the vulgar monotony of those antiquated flirtations which in Hermanstadt did duty for society, and to be reminded of things one was in danger of forgetting—of fresh young faces, light pretty dresses, and real dancing.

---

* As a curious instance of the precariousness of human life, I may here make mention of Colonel P——, a distinguished countryman of ours, then occupying a diplomatic post at Vienna. This gentleman, who had an unwholesome liking for witnessing executions, having accidentally learned that Hermanstadt boasted two candidates for the gallows, had requested a Transylvanian acquaintance to send him timely notice of their hanging, in order that he might assist at the spectacle. This morbid desire was, however, not destined to be satisfied, as long before the slow march of justice had culminated in a death-warrant, Colonel P—— himself had been carried off by the far more rapid Egyptian fever.

Nor was I disappointed in what I saw during my fortnight's stay at Klausenburg: pretty dresses in plenty; prettier faces, for the girls of the place are justly celebrated for their good looks; and as for dancing—why, I do not think I ever knew before what it was to see real, heartfelt, impassioned, indefatigable dancing. An account of the three last carnival days, as I spent them at Klausenburg, will convey some notion of what is there understood by the word dancing.

We had arrived late on the evening of the Saturday preceding Ash-Wednesday, therefore only the gentlemen of the party, unwilling to lose a single instant of their precious holiday-time, rushed off to a large public ball or *redoute*.

The following evening—Carnival Sunday—assembled the whole society in the *salons* of the military commander, Baron V——, whose guest I was at the time. There were from thirty to thirty-six dancing couples, and the first thing to strike a stranger on entering the room was, that not a single plain face was to be seen among them. Almost all the young girls were pretty, some of them remarkably so; dark beauties mostly, with a wealth of black plaits, glorious eyes, and creamy complexions, and with the small hand and high-curved instep which characterize Hungarian ladies. The faintest suspicion of a dark shade on the upper lip was not without charm in some cases; and when viewed against a strong light, many of the well-cut profiles had a soft, downy appearance, which decidedly enhanced their *piquante* effect. Side by side with these, however, were one or two faces fair enough to have graced any English ball-room.

What pleased me here to see was, that the married women, as a matter of course, leave the dancing-field to the young girls, and do not attempt, by display of an outrageous luxury in dress, to concentrate attention on themselves: the particular type of exquisite *élégante* never missing from a French or Polish *salon* has no place here. This is surely as it should be and as nature intended; pleasure, dancing, flirtation are for the young and the unmarried, and those who have had their turn should be content to stand aside and look on henceforth; but when, as is too often the case, it comes to be a trial of strength between matrons and maidens as to which shall capture the best partners and carry off the greatest number of trophies, the result can only be an unnatural and distorted state of society.

What Edinburgh society was to London some fifty years ago, so does Klausenburg stand to-day with regard to Pesth. As nearly all the people here are connected by ties of blood as well as of friendship, something of the privacy of a family circle marks their intercourse; and while lacking none of the refining touches of modern civilization, a breath of patriarchal *sans gêne* pervades the atmosphere.

The weak side of Klausenburg society at present is a minority of gentlemen, as of late years many members of distinguished families have got to prefer the wider range of excitement offered by a season at Buda-Pesth to the more restricted circle of a purely Transylvanian society which satisfied their fathers and grandfathers. On this occasion, however, there was no lack of dancers, for the young hussars who had come with us from Hermanstadt efficiently filled up the social gaps, restoring the balance of sex in the most satisfactory manner.

What interested me most in the ball-room was to watch the expression of the Tzigane musicians crowded together in a door-way; their black eyes rolling restlessly from side to side, nothing escapes their notice, and they are evidently far better informed of every flirtation, mistake, coolness, or quarrel in the wind, than the most vigilant chaperon.

Of course here, as at every Hungarian ball, the principal feature was the csardas; and it was curious to see how, at the very first notes of this dance, the young people all precipitated themselves to the end of the room where the musicians were placed, jostling one another in their anxiety each to get nearest to the music. To an uninitiated stranger it looks most peculiar to see this knot of dancers all pressed together like herrings in a barrel in one small corner, while fully two-thirds of a spacious ball-room are standing empty; but the Hungarians declare that the Tziganes only play the csardas with spirit when they see the dancers at close quarters, treading on their very toes and brushing up against the violins. Sometimes the band-master, unable to control his excitement, breaks loose from the niche or door-way assigned to the band, and, advancing into the room, becomes himself the centre of the whirling knot of dancers.

Whenever the csardas comes to an end there is a violent clapping of hands to make the music resume. Hungarians are absolutely insatiable in this respect, and, however long the dance has lasted, there will always be eager cries for more and more and more.

The cotillon, which was kept up till seven in the morning, was much prettier than any I remember to have seen danced before, for

Hungarians are as superior to Germans or Englishwomen in point of grace as they are to Poles in the matter of animation—and they executed all the usual figures demanding the introduction of a cushion, a mirror, a fan, India-rubber balls, etc., in a manner equally removed from boisterous romping as from languid affectation.

The following evening (Monday) the society reassembled at the pleasant and hospitable house of Mme. de Z——, whose dark-eyed daughters take a foremost rank among Transylvanian beauties. In order to have some strength remaining for what was still to come, dancing was on this occasion reduced to the modest allowance of six hours, the gypsies being compulsorily sent away soon after three o'clock, in order to force the young people to take some rest.

On Tuesday we all met again at the Casino for the bachelor's ball, given by the gentlemen of the place, and where, with the exception of supper and occasional snatches of refreshment, dancing was kept up uninterruptedly till near eight o'clock next morning. At the conclusion of the cotillon each lady received from her partner a pretty white and silver fan, on which her initials were engraved—a souvenir which I have much pleasure in preserving, in remembrance of the happy days I passed at Klausenburg.

An old traditional dance, which they here call *Écossaise* (but which in reality is simply a *pot-pourri* of several English country-dances), is danced at Klausenburg after midnight on Shrove-Tuesday, or rather Ash - Wednesday morning.* This dance having been somewhat neglected of late years, the young people blundered sorely over some of the figures, and the dance would have lapsed into hopeless chaos had not the former generation gallantly thrown themselves into the breach. Respectable fathers of grown-up daughters, and white-haired grandmothers, now started to their feet, instinctively roused to action by vivid recollections of their own youth ; and such is the power of memory that soon they were footing it with the nimblest dancers, going through each figure with unerring precision, and executing the complicated steps with an accuracy and grace which did honor to the dancing-masters of half a century ago.

One of these figures was the old one of cat and mouse, in which

---

* I failed to obtain any reliable information as to when and how this dance had been here imported, but it seems to have been in use for a good many generations past.

the girl, protected by a ring of dancers, tries to escape the pursuit of her partner, who seeks to break through the line of defenders—the moment when the cat seizes its prey being always marked by the band-master causing his violin to give a piteous squeak, imitating to perfection the agonized death-shriek of a captured mouse.

It is *de rigueur* that the last dance on Ash-Wednesday morning should be executed by daylight. This was about seven o'clock, when, the lights being extinguished and the shutters flung open, the gypsies threw all their remaining energies into a last furious, breathless galop —a weirder, wilder scene than I ever witnessed in a ball-room, to look at this frenziedly whirling mass of figures, but dimly to be descried in the scarcely breaking dawn—gray and misty-looking as ghosts risen from the grave to celebrate their nightly revels, and who, warned by the cock's crow of approaching daybreak, are treading their last mazes with a fast and furious glee; while the wild strains of the Tzigane band, rendered yet more fantastic by the addition of a monstrous drum (expressly introduced for the purpose of adding to the turmoil), might well have been borrowed from an infernal orchestra.

When the galop came to an end at last, from sheer want of breath on the part of both players and dancers, daylight was streaming into the room, disclosing a crowd of torn dresses, crushed flowers, and flushed and haggard faces, worn with the dissipation of the previous hours—a characteristic sight, but not a beautiful one by any means. Each one now rushed to the tea-room to receive the cups of fresh steaming *kraut suppe*, served here at the conclusion of every ball. It is made of a species of pickled cabbage, and has a sharp acid flavor, most grateful to a jaded palate, and supposed to be supreme in restoring equilibrium to overtaxed digestions.

While the ladies were resting till their carriages were announced, the gentlemen began to light their cigars, and the Tziganes, having recovered strength, resumed their bows; but what they now played was no longer dance music, but wild, fitful strains and melancholy national airs, addressed now to one, now to another of the listeners grouped about.

In other Continental towns dancing is brought to an end on Ash-Wednesday morning, and most people would suppose that having danced for three nights running, even the youngest of the young would be glad to take some rest at last. Not so at Klausenburg: nobody is ever tired here or has need of rest, as far as I can make out;

and it is a special feature of the place that precisely Ash-Wednesday should be the day of all others when gayety runs the wildest. The older generation, indeed, lament that dancing is no longer what it used to be; for in their time the Shrove-Tuesday party used never to break up till the Thursday morning, dancing being kept up the whole Wednesday and the following night, people merely retiring in batches for an hour or so at a time to repair the damages to their toilets.

Such desperate dissipation has now been modified, in so far as the party, separating towards 8 or 9 A.M., only meet again at 6 P.M., first to dine and then to dance. I could not get any one to explain to me the reason of this Ash-Wednesday dissipation, which I have never come across in any other place. Most of those I asked could assign no reasons at all, except that it had always been the custom there as long as any one could remember; but one version I heard was that in 1848 the Austrian Government took into its head to forbid dancing in Lent. "So, naturally, after that we had to make a point of dancing just on Ash-Wednesday to show our independence," said my inform-ant. The delicate flavor of forbidden fruit, which, no doubt, adds so much to the sweetness of these Ash-Wednesday parties, is kept up by the Klausenburg clergy, who, after having for years vainly attempted to put a stop to this regularly recurring Lenten profanation, now con-tents itself with a nominal protest each year against the revellers. Thus, as often as the day comes round, a black-robed figure, sent hither to preach sackcloth and ashes, makes his appearance on the ball-room premises; but, more harmless than he looks, his bark is worse than his bite, and he interferes with no one's enjoyment. He does not indite maledictions in letters of fire on the wall; neither does he act the part of Banquo's ghost at the banquet. Probably he has in former years too often acted this part in vain, so finds it wiser now to compromise the matter by accepting a modest sum as alms for his church, and abandoning the sinners to their own devices.

In place of the limp and crushed tulles and tarlatans of the previ-ous night, the young girls had now appeared mostly in pretty muslin and fresh summer toilets adorned with natural flowers. Some of them looked rather pale, as well they might after their previous efforts; but at the first notes of the csardas every trace of fatigue was gone as if by magic, and not for worlds would any one of them have consented to sit through a single dance. "Of course I am tired," said a young girl to me, very seriously, "but you see it is quite impossible to sit still when you hear the csardas playing; even if you are dying you must get up and dance."

For my part, I confess that the mere effort of looking on this fourth night was positive exhaustion. Long after midnight they were still dancing away like creatures possessed—dancing as though they never meant to stop, and as though their very souls' salvation depended on not standing still for a single moment. My brain began to reel, and feeling that worn-out Nature could do no more, I made the best of my way to carriage and bed, pursued by nightmares of a never-ending csardas.

After Ash-Wednesday Klausenburg society settled down to a somewhat calmer routine of amusement, consisting in skating, theatre-going, visiting, and parties.

There is a pleasing elasticity about Klausenburg visiting arrangements, people there restricting themselves to no particular hour, and no precise costume for going to see their acquaintances; so that ladies bound for the theatre or a party may often be seen paying two or three visits *en route*, not at all embarrassed by such trifles as short sleeves or flowers in the hair.

About two parties a day seemed to be the usual allowance here in Lent. Some of these reunions, beginning at five o'clock, were accompanied by cold coffee, ham sausages, and cakes; others, commencing at nine in the evening, were connected with tea and supper, so that frequently the self-same party might be said to begin in one house and terminate in another.

The gypsies were everywhere and anywhere to be seen, for most of these social gatherings end in dancing, and without the Tzigane no pleasure is considered complete. Pongracz, the present director of the Tzigane band at Klausenburg, has, so to say, grown up in society, his father having filled the post before him, and he himself, a man well on in middle-age—with such a delightfully shrewd, good-natured, rascally old face—has played for another generation of dancers, fathers and mothers of the young people who now fill the ball-room. There are other Tzigane bands as good, but his is the only one " in society," and it is most amusing to note the half-impudent familiarity of his manner towards both gentlemen and ladies who have grown up to the sound of his fiddle. It is positive agony to him to witness bad dancing, and he was wont to complain most bitterly of one gentleman to whom nature had denied an ear for music (a rare defect in any Hungarian).

22

"None of you young people dance particularly well nowadays," he remarked, with frank criticism, "but among you there is one who makes me positively ill to look at. If I were not to play *at* him and send my violin into his feet, he would never be able to get round at all."

On another occasion, when the figures of the *Écossaise* threatened to melt away into hopeless confusion, Pougracz angrily turned round and apostrophized a married lady who was sitting near me. "How can you sit there and see them making such a mess of it all ?" he said. "It is not so long ago that you were dancing yourself as to have forgotten all about it, so go and make order among them !"

The pretty old-fashioned custom of serenades being still here *en vogue*, sometimes on a dark winter's night, between two and three o'clock, one may hear the Tzigane band strike up under the window of some fêted beauty, playing her favorite air or *nota*. The serenade may either have been arranged by a special admirer, or merely by a good friend of the family. Often, too, several young men will arrange to bring serenades to all the young ladies of their acquaintance, going from one house to another. The lady thus serenaded does not show herself at the window, but if the attention be agreeable to her, she places a lighted candle in the casement in token that the serenade is accepted.

Such acceptance is, however, by no means compromising, no serious construction being necessarily put upon what may simply be intended as a friendly attention.

There is something decidedly refreshing about such frank ovations nowadays, when the lords of creation have become so extremely chary of their precious attentions towards the fair sex. To offer a nosegay to a girl is in some places so fraught with ominous meaning as to be considered equivalent to a marriage proposal, and exquisite young dandies are apt to feel themselves seriously compromised by the gift of a single rose-bud.

Only, the Klausenburg roses have no such treacherous thorns, it seems; and methinks society must surely be healthy in a place where any gentleman may, without laying himself open to the charge of lunacy, wake up a whole street at 3 A.M. by instigating a musical row beneath the window of a young lady acquaintance.

CHAPTER XLVII.

JOURNEY FROM HERMANSTADT TO KRONSTADT.

THE railway from Hermanstadt to Kronstadt takes us mostly through a rich undulating country, for, leaving the mountains always farther behind us, we near them again only as we approach the end of our journey.

Salzburg, or Vizkana as it is named in Hungarian, renowned for its salt-mines, is the first station on the line on leaving Hermanstadt— a melancholy, barren-looking place, seemingly engendered by Nature in one of her most stagnant moods. A wearisome stretch of sandy hillocks, their outlines broken here and there by unsightly cracks and fissures, is all that meets the eye; not a tree or bush to relieve the monotony of the short stunted grass, where starved-looking daisies, and spiritless, emaciated chamomiles, are all the flowers to be seen. No wonder the great white cattle look moody and dissatisfied, as from the sandy cliff above they sullenly gaze down at their own reflections in the dull green waters of the Tököli Bath. This bath, highly beneficial in cases of acute rheumatism, is nothing more than an old salt-mine dating back to the time of the Romans, and which, through some accident or convulsion of nature, has been flooded. The brine it contains is so strong as to bear up the heaviest bodies and render sinking an impossibility, so that, though of tremendous depth, persons absolutely ignorant of swimming can walk about in it in perfect safety, with head and shoulders well above the surface.

There are various other baths in the place, all somewhat weaker than the Tököli and other salt-mines, which, only worked in winter, yearly furnish some eighty thousand hundred-weight of salt. But the weirdest and gloomiest spot about Salzburg is an old ruined mine, deserted since 1817, and where over three hundred Honved soldiers found their grave in 1849. They fell in battle against the revolutionary Wallachians, and, as the simplest mode of burial, their bodies were thrown down the old shaft, which is over six hundred feet deep and filled with water to about a quarter of its depth.

A magnificent echo can be obtained by firing a gun or pistol down the shaft; but it is dangerous to approach the edge, because of earth-slips, for which reason the place is enclosed by a wire railing. However, neither this danger nor the fear of the three hundred ghosts who may well be supposed to haunt the spot is sufficient to restrain the Roumanians from prowling about the place. On fine moonlight nights—as I was told by the revenue officials, whose guard-house is close by—they will let themselves down by ropes to chip off whole sackfuls of salt. Sometimes they are caught in the act by some wide-awake official, who then threatens to cut the rope and send the culprits to rejoin the Honveds below, till the unfortunate wretches are forced to sue for their lives in deadliest fear.

The prettiest of the Saxon towns we passed on our way to Kron-stadt is Schässburg, situated on the banks of the river. Towers and ramparts peep out tantalizingly from luxurious vegetation, making us long to get out and explore the place; particularly inviting is a steep flight of steps leading to an old church at the top of a hill.

It is here that Hungary's greatest poet, Petöfi, perished in the battle of Schässburg on the 31st of July, 1849, when the revolted Hungarians, led by the Polish general Bem, were crushed by the superior numbers of the Russian troops come to Austria's assistance.

Petöfi's body was never found, nor had any one seen him fall, and for many years periodical reports got afloat in Hungary that the great poet was not dead, but pining away his life in the mines of Siberia. There seems, however, to be no valid reason for believing this tale, and more likely his was one of the many mutilated and unrecogniz-able corpses which strewed the valley of Schässburg on that disastrous day.

To the west of the town we catch sight of a solitary turret perched on the overhanging cliff above the river; it is said to mark the place where a Turkish pacha, besieging the town with his army, was slain by a shot fired from the goldsmiths' tower. The pacha was buried here sitting on his elephant, and this tower raised above them, while that other tower from whence the shot was fired, held ever since in high honor, was decked out with a golden ceiling. This latter has now fallen into ruin, and the inscription on the pacha's resting-place has become almost illegible, but the legend still runs in the people's mouths, and is told in verse as follows:

> "By Schässburg, on the mountain
> A turret gray doth stand,

SCHÄSSBURG.

(Reprinted from publication of the Transylvanian Carpathian Society.)

And from the heights it gazes
    Down on the Kokel land.
And ne'er a passing wand'rer
    This turret who doth see,
But pauses to inquire here
    What may its meaning be.

"It is a proud remembrance
    Of doughty deeds and bold.
Still faithfully the people
    Relate this legend old:
In by-gone days of trouble
    Went forth, with sword and brand,
A mighty Turkish pacha,
    To devastate the land.

"Thus also would he conquer
    This ancient Saxon town;
But here each man was ready
    To die for its renown.
And there upon the mountain
    The pacha took his stand,
An elephant bestriding,
    And cimeter in hand.

"The mighty Ali Pacha,
    He swears with curses wild,
That by his beard will he destroy
    The Saxon, chick and child.
Then struck the haughty Moslem
    Full in the breast a ball;
With curses yet upon the lip,
    A death-prey he must fall.

"The leaden ball came flying,
    Full thousand paces two,
From out a fortress turret,
    With deadly aim and true.
A sturdy goldsmith was it
    Who fired this famous shot;
The Turkish horde, which seeing,
    Their courage all forgot.

"And panic-struck escaping,
    Their pacha left to die,
The elephant still bestriding,
    With fixed and glassy eye.
Then sallied forth the Saxons
    As thus the Moslems fled,

And gazed on the dead pacha
　With joy and yet with dread.

"They built up Ali Pacha
　Within that turret gray,
From head to foot still armed
　In battle-field array;
His elephant beside him
　Was buried here as well,*
And outside an inscription
　Their history doth tell.

"By times a plaintive wailing
　May here be heard at night;
Or chance you to see flitting
　A phantom figure white,
The pacha 'tis, who cannot
　Find lasting rest, they say,
Because 'mid heavy curses
　His spirit passed away."

Another point of interest we see from the railway is the ruined castle of Marienburg, crowning a bare hill to our right hand, about half an hour before reaching Kronstadt, built by the knights of the Teutonic order during their occupation of the Burzenland in the early part of the thirteenth century.

These knights, whose order unites some of the conditions of both Templars and Maltese knights, had been founded in Palestine about the year 1190, for the double purpose of tending wounded crusaders, and, like these, combating the enemies of the Holy Sepulchre. Only Germans of noble birth were admitted as members, under condition of the customary vows of chastity and obedience. They had, however, not been long in existence when their position in Palestine began to grow insecure; and casting about their eyes in search of some more tenable position, they were met half-way by the King of Hungary, Andreas II., who, on his side, was in want of some powerful alliance to secure the eastern provinces of Transylvania against the repeated invasions of the Kumanes.

The negotiations between the monarch and the Teutonic order seem to have lasted several years, being finally brought to a conclusion

---

* Why the elephant was also buried is not very apparent, as it is hardly to be supposed that it was killed by the same shot which slew the pacha.

in 1211 in a treaty signed by the King in the presence of eighteen distinguished witnesses. This treaty distinctly sets forth that the part of
the country called the Burzenland, and whose boundaries are exactly
defined, is bequeathed as an irrevocable gift to the knights of the Teutonic order by the King, who, hoping thereby to obtain pardon of his
sins and secure eternal salvation for himself and his ancestors likewise,
intrusts to them the defence of the eastern frontier of his kingdom
against barbaric invasions. In this document, which is lengthy and
involved, are likewise set forth all the rights, obligations, privileges,
and restrictions of the said knights. They were exempted from all
the usual taxes and tributes to the King, who, however, did not resign
his claim to the sovereignty of the land, reserving to himself on all
occasions the right of ultimate decision in cases of contested justice.
Whatever gold or silver was discovered in the soil was to belong, half
to the King, half to the order. Though granting the utmost freedom
in all matters relating to trade and commerce, the Hungarian monarch
retained the sole right of coinage; and while permitting the knights
to erect the wooden fortresses and citadels which were amply sufficient
to resist attacks from the barbarians, it was distinctly stipulated that
they were not to build castles or fortifications of stone.

Barring these few restrictions, the land was to be absolutely their
own; and had the knights been wise enough to keep to the compact,
no doubt the Teutonic order might yet be flourishing to-day in Transylvania, instead of having been ignominiously expelled after scarce a
dozen years' residence.

At first the new arrangement seems to have been most beneficial to
the country, for we hear of growing prosperity and of flourishing agriculture and commerce; and many German villages which acknowledged
the Teutonic knights as their feudal masters were founded at that time.

But the good understanding between King Andreas and the
knights was of short duration, for before ten years had elapsed we
already read of dissensions cropping up; the knights are accused of
extending their boundaries beyond the prescribed limits, of issuing an
independent coinage, of building stone castles, and of bribing away
German colonists to settle on their own land to the detriment of other
provinces—all of which things were distinctly interdicted by the terms
of agreement. Many stories, too, are told of their cruel tyranny
towards unfortunate serfs—such, for instance, as compelling several
hundreds of them to pass whole nights in the marshes round Marien-

burg, each man armed with a long switch wherewith to flog the troι
blesome frogs, whose croaking disturbed the slumbers of the holy me
up in the castle.

King Andreas, who was of a weak, vacillating disposition, wε
easily persuaded by counsellors antagonistic to the order to revoke th
deed of gift, which proclamation was issued in 1221, accompanied b
an order to the knights to evacuate the territory and the stronghold
they had built. Before, however, this had been effected, the Popε
Honorius III., himself a special protector of the order, intervenec
effecting a reconciliation, the result of which was a fresh treaty coι
firming the previous donation. This renewed deed of gift not onl
ratified all the terms of the previous document, but actually increase
the privileges enjoyed by the knights, granting them among othε
things the much-coveted right of building stone castles.

In spite, however, of some notable victories over the Kumanes i
1224, and the brilliant prospects thereby opened of enlarging thei
domains, the Teutonic knights were not destined to shine muc
longer in the land they had thus successfully civilized and made arε
ble. No doubt they hastened their own downfall by the signε
short-sightedness of their grand-master, Hermann von Salza, wh
committed the error of taking upon himself, to offer the supremac
of the Burzenland to the Holy See, begging the Pope to enroll thι
province among the Papal States. Of course the knights had n
right thus to dispose of a domain which they only held as subjecι
of the Hungarian Crown; and though the Popè, as was to be eι
pected, gladly accepted the handsome donation, the King as naturall
resented a proceeding which could only be regarded as the blackeι
high-treason. This time the breach was such as could no longer b
bridged over by any attempt at reconciliation. The Teutonic knighι
had made themselves too many enemies, and especially the King
eldest son (afterwards Bela IV.) was strenuous in urging his father t
eject the order from the land. This sentence was carried out, nι
without much trouble and bloodshed; for the knights were little di
posed to disgorge this valuable possession. Even when at last con
pelled to turn their backs on Transylvania, which appears to haν
been about 1225, it was long before they relinquished the hope ι
ultimately regaining their lost paradise. But all efforts in this dire
tion proved unavailing; for it was decreed that the German knighι
were to behold the Burzenland no more.

I have not been able to obtain any picture of Marienburg, and to the best of my knowledge none such has ever been executed, which is all the more to be lamented, as this interesting ruin, like so many others in the country, bids fair to vanish ere long without leaving any trace behind. In default, therefore, of Marienburg, I offer a picture of the Castle of Törzburg, another of those seven fortresses raised by the Teutonic knights during their brief but brilliant reign. This castle, lying south of Kronstadt, at the entrance of the similarly

CASTLE OF TÖRZBURG.

named pass, has, however, lost much of its former romantic appearance. Since 1878, when the Hungarian Government thought necessary to guard the frontier against Roumania, it was converted into a soldiers' barracks; and though no longer used for that purpose, no steps have yet been taken to restore the edifice to its original form by rebuilding the slender turrets of which it had been divested.

Shortly before reaching Kronstadt our train came to an unexpected stand-still in the midst of a wide-stretching plain. Some flocks were grazing on either side of the rails, but there was no

station or guard‑house in sight to explain this unaccountable stop
page, and there seemed to be nothing to suggest an accident, til
stretching our heads out of the window, we saw a group of peopl
bending over a formless mass which lay on the rails some hundre
yards to our rear. One of the passengers who happened to be
doctor was hastily summoned to the spot, but he returned shakin
his head, for his science could do nothing here. A shepherd la
aged twelve or thirteen had been lying across the rails seemingl
asleep in the sun. He lay so flat that the engine‑driver had faile
to perceive him till the last moment, and then only had seen how
white figure had jumped up in front of the engine, but instantane
ously caught by a blow from the engine‑fliers, was stricken down t
rise no more.

Had the boy been asleep or intoxicated, or whether it were an acc
dent or a suicide, none could tell. We were thankful to be far enoug
from the scene to be spared the sight of the horrible details—how ho
rible could be guessed from the expression of those who were no
slowly returning to resume their places in the train.

As we moved away I could only discern how two men were liftin
the body from the rails, and how a woman with uplifted arms wa
running across a field towards them.

CHAPTER XLVIII.

KRONSTADT.

It needed the sight of beautiful Kronstadt to efface the impressio
of this ghastly picture — beautiful, indeed, as it clings to the stee
mountain‑side, looking as though the picturesque houses and turre
had been carved out of the rocks which tower above them.

At Hermanstadt the view of the mountain‑chain is grander an
more sublime, but Kronstadt has the advantage of being in itself pa
and portion of the mountain scenery, the fashionable promenade win
ing in serpentine curves up the Kapellen Berg to the back of the tow
being but the beginning of an ascent which, if pursued, will lead us
a height of wellnigh seven thousand feet.

Without, however, going any such desperate distance, merely fro the top of the Kapellen Berg or Zinne (thirteen hundred feet above the town), to be reached without perceptible effort, we can enjoy one of the finest views to be seen throughout Transylvania, offering as it does a singularly harmonious blending of wild, uncultured nature and rich pastoral scenery.

Not far below the highest point of the Kapellen Berg is a small cave which goes by the name of the Nonnenloch (nun's hole). A hermit is said to have lived here for many years; but it is more celebrated as having been the haunt of a monstrous serpent, which hence used to pounce down upon inadvertent wanderers. On one occasion it is said to have carried off and devoured a student who was reading near the town-wall; but tormented by thirst after this plentiful repast, the monster drank water till it burst. The portrait of this gigantic snake may still be seen painted on the old town-wall near the barracks.

There is another legend relating to the Kronstadt Kapellen Berg, which, though somewhat lengthy, is too graceful to be refused a place here:

"Many, many years ago there lived at the Kronstadt gymnasium a student who was uncommon wise and God-fearing, and who could preach so well that it often happened that he was delegated by any one of the town clergymen, when indisposed with a cold or toothache, to preach in his stead. And this the student did right willingly; for he received for each sermon half a Hungarian florin, which was good pay for those times. But still more for the honor and glory did he like to do it; and the most praiseworthy thing about it was, that he did not copy out his sermons from a book, but that he composed them unaided out of his own mind and learned them by rote; and as, moreover, he had a fine manner of delivery, it was a pleasure to listen to him. Whenever he had to learn a sermon by heart, it was his custom to seek out solitary places where he might be undisturbed, but his favorite haunt used to be the steep, wooded hill behind the town.

"Thus one day, having to learn a sermon to be preached on the morrow at the Johannis Kirche (the present Catholic Franciscan church), our student as usual repaired to his favorite haunt. He had just finished his self-allotted task, and was preparing to go home, when he espied a beautiful bird, which, hopping about on an overhanging branch, seemed to be intently gazing at him. The student approached the bird, but when he had reached it so close as almost to touch it with his hand, it flew off some paces farther up the hill, alighting on an-

other branch and gazing on him as before. Again he followed th
bird, which, repeating its former manœuvre, led him on by degree
almost to the top of the hill to the spot now known as the Nonnei
loch. Here the bird disappeared into a thicket, still followed by th
student, who, bending aside the branches, saw a broad cleft in th
rock, wide enough to admit a man's body. He could still descry th
bird, which, flying in through the opening, was soon lost to sight i
the cavernous depths within.

"Wonderingly he entered the cave and penetrated a considerabl
way into the mountain, not understanding, however, how it was tha
though so far removed from the light of day, he was yet perfectl
able to distinguish his surroundings as in a sort of twilight. Sudder
ly at the end of the cave, which had now contracted to a narrow pa
sage, he was confronted by the figure of a dwarf with pale face an
long gray beard, who cried in a deep, angry voice, 'Who art thou
and what seekest thou here?'

"The student felt sorely afraid, but took heart, seeing that h
conscience was clear and he had done no harm; so he related to th
dwarf how, having come hither to learn his sermon, which by th
help of God he hoped to preach next day in the Johannis Kirche, h
had been led by the bird ever up the hill and deeper into the fores
till he reached this cave.

"At the very first word the manikin's face grew mild and benev
lent. 'So thou art he?' he said, in a gentle voice, when the other ha
finished speaking. 'Often have I listened to thee reciting thy se
mons down in the forest, and have been rejoiced and edified by th
beautiful words. I am the *berg-geist* (mountain-spirit), and the bir
which enticed thee hither is in my service, and did so by my orde
for I wished to know thee. Thou shalt not repent having come hithe
for I will show thee what no mortal eye has seen.'

"At a sign from the dwarf an invisible door at the extremity (
the cave flew open, and following his guide, the student gazed abou
him in speechless wonder. He now found himself in a vault far wid
and loftier than the church nave, and though there were here neith
windows nor torches, the whole building was pervaded by a rosy, tran
parent twilight. What a gorgeous and splendid sight now met h
eyes! The arches on which the vault rested were of massive silve
and of silver, too, the pillars which supported them. The ribs of th
arches were of gold, as likewise the ornaments on the columns. Mor

over, these columns were encircled by flower-garlands composed of many-colored precious stones—diamonds, rubies, emeralds, sapphires, and topazes; while hundreds more of the same stones lay strewn about on the ground. How all this glittered and sparkled before the eyes of the wondering student!

"'See,' spoke the dwarf, 'this is a workshop, and there are many more such in the heart of the mountains, where, out of gold, silver, and precious stones, we spirits fashion the flowers that deck the surface of the earth. You foolish mortals no doubt believe the flowers to sprout of themselves in spring to enamel meadow and forest in blue, red, and yellow tints. But learn that this is the work of us, the mountain-spirits, who by order of the Creator wander over the surface of the earth, unseen by men, sowing broadcast the mountain treasures which glitter in the sunshine in manifold shapes and colors. And in autumn, when the flowers wither, we go forth again to gather in the gems we have strewn, and hide them in rocky strongholds till spring comes round again. Thus do we strive to rejoice the hearts of men by letting their eyes feast on the works of the Creator. But,' he continued, laughing maliciously, 'we feel but contempt and derision for such foolish mortals as, having become possessed of some stray grains of our flower-seed, which they have perchance discovered in a torrent-bed or rocky fissure, set great store on their possession, decking themselves out with it as though each simple field-flower were not more beautiful by far than the gem from which it has sprung.'

"The words of the mountain-spirit well pleased the student, and he thought of the text of the sermon he was about to preach on the morrow, treating of the lilies of the field, which neither toil nor spin, and are yet more gorgeous than Solomon in all his glory. But at the same time there went through his brain other thoughts of less lofty nature. To a poor devil such as he a pocketful of these glittering stones would be a most acceptable present—sufficient probably to relieve him of all material anxiety, and enable him to go to Germany to finish his studies. Vainly he hoped that the gray-bearded dwarf might tender some such gift, but to his discomfiture the berg-geist betrayed no such intention.

"Something more than an hour the student spent in contemplation of the riches of the cavern; then he bethought himself of home, and begged the dwarf to let him out.

"'The little bird,' spoke the spirit, 'which brought thee hither will

conduct thee back through the cleft.' But as they neared the ⟨
trance of the vault the student made a feint of stumbling, and as
did so, surreptitiously caught up a handful of gems, which he secret
in the pocket of his dolman. The old dwarf said nothing, but smil
sarcastically, and the student deemed his manœuvre to have pass
unnoticed.

"Suddenly the dwarf had disappeared, and the student found hi
self again in the cleft of rock where an hour previously the bird h
lured him; and here, too, the bird itself was waiting for him, an
hopping cheerfully in front, soon conducted him back to the light
day, whereupon it disappeared into the bushes.

"Our student felt heartily thankful to be delivered from the son
what uncanny surroundings, and to see the blue sky and the gold⟨
sunshine once more. But, strange to say, as he pursued his way hon
ward down the hill to regain the town by the upper gate, sevei
things struck him as unknown and unfamiliar. The people he m
were not attired according to the fashion of the day; the path w
smoother and better kept; even the very trees seemed changed, ai
no more the same he had seen growing there when he had gone ι
the hill that morning. He specially remembered a slender your
lime-tree which had been planted only the spring before; where hi
it now gone to? and how came there to be an aged and majestic tr⟨
in its place?

"As he entered the town-gate that leads into the *Heilig-leichnar*
Gasse (Corpus Christi Street), many things likewise appeared strang⟨
the houses had foreign shapes, and out of their windows there peep⟨
unknown faces.

"While ruminating over these puzzling facts he bethought himse
of the treasure he carried in his pocket, and his conscience began
prick him, that he, who until now had been careful to keep the T⟨
Commandments, had now made himself guilty of breaking the eighι
one. It seemed to him as though the purloined gems were burnir
through the coat into his heart. Thus thinking, he approached tl
river in order to ease his conscience by throwing in the stolen prope
ty. He put his hand into his pocket and drew it out full, but befo:
throwing away the treasure he wished to take a last look at the glitte
ing stones. But what was this? A handful of coarse gravel was ⟨
he held. Some witchcraft must be here at work; and a cold shudder ra
over his frame, but he was thankful to be rid of the accursed jewels.

"At last he had reached the school, and stepped over the threshold of the door. Several students met him in the corridors or coming down the staircase; but he, who knew every one about the place, was surprised to see naught but strange faces, who stared back at him with astonishment equal to his own.

"He entered his little bedchamber, but here also all was different: no press, no table, no chair remained of those he had left there that morning; the very bed was another one, and the occupants of the room knew him as little as he knew them.

"This was surely a greater wonder than all that had happened to him up yonder at the cavern. It needed all his self-control to keep his faculties together and prevent himself from going mad. And he must keep his reason; for was he not to preach his sermon next day in the Church of St. John?

"He fared no better when, hoping to find a way out of his dilemma, he rushed wildly to the rector's abode. The voice which responded '*Intra*' to his modest knock was a strange one; and as he, entering, saw a stranger sitting at the writing-table, he timidly said that he wished to speak to the *Virum pereximium*. 'I am he,' was the answer; 'who are you, and what seek you here? I am acquainted with all the students of the gymnasium. How come you to be wearing their dress?'

"Our student now mentioned his name, and related how he had been delegated by the reverend and worthy minister such-and-such to preach on the following day; how he had gone out early on to the hill to learn his sermon by rote, and all that subsequently happened to him. Everything he related faithfully, excepting the episode regarding the handful of glittering stones, which he thought better to conceal. Then he told how on his return he found everything changed as by an evil charm—how he knew nobody, and was known by none in return.

"When the student had first named himself, and likewise mentioned the name of the preacher whose place he was to take next day, an expression of wondering astonishment had dawned on the rector's face, which grew more intense as the narrative proceeded. When the student had finished his story, he turned round hastily and took from the bookcase behind him an ancient volume in pig-skin binding.

"'Yes; here it stands in the *Albo studiosæ juventutis gymnasii*,
23

anno Domini 1——: "On the —— of the month of August did tl
Studiosus Togatus N—— N—— ex œdibus gymnasii, absent himse
from here and did not again return, which defalcation caused all tl
greater consternation as the said *studiosus* had been delegated
preach next day, being the fifteenth Sunday after Trinity, in tl
church of St. Johannes, and in lieu of the sermon a *lectio biblica* had
be held instead." And this happened,' wound up the rector, turnir
to the student, ' exactly a hundred years ago to-day.'

"And so it was in truth; the time he had spent in the cave ha
seemed but an hour to the young man, and in reality a hundred yea
had passed! Everything around him had changed except his ow
self; for the years that had fled had left no mark on him, and I
looked young and strong as a youth of scarce twenty years.

"It is easy to conceive how this wonderful story was swiftly spree
throughout the town, and especially what sensation it caused amid tl
Kronstadt students, among whom the centenarian youth was now pe
mitted to resume his place. Then as the mid-day bell had just tolle
and our student felt a mighty craving of hunger within him (whic
was not wonderful, considering that he had fasted for a century), I
did not require much pressing to sit down at the dinner-board wit
his companions.

"But oh, wonder of wonders! hardly had he swallowed the fir
spoonful of the dish before him, when his whole appearance began
change: his dark hair turned gradually white, and fell from his hee
like snow-flakes; his features shrank perceptibly, and the bloom of h
cheek gave place to an ashy pallor; his eye grew dim; and scarce
had his comrades, hastening to support his sinking frame, laid hi
upon a bed, when with a last deep-drawn breath he expired.

"For some years after this many Kronstadt students used to hau
the hill along the town, in hopes that the bird might appear and lee
them into the enchanted cavern, secretly resolving well to line the
pockets with the riches it contained—for that the jewels were subs
quently changed to gravel they had not been informed. But thou;
many have searched for the spot, none ever succeeded in finding
again, so that by degrees the love of reciting sermons on the moui
ain died out, and the whole story lapsed into oblivion. Also, the pa
from the *Albo scholastico* where mention is made of this is said to
missing, so that now but a few old people are acquainted with tl
legend, and fewer still there are who yet believe it."

Kronstadt, or Brasso, as it is called in Hungarian, lying at a height of 1900 feet above the sea-level, is of more mixed complexion than other Transylvanian towns, and is already mentioned in the thirteenth century as having a mixed population of Saxons, Szeklers, and Wallachs. Whereas Klausenburg is exclusively a Hungarian, and

KING MATTHIAS CORVINUS.

Hermanstadt a Saxon city, Kronstadt partakes a little of both characters, and has, moreover, a dash of Oriental coloring about it. In the streets, besides the usual contingent of fiery Magyars, stolid Saxons, melancholy Roumanians, ragged Tziganes, and solemn Armenians, we pass by other figures, red-fezzed, beturbaned, or long-robed, which, giving to the population a kaleidoscopic effect, make us feel that we are next door to the East, and only a few steps removed from such things as camels, minarets, and harems.

Kronstadt is said to derive its name from a golden crown found suspended on a broken tree-stump about the year 1204. A fugitive king—such is one version of the story—had here deposited his head-gear, no doubt finding it inconvenient when flying through the for-est. On the spot where the royal insignia was found was raised the present town of Kronstadt, whose arms consist of the image of a crown suspended on a stump. The tree-stump represents the town, we are told, its roots the *Burzen*, or *Wurzel, land,* while the crown is figurative of the Hungarian monarch.* The original crown is said to have been long treasured up in the guildhall of Kronstadt, and jealously guarded by the citizens, who showed it but rarely, and as special mark of favor to some potentate. An old writer of the year 1605 described this crown as being of gold and decorated with golden plumes, and mentions that it was Gregory, the despotic king of Mœsia, who, obliged to withdraw from the siege of Kron-stadt, and defeated by the Turkish pacha Mizetes, laid down his crown on the stump where it was afterwards found by Kronstadt citizens.

There is another story, which relates that this crown belonged to Solomon, King of Hungary, who died dethroned in the eleventh cen-tury, and spent his last years living as a hermit in a romantic valley near Kronstadt which still bears his name. Feeling his death ap-proach, he concealed his golden crown in a hollow beech-tree, where long afterwards it was discovered by some shepherds, when the tree becoming old and rotten, had fallen to the ground.

The Feast of St. John the Baptist (June 24th) was generally regarded as the anniversary of the crown-finding, to commemorate which it used to be customary to hoist up at the end of a high May pole a crown woven together of ripe cherries, roses, and rosemary and adorned with gingerbread figures and cakes of various sorts. The youth of both sexes danced round this pole to the sound of music, and whoever succeeded in scaling the height and carrying of the crown received a handsome prize.

A dilapidated crown carved in the stone façade of an old house in the *Purzelgasse* at Kronstadt gives evidence that here King Matthias once travelling *incognito*, as was his wont, entered and consumed the

---

* According to others, the name of Kronstadt would be derived from the *Krа-nenbeeren* (cranberries) which grow profusely on the surrounding hills.

frugal meal of six eggs, leaving behind him on the table-cloth a paper on which were written the Latin words:

"Hic fuit Matthias rex comedit ova sex."*

The principal church at Kronstadt, dating from the end of the fourteenth century, contains many objects of interest, besides an organ which is of European reputation. In the sacristy are preserved rich old vestments remaining from Catholic times, perfect masterpieces of elaborate embroidery, such as I have not anywhere seen surpassed. Sometimes a cope or chasuble is covered with a whole gallery of figures executed in raised-work, each detail of expression and every fold of the drapery being rendered in a manner approaching the sculptor's art.

In the church itself hang some of the most exquisite Turkish carpets I have ever seen — such tender idyllic blue-green tints, such gloomy passionate reds, such pensive amber shades, as to render distracted with envy any amateur of antique fabrics who has the harrowing disappointment of ascertaining that these masterpieces of the Oriental loom are not purchasable even for untold sums of heavy gold!

"There was *ein verrückter Engländer* (a mad Englishman) here some years ago," I was told by a church-warden, "who would have given any price for that pale-blue one up yonder, and he remained here a whole month merely to be able to see it every day; but he had to go away empty-handed at last, for these carpets, like the vestments, are the property of the Church, and not even the bishop himself has power to dispose of them."

CHAPTER XLIX.

SINAÏA.

From Kronstadt we made an excursion to Sinaïa, a fashionable watering-place and summer residence of the King of Roumania, about two hours' distance over the frontier.

---

* It is of this monarch that the people still say, 'King Matthias is dead, and Justice along with him." He was, in fact, a sort of Hungarian Haroun-al-Raschid, going about in disguise among his people, rewarding them according to their deserts.

We had provided ourselves with a passport from Hermanstadt, for just at that particular moment the regulations about crossing the frontier were rather strict, in consequence of some temporary coolness between the two crowned heads on either side. Usually the *entente cordiale* between both countries is most satisfactory, and Austrian officers wishing to pay their respects to his Roumanian Majesty can always count on a gracious reception; but we happened, unfortunately, to have hit off a brief period of international sulks. Austrian officers were forbidden to show themselves in uniform within the kingdom, or, indeed, to cross the frontier at all, and were consequently reduced to the subterfuges of passports and plain clothes.

It ultimately proved to be much easier to cross from Hungary to Roumania than *vice versa;* for on our way back that same evening, we were detained an eternity by the suspicious pedantry of the Hungarian officials, contrasting unfavorably with the genial simplicity of arrangements on the other side.

The whole route from Kronstadt to Sinaïa is very beautiful, the railway running through a deep valley which sometimes narrows to the dimensions of a close mountain gorge, densely wooded on either side by noble beech forests, bordered by fringes of wild sunflowers, which marked the way in a line of unbroken gold. One might almost have fancied that some munificent fairy had thus chosen to show the way to the King's abode, by strewing gold-pieces along the road.

The glimpses of peasant life we got by looking out of the carriage-window already showed us costumes more varied and fantastic than on the Hungarian side; an air of Eastern luxury as well as of Eastern indolence pervaded everything, and it was impossible not to feel that we had entered another country—the land *beyond* the land beyond the forest.

At Sinaïa itself the valley has somewhat widened out, affording room for numerous handsome villas and luxurious hotels which have sprung up there of late years. On a low hill stands the convent where the royal family have taken up their residence till the new-built castle is ready to be inhabited.

Proceeding on our way towards the convent, we were puzzled for a moment by the appearance of the peasant women we met—their surprising richness of costume and profusion of ornament surpassing the limits of even Roumanian gorgeousness. Their straight-cut scarlet aprons were literally one mass of rich embroidery, and each move

CASTLE PELESCH AT SINAÏA. SUMMER RESIDENCE OF THE KING OF ROUMANIA.

ment of the arm caused the sleeve to glitter in the sun like the scales of gold and silver fish; but why, in place of the customary sandals, did they wear delicate high-heeled *chaussure* strongly suggestive of Paris? Why, instead of the twirling distaff, did we see Japanese fans in their hands? And why, oh why, as we came within ear-shot, did we make the startling discovery that they were not talking Roumanian at all, but speaking French with more or less successful imitations of a Parisian accent?

These various "whys" were soon put to rest by the information that these were not peasants at all, but Roumanian Court ladies, who, following the example of their queen, adopt the national dress for daily wear during the summer months.

It being Sunday, mass had just finished as we reached the convent, whence a motley congregation of officers and ladies, soldiers, peasants, and monks came pouring out. A sentry walking up and down in a somewhat *nonchalant* manner, as though merely taking a mild constitutional, and a red-and-blue flag waving above the low roof of the old-fashioned, shabby building, were the only symptoms of royalty about the place.

Presently a low basket-carriage, drawn by two handsome cream ponies with distressingly long tails and ill-cut manes, came round to the convent door, close to where we were standing, and was entered by a slender lady attired in the national costume, bareheaded, and holding up a Chinese parasol to protect herself from the broiling sun. She appeared to be on easy, cordial terms with the respectable-looking family servant who assisted her to get in, and had quite a pleasant chat with him as he stood on the door-step. It was evident, from the way she was saluted on her passage, that the Queen is a great favorite with people of all classes.

The King, whom we came across a little later in the day, seemed of more unapproachable species, and the little incident connected with his appearance savored rather of Russian than of Roumanian etiquette.

We were walking in the direction of the newly built castle, which, situated on the banks of a torrent at the opening of a steep mountain ravine, and deliciously shrouded in gigantic trees, is the most perfect beau-ideal of a summer chateau I ever saw. Already I had had occasion to remark the appearance of several semi-military-looking beings (whether policemen or soldiers I cannot precisely define) dodging about mysteriously in and out between the tree-stems, when suddenly one of them came rushing towards us, waving his arms aloft like a windmill gone mad, and with an expression of the wildest despair hurriedly repeating something we failed to understand, but which evidently was either a warning or a threat. Before we had time to request this curious being to explain himself more intelligibly, he had disappeared, jumping over the steep, precipitous bank of the ravine, and vanishing in the brushwood.

We now looked round in alarm, half expecting to see a furious wild-boar, possibly even a bear, appearing from the mountain-side, but could only perceive a tall, dark, handsome officer approaching us, and behind him a correct-liveried servant carrying a railway rug. The meaning of the mysterious warning now began to dawn on our comprehension; this could only be the King, from his resemblance to the portraits we had seen, and we had probably no business to be here prying on his private premises. Our feeling of tact was, however, not exquisite enough to induce us to risk our necks in endeavoring to conceal ourselves from his august gaze, so we bravely stood our ground, and nothing worse happened than our bow being very politely returned.

When his Majesty had disappeared I went to the bank to see what had become of the unfortunate soldier or policeman who had effaced himself in so foolhardy a manner; but though I half expected to see his corpse lying shattered at the foot of the rock, no trace of him was there to be seen.

The castle, now completed, and since 1884 inhabited every summer by the royal family, is built in the old German style, and has, I hear, been fitted up and furnished in most exquisite fashion—each article having been carefully selected by the Queen herself, whose artistic taste is well known. Deeper in the forest, at a little distance from the castle, is a tiny hunting-lodge, where in the hot weather the Queen is wont to spend a great part of the day. It is here that she loves to sit composing those graceful poems in which she endeavors to reflect the spirit and heart of her people; and visitors admitted to this royal sanctuary are sometimes fortunate enough to see the latest rough-cast of a poem, bearing the signature of Carmen Sylva, lying open on the writing-table.

The villas about Sinaïa are rather bare-looking as yet, especially on a burning summer day; for parks and gardens have not had time to grow in proportion to the hot-headed mushroom speed with which this whole colony has sprung into existence. The bathing establishment is one of the most delightful I ever saw—a large marble basin, roofed in and lighted from above, framed with a luxuriant fringe of feathery ferns and aquatic plants trailing down on to the surface of an exceptionally clear and crystal-like water. When the Queen comes hither to bathe the walls are further adorned by hangings of Oriental carpets and embroidered draperies.

There are in the place several good restaurants whose cookery might rival any Vienna or Paris establishment, and, for prices, indeed surpass them. Everything we found to be very dear at Sinaïa. As we were returning to Kronstadt in the evening and intended to walk about all day, we did not engage a bedroom at the hotel, but merely asked for some place where we might deposit our wraps and umbrellas. For this purpose we were given a sort of small closet, semi-dark, being only lighted from the staircase, and containing, besides a broken table, but two deal chairs and an unfurnished bedstead. Yet for this luxurious accommodation, which our effects enjoyed during a period of about eight hours, we were charged the modest sum of fifteen francs.

I spent some time at a very fascinating bazaar, where I purchased a few specimens of Roumanian pottery, dainty little red-and-gold cups for black coffee, some grotesque birds, and an impossible dog, which have somewhat the appearance of ancient heathen household gods. There were also carpets for sale, but mostly over-staring in pattern, and of terrifically high prices.

We had brought with us a letter of introduction to a *ci-devant* Austrian officer settled here, and married to a daughter of Prince G——, one of the principal notabilities of the place, which introduction procured us a very pleasant invitation to dine with his family on the terrace overlooking the public gardens.

Our beautiful dark-eyed hostess, whose graceful *élancée* figure seemed made to show off to perfection all the fascinations of the national costume, was kind enough to dress expressly for my benefit before dinner, putting on a profusion of jewellery to heighten the effect of robes fit for Lalla Rookh or Princess Scheherezade. One can hardly wear too much jewellery with this attire: three jewelled belts, one adorned with turquoises, another with garnets, and a third with pearls and emeralds, were disposed across the hips one above the other, like those worn in old Venetian paintings; several necklaces, forming a bewildering cascade of coral and amber over the bosom; a perfect wealth of bracelets; and more jewelled pins than I was able to count held back a transparent veil, further secured by loose golden coins falling low on the forehead.

Her father, Prince G——, gave us some interesting details about the foundation of this promising colony, which is the only establish ment of the sort in the kingdom. He himself was the principal moving spirit in its foundation, and it was owing to his persuasions chiefly that the King formed the resolution of founding a national watering place, which, by becoming the resort of the Roumanian *noblesse*, would keep them at home, instead of spending their money at French or German baths.

Gladly would I have prolonged my stay in Roumania by some days, or even weeks; and it was tantalizing to have to leave these attractive unknown regions after such a cursory glance. Still more so was it to be obliged to refuse a friendly invitation to return there to join a projected expedition of eight to ten days across the mountains to be organized as soon as the weather had grown cooler. It was to be a large cavalcade—about twenty persons in all—the ladies in Rou manian dress and riding in men's saddles. "Perhaps it is because of this you refuse," said my hostess. "I have heard that you English are always so very particular; but here everybody rides so—even the Queen herself has no other saddle."

I had, alas! no opportunity to correct this impression, by showing that an Englishwoman may be as enterprising as a Roumanian queen

---

CHAPTER L.

UP THE MOUNTAINS.

"When I was young our mountains were still locked up," I was told by a gentleman native of the place, who accompanied me on my first mountain excursion in Transylvania. "Whoever then wanted to climb hills or to shoot chamois had to travel to Switzerland to do so and at school they used to teach us that there were no lakes in the country."

It is, in fact, only within the last half-dozen years that some attempt has been made to unlock the long range of lofty mountains which tower so invitingly over the Transylvanian plains, and render practicable the access to many a wild, rocky gorge and secluded loch hitherto unknown save to wandering Wallachian shepherds. A most praiseworthy institution, somewhat on the principle of the Alpine Club, has been formed, thanks to whose energy suitable guides have been secured and rough shelter-houses erected at favorable points.

THE NEGOI—THE HIGHEST MOUNTAIN IN TRANSYLVANIA, 8250 FEET HIGH.*

All this, however, is still in a very primitive state, and the difficulties and inconveniences attending a Transylvanian mountain excursion are yet such as will deter any but very ardent enthusiasts from the attempt. It is not here a question, as in Switzerland, of more or less hard walking or clambering before you can reach a good supper and a comfortable bed. Here the walking is often hard enough, but with this essential difference—that no supper, whether good or bad, can be obtained by any amount of effort; and that the bed, if by good-luck you happen to reach a hut, consists at best of a few rough boards with a meagre sprinkling of straw. You cannot hope to purchase so much

---

* Reprinted from a publication of the Transylvanian Carpathian Society.

as a crust of bread on your way, and the crystal water which gurgles
in each mountain ravine is the only beverage you will come across.
Everything in the way of food and drink, as well as cooking utensils,
knives, forks, cups, and plates, along with rugs and blankets for the
night, must be carried about packed on baggage-horses. Therefore,
when a party consists of half a dozen members, and when the length
of the expedition is to exceed a week, the caravan is apt to assume
somewhat imposing proportions. Luckily, in the land beyond the
forest prices are still moderate in the extreme, and without rank extravagance one may indulge in the luxury of two horses and one guide
apiece. One florin (about 1*s.* 8*d.*) being the usual tax for a horse per
diem, and the same for a man, the daily outlay thus amounts to five
shillings only—a very small investment indeed for the enjoyment to
be derived from a peregrination across the mountainous parts of the
country. I have no doubt that all true lovers of nature will agree
with me in thinking that precisely the rough and gypsy-like fashion
in which these excursions are conducted forms their greatest charm,
and that beautiful scenery is more thoroughly appreciated undisturbed
by any seasoning of French-speaking waiters, *table-d'hôte* dinners, and
wire-rope tram-ways.

This way of travelling has, moreover, the incontestable advantage
of being select, and escaping the inevitable discords which continually
jar upon us when moving in a tourist-frequented country. What
beautiful view does not lose half its charm if its foreground be marred
by a group savoring of cockneyfied gentility? Which magnificent
echoes do not become vulgar when awakened by the shrieking chorus
of a band of German students? Does not even a broken wine-bottle
or a crumpled sheet of newspaper, betraying the recent presence of
some other picnicking party, suffice to ruin miles of the finest landscape to an eye at all fastidious?

Here we may walk from sunrise to sunset without meeting other
sign of life than some huge bird of prey hovering in mid-air above a
lonely valley; and once accustomed to the daily companionship of
eagles, one is apt to feel very exclusive indeed, and to regard most
other society as commonplace and uninteresting.

From the moment we set foot on the wild hill-side, we have left
behind us all the mean and petty conditions of every-day life. At
least we have no other littlenesses to bear with than what we bring
with us ready-made—our own stock-in-trade (which, of course, we can

not get rid of) and that of our chosen companions. Therefore, if I may offer a friendly piece of advice to any would-be mountaineer in these parts, let him look at his friends—not twice, but full twenty times at least—before he contemplates cultivating their uninterrupted society at an altitude of six thousand feet above sea-level. Indeed a Transylvanian mountain excursion is not a thing to be lightly entered upon out of simple *gaieté de cœur*, like any other pleasure-trip. It is a serious and solemn undertaking—almost a sort of marriage-bond—when you engage to put up, for better for worse, with any given half-dozen individuals during an equal number of days and nights. Like gold, they must previously have been tried by fire; and you will find very, very few people, even among your dearest friends, who, when weighed in the balance, will not be found wanting in one or other of the many qualifications which go towards making up a thoroughly congenial companion.

The pure ozone of these upper regions seems to act like the lens of a powerful microscope, bringing out into strong relief whatever is mean or paltry. Sweetly feminine airs and graces which have so entranced us in the ball-room develop to positive monstrosities when transplanted to the mountain-top; an intellect which amply sufficed for the requirements of small-talk on the promenade or at morning calls shows pitiably barren when brought face to face with the majesty of nature; and a stock of amiability always found equal to the exigencies of conventional politeness very soon runs dry under the unwonted strain of a genuine demand. As in the palace of truth in the fairy tale of Madame de Genlis, nothing artificial can here remain undiscovered. You can as little hope to hide your false chignon while camping-out at night as to conceal the exact quality of your temper; and defects of breeding will leak out as surely as the rain will leak in through the inferior fabric of a cheap water-proof cloak.

On the other hand, however, be it said, that many people who in town life have appeared dull and commonplace now rise in value under the action of this powerful microscope; sterling qualities, whose existence we had never suspected, now come to light; and hidden delicacies of thought, which have had no room for expansion in the muggy atmosphere of conventionality, put forth unexpected shoots.

Such reflections are, nevertheless, but pointless digressions from the subject in hand, having nothing whatever to do with my own individual experiences; and present company being always excepted, I

would have it distinctly understood that we were *all* amiable, *all* enter
taining, *all* refined and noble-minded, when in the second week of
September we started on one of these excursions—a long-cherished
wish of mine whose execution had been hitherto baffled by the diffi
culty of finding suitable companionship.

Our party consisted of four gentlemen and two other ladies be
sides myself, and a six hours' drive had taken us from Hermanstadt
to the foot of the hills, where horses and guides awaited us—an im
posing retinue of fully a dozen steeds and nearly as many men: the
former starved, puny-looking animals, weak and spiritless at first sight,
but sure-footed as goats and with endless resisting power; the latter
wild, uncouth fellows, with rolling black eyes and unkempt elf-locks,
attired in coarse linen shirts, monstrous leather belts, and wearing the
national opintschen on their feet.

Our provisions and utensils were packed, according to the custom
of the country, in double sacks made of a sort of rough black-and
white checked flannel, and these, along with our bundles of wraps
secured to the backs of the pack-horses—a somewhat complicated busi
ness, as the weight requires to be extremely nicely balanced on either
side. It was wonderful to see how much could be piled up upon one
small animal, which wellnigh disappeared beneath its bulky freight.

While this packing was going on we rested by the river-side, al
ready enjoying a foretaste of the beauties in store for us. Dense
beech woods clothed the sides of the valley down to the water's edge,
terminating as usual in a golden fringe of wild sunflowers standing
out in broad relief from the dark background; clumps of bright-blue
gentians and rosy rock-carnations were sprouting between the stones,
and here and there the luxuriant trails of the wild hop hung down
till they touched the water; a pair of water-ousels perched on oppo
site banks were making eyes at each other across the roaring torrent,
and the deep quiet pools were occasionally stirred by the leap of a
silvery trout.

At last we were told that all was ready; so, mounting our riding
horses, we commenced the ascent. The saddles were the usual rough
Hungarian wooden ones, only softened by a plaid or rug strapped
over. Side-saddles are here useless, as the horses cannot be tightly
girthed for climbing, and are not accustomed to the one-sided weight,
so the only way to ride with comfort and safety is to imitate the ex
ample of the Roùmanian queen. A very little contrivance about the

costume is all that is necessary in order to sit comfortably on a man's saddle; but I found the unwonted position rather trying at first, and sought occasional relief by sitting sidewise, using the high wooden prominence in front as the pommel of a lady's saddle. However, I soon relinquished these experiments, having very nearly come to serious grief from the saddle turning abruptly, which undoubtedly would have landed me on my head had I not extricated myself by a frenzied evolution. After this experience I thought it wiser to tempt fate no further and meekly resign myself to the degradation of a temporary change of sex.

On this particular occasion, however, I did not for long tax the powers of my steed, it was so much pleasanter to walk up the mountain-path step by step, and enjoy at close quarters all the wonders of the forest.

For upwards of two hours our way led us through splendid beech woods richly carpeted with every species of ferns and mosses, an endless vista of shining gray satin and soft emerald velvet. Then by-and-by the first shy irresolute fir-tree appears on the scene, like a bashful rustic strayed unawares into the presence of royalty. The tall majestic beeches look down contemptuously on the puny intruder; for, like ancient monarchs fallen asleep on their thrones, they do not conceive it possible that their reign should ever come to an end.

"What means this rough interloper?" they seem disdainfully to ask, as they nod in the evening breeze. "Are not we the sole lords in these realms? What seeks this insolent upstart in our royal presence?"

But scarcely have we gone a hundred paces farther, than again we meet the intruding pine, larger and stronger this time; nor is he alone, for he has brought with him a motley group of his prickly brethren. Onward they press from all sides, impudently sprouting up at the very feet of the indignant beeches—their rough green arms ruthlessly brushing against the delicate gray satin of those shining pillars, trampling down the emerald velvet of the carpet, like revolutionary peasants broken into a palace.

The lordly beeches make a last effort to assert their supremacy, but the limits of their kingdom are reached; the sharp wind sweeping over the mountain-top, making them shake with impotent rage, is too keen for their delicate constitutions. They dwindle away, perish, and die, leaving the field to their hardier foe.

24

And now King Pine has it all his own way. *Le roi est mort.
Vive le roi!* A minute ago we had been revelling in the beauties of
the beech forest, and now, courtier - like, we find ourselves thinking
that the pine woods are more beautiful yet by far. What can be
more exquisite than those feathery branches trailing down to the
mossy carpet? what more glorious than those straight-grown stems,
each one erect and strong, worthy to be the mast of a mighty
ship? what scent more intoxicating than the perfume they breathe
forth?

Our reflections are presently broken in upon by a scramble close
at hand. One of our baggage-horses has trod upon an underground
wasp's-nest, which intrusion having been duly resented by the indignant insects, the horse takes to kicking violently, and finally rolls
down the wooded incline, scattering our baggage as he goes. Luckily,
nothing is lost or damaged, and after a little delay, the fugitive being
captured and reladen, we are able to proceed on our way. A little
more climbing, and then at last the forest walls unclose, and we stand
on an open meadow of short-tufted grass, where is built the rough
wood hut which is to give us shelter. To the right and left the pine
woods slope upward, their shadowy outlines gradually losing themselves in the fast-gathering twilight; and in front, at a distance of
some five hundred yards, is a wall of rock overwashed by a foaming
cascade, whose music has been growing on our ears during the last
few minutes.

The horses are relieved of their respective burdens and set loose
to graze; neither hay nor oats has been provided, nor do they expect
it. Our Wallachian guides busy themselves in collecting firewood
and kindling a large camp-fire, for the triple purpose of cooking the
supper, keeping themselves warm, and scaring off possible bears or
wolves that may come prowling about at night in quest of a horse.
There is here no difficulty in providing firewood enough for a splendid bonfire, and no tree burns with such spirit as a dead fir-tree.

It is my duty here to forestall all possible anticipation, by frankly
acknowledging that no bear ever did come to disturb us on this occasion. Yet the thought of the shaggy visitor who might at any moment be expected to drop in upon us went a long way towards en-
hancing the romance of the situation. During our whole stay in
the mountains Bruin was like a vague intangible presence hovering
around, and causing us delicious thrills of horror at every step. If

we plucked a branch of late raspberries on our path, it was with a trembling hand, lest a furry paw should appear at the other side of the bush to claim its rightful property; and we lay down to rest half expecting to be wakened by an angry growl close at hand. Consequently, the raspberries we ate and the sleep we snatched were sweeter far than common raspberries and every-day sleep, feeling, as we almost got to do, as though each had been fraudulently extorted from the bear.

Our shelter-hut, roughly put together of boards, consisted of a small entrance-lobby with stamped earth floor, and of one moderate-sized room about six paces long. All down one side, occupying fully half the depth of the apartment, ran a sort of shelf covered with straw, supposed to act as bed, where about a dozen persons might have room lying side by side. A long deal table, a wooden bench, and a row of pegs for hanging up the clothes completed the furniture. Besides the wooden shutters, there were movable glass windows, which were regularly deposited in a hiding-place under the foot-boards, lest they should be wantonly broken by the all-destroying Wallachians. Each authorized guide only is apprised of their place of concealment, to which he is careful to restore them when the party breaks up.

This particular shelter-hut is an exceptionally well-built and luxurious one, most such being devoid of windows, and often closed on one side only.

By the time we had prepared our supper and cheered ourselves with numerous cups of excellent tea it had grown quite dark, and we were thankful to seek our hard couches. A railway rug spread over the straw-covered boards rendered them quite endurable, and all superfluous coats and jackets were pressed into the pillow service. All of us lay down in our clothes, merely removing the boots; for it is hardly possible to dress too warmly for a night passed in these Carpathian shelter-huts; and despite the day having been so warm as to necessitate the thinnest summer clothing for walking, the nights were piercingly cold, and even a heavy fur sledging-cloak was not superfluous.

Though the splash of the water-fall and the tinkling bell of a grazing horse were the only sounds which broke the stillness of the night, yet our unwonted surroundings did not allow of much uninterrupted slumber. But it is surprising to note to what a very minimum the necessary dose of sleep can be reduced on such occasions; the body, renovated as by a magic potion, seems unaccountably delivered from all physical weakness; even the sore throat we had brought with us from the lower world has vanished in the pure atmosphere of the upper regions.

CHAPTER LI.

THE BULEA SEE.

NEXT morning we proceeded to the real object of our excursion, the Bulea See, a lake which lies at the foot of the Negoi, 6662 feet above the sea-level, and situated about three hours distant from our shelter-hut.

There was a steep climb till we had reached the top of the water-fall, and then we found ourselves in a second valley, larger and wider than the first, and of a totally different character. Here were neither moss nor ferns, neither beech nor pine woods—only a deep and lonely valley shut in by pointed rocks on either side, and thickly strewn throughout with massive bowlder-stones, each of which would seem to mark the resting-place of a giant. The only form of vegetation here visible, besides the short scraggy grass sprouting in detached patches betwixt the stones, were the stunted irregular fir-bushes (called *krumm-holz*), which, blown by ever-recurring gales into all sorts of fantastic shapes, resemble as many wizened goblins playing at hide-and-seek among the giant tombstones, crawling and creeping into every hollow which can afford them shelter from the inclemency of the winter storm; for now we have entered a third kingdom, and the reign of the pine-tree is at an end. Having once overpassed the height of 1800 metres (5905½ feet), above which fir-trees do not thrive, these once stalwart and overbearing giants have degenerated to the misshapen and crooked goblins we see.

Yet here again we are forced to acknowledge this new metamorphosis to be but another step in the scale of loveliness. We had been enchanted by the beech woods, ravished by the pine forest, yet now all at once we feel that with the desolate wildness of these upper regions a yet higher note of beauty has been struck; for here Nature, seeming to disdain such toilet artifices as trees or ferns or cunningly tinted mosses, like a classical statue, boldly reveals herself in her glorious nudity, with naught to distract the eye from the perfection of her sublime curves.

Something of the charm of this desolate stony valley lay no doubt, for me, in its marked resemblance to Scottish scenery, recalling to my mind some of the wilder parts of Arran, the upper half of Glen Rosa, or portions of Glen Sannox, seen long ago but never forgotten; and for a moment I experienced the pleasurable sensation of recognizing the face of a beloved old friend in a strange picture-gallery.

The fierce barking of dogs aroused me from my comparisons, and now for the first time I perceived that at one place the large loose stones had been piled together so as to form a rude sort of hovel or cavern, the headquarters of some shepherds come hither to find pasture for their flocks during the brief mountain summer.

We approached the *stina,* as these *bergeries* are called, and made acquaintance with the shepherd, some of the gentlemen at my request cross-questioning him as to his habits and occupation. He was ready enough to enter into conversation with us and our guide, seemingly rejoiced at the sight of other human beings after a long period of isolation. We learned from him that the shepherds are in the habit of coming up here each summer about the end of June, to remain till the middle of September, after which date snow may be expected to set in, and the shepherd, proceeding southward as the year advances, leads his flocks into Wallachia and Moldavia to pass the winter. These flocks are not the property of one individual, but each village inhabitant has his particular sheep marked with his own sign. All the mountain pastures in these parts belong to a Count T——, who receives forty-five kreuzers (about 9*d.*) per sheep for its summer pasturage.

This particular flock consisted of about eight hundred head, herded by four shepherds only, and six or eight large wolf-dogs. The men receive thirty florins (£2 10*s.*) yearly wages, besides a pair of sandals each, and a certain proportion of food, principally maize-flour, to be cooked into *mamaliga,* and whatever cheese and sheep's milk they require. These wages are considered high enough in these parts, but the work required is hard and fatiguing. The whole day the shepherd must creep along the crags with his flock, at places where scarce a goat could obtain footing, and at night he must sleep in the open air whatever be the weather, ready to spring up at the slightest alarm of wolf or bear.

"When did you last see a bear?" inquired our interpreter of the solitary shepherd.

"This very night, *dommu*" (master), he replied, "the *ursu* came prowling about the camp, and had to be driven away by the dogs. Most nights he does come, and four of my sheep has he carried off this year. Not one of our dogs but has been torn or wounded by him in turn."

"And where are your sheep at present?" was the next question, as we looked round at the deserted camp.

The man pointed upward and uttered a shrill, unearthly cry, which presently was repeated as by an echo coming from the topmost ledges of the crags overhead; and there, looking up to where the jagged peaks were sharply defined against the blue sky, we could see the white sheep clinging all over the face of the precipitous cliffs like patches of new-fallen snow. It was wonderful to see how these seemingly sense-less animals obey the slightest call of their shepherd, who by the inflec-tions of his voice alone guides them in whatever direction he pleases; and it is almost incredible that out of a flock of eight hundred sheep the shepherd should be able to recognize and identify each separate animal.

When we came to see those sheep at close quarters later in the day, we were surprised at the whiteness and fine quality of their wool— each single animal looking as though it had been freshly washed and carefully combed out, like the favorite poodle of some fine lady, and presenting therein a striking contrast to the flocks down below on the plains, whose appearance is dirty and unkempt. This superior toilet of the mountain sheep seems due to the constant mists and vapors ever flitting to and fro in these upper regions, which thus enact the parts of cleansing spirits; but why, when they are about it, do not these benev-olent *kobolds* wash the shepherd as well?

Besides the dogs, there is usually a donkey attached to each shep-herd's establishment. It serves to carry the packs of cheese and milk, or the heavy *bunda* (sheepskin coat) of the shepherd, and follows the flock about wherever its legs permit. On this occasion we met the in-evitable ass some few hundred yards farther up the valley, standing on one of the giant tombstones, and with head thrown back, loudly braying up in the direction of the mountain heights. He, too, had caught sight of his beloved sheep scrambling so far out of reach up there, and weary of his loneliness, was thus passionately entreating his eight hundred sweethearts to return to his faithful side.

Two hours more up the lonely valley brought us to our destination. There was one last rocky wall to be overcome, and, having scaled it, we stood with panting breath before the Bulea See, a curiously suggestive little loch, dark greenish-blue in color, which nestles in the stony chalice formed by the rocks around.

Nothing but gray bowlder-stones lying here cast about; no plant save the deadly monk's-hood growing rank in thick, short tufts of deep sapphire hue; no sign of life but one solitary falcon soaring overhead, and some scattered feathers lying strewn at the water's edge.*

The brooding melancholy of this solitary spot has a charm all its own. This would be the place, indeed, for a life-sick man to come and end his days, and if there be such a thing as a voluptuous suicide, methinks these were the proper surroundings for it. Death must come so swiftly and so surely in those still green waters, which have such an insinuating glitter; no danger here of being saved and brought back to unwelcome life by a meddlesome log of floating wood, or the officious arm of an out-stretched branch. Everything here seems to breathe of the very spirit of suicide; the cold green waters, the deadly monk's-hood, the hovering falcon, all seem to agree, " This is the end of life—come here and die !"

But let the hapless wretch bent on leaving this world beware of looking round once more before executing his resolve, for if he but turn and gaze again at the magnificent panorama at his feet, he will assuredly be violently recalled to life.

I do not recollect having seen any single view which in its glorious variety ever impressed me as much as what I saw that day, looking from the platform beside the Bulea See; neither a framed-in picture nor yet a bird's-eye view, it rather gave me the feeling as though I were standing at the head of a giant staircase whose balustrades are formed by the nicked-out peaks of the crags on either side, and whose separate steps present as many gradations of variegated beauty.

Close to our feet lay the stony valley we had just been traversing, with its gigantic tombstones and wizened dwarf bushes, and the flashing crest of the water-fall, just visible, like a silver thread, at the farthest point. Then, after a sudden drop of several hundred feet, our

---

* These feathers, of a bluish color, we identified as those of the garrulous roller, *Coracias garrula;* and as this bird is never to be found at the aforementioned height, it must apparently have been crossing the mountains to migrate southward, when its travelling arrangements were disturbed by the watchful falcon.

eye lights upon the pine valley, with the shelter-hut where we had passed the previous night. With a telescope we could just make out the place of the camp-fire and the figures of some grazing horses. Of the third step of this giant ladder—namely, the beech forest—we could see only the billowy tops of the close-grown trees, a mass of waving green, touched here and there by the hand of autumn into russet and golden tints; then far, far below lay stretched the smiling plain, streaked with occasional dark patches we knew to be forests, and sundry white dots we guessed at as villages, and the serpentine curves of the river Alt, winding like a golden ribbon between them.

A long bank of clouds which had been hovering over the plain now sank down, gradually obscuring that part of the view, but not for long. This was but another freak of nature, one more turn in the kaleidoscope; for now the mist has sunk so low that the plain itself appears above it, and we behold the landscape framed in the clouds, like a delusive *Fata Morgana.*

This is indeed a picture never to weary of, and after gazing at it for ten ecstatic minutes, I defy the life-sick man to turn away and carry out his suicidal intentions. The cold green waters have lost their attraction for him, and the spell of the deadly monk's-hood is broken; for another voice whispers in his ear, and it tells him of life and of hope: a few minutes ago he had felt like a condemned criminal in sight of his grave, but now, with this glorious world at his feet, he is fain to think himself monarch of all he beholds.

The giant's ladder contains one more step, for by scrambling up the rocks at one side of the loch one may reach the crest of the mountains, and walking there for hours on the confines of Roumania, gain an extensive view into both countries.

This is what some of the gentlemen of our party did, in hopes of coming across chamois; while the rest of us remained below, well content with what we had achieved, settling down, not to suicide, but to such healthier, if more commonplace, pursuits as luncheon and sketching. At least the luncheon was eaten and the sketch was begun ; but beginning and finishing are two very different things in these regions, and one cannot reckon without the mountain-sprites, who were this day mischievously inclined.

A tiny white cloudlet, snowy and innocent-looking as a tuft of swan's-down, had meanwhile detached itself from the bank of clouds below the plain, and was speeding aloft in our direction. Incredibly fast this mountain-sprite ascended the giant staircase—gliding over the space it had taken us three hours to traverse in not the tenth part of that time; jumping two steps at once, it seemed in its malicious haste to spoil our pleasure. Now it has reached the terrace where we are sitting; we feel its cold breath on our cheek, and in another minute it has thrown its moist filmy veil over the scene. The lake at our side has disappeared; we cannot see ten paces in front, and we shiver under the warm wraps we just now despised.

The mist, which feels at first like a soft, invisible rain, gradually becomes harder and more prickly; there is a sharp, rattling sound in the air, and we realize that we are sitting in a hail-storm, from which we vainly try to escape by dodging under the overhanging rocks.

As quickly as it came it is gone again, for scarce ten minutes later the sun shone out triumphant, dispersing the ill-natured vapors. Yet a little longer will the sun lord it up here as master, and come victorious out of all such combats; but these impish cloudlets are the outrunners of the army of the dread ice-king, and will return again day by day in greater numbers, soon to be no more driven away from these regions.

CHAPTER LII.

THE WIENERWALD—A DIGRESSION.

I SHALL never forget the shock to my feelings when, shortly after leaving Transylvania, I went to spend the summer months in the much-famed Wienerwald near Vienna. In former years I had often visited this neighborhood, and had even retained of it very pleasant recollections; but now, fresh from the wild charm of undefiled and undesecrated nature, the Wienerwald and everything about it appeared in the light of a pitiable farce. In fact, I do not think I had ever rightly appreciated the Transylvanian mountain scenery till forced to compare it with another landscape.

The country about Vienna—of which its natives are so proud—is beautiful, it is true, or rather it has been beautiful once; but, alas! how much of its charm has been destroyed by that terrible *Verschönerungs Verein* (Beautifying Association), as those noisome institutions are called, loathsome abortions of a diseased German brain, which have the object of teaching unfortunate mankind to appreciate the beauties of nature in the only correct fashion authorized by science.

Viewed in the abstract, an ignorant stranger unacquainted with the habits of the country might be prone to imagine taking a walk up any of those beautiful wooded hills to be a comparatively simple matter, provided his lungs and his *chaussure* be in adequate walking trim. Ridiculous error! to be speedily rectified by painful experience before you have spent many days in the neighborhood of the Austrian capital. It is here not a question of boots, but of books; of science, not of soles; your lungs are useless unless your mind be rightly adjusted; and the latest edition of Meyer's "Conversations Lexicon" will be far more necessary to fit you for a walk in the Wienerwald than a pair of Euknemida walking-shoes.

To go into a civilized Austrian forest requires at least as much preparation as to enter a fashionable ball-room; and unless you have been thoroughly grounded in contemporary literature, general history, and the biographies of celebrated men, you had far better stay at home.

There you are not left to yourself to make acquaintance with trees and flowers, as your ignorant rustic fashion has hitherto been; but your exact relations to the botanical world around you are precisely defined from the very outset. At every step you make you are overwhelmed with alternate doses of advice, admonition, entreaty, or threat; but never, never by any chance are you left to your own devices! You cannot feel as if you were alone even in the most hidden depths of the forest, for the tormenting spirit of the *Verschönerungs Verein* will insist on following you about step by step, its jarring voice ever breaking in on your most secret reveries. It *warns* you not to tread on the grass; it *entreats* you to spare the pine-cones; it *instructs* you to avoid meddling with the toadstools; it *recommends* the flowers to your protection; it *advises* you to be careful with your cigar-ashes; it *commands* you to muzzle your unhappy terrier; it weighs you down with a crushing sense of your own unworthiness by appealing to your sense of honor, of probity, of refinement, of patriotism, and to a hundred other noble qualities you are acutely conscious of *not* possessing; then passing from fawning flattery to brutal menace, it growls dark threats against your liberty or your purse, should you have remained deaf to its hateful voice, and presume to have overstepped the limits of familiarity prescribed towards an oak-tree or a bush of wild-rose.

If, chafing in spirit at these reiterated pinpricks, you would take some rest by sitting down on one of the numerous benches placed there for the accommodation of exhausted but perfectly educated individuals, you are abruptly called upon to choose between Goethe and Schiller, Kant or Hegel, Lessing or Wieland, to the immortal memory of each of which celebrities the proud monument of six feet of white-painted board has been dedicated.

A harmless enough looking little bridge is designated as Custozza bridge, and a delicious opening in the forest redolent of wild cyclamen desecrated by the base appellation of *Philosophen Wiese* (Philosopher's meadow). Even the source where you pause to slake your thirst has been christened by some such preposterous title as the fountain of friendship or the spring of gratitude. You cannot, in fact, move a hundred yards in any given direction without having the names of celebrated men, cardinal virtues, or national victories forced down your throat *ad nauseam*, and—what to my thinking is the cruelest grievance of all—you are there debarred the simple satisfaction of losing your way in a natural unsophisticated manner, every second tree having been converted into a sign-post, which persists in giving information you would much rather be without.

Latitude and longitude are dinned into your ears with merciless precision; staring patches of scarlet, blue, and yellow paint, arranged to express a whole series of cabalistic signs, disfigure the ruddy bronze of noble pine-stems; gaunt pointing fingers, multiplied as in a delirious nightmare, meet you at every turn, informing you of your exact bearings with regard to every given point of the landscape within a radius of ten miles. "Two hours from Bürgersruhe," they tell you; "Five hours from Wienerlust;" "An hour and a half from Philister Berg"—and oh, how many weary miles away from anything resembling nature and freedom, eagles and poetry!

You long to be gone from the mournful spectacle of nature profaned and debased; your independent spirit chafes and frets under the oppressive tyranny of a vulgar despot, who, not content with directing your movements and restricting your actions, would further extend his detested interference to the inmost regions of your thoughts and feelings. Why should I be confronted with Hegel, when I wish to cultivate the far more congenial society of an interesting stag-beetle? Wherefore disturb the luxurious feeling of gloomy revenge my soul is brooding by the suggestion of any sentiment as sickly and as utterly fabulous as friendship or gratitude? Why dishonor the fragrance of pale cyclamen by a bookworm odor of mustiness and mildew? Why, O cruel *Verschönerungs Verein*, skilful annihilator of all that is beautiful and sublime, have you left no margin for poetry or imagination, romance or accident, conjecture or hope, in visiting these regions? "*Lasciate ogni speranza voi ch' entrate*" it is indeed the case here to say; or rather, if you be wise, do not enter these hopeless regions at all, but turning your back on all such, go straight through to Transylvania, where you will find in profusion all those charms of which the Wienerwald has been so cruelly robbed!

CHAPTER LIII.

A WEEK IN THE PINE REGION.

Our quarters at the shelter-hut in the pine valley were so satisfactory, and its situation so delightful, that instead of remaining only two nights, as had been originally intended, we stayed there a whole week, exploring the valley in all directions, making sketches of the principal points, and collecting supplies of the rare ferns and mosses with which the neighborhood abounded, along with the alpen-rose, which we often discovered still flowering at sheltered places.

A thorough dose of nature enjoyed in this way acts like a regenerating medicine on a mind and body wearied and weakened by a long strain of conventionalities. It is refreshing merely to look round on a beautiful scene as yet untainted by the so-called civilizing breath of man, who, too often attempting to paint the lily, invariably vulgarizes when he seeks to improve the work of the Creator. What unmixed delight to see here everything unspoiled and unadulterated, each tree and flower living out its natural life, or falling into beautiful decay, without having been turned aside from its original vocation, or distorted to an unnatural use to minister to some imaginary want of sensual, cruel, greedy, rapacious man; to find one little spot where nature yet reigns supreme; to be able to gaze around and say that those splendid fir-stems will *not* be cut up in a noisy saw-mill, nor yet defiled by vulgar paint; those late scarlet strawberries hanging in coral fringes from pearl-gray rocks will *not* be sold at so much a pint and cooked into sickly jams ; those prickly fir-cones will *not* be abstracted from their rightful owners, the red-coated squirrels, to adorn the tasteless veranda of some popular beer-house ; the swelling outlines of those glorious blue gentians will be flattened in *no* improved herbarium, nor those gorgeous butterflies invited to lay down their young

THE PINE VALLEY.*

lives to further the interests of science ; those brown leaping trout will, thank Heaven, never, never figure on an illuminated *menu* card as *truites à la Chambord*, to flatter the palate of some dissipated sybarite! The pure light of the north star alone will point out my direction, and neither Kant nor Hegel will rise from his grave to torment me here.

It is wonderful how soon one gets accustomed to roughing it, and doing without the comforts and luxuries of daily life, and it is delightful to discover that civilization is only skin-deep after all. On the second morning it seemed no hardship to perform our toilet at a mountain spring shrouded in a pine-tree boudoir ; empty bottles were very worthy substitutes for silver candlesticks ; and for brushing our

* Reprinted from a publication of the Transylvanian Carpathian Society.

dress and cleansing our boots, a wild Wallachian peasant quite as useful as a trained *femme de chambre.*

Dress and fashion, uniforms and coffee-houses, the wearisome chit-chat of a little country town, as well as the intricacies of European politics, had all passed out of our lives as though they had never existed, leaving no regret, scarcely even a memory. It seemed hardly possible to believe that such useless and unnatural things as false hair, diamond ear-rings, military parades, cream-laid note-paper, calling-cards, sugar-tongs, intrigue, envy, and ambition existed somewhere or other about the world. Were there really other forms of music extant than the lullaby of the water-fall, and the wild pibroch of the wind among the fir-stems? other sorts of perfumes than the pine wood fragrance and the breath of wild thyme?

While we were thus revelling in the pure ozone above, two emperors were meeting in some dull corner of the dingy earth below,* and all Europe was looking on and holding its breath, in order to catch some echo of the royal syllables interchanged.

For our part, we completely skipped this page of European history, and felt none the worse of it. Everything changes proportion up here, and a real eagle becomes of far more absorbing interest than a double-headed one. We were virtually as isolated as though cast on a desert island in the Pacific; and but for one messenger despatched to assure us of the welfare of our respective families, we had no communication with the world we had left.

Here we had a hundred other sources of interest of more absorbing and healthier kind than the so-called pleasures we had left below. First there was the water-fall, a never-failing element of beauty and interest. It was delightful to sketch it, sitting on a moss-grown stone at the edge of the torrent; it was yet more delightful to clamber up to its base, and clinging on to a rock, receive the breath of its spray full on our face, and enjoy at close quarters the musical thunder of its voice. Not far from this was the place where, three years previously, the great avalanche had swept over the valley, felling prostrate every tree which came in its passage. All across one side of the glen, and half-way up the opposite hill, can still be traced the ravaging march of the destroying forces; for here the woodman never comes with his

---

* The meeting of the Emperors of Austria and Russia at Skiernevice, in September, 1884.

axe, and each tree still lies prostrate where it was stricken down, like giant ninepins overthrown; and here they will lie undisturbed till they rot away and turn to soft red dust, mute vouchers of the terrible power of unchained nature. One felt inclined to envy the bears and eagles for this glorious sight, of which they alone can have been the fortunate spectators.

Another point of interest indicated by our guides was the bridge of fir-stems over a steep ravine, where years ago a terrified flock of sheep, pursued by a bear in broad daylight, had leaped down over the precipitous edge, upwards of three hundred breaking their legs in their frenzied attempts to escape.

The shepherds who lived above in the stony valley came frequently down to our shelter-hut, and we used to find them comfortably ensconced at our camp-fire, in deep conversation with the guides. In their lonely existence it must have been a pleasant experience to have neighbors at all within reach, and our hospitable camp-fire was doubtless as good as a fashionable club to their simple minds. They brought us of their sheep's milk and cheese. The latter, called here *brindza*, was very palatable, and the milk much thicker and richer than cow's milk, but of a peculiar taste which I failed to appreciate.

There was a shepherdess, too, belonging to the establishment; but let no one, misled by the appellation, instinctively conjure up visions of delicate pastel-paintings or coquettish porcelain figurines, for anything more utterly at variance with the associations suggested by the names of Watteau and Vieux Saxe, than the uncouth, swarthy, one-eyed damsel who inhabited the bergerie, cannot well be imagined. The male shepherds were four in number—two of them calling for no special description; the third, a boy of about fourteen, with large, senseless eyes and a fixed, idiotic stare, looked no more than semi-human. The most distinguished member of the party, and, as we ladies unanimously agreed, decidedly the flower of the flock, was a good-looking young man of some twenty years, with straight-cut, regular features, a high brown fur cap, and a wooden flute on which he played in a queer, monotonous fashion, resembling the droning tones of a bagpipe. He had come from Roumania, he told us, and had been for a time tending flocks in Turkey, where he had picked up something of the language. It was a curious country, he observed, and the people there had curious habits — such, for instance, as that of keeping several wives; the richer a man was, the more wives he kept.

Our young shepherd shrugged his shoulders as he made this remar: in a supercilious manner, evidently of opinion that women were a evil which should not be unnecessarily multiplied; and certainly, judg ing from the solitary specimen of female beauty which the stony val ley contained, no man could feel tempted to embark in a very exten sive harem.

We afterwards ascertained that the interesting shepherd with th fur cap and wooden flute had committed a murder over in Roumania and been obliged to fly the country on that account. This disclosur rendered us somewhat more reserved in our intercourse with our ro mantic neighbor, and though we could not exactly put a stop to hi visits, we avoided over-intimacy, and always felt more at ease in hi society when there was a gun or revolver within handy reach.

Our Wallachian guides proved thoroughly satisfactory in ever: way — active, obliging, and full of inventive resources. They wer: very particular about keeping their fast-days as prescribed by th Greek Church, and would refuse all offers of food at such times When not fasting they were easily made happy by any scraps o cheese or bacon left over from our meals, or by a glassful of spirits o wine judiciously adulterated with water. On one occasion a parce containing a dozen hard-boiled eggs, grown stale (to put it mildly from having been overlooked, was received with positive rapture b; one of these unsophisticated beings, who devoured them every on with a heartfelt relish not to be mistaken.

Ham, sausages, and bread and cheese, formed the staple of ou nourishment in this as in other Transylvanian mountain excursions— for after the first day, of course, no fresh meat could be procured Also, the Hungarian *paprica speck*—viz., raw bacon prepared with re: pepper—is useful on these occasions, as it gives much nourishmen in a very small compass. I never myself succeeded in reaching th point demanded by Hungarian enthusiasm for this favorite nationa food; so that all I can conscientiously say for it is that, given th circumstances of a keen appetite, bracing mountain air, and no othe available nourishment, it is quite eatable, and by a little stretch o indulgence might almost be called palatable. The Magyars, howeve: pronounce this bacon to be of such superlatively exquisite flavor a only to be fit for the gods on a Sunday! So I suppose it can only b by reason of some peculiarly ungodlike quality in my nature that I an unable to appreciate this Elysian dish as it deserves.

The Roumanians have, like the Poles, a certain inbred sense of courtesy totally wanting in their Saxon neighbors; it shows itself in many trifling acts—in the manner they rise and uncover in the presence of a superior, and the way they offer their assistance over the obstacles of the path. One day that I had hurt my foot, and was much distressed at being unable to join a longer walk, I found in the evening a large nosegay of ripe bilberries, surrounded by red autumn leaves, lying at the foot of my sleeping-place—a delicate attention on the part of our head guide, who wished thereby to console me for the pleasure I had lost.

The peasants were always pitying us for the disadvantages of our *chaussure:* how could we be so foolish as to submit to the torture and inconvenience of shoes and stockings, instead of adopting the comfortable opintschen they themselves wore? And they almost succeeded in persuading me to make the attempt on some future occasion, although I feel doubtful as to how far a foot corrupted by civilization could be induced to adapt itself to this unwonted covering.

We celebrated our last evening in the pine valley by ordering an extra large bonfire to be made. Accordingly, three good-sized fir-trees were felled, and bound together to form a sort of pyramid. A glorious sight when the flames had scaled the heights, turning each little twig into a golden brand, and drawing a profusion of rockets from every branch—far more beautiful than any fireworks I had seen.

One of our guides, called Nicolaïa—the tallest and wildest-looking of the group—especially distinguished himself on this occasion. He had evidently something of the salamander in his constitution, for he seemed to be absolutely impervious to heat, and to feel, in fact, quite as comfortable inside the fire as out of it. By common consent he was generally assigned the part of cat's-paw, to him being delegated the office of taking a boiling pot off the fire or picking the roasted potatoes from out the red-hot embers. Standing as he now was, almost in the centre of the glowing pile, supporting the burning fir-trees with his sinewy arms, while a perfect shower of sparks rained thickly down all over his ragged shirt and bare, tawny chest, it required no stretch of imagination to take him for a figure designed by Doré and stepped straight out of Dante's Inferno.

Our last morning came, and with heartfelt regret we prepared to leave the lovely valley where we had spent such a truly delicious

25

week. An additional pack-horse having been sent for from the village below, we were surprised to see the animal in question make its appearance led by the Roumanian cure of the parish, who, having heard that a horse was required, had bethought himself of earning an honest penny by hiring out his beast and enacting the part of driver. Anywhere else it would be a strange anomaly to see a clergyman putting himself on a level with a common peasant, attired in coarse linen shirt and meekly carrying our bundles; but here this is of every-day occurrence. The Roumanian peasant, however rigorously he may adhere to the forms of his Church, has, as I said before, no inordinate respect for the person of his clergyman, whose infallibility is only considered to last so long as he is standing before the altar; once outside the church walls he becomes an ordinary man to his congregation, and not necessarily a particularly respected or respectable individual. This particular popa was, as it appeared, not only accustomed to serve as driver, but likewise as beast of burden himself—as he genially volunteered to carry all the mosses and ferns we collected on the way. I am ashamed to say that we basely accepted his services, and loaded him unmercifully with the spoils of the forest, thus unceremoniously apostrophizing him: "Here, popa, another hart's-tongue;" or, "Take this ivy trail, will you?" till he was wellnigh smothered in sylvan treasures.

Our path to the foot of the mountains, where our carriages were to await us, was a walk of about three hours; but soon after starting, our sacerdotal porter having volunteered to show us a short cut, which should take us down in two-thirds of that time, we gladly grasped at this proposition and at the prospect of seeing a new part of the forest; and our other guides being on ahead with the horses, we blindly intrusted ourselves to the guidance of the holy man, who forthwith began to lead us through the very thickest forest-mazes, over rocks and torrents, through bogs and brier, up hill and down dale, till our clothes were torn, our hands were bleeding, and our tempers were soured. "The way must be very short, indeed, if it is so bad," was the reflection which at first kept up our spirits; but we had yet to learn that brevity and badness do not always go hand in hand, and that an execrable path may be lengthy as well. Like jaded warriors overcome by the fatigue of an excessive march, we now disburdened ourselves of our rich spoils, having no further thought but to find our way from out this bewildering labyrinth of smooth beech-stems. Clumps of exquisite maidenhair ferns, but now so tenderly dug up, were callously cast aside, and the much-prized layers of velvety moss were brutally left to perish. All noble instincts seemed dead within us, our weary limbs and empty stomachs being all we cared for. The forest had suddenly grown hideous, and we wondered at ourselves for ever having thought it beautiful. The priest was a ruffian luring us on to our destruction. Utterly losing sight of his sacerdotal character, we abused him in harsh and vigorous language, which he meekly bore—I must say that much for him. Perhaps he had heard similar language before, and was accustomed to it.

Whether the popa had lost his way and did not wish to acknowledge it, or whether, as I rather suspect, he had never been in the forest before, remains an unsolved mystery; the result was, however, that after nearly seven hours of remarkably hard walking we were still lost in the depths of the forest, and apparently no nearer our destination than when we had set out.

At this juncture one of the ladies lay down on the ground, declaring herself incapable of going a step farther. She was nearly fainting with fatigue and hunger, for all our provisions had been sent on with the horses. The predicament was a most unpleasant one; for although the popa swore for at least the twentieth time that we should arrive in less than half an hour, we had been too cruelly deceived, and our confidence in him was gone. Half an hour might just as well mean three or four hours farther; and even if he spoke the truth our unfortunate companion was far too much exhausted to proceed.

After a brief consultation we determined that, leaving two gentlemen in charge of the invalid, some of us should go on with the miscreant priest as guide, sending back a horse and some restoratives to the spot. This plan proved successful; for after about three-quarters of an hour more of clambering and climbing, we reached the forest edge, and found our guides waiting for us and much perplexed at our nonappearance.

"The devil take the popa!" was their hearty and unanimous exclamation when we had related our adventure; "who could be fool enough to follow the priest? Did we not know that it was bad-luck even to meet a popa?" they asked us pityingly; and certainly, under the circumstances, we felt inclined for once to attach some weight to popular superstition, and inwardly to resolve never again to trust ourselves to the guidance of a Roumanian popa.

CHAPTER LIV.

LADUS AND BISTRA.

THIS first taste of the delights of a Transylvanian mountain excursion had but stimulated our desire for more enjoyment of the same kind. After revelling so unrestrainedly in the pure mountain air, it was not possible to settle down at once to the monotony of every-day life. Some touch of the restless, roving spirit of the gypsies had come over me, and I began to understand that the life they lead might have a fascination nowhere else to be found. I positively hungered for more air, more sunshine, for deeper draughts of the pine wood fragrance, further revelations of the mountain wonders. I could not afford to waste the very last days of this glorious summer weather cooped up within narrow streets; and as one or two of my late companions were of the same way of thinking, another expedition was speedily resolved upon.

It was, however, not without difficulty that we organized this second excursion, which could not possibly be attempted by two ladies without at least an equal number of gentlemen. Especially if there were going to be any more fainting-fits, a second protector was an imperative necessity; and who could tell (women being proverbially incalculable in their doings) whether we might not both select the self-same moment for swooning away? As yet only one of the stronger sex had been secured, and a second seemed to be nowhere forthcoming. As I before remarked, it is no easy matter to find a person with exactly the requisite qualifications for a mountaineering companion, and I am inclined to believe that Diogenes must have been contemplating some such ascent when he ran about the streets of Athens with a lantern. We had gone over the list of our dearest friends, and had rejected most of them, feeling convinced that we should get to detest them in the course of the first forty-eight hours. Of those few who remained some were unwell and others unwilling; some had no time and others no boots; the cavalry officers rarely cared to walk at all, and infantry officers were of opinion that they had quite enough walking already in their usual routine of military duty; and it is mournful to have to record that out of a population of about twenty-two thousand inhabitants, not another man could be found both willing and able to walk up a hill with a couple of ladies.

Our plan, therefore, seemed doomed to dire disappointment, when a bright thought struck me—the very brightest I ever had. Besides the population of 13,000 Germans, 3737 Roumanians, 2018 Magyars, 238 Jews and Armenian gypsies, and 443 infants, shown by the latest statistical return of the town, Hermanstadt could boast of something else—namely, one Englishman; and on this one solitary countryman all my hopes were accordingly fixed.

The gentleman in question, who had made his appearance here some months previously along with his wife and child, had long been a source of deep and perplexing interest to the inhabitants of Hermanstadt. None of them knew his name, and no name was required, " Der Engländer" being sufficient to describe the fabulous stranger who had found his way to these remote regions. No one spoke of him in any other way, and his bills and parcels were sent to him invariably addressed to " Der Engländer." His wife and his hat, his umbrella and his stockings, his boots and his baby, were as many sources of puzzling conjecture to these worthy people, who regarded him with all the deeper suspicion just because the life he led was so apparently harmless.

What had brought him to this out-of-the-way corner of Europe? was the question which troubled many a Saxon mind; and more than one was of opinion that he was a British spy sent by Mr. Gladstone for the express purpose of studying the military resources of the country and corrupting the population. No one would, I think, have been much surprised if some dark crime had been brought home to him, or if a supply of nitro-glycerine had been found concealed in the baby's perambulator — the two most suspicious circumstances about him being, that he had occasionally been seen looking on at the military parade, and had an uncanny habit of taking long walks in the country. It was, however, precisely this last ominous symptom which had directed my thoughts to him on this occasion; and having formed a slight acquaintance with Mr. P—— and his wife, I felt sure that he would prove equal to the occasion.

A deep analysis of international character has led me to the conclusion that, in a contingency like the present, one Englishman may be fairly balanced against a trifling majority of some twenty thousand

other mixed races; so I put forward my candidate, expressing a con-
viction that my countryman would in no way fall short of the national
standard which demands that every Englishman shall do his duty.

"Very well," said my friend, half reluctantly, "let us ask 'Der
Engländer,' if you really think it safe." So after I had pledged my
honor that the country's security would in nowise be imperilled, I
secured the valuable and agreeable companionship of Mr. P——; and
we set out once more, a small party of four people, with the requisite
number of guides and baggage-horses.

This second expedition was to be conducted on a somewhat different principle from the first; for, instead of taking up our quarters at
one given point, we proposed wandering over the mountains in true
gypsy fashion, sleeping wherever we happened to find shelter in shepherds' huts or foresters' lodges, or, in the absence of these, camping
under a sail-cloth tent we carried with us. It had been planned that
we were to remain out fully ten days, returning by a different route,
and making a short excursion into Roumania.

We drove to the foot of the hills, and then commenced our ascent
from a Roumanian village, where the white-veiled women plying the
distaff in front of their doors sent us courteous salutations as we
passed. The weather was radiantly beautiful, the atmosphere of a
faultless transparency, without a breath of air to hasten the falling
leaves, or a cloud to mar the effect of the deep-blue vault. There
were still wild flowers enough—campanulas, gentians, and wild carnations—growing on the steep grassy slopes, to make us fancy ourselves
in midsummer; and the gaudy insects disporting themselves thereon
—butterflies blue and purple, gold and scarlet grasshoppers, and shining bronze beetles—were as many brilliant impostors luring us on to
the belief that winter was still far away.

But the furry caterpillars scuttling across our path at headlong
speed, in their haste to wrap themselves up in their warm winter
cocoons, knew better; and so did the ring-doves and martens, which,
with other tribes of migrating birds, were all winging it swiftly towards the south, making dark streaks in the blue sky overhead.

For our part, we felt it almost too hot to walk uphill in the sun,
and were thankful when, after an hour's ascent, we gained the shade
of the dense pine forests which, without admixture of beech, clothe all
this part of the country.

There is no sense of monotony in these beautiful pine woods, though one may walk in them for many days without reaching the end of the forest, for no two parts of it are alike, and surprises await us at every turn. Thus one region is distinguished by a profusion of coral ornaments, the huge red toadstools, sprouting everywhere on the emerald moss, looking like monster sugar-plums which have fallen from these gigantic Christmas-trees; then suddenly a new transformation takes place, and we are walking in a mermaid's grove far beneath the sea—for are not the trees here adorned with tremulous hangings of palest green sea-weed? Yet this is no other than a lichen, the *Usnea barbata*, or bearded moss, also called Rübezahl's hair, which with such strange perversity will sometimes seize upon a whole forest district, thus fantastically decking it out in this long, wavy fluff, hanging from each twig and branch in fringes and bunches like a profusion of gray-green icicles; while elsewhere, under apparently the self-same conditions of soil and vegetation, we may seek for it in vain.

Farther on we come upon a scene still more weird and suggestive, as we seem to have stepped unawares into a land of ghosts. Hundreds of dead fir-trees, bleached and dry, are standing here upright and stark. Untouched by the storm, and unbroken by old age, with every branch and twig intact, they have been stricken to the heart's core by a treacherous enemy, the *Borkenkäfer* (*Bostrichus typographus*), a small but baneful insect, which for years past has been plying its deadly craft, and, vampire-like, sapping their life away. It is a relief to quit this death-like region, and return to the exuberant life expressed in every line of those gorgeous trees, growing scarce fifty paces ahead of their stricken brethren, whose lower branches, weighed down beneath the burden of their own magnificence, have sunk to the ground, where they lie voluptuously embedded in the rank luxuriance of the moss-woven grass. Yet here, too, the deadly insect will come, in scarce half a dozen years, to turn those emerald giants into staring white ghosts. Day by day it is creeping nearer, and though they know it not, those deluded trees, their days are already counted. Let us pass on; life is not blither than death after all!

Our first halt was made at La Dus, a small group of huts tenanted in summer by Hungarian gendarmes, there stationed for the purpose of keeping a lookout on smugglers and possible military deserters, who may hope to evade service by concealing themselves among the shepherds, or going over the frontier into Roumania. The immediate surroundings of this little establishment are somewhat bleak and desolate, the forest having been of late much cleared out at this spot. A tiny cemetery behind the houses seems to act the part of pleasure-ground as well; for right in its centre, separating the seven or eight graves into two rows, is a primitive skittle-ground—which curious arrangement can only be explained by the supposition that here the skittles had the right of priority, the dead men being but dissipated interlopers, who, having loved to play at skittles during their life-time, desired to be united to them even in death. The remains of a camp-fire I observed in one corner was another sign of the peculiar way the defunct are treated in this obscure church-yard, the ashes on closer investigation showing the charred wrecks of some of the crosses and railings missing from more than one grave.

In a wooden *châlet* reserved for the occasional visits of inspection of a head forester we obtained night-quarters, proceeding next morning on our way, which again took us through similar pine woods, reaching this time a comfortable shooting-lodge lying deep in the forest of Bistra, where we were made welcome by a hospitable Roumanian game-keeper and four or five remarkably amiable pointers, which threatened to stifle us with their affectionate demonstrations.

The weather had now begun to change, and a small drizzling rain had already surprised us on the way. Reluctantly we acknowledged that the caterpillars were by no means so devoid of sense as had appeared at first sight; and those migrating winged families, which had seemed so unreasonably anxious to start for Italy, were now slowly rising in our estimation, and as we were very comfortably installed at the game-keeper's lodge, we resolved to stay there two nights in order to give the weather time to improve before venturing on to higher ground.

This intervening day of rest was spent pleasantly enough in walking about and sketching, despite occasional showers of rain; while the gentlemen proceeded to shoot *haselhühner* in the forest. For the benefit of those unacquainted with these delicious little birds, I must here mention that they are about the size of a partridge, but of far superior flavor. They are mostly to be found in pine forests, where they feed on the delicate young pine-shoots, along with juniper-berries, sloes, and heather-nibs, which gives to them (in a fainter degree) something of the sharp aromatic taste of the grouse.

Close to the game-keeper's lodge there was a dashing mountain torrent of considerable volume, and this point had been selected for the construction of a *klause* (literally cloister) — or to put it more clearly, a monster dam—across the torrent-bed, with movable sluices. By means of the body of water obtained in this way, the wood of the forest is conveyed to the lower world. The river - banks are here enlarged till they form a small lake, and the dam, built up securely of massive bowlder-stones, is, for greater preservation against wind and weather, walled and roofed in with wooden planking, which gives to it the appearance of a roomy habitation. In connection with this lake are numerous wooden slides or troughs, which, slanting down from the adjacent hills, deposit whole trunks at the water's edge, there to be hewn up into convenient logs and thrown into the water. When a sufficient quantity of wood has been thus collected the sluices are opened, and with thunder-like noise the cataract breaks forth, easily sweeping its wooden burden along.

Even greater loads sometimes reach the lower world by this watery road, and occasionally twenty to twenty - five stems, roughly shaped into beams for building purposes, are fastened together so as to form a sort of raft, firmly connected at one end by cross-beams and wooden bands, but left loose at the opposite side to admit of the beams separating fan-like, according to the exigencies of the encountered obstacles, as they are whirled along. Two men furnished with lengthy poles act as steersmen, and it requires no little skill to guide this unwieldy craft successfully through the labyrinth of rocks and whirlpools which beset the river's bed. The perils of such a cruise are considerable, and used to be greater still before some of the worst rocks were blasted out of the way. Sometimes the whole craft goes to pieces, dashed against the bowlders, or else a fallen tree-stem across the river may crush the sailors as they are swept beneath. From this fate the navigators may sometimes barely escape by throwing themselves prostrate on the raft, or by leaping over the barrier at the critical moment; or else, when the obstacle is not otherwise to be evaded, and seems too formidable to surmount, they find it necessary to make voluntary shipwreck by steering on to the nearest rock. The thunder-like noise of the cataract renders speech unavailing, so it is only by signs that the men can communicate with each other.

This particular klause is not in use at present, as there are similar ones in neighboring valleys; so the little colony of log-huts built for the accommodation of workmen is standing empty, and single huts can be rented at a moderate price by any one who wishes to enjoy some weeks of a delightful solitude in the midst of fragrant pine forests.

CHAPTER LV.

A NIGHT IN THE STINA.

As on the second morning the rain had stopped, we thought we might venture to proceed on our way, the next station we had in view being the Jäeser See, a mysterious lake lying high up in the hills, of which many strange tales are told. This *meeresauge* (eye of the sea, as all such high mountain lakes are called by the people) is the source of the river Cibin, and believed by the country-folk to be directly connected with the ocean by subterraneous openings. The bones of drowned seamen and spars from wrecked ships are said to have been there washed ashore; and popular superstition warns the stranger not to presume to throw a stone into its gloomy depths, as a terrible thunder-storm would be the inevitable result of such sacrilege. According to some people, the Jäeser See would be no other than the devil's own caldron, in which he brews the weather, and where a dragon sleeps coiled up beneath the surface.

No wonder we felt anxious to visit such an interesting spot, and that we pressed onward without heeding the driving mists which every now and then obscured our view. We had now reached the extremity of the pine region, and were walking along a mountain shoulder where short stunted bushes of fir and juniper afforded shelter for countless *krametsvögel* (a sort of fieldfare), which flew up startled at our approach, uttering shrill, piercing cries. Several birds were shot as we went along; but as we had no dog to seek them out, they were mostly lost in the thick undergrowth where they had fallen.

The sun had now hidden itself, and a sharp piping wind was blowing full in our faces. We struggled on manfully notwithstanding, for some time, in face of discouragement; but when at last the mist had turned to a driving snow-storm, blinding our eyes and catching our breath, we forcedly came to a stand-still, to consider what next was to be done. There was no shelter to be obtained by going on, as our guides explained; even did we succeed in reaching the lake, which was doubtful in this weather, there was neither hut nor hovel near it, nor for many miles around, and we ruefully acknowledged that our much-vaunted sail-cloth tent would afford but scanty shelter against such a storm as was evidently coming on. It was too late to think of returning to the forester's lodge, being near four o'clock, and darkness set in soon after six. By good-luck, as we happened to remember, we had passed a seemingly deserted shepherds' hut about half an hour previously, the only habitation we had seen that day. By retracing our steps we might at least hope to pass the night under cover.

It proved no such easy matter, however, to find the place in question, for the heavy mists which accompanied the snow-storm enveloped us on all sides as with a veil, and we could not distinguish objects only twenty paces off; and although the hut stood out upon an open slope of pasture, we passed it close by more than once without suspecting. At last, despatching a guide to ascertain the exact bearings, we waited till his welcome shout informed us that our place of refuge was found, and a few minutes later we had reached the stina.

This hut, very roughly put together of logs and beams, had been evacuated by the shepherds some ten days previously; its walls were very low, the roof disproportionately high; there were no windows, and none were required, for there were as many chinks as boards, and fully more holes than nails about the building, and these, in freely admitting the wind and the rain, furnished enough daylight to see by as well. Yet such as it was, it was infinitely better than our flimsy tent, and we felt heartily thankful for the shelter it afforded.

The hut inside was divided off into two compartments, one for living and sleeping, the other a sort of store-room where the shepherds are in the habit of keeping their milk and cheeses. Some rude attempt at furnishing had also been made; one or two very primitive benches, some slanting boards to serve as beds, and a rickety table, weighted down by stones to keep it together. Bunches of dried juniper were stuck at regular intervals along the eaves of the roof inside by way of decoration; perhaps, also, as a charm to keep the lightning away. Some little objects carved out of wood, knives, spoons, etc., came likewise to light in our course of investigation.

There was no such thing as a fireplace or chimney, but a heap of gray wood-ashes in the centre of the stamped earth floor testified that a fire could be made notwithstanding, and only the patient smoke of many summers could have polished those beams inside the hut into that shiny surface of rich brown hue.

We took the hint, and presently the welcome sight of dancing flames lit up the scene. At first a dense smoke filled the building, and there seemed really no choice between freezing and suffocation, when some inventive spirit bethought himself of knocking out a portion of the roof by means of a long pole, and so making an improvised chimney. The current of air thus effected instantaneously carried off the dense smoke-clouds, and left the atmosphere comparatively clear.

Like fire-fly swarms the sparks flew upward, probing the mysterious darkness of the cavernous roof; and now as the blast swept by outside, shaking the walls and fanning the flames to an angry growl, the dead wood-ashes were likewise stirred to life, and, wafted aloft in the guise of fluttering white moths, they joined in a whirling dance with the golden fire-flies.

We had suspended our drenched cloaks from the cross-beams near the fire, and were beginning to prepare our supper, when a startling interruption gave a new current to our thoughts. One of the guides who had been collecting firewood outside now rushed in, exclaiming, "A bear! a bear! There is a young bear up there among the rocks."

Breathless we all hurried to the door, and Count B—— seized his gun, trembling with joyful anticipation, and almost too much agitated to load. The snow-storm had momentarily relaxed its violence, and there, sure enough, on the rising ground a little above the hut, we espied a black and shaggy animal gazing at us furtively from over a large bowlder-stone. It could be nothing else but a bear.

With palpitating hearts we watched the huntsman steal upward till within shot, terrified lest the bear should take alarm too soon. But no; this was not the sort of disappointment in store for us! The animal let itself be approached till within a dozen paces; it was a perfectly ideal bear in all respects, coming as it seemed with such obliging readiness to be shot at our very threshold.

Delusive dream! too beautiful to last! One moment more and the shot would be fired; we held our breath to listen—and then—oh, woful disappointment!—the gun was lowered, and the would-be bear-hunter called out in heart-rending accents, "It is only a dog!"

Only a poor half-starved dog, forgotten by the shepherds on their descent into the valley, and which probably had been prowling round the hut ever since in hopes of seeing his masters return. The animal was shaggy and uncouth in the extreme, gaunt and wild-looking from hunger, with glaring yellow eyes which gazed at us piteously from out its bushy elf-locks. Even at a very short distance the resemblance to a bear was striking.

We called the poor outcast, and would fain have given him food and shelter; but he was scared and savage, and misunderstanding our benevolent intentions, could not be persuaded to approach. We had therefore to content ourselves with throwing food from a distance, which he stealthily devoured whenever he thought himself unobserved.

After this bitter disappointment we returned to the hut, and there made ourselves as comfortable as circumstances would permit, completing our cooking arrangements, not without a sigh of regret for the delicate bear's-paws we had just now been expecting to sup upon; though a brace of haselhühner shot the previous day in the Bistra forest, and now roasted on a spit, gave us no cause to complain of the quality of our food.

Our next care was to prepare our sleeping-couches, for here there was not even a sprinkling of straw to soften the hard boards. Luckily, these forests contain an endless supply of patent spring mattresses, and a few armfuls of fresh-cut fir-branches, with a rug spread over, makes as good a bed as any one need desire. A Scotch plaid (my faithful companion for many years) hung along the wall kept off the worst draughts, and a roaring fire sustained the whole night prevented us from perishing with cold. Our sleeping-boards were close alongside this improvised hearth, with barely room enough to pass between without singeing one's clothes; yet while our faces were roasting, our backbones were often as cold as ice, so it became necessary to turn round from time to time when in imminent danger of getting overdone at one side. Opposite us slumbered the guides, taking turns to sit up and tend the fire.

Many a massive log was burned that night, and not only trunks and branches, but much of the rustic furniture as well, was pressed into service as fuel. The shepherds will require to furnish their house anew next summer.

It was late ere sleep came to any of us, and when it came at last it brought strange phantoms in its train; visions of ghosts and sorcerers, of bears and bandits, flitted successively through our brain; and scarcely less strange than dream-land was the reality to which we were occa-

sionally roused by alternate twinges of cold and heat—the smouldering fire at our elbow, the slumbering guides, and the white moths and
fire-flies whirling aloft in the frenzied mazes of a wild Sabbath dance,
to which the moaning wind, like the wailing voice of some unquiet
spirit, played a mournful accompaniment.

When morning came we reviewed our situation dispassionately.
The storm was over, and the day, though dull, was fair as yet; but
the horizon was clouded, and some peasants coming by told us of snow
lying deep on the mountains we were bound for. We could no longer
blind ourselves to the fact that summer was over, and that the troublesome mists, which but a fortnight ago could easily be dispersed by the
sun's disdainful smile, were now the masters up here.

It was clearly impossible to proceed farther under the circumstances; so, remembering that discretion is often the better part of
valor, we resolved to cut short our expedition, postponing all further
explorations to a more favorable season.

When our little caravan was set in motion, I turned round to take
a last look at the hut which had sheltered us, and which most likely I
shall never see again. There, motionless on a neighboring rock,
crouched the gaunt figure of the hungry dog, gazing intently before
him. Then, as I watched, he crept stealthily down till he had reached
the half-open door of the empty stina, where, after a cautious investigation to assure himself of the coast being clear, he entered, and was
lost to my sight. Doubtless he thought to warm himself by the fire
we had left, and to discover some food-scraps remaining from our
meals.

That dog haunted my thoughts for many days afterwards, and I
could not refrain from speculating on its fate, which can only have
been a tragic one. Did it perish of cold and hunger, or else fall a
prey to the wild beasts of the forest? After having but yesterday unconsciously enacted the part of the bear, perhaps Bruin himself came
to fetch it on the morrow. It would, after all, have been more merciful if the error had lasted a little longer, and a kindly bullet been
lodged in its unsuspecting heart.

CHAPTER LVI.

FAREWELL TO TRANSYLVANIA—THE ENCHANTED GARDEN.

So the end of our Transylvanian sojourn had actually come, and like many things whose prospect appears so unconditionally desirable when viewed in the far distance, the realization of this wish now failed to bring altogether the anticipated satisfaction.

Whoever has read Hans Andersen's exquisite tale of the fir-tree will understand the indescribable pathos assumed by commonplace objects as soon as they are relegated from the present tense into the

THE CAVERN CONVENT, SKIT LA JALOMITZA.*

past; and those who have not read this fairy tale will understand it equally well, for is not the story of the fir-tree the history of each of our own lives?

I had indeed often longed to be back again in the world; I had yearned to be once more within reach of newspapers and lending-

* Reprinted from a publication of the Transylvanian Carpathian Society.

libraries, and to be able to get letters from England in three days
instead of six. Of course I would return to the world some day or
other; but that day need not have come just yet, I now told myself,
and I should have liked to spend one more summer in face of that
glorious chain of mountains I had got to love so dearly.

All at once I became acutely conscious of a dozen projects not yet
accomplished—of points of interest as yet unvisited, of pictures I had
not yet looked upon, of songs I had not heard. The proud snowy
Negoi I had so often dreamed of ascending now smiled down an icy
smile of unapproachable majesty upon my disappointment; the dark
pine forests I had expected to revisit seemed to grow dim and shadowy as they eluded my grasp, and with them many other objects of
my secret longing. That other mountain, the Bucsecs, where live
those solitary monks, snowed up during the greater part of the year
in their cavern convent scooped out of the rock; the noble castle of
the great Hunyady, pearl of mediæval citadels; those wondrous salt-
mines of Maros-Ujvar, whose description reads like a vision in a fairy.
tale; and those rivers whose waters may literally be said to " wander
o'er sands of gold "—the thought of these, and of many other such
items, now rose up like tormenting spectres to swell the mournful list
of my blighted hopes. There were dozens of old ruined towers
whose interior I had not yet seen, scores of little way-side chapels I
had proposed to investigate. Why, even in this very town of Hermanstadt there were nooks and corners I had not explored, church-
towers I had not ascended, and mysterious little gardens as yet unvisited. Precisely the most inviting-looking of these gardens, the most
mysteriously suggestive, and the one which showed the richest prom-
ise of blossom peeping over the wall, had hitherto baffled all attempts
at entrance. Nearly every day for the last two years I had passed
by that garden, which towered over my head like a sea-bird's nest
perched on a steep rocky island, and always had I found the gate to
be persistently locked against the outer world. Was I actually going
to leave the place without having set foot within its enchanted precincts? without having plucked that head of golden laburnum just
breaking into flower, which nodded so mockingly over the wall? and
all at once an irresistible longing came over me; I felt that I *must*
enter that garden, *must* gather that flower, even were it defended by
dragons and witches.

And my wish did not seem to be impracticable at first sight—the garden, as I knew, belonging to the cure, a jovial-faced old man, with whom I had merely a bowing acquaintance, but who, I felt sure, would be delighted to show me his garden. Accordingly one forenoon, about a week before my departure from Hermanstadt, I sent my two boys with a calling-card, on which was indited my request in the politest terms and most legible handwriting at my command.

The small messengers I had despatched to the presbytery came back even sooner than I had expected, but their mien was crestfallen, and their eyes suspiciously moist.

"What is the matter?" I asked, in surprise. "Have you not brought me the key of the garden? Did not the cure say Yes?"

CASTLE VAJDA HUNYAD BEFORE ITS RESTORATION.

"He said nothing; we never saw him. The whole house was full of doctors and of pails of ice," was the somewhat incoherent explanation. "And then there came an old woman with a broom and made us go away."

Evidently the subject of the broom was too painful to be dwelt upon, for the moisture in the eyes showed symptoms of reappearing.

Further inquiries elucidated the situation. Alas! it was but too true; the cure had been seized with a stroke of apoplexy that morning; and after waiting for two whole years, I had appropriately selected that very moment to request the loan of his garden key!

Two days later he died, and was buried with much pomp; and then, after waiting for three days more, I thought I might without indelicacy repeat my request, applying this time to the sacristan.

The branch of laburnum had now burst into full flower, and the more I gazed the more absolutely impossible it seemed to leave the place without it.

This time, in consideration of the broom and the old woman, I had despatched a full-grown messenger, desiring him on no account to presume to return without the key; but the answer he brought, though polite, was yet more hopeless, and he, too, had come back empty-handed. "Have you been to the sacristan?" I sternly inquired. He had, as he humbly informed me, and not only to him, but likewise to the next priest in rank, as well as to the sister and nephew of the deceased, and to his best friend.

"The gentlemen were all very polite, and much regretted not being able to oblige me," he said; "but the garden gate had been closed with the official seal immediately after the death, and this key, along with all others, deposited at the *gericht* (court of justice) till a successor should be elected."

"And when will that be?"

"In about six months probably."

In six months! They dared talk to me of six months, when I should be gone before as many days! And what cared I for their hypocritical expressions of regret, now that I knew them to be dragons in disguise? Hope was now dead within me, for even British pertinacity cannot cope with supernatural agency, and expect to penetrate realms defended by witches and dragons.

Driving to the station, we passed for the last time by the impenetrable stone-wall which masked the object of all this useless longing and effort, and which, like all unattainable things, looked more than ever desirable on the balmy May evening we turned our backs upon Hermanstadt. In vain my eyesight strove to penetrate the dense screen of flowery shrubs hiding from my view—I know not what. Perhaps an old temple with shattered columns, or a fountain which has ceased to play? Maybe an ancient statue draped in ivy, or a tombstone bearing some long-forgotten name?

Naught could I see but the dense-grown tops of gelder-rose and bird - cherry pressed tightly together, and one clustering branch of overblown laburnum dropping its petals in amber showers on to the road.

Were you mocking me, or weeping for me, enigmatical golden flower? Shall I ever return to gather you?

THE END.

TRANSYLVANIA.

Milton Keynes UK
Ingram Content Group UK Ltd.
UKHW021347300923
429700UK00008B/44